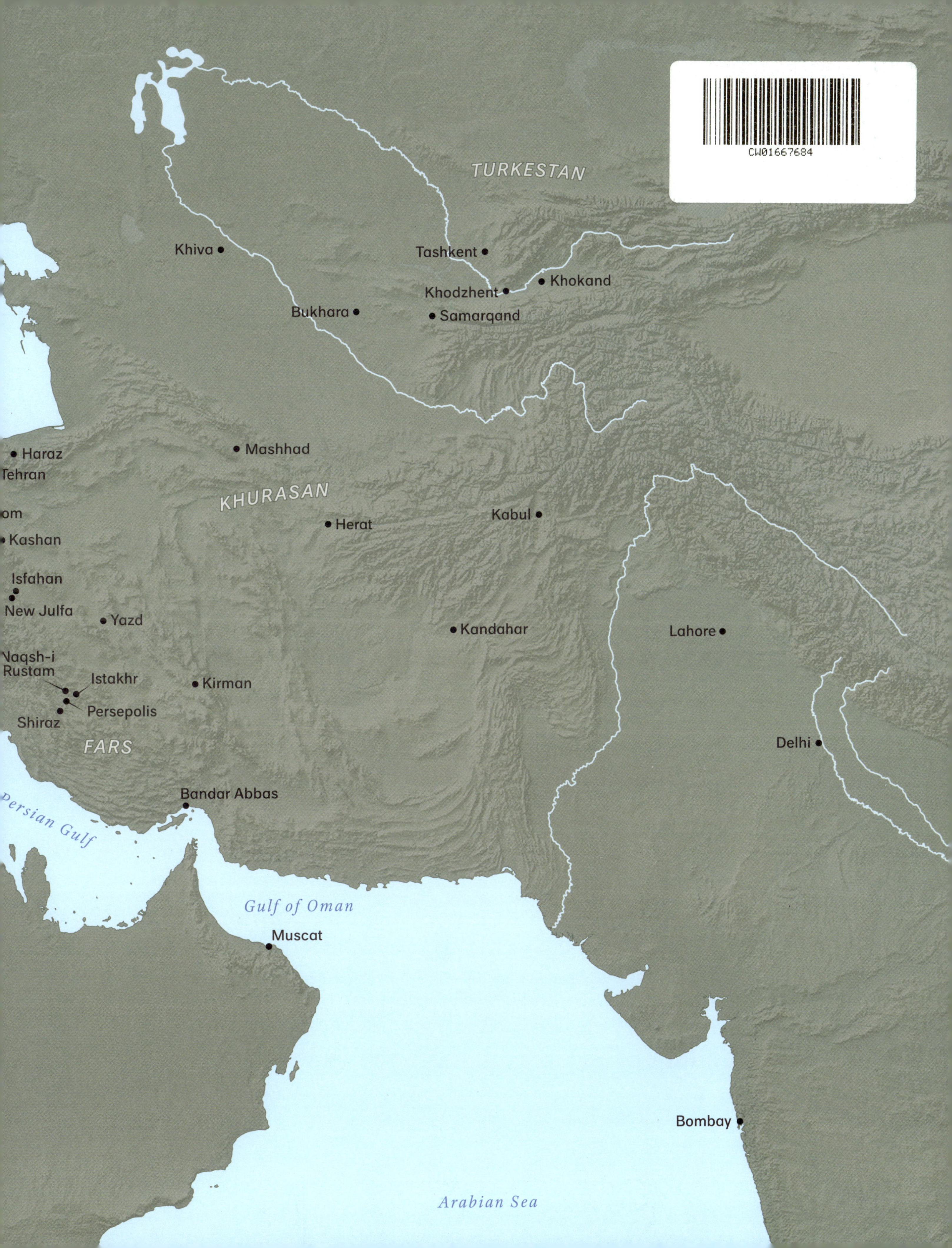
TURKESTAN
Khiva
Tashkent
Khokand
Khodzhent
Bukhara
Samarqand
Haraz
Tehran
Mashhad
KHURASAN
om
Herat
Kabul
Kashan
Isfahan
New Julfa
Yazd
Kandahar
Lahore
Naqsh-i
Rustam
Istakhr
Kirman
Persepolis
Shiraz
FARS
Delhi
Bandar Abbas
Persian Gulf
Gulf of Oman
Muscat
Bombay
Arabian Sea

Technologies of the Image

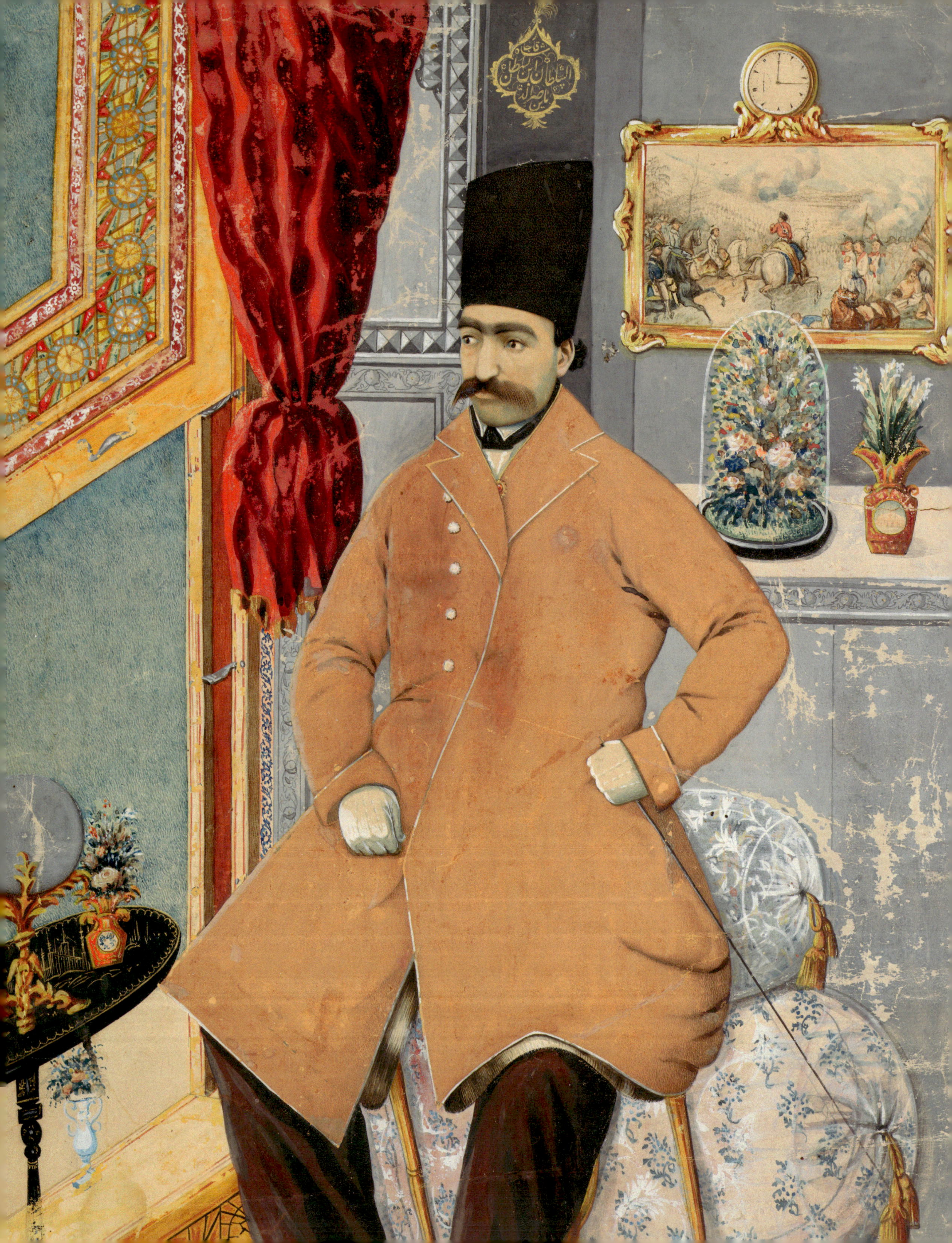
شاه قاجار
السلطان ابن السلطان
ناصرالدین

Technologies of the Image

Art in 19th-Century Iran

Edited by
David J. Roxburgh **and**
Mary McWilliams

With contributions by
Farshid Emami,
Mary McWilliams,
David J. Roxburgh, **and**
Mira Xenia Schwerda

HARVARD ART MUSEUMS
Cambridge, Mass.

Distributed by

YALE UNIVERSITY PRESS
New Haven and London

This catalogue accompanies the exhibition *Technologies of the Image: Art in 19th-Century Iran*, on view at the Harvard Art Museums, Cambridge, Massachusetts, from August 26, 2017, through January 7, 2018.

PUBLISHED BY
Harvard Art Museums
32 Quincy Street
Cambridge, MA 02138-3847
harvardartmuseums.org

DISTRIBUTED BY
Yale University Press
302 Temple Street
PO Box 209040
New Haven, CT 06520-9040
yalebooks.com/art

PRODUCED FOR THE HARVARD ART MUSEUMS BY
Lucia | Marquand, Seattle
luciamarquand.com

AT HARVARD ART MUSEUMS
Managing Editor: Micah Buis
Editors: Sarah Kuschner and Cheryl Pappas
Design Manager: Zak Jensen
Designers: Becky Hunt, Adam Sherkanowski

AT LUCIA | MARQUAND
Editorial Director: Melissa Duffes
Designer: Thomas Eykemans

Edited by Andrew Halladay
Typeset in Adobe Text and Neutral by Marie Weiler
Indexed by Enid Zafran
Printed on 157 gsm Chinese OJI matte artpaper
Printed in China by Artron Art Group

Cover image: *The Persian Family* (details). For full information, see cats. 30 and 31, p. 142.
Page ii image: *Nasir al-Din Shah Qajar* (detail); page vi image: *A Photographer's Room* (detail). For full information, see cat. 2, p. 131, and cat. 28, p. 140.

LIBRARY OF CONGRESS CATALOGING-IN-PUBLICATION DATA
Names: Roxburgh, David J., editor, author. | McWilliams, Mary, 1954– editor, author. | Emami, Farshid, author. | Schwerda, Mira Xenia, author. | Harvard Art Museums, host institution.
Title: Technologies of the image : art in 19th-century Iran / edited by David J. Roxburgh and Mary McWilliams ; with contributions by Farshid Emami, Mary McWilliams, David J. Roxburgh, and Mira Xenia Schwerda.
Description: Cambridge, Mass. : Harvard Art Museums, 2017. | "This catalogue accompanies the exhibition Technologies of the Image: Art in 19th-Century Iran, on view at the Harvard Art Museums, Cambridge, Massachusetts, from August 26, 2017 through January 7, 2018." | Includes bibliographical references and index.
Identifiers: LCCN 2017011017 | ISBN 9781891771736 (Harvard Art Museums : alk. paper) | ISBN 9780300229196 (Yale University Press (distributor) : alk. paper)
Subjects: LCSH: Art, Iranian—Exhibitions. | Islamic art—Iran—Exhibitions. | Photography—Iran—Exhibitions. | Lacquer and lacquering—Iran—Exhibitions. | Painting, Iranian—Exhibitions.
Classification:
LCC N7280 .T37 2017 | DDC 709.55—dc23
LC record available at https://lccn.loc.gov/2017011017

Dedicated to the memory
of Kazem Kooros

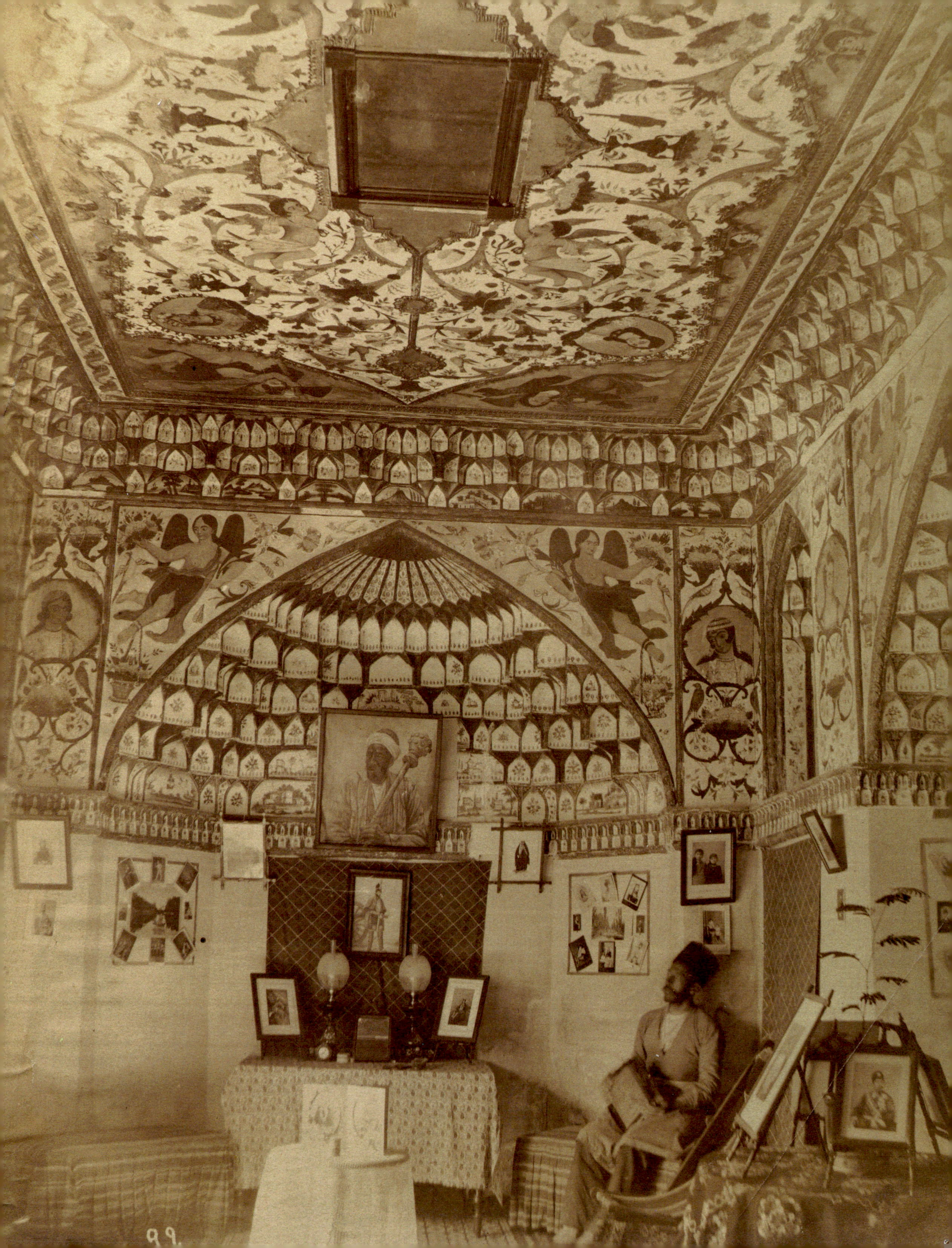
۹۹.

Contents

گزینش بدیدند شاهان همه / بپیشش دل نیکخواهان همه

گزینش نپذرفت و نشنید پند / اگر پند نشنید از او دید بند

اگر شاه ارجاسب توران خدای / که دیوان بتندی بپیشش بپای

از او بستدی نیز هر سال باژ / چرا داد باید بها مال ساژ

پیدا شدن زردشت و گزیدن گشتاسب و لهراسب و همگی سرداران ایران کیش اورا

چو یکچند گاهی برآمد برین / درختی پدید آمد اندر زمین

از ایوان گشتاسب تا پیش کاخ / درختی گشن بیخ و بسیار شاخ

همه برگ او پند و بارش خرد / کسی کو چنان برخورد کی مرد

یکی پاک پیدا شد اندر زمان / بدست اندرش مجمر عود دیان

خجسته پی و نام او زردهشت / که اهرمن بدکنش را بکشت

بشاه جهان گفت پیغمبرم / ترا سوی یزدان همی رهبرم

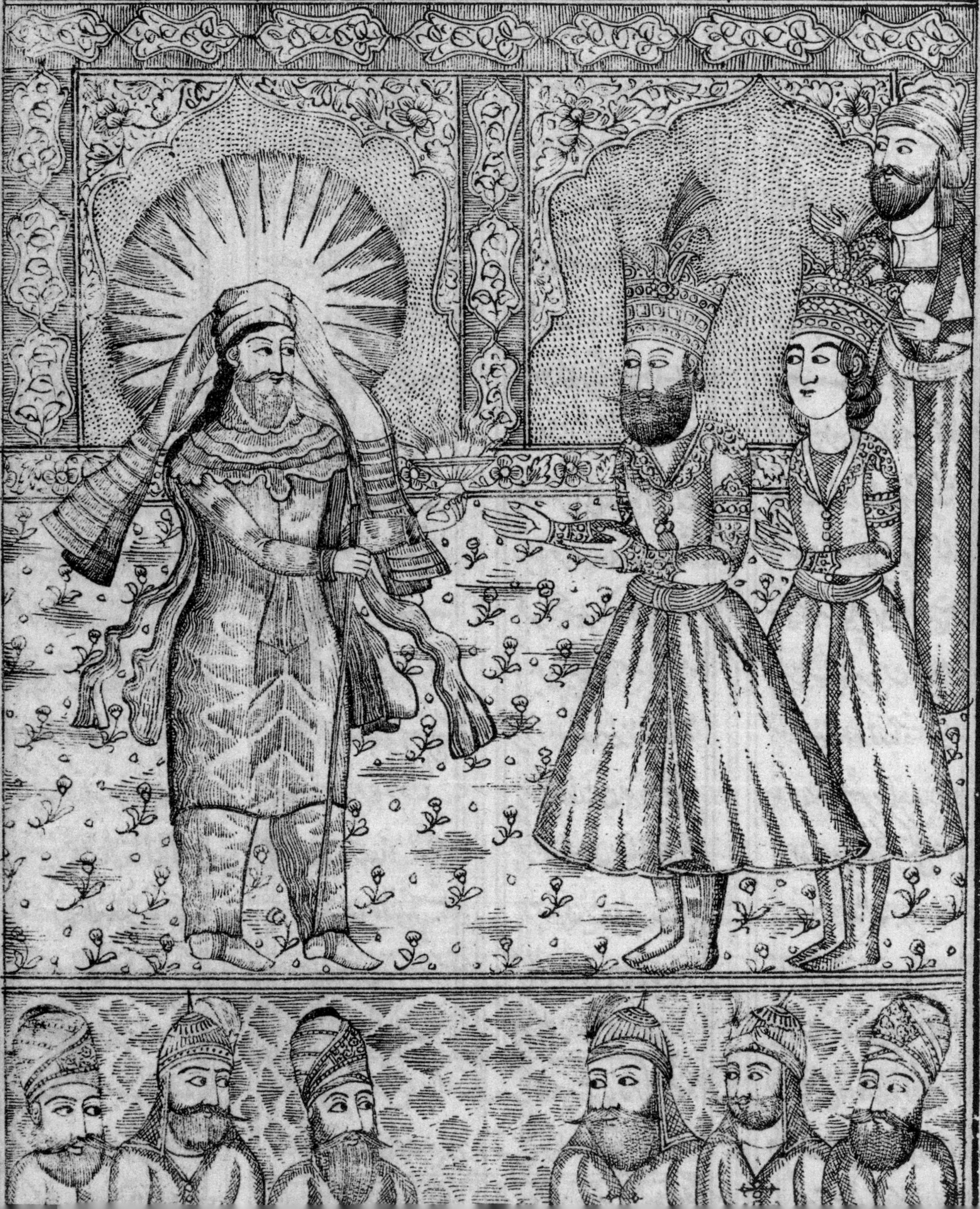

Foreword

Iran emerged from decades of isolation and internal warfare in 1796, when Aqa Muhammad Khan was officially crowned shah. The new Qajar dynasty he established, which would endure until 1925, strove to formulate a court culture and consolidate control over the land and its peoples, even as Iran rapidly became enmeshed in the broader world as the 19th century unfolded. The expansionist ambitions and technological advances of European powers—primarily the British and Russian Empires—brought Westerners and their innovations, intrigues, and industrial products to Iran, and to some degree, drew Iranians to the West. Stimulated and challenged by developments both inside and far beyond their country, 19th-century Persian artists not only mastered new image-making technologies, they also readily assimilated an unprecedented influx of pictorial material from abroad into their traditional art forms.

Images crossed borders and circulated in diverse socioeconomic milieus during the 19th century, serving an ever widening spectrum of interests and purposes in Iran. To project prestige and stability, shahs commissioned portraits in a range of mediums, revived the pre-Islamic tradition of rock reliefs, and became the first Iranian rulers since the Sasanians to stamp their likenesses on coins. And yet while kingly precedent, taste, and patronage remained influential throughout the century, the currency of pictures ultimately depended neither on coinage nor on royal prerogative. Alone or in combination with illumination and calligraphy, pictorial art saw a much broader deployment: on objects intended to serve as official gifts, to celebrate marriages and births, to document events or sites, to illustrate works of literature, to amuse, to inspire, and to foment political change. Together with their patrons and customers, talented and resourceful Qajar artists fashioned this most interesting century into an era of heightened picture-making.

With a few notable exceptions, scholars have historically understudied and often underappreciated the art of Iran in the Qajar era. *Technologies of the Image: Art in 19th-Century Iran* offers fresh perspectives on the period by foregrounding the inherent relationship and movement among mediums and

Detail: *Zoroaster Offering the Eternal Fire to Gushtasb,* dated 1265–67 H (1848–50). For full information, see cat. 45, p. 146.

images, both traditional and new, while deflecting primary attention from royal patronage to more public and widely accessible forms of image-making. David J. Roxburgh and Mary McWilliams have brought together four principal art forms—lacquer, lithography, photography, and painting—to explore their separate and convergent histories, contexts of production, and means of dissemination across an expanded range of socioeconomic levels. This catalogue and the Harvard Art Museums exhibition it accompanies are organized to consider artistic processes, systems of duplication and translation, image mobility, as well as the sociocultural implications of accelerated production and wider distribution.

Befitting its focus on interplay and interaction, *Technologies of the Image* has been an intensely collaborative endeavor. Initiated by a professor, a curator, and a private collector, the project was enriched—and its horizons wonderfully expanded—by the participation of two senior graduate students, a conservation scientist, a paper conservator, and additional lenders both private and public. The Harvard Art Museums' Art Study Center and Straus Center for Conservation and Technical Studies greatly facilitated the exchange of ideas and discoveries between museum staff, students, and faculty involved in the project. As the thought-provoking catalogue essays by Farshid Emami and Mira Xenia Schwerda demonstrate, our mission to create new knowledge about art dovetailed quite easily with another of our primary goals: to train the next generation of scholars. Indeed, the museums' ability to draw not only on the expertise of our own staff, but also on the research and vibrancy of Harvard faculty and graduate students is further evident in two additional, related publications that will also appear in 2017: *An Album of Artists' Drawings from Qajar Iran*, edited by David J. Roxburgh; and *A Collector's Passion: Ezzat-Malek Soudavar and Persian Lacquer*, edited by Massumeh Farhad and Mary McWilliams and co-published with the Smithsonian's Freer and Sackler Galleries.

There are many people to thank for the success of this project, but special gratitude is due to Vahid Kooros, Abolala Soudavar, and Elmar Seibel, three individuals whose lives have been shaped by a deep engagement with Persian art. *Technologies of the Image* would not have been possible without generous loans from private collectors and from institutions. We are grateful to the descendants of ʿAli Khan Vali, to Harvard University's Houghton Library, Fine Arts Library, and Ernst Mayr Library, and to the Museum of Fine Arts, Boston, the Museum für Lackkunst, Münster, and the Freer Gallery of Art and Arthur M. Sackler Gallery of Art, Smithsonian Institution, Washington, D.C. Finally, we acknowledge the visionary support of Stan and Norma Jean Calderwood and the Curatorial Support Fund they established at the Harvard

Art Museums; it provides key financial support for so many of our projects in the fields of Islamic and later Indian art.

With a long tradition of teaching, collecting, and exhibiting Islamic art, the Harvard Art Museums are pleased to present a new chapter in that history. McWilliams and Roxburgh have adopted an innovative approach to the Qajar period; their exhibition and catalogue alike shed exciting new light on this transformative era for Iranian art.

Martha Tedeschi
Elizabeth and John Moors Cabot Director
Harvard Art Museums

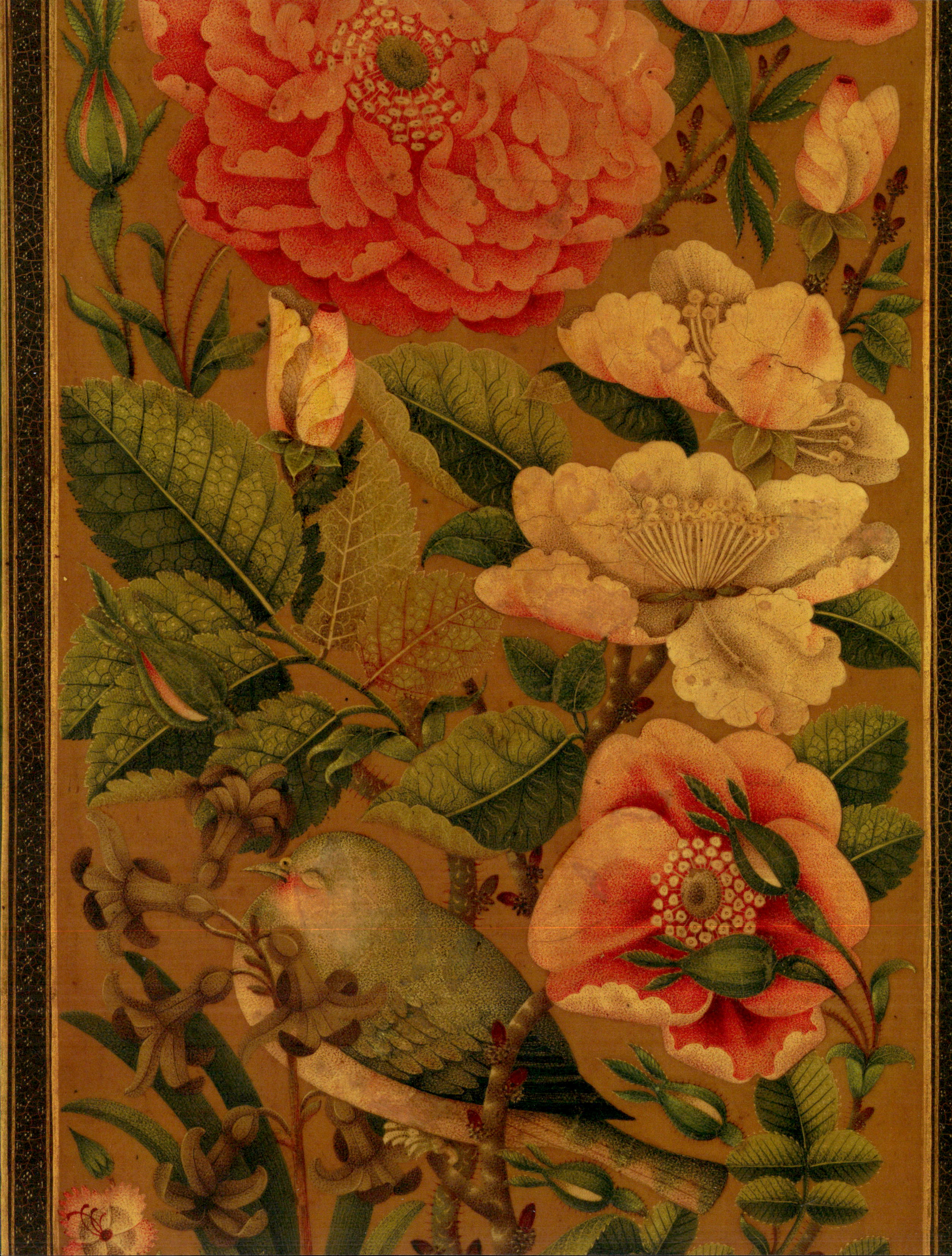

Preface and Acknowledgments

The genesis of this exhibition was a visit to the Houston home of Kazem Kooros more than a decade ago. We were at the time working on the exhibition *Traces of the Calligrapher: Islamic Calligraphy in Practice, c. 1600–1900*, for the Museum of Fine Arts, Houston. Our Texan host, Vahid Kooros, arranged a meeting with his father, who graciously shared with us his extensive collection of Persian art of the Qajar era and his equally wide knowledge of the field. It was in this house that we first came to know many of the objects later selected for the exhibition *Technologies of the Image: Art in 19th-Century Iran*. In grateful remembrance of this meeting, we dedicate this catalogue to the memory of Kazem Kooros.

A distinguished collector of Persian art, Kazem Kooros was also a cultured patron of poets, musicians, and educational and medical institutions in Iran. Over the course of a long life that began during the reign of Muzaffar al-Din Shah Qajar, Mr. Kooros witnessed profound changes in his native land, while serving as an industrialist, businessman, philanthropist, senator, and member of parliament. Our gratitude to this remarkable gentleman extends to his sons, Saeed, Hamid, and Vahid, and to their families for their continuing encouragement and support. The sons have inherited from their father not only a very fine collection, but also his generous spirit, culture of hospitality, and dedication to the arts.

Our initial concept for the exhibition had been to join selections from the Kooros collection with works from the Qajar era at Harvard University. Among the most notable of the Qajar works available at Harvard is an extraordinary album of photographs by ʿAli Khan Vali, which his descendants have most kindly placed on long-term loan to the Fine Arts Library. Frequently used in teaching at Harvard, the *ʿAli Khan Vali Album* is on public view for the first time in this exhibition (cat. 24). Also of great importance, but hitherto little studied, is *An Album of Artists' Drawings from Qajar Iran* (Harvard Art Museums, 1960.161), which became the focus of David J. Roxburgh's graduate seminar in the spring of 2015. Published simultaneously with this catalogue is a monographic facsimile of the Harvard Qajar Album, which shares the research

Detail: *Rectangular Mirror Case with Flowers, Butterfly, and Sleeping Bird*, dated 1263 H (1847–48). For full information, see cat. 57, p. 150.

and insights of the graduate students and museum colleagues who participated in the seminar. Because this album was temporarily disbound for the seminar, we have been able to include 12 of its folios in the exhibition. The experience and perspectives gained through the seminar have enriched this exhibition and catalogue to an incalculable degree.

Apart from the album of drawings and sketches, the Qajar holdings in the permanent collections of the Harvard Art Museums were relatively spare until 2014, when we received a splendid gift from Abolala Soudavar. We cannot overstate our gratitude for the donation of more than one hundred works of Persian art drawn from the collection of Mr. Soudavar's mother, Ezzat-Malek Soudavar (d. 2014). Born in the turbulent final years of the last Qajar ruler, Ahmad Shah Qajar, Mrs. Soudavar was devoted to Persian art and poetry and a respected figure in scholarly and collectors' circles. At the Harvard Art Museums, we are honored by Mr. Soudavar's decision to divide this collection between Harvard and the Smithsonian Institution's Freer and Sackler Galleries, and proud to have joined with the Smithsonian to publish the catalogue *A Collector's Passion: Ezzat-Malek Soudavar and Persian Lacquer* (2017).

Both Ezzat-Malek Soudavar and Kazem Kooros lived more than a century. They were friendly rivals in the small world of connoisseurs of Qajar art, and it is deeply gratifying that this exhibition brings works of art from their collections into dialogue for the first time. As demonstrated by catalogue numbers 69 and 70, their collections have much to say to one another.

To realize our goal of exploring the mobility of images and the interplay of old and new technologies and artistic practices in the Qajar period, we invited two advanced graduate students at Harvard, Farshid Emami and Mira Xenia Schwerda, to explore the arts of lithography and photography. Their resourcefulness and boundless intellectual curiosity augur well for the future of the field, and their energetic research uncovered further sources of Qajar art within the university and brought additional collectors into the project. The photography section would not have been possible without the encouragement and generosity of Elmar W. Seibel, who shared with us his impressive collection, his broad knowledge, and his time. We are deeply grateful to Elmar and his wife, Azita Bina-Seibel, for contributing the digital photography of their loan objects for the catalogue. We would also like to thank Kenneth Robbins, who kindly lent Qajar postcards, shared his expertise of this medium, and contributed digital images for the catalogue. Our Qajar project has been immeasurably enhanced by additional loans granted from the Houghton Library and the Ernst Mayr Library at Harvard and from the Museum für Lackkunst in Münster and the Freer and Sackler Galleries Archives, Smithsonian Institution, Washington, D.C.

With four main contributors to the project, there is necessarily a lengthy list of individuals and institutions to whom we are deeply indebted; all have generously shared both time and knowledge. Any errors in the catalogue are ours alone.

At the Harvard Art Museums, this project could not have succeeded without the support and leadership of former director Thomas W. Lentz and former chief curator Deborah Martin Kao. We are grateful for the continuing encouragement of Martha Tedeschi, the new Elizabeth and John Moors Cabot Director, and Susanne Ebbinghaus, the George M.A. Hanfmann Curator of Ancient Art and Head of the Division of Asian and Mediterranean Art. Our work has depended on the expertise and good will of colleagues in the Straus Center for Conservation and Technical Studies, including Angela Chang, Anne Driesse, and Charlotte Karney. Special recognition is due to the Straus Center's ever gracious Katherine Eremin, Penley Knipe, and former Australian Conservation Science Fellow Claire Grech, whose analyses have clarified and broadened our understanding of the works of art explored in the catalogue and exhibition. Credit is due to Katherine for the photomicrographs of lacquer objects. Elizabeth Rudy, the Carl A. Weyerhaeuser Associate Curator of Prints, provided insights and contacts for the realm of European prints, and graduate student Bronwen Gulkis contributed object research and coordinating support as a summer assistant. We wish to thank Katya Kallsen, Natalja Kent, and Katie Kujala for photography; Jessica Martinez and Francesca Bewer for engaging both academic and public audiences; Micah Buis for editorial advice and guidance; Zak Jensen for overseeing the catalogue design; and Justin Lee for inspired installation design. Amy Brauer, Monique Goodin, Ayşin Yoltar-Yıldırım, Stephanie Rozman, and Rachel Parikh provided steadfast curatorial and administrative support in the Division of Asian and Mediterranean Art. A multitude of tasks were expertly coordinated and carried out by Jennifer Allen, Mary Lister, Jessica Diedalis, Karen Gausch, and their colleagues in the Division of Collections Management. Finally, the unflappable Matthew Rogan, curatorial assistant for special exhibitions and publications, proved himself the indispensable man in all aspects of the project.

Within Harvard University, we would like to thank András J. Riedlmayer and Emily Una Weirich of the Fine Arts Library; Thomas Hyry and Hope Mayo of the Houghton Library; Constance Rinaldo, Robert Young, and Dana Fisher of the Ernst Mayr Library of the Museum of Comparative Zoology; Judith Warnement and Kanchi Gandhi at the Harvard University Herbaria; C. Scott Walker of the Harvard Map Collection; and Elena Bulat of the Weissman Preservation Center. Graduate students Maria Blackwood and Mohsen Goudarzi generously shared knowledge and research.

To our colleagues beyond Cambridge, we extend sincere thanks for providing answers and advice, information and images, and for spending their precious hours, even days, granting access to public and private collections. In the United States, we have been assisted by Yael Rice of Amherst College;

Amy Landau of the Walters Art Museum, Baltimore; Richard Newman of the Museum of Fine Arts, Boston; Houchang Chehabi of Boston University; Sassan Pejhan of the Iran Philatelic Study Circle, Los Angeles; Shabnam Rahimi-Golkhandan of Yale University; Joan Cummins and Caitlin McKenna of the Brooklyn Museum; Sheila Canby and Maryam Ekhtiar of the Metropolitan Museum of Art, New York; Houman Sarshar of the Kimia Foundation, New York; Massumeh Farhad, Simon Rettig, and David Hogge of the Freer and Sackler Galleries, Smithsonian Institution, Washington, D.C.; and independent scholars Shreve Simpson and Reza Sheikh. We are deeply grateful to colleagues in Europe who have furthered our research, including Alban von Stockhausen and Martin Schulz of the Bernisches Historisches Museum, Bern; Arnoud Vrolijk of the Leiden University Library; Ladan Akbarnia of the British Museum, London; Moya Carey and Behnaz Atighi-Moghaddam of the Victoria and Albert Museum, London; Monika Kopplin of the Museum für Lackkunst, Münster; Natalia Avetyan of the State Hermitage Museum, St. Petersburg; Iván Szántó of the Austrian Academy of Sciences, Vienna; Sona Baloyan of the Matenadaran Museum, Yerevan; and Axel Langer of the Rietberg Museum, Zürich. We can only hope to pay forward these many debts of gratitude. We also wish to acknowledge the individuals at Lucia | Marquand who helped edit, design, and produce this volume: Melissa Duffes, Tom Eykemans, and Andrew Halladay.

Finally, we speak for Mira and Farshid as well in offering heartfelt thanks to our family members for their patience, understanding, and steadfast support.

David J. Roxburgh and *Mary McWilliams*
Harvard University, December 2016

Note to Reader

Dates, Transcriptions, and Transliteration

Year 1 in the Islamic calendar corresponds to 622 CE. Throughout the catalogue, dates are given in CE years, unless otherwise indicated. When hijri (H) dates are provided, they are placed first, followed by CE dates in parentheses.

Foreign words and proper nouns that have entered the English language or have a generally recognized English form are anglicized in the text. Place names follow English usage, and false English plurals for Persian, Arabic, and Turkish words are used. Place names and names of historical personages with no English equivalent are transliterated, but aside from *'ayn* (ʿ) and *hamza* (ʾ), diacritical marks are omitted within the body of the text. Quoted passages and titles of published works are fully transliterated, as are specific foreign words or phrases, which are preceded or followed by their English equivalent.

Arabic, Persian, Turkish, and Ottoman Turkish are transliterated according to the system used in the *International Journal of Middle East Studies*. Diphthongs are indicated by aw and ay. Translations are the work of individual authors, unless otherwise stated. For Russian inscriptions, the Cyrillic script is romanized. Particularly lengthy inscriptions are summarized in the checklist, and the full inscription can be found by searching for the individual object on the Harvard Art Museums' website at harvardartmuseums.org/collections.

Geographical and Place Names

The names of modern countries have been used when possible in place of older cultural and dynastic designations. Thus, for example, Persian objects have been assigned to Iran, and Mughal objects to India or Pakistan. For broader cultural designations, as for traditional poetry or painting, the term *Persian* is used synonymously with *Iranian*.

In the case of the map printed on the front and back endsheets, older names have been used for cities and regions.

Illustrated Checklist

The checklist is divided by medium and then chronologically within divisions. The sequence of mediums follows the layout of the exhibition.

Measurements for three-dimensional objects are height × width × depth. In the case of a pen box: height measures the distance from the ground to the highest point on the object (e.g., the apex of the convex lid); width measures the lateral dimension from left to right; and depth measures the longitudinal distance (from bow to stern, if the pen box were a ship). Where a dimension varies, the maximum is recorded. For works on paper, the dimensions are for the entire folio, including mounting pages and margins, unless otherwise indicated.

Media and materials have been determined through examination and analysis by staff in the Harvard Art Museums' Straus Center for Conservation and Technical Studies: Katherine Eremin, the Patricia Cornwell Senior Conservation Scientist; Claire Grech, former Australian Conservation Science Fellow; and Penley Knipe, the Philip and Lynn Straus Senior Conservator of Works of Art on Paper and Head of the Paper Lab. The term "watercolor" is used to indicate the use of a water-based medium; it may be applied in transparent or opaque films.

Website

For works of art in the permanent collections, the Harvard Art Museums' website provides additional information and images: harvardartmuseums.org/collections.

Technologies of the Image

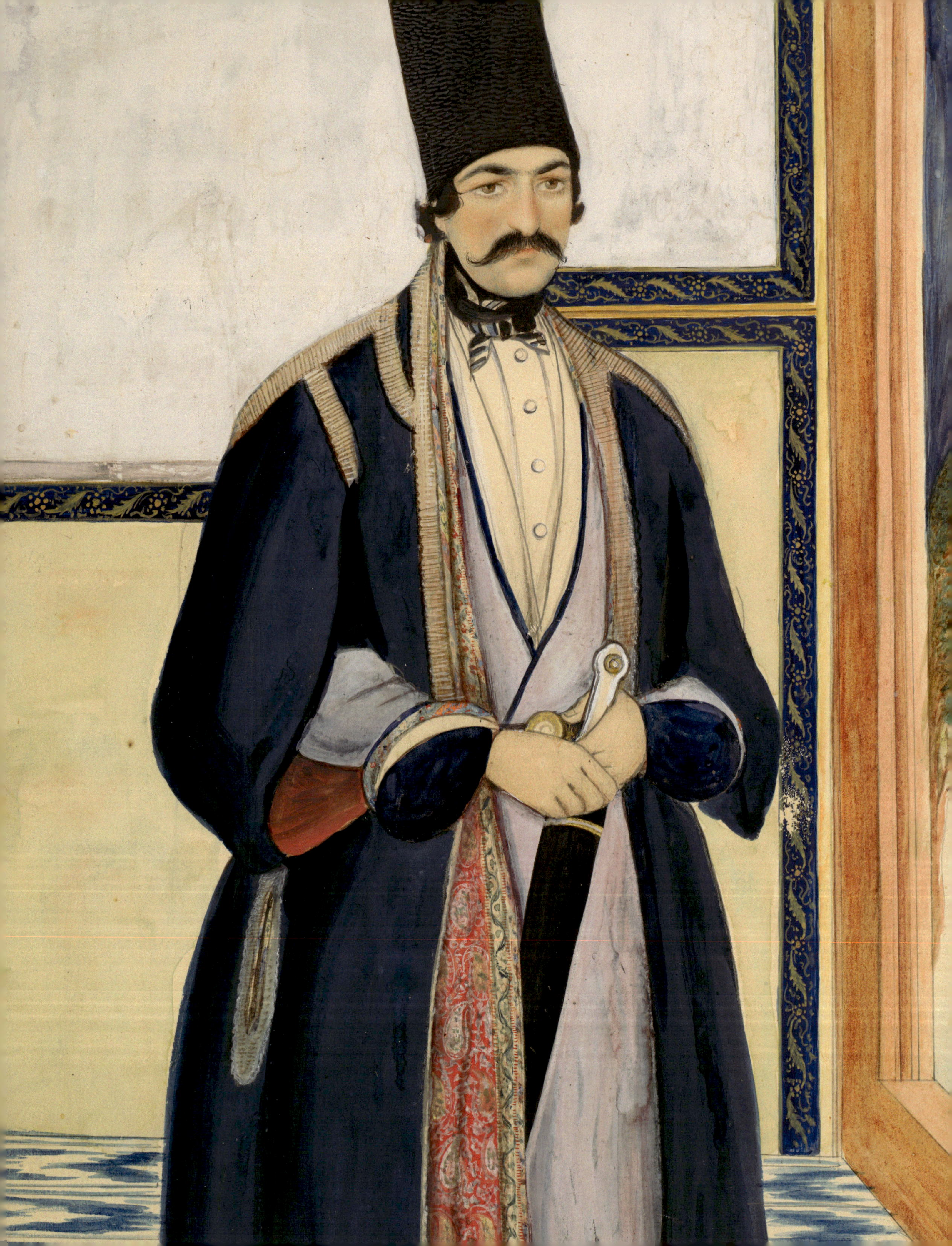

1 Technologies of the Image

ART IN 19TH-CENTURY IRAN

David J. Roxburgh

The exhibition *Technologies of the Image: Art in 19th-Century Iran*, together with this accompanying catalogue, examines the complex artistic trends and developments of a period observed and commented upon by members of Qajar society and foreign visitors to Iran alike. The overwhelmingly negative assessments of art made under the rule of the Qajar dynasty (r. 1779–1925), especially by European travelers—reflective of cultural biases of differing magnitudes—have had the unfortunate effect of stifling art historical scholarship on the period.[1] Though the field of Qajar art and architecture has grown considerably in recent years, revealing a greater interest in the modern period of the Islamic lands, some evaluations and approaches remain affected by frameworks formed in the 19th century. This exhibition and catalogue differ from earlier studies about Qajar art by a shift of emphasis and approach. *Technologies of the Image* not only examines the effects and results of new technologies of representation across a variety of mediums, their contexts of production, and sectors of society that range from the courtly elite to the citizenry at large, but also suspends the value judgments that shaped and framed the majority of responses to Qajar art during the 19th century and after. While the histories of lithography, chromolithography, and photography as new technologies of the image fostered in Iran—and as mass-produced items also imported into Qajar domains from Europe, Russia, and India—have been widely acknowledged, focused studies

Detail: *Standing Courtier*, mid-19th century. For full information, see cat. 5, p. 132.

about the results and implications of their emergence and interactions are thus far lacking.

The exhibition and catalogue essays examine the mediums of lacquer wares, lithography, photography, and painting; their separate, intertwined, and co-dependent histories; as well as their contexts of invention and production and their means of dissemination. Collectively, the objects in the exhibition comprise portable objects including lacquer wares (e.g., pen boxes, mirror cases), handmade and printed illustrated books, albums (composed of collections of drawings, paintings, and photographs), single-sheet painted and printed images, photographs, and postcards. The breadth of mediums and subject matters evidenced by these objects matches the diverse formats through which images were embodied and circulated in the world.

While each essay in the catalogue is organized around a single medium—introducing its distinctive material properties, particular techniques of production, favored subject matters, and histories—the individual medium is also examined in light of its exchanges with others. The vast array of objects made in Iran during the reign of the Qajar dynasty indicates complex intersections of mediums and their remediation.[2] The term "remediation" refers to a common understanding that successive forms of representation always involve the mediation and refashioning of prior mediums (e.g., perspective painting, photography, and television). Thinking about this process entails the consideration of a host of elements that includes, for example, subject matters, means of presentation, composition, the integration of text and image, and the material properties and effects of distinct mediums that to various degrees could be preserved—if that was, in fact, sought after—despite the process of translation.

The free mobility of the image across mediums and systems of duplication and translation in 19th-century Iran—a process that did not worry Qajar artists and patrons, unlike their frequently distraught European contemporaries—is already fully apparent in even the most characteristic of forms, the lacquer object. Lacquer in the Islamic lands, developed in the late 15th century, consisted of an object made from pasteboard or papier-mâché that was decorated with layers of watercolor, metallic substances, and oil-and-resin-based lacquer. The material durability of lacquer wares permitted images to appear in richly developed and detailed schemes and on exterior surfaces. In her essay, Mary McWilliams examines the methods and materials developed by artists of lacquer wares—many of whom worked in other mediums—and the procedures and concepts through which image programs were formed. Artists of lacquer wares in the Qajar period eagerly sourced images from different mediums in an inventive system of recycling, adaptation, and reformulation. While this self-referential process of conceptualizing new images through a repertoire of existing models held sway in earlier periods in Iran, its continuity across the Qajar era facilitated increased production to meet market demands. It also introduced novel types inspired by European models from printed sources including engravings, lithographs, chromolithographs, and photographs.

Lithography appeared in Iran in the early 19th century shortly after its invention by Alois Senefelder and eclipsed the use of movable type for much of the period. While the acquisition of equipment and know-how necessary for lithography was supported by the Qajar elite as part of a modernization program, the developing print culture extended access to images and texts—as printed books, journals, single-sheets, and posters—in an unprecedented manner. Farshid Emami surveys the emergence of lithography, the relation between lithographed works and precedent and antecedent techniques and forms (the manuscript and photograph, respectively), and gauges some of the effects of the modern culture of print. He demonstrates, for example, how expanded access to texts and images propagated new habits of reading among a broader sector of society.

The Qajar elite also embraced photography after its invention in Europe. Its use expanded from courtly circles to the cities and streets of Iran over the course of the 19th century. Mira Xenia Schwerda presents the history of photography and attends to its propagation, successive technological developments, and steady spread as it was freed from the limitations of the unique image and emerged as a mass-produced commodity of visual expression and documentation. In addition, Schwerda considers the social, cultural, and political uses and values of the photograph, the invention of new subjects and image types, and interrelations between diverse kinds of photographs and other mediums.

In the final essay, I examine the historical medium of painting—including single-sheet paintings in watercolor on paper and lacquer wares—in light of the impact of photography and the intermedial role of lithography. Rather than marking a break with traditional practice, the effect that photography had on painting can be understood as a continuity in the Qajar artists' working methods. The approach of earlier generations of Persian painters was little different conceptually and practically; they similarly preferred to work from and after images seen on objects rather than from the direct study of life.

Given the nature of our subject matter and our approaches to it, some level of repetition among the essays is inevitable, perhaps even desirable. Though they are intended to generate productive synergies that hopefully will stimulate further research, each essay is written in a manner that permits separate reading.

The Qajars: Frameworks for the History of Their Art

The Qajars had a deep history in Iran as a Turkmen tribe that had been settled there since the advent of the Mongols in the 1200s. From the 1780s, Qajar leader Aqa Muhammad Khan (r. 1779–1797) steadily expanded his territories in northern Iran and made his major bid for power by waging war against Lutf ʿAli Khan (r. 1751–1794), the last leader of the Zand dynasty, whose capital was in Shiraz. The major southern cities of Shiraz and Isfahan now lay in Qajar hands. In 1796, Aqa Muhammad Khan also succeeded in rooting out the last representative of the Afsharid dynasty (r. 1736–1796), Shahrukh b. Nadir Shah, at Mashhad, located in the province of Khurasan, northeastern Iran. During his reign, Aqa Muhammad Khan restored a political unity to Iran that had not been seen since the zenith of Safavid dynastic power in the 1600s. Beginning with his nephew, six Qajar rulers followed Aqa Muhammad Khan, with succession passing through the first-born son, until the dynasty came to an end in 1925. The long reigns of two kings, Fath 'Ali Shah (r. 1797–1834) and Nasir al-Din Shah (r. 1848–1896), occupied the better part of the 19th century.

Qajar rulers faced many opportunities and challenges over the course of the 1800s, which is not at all surprising given the obvious strategic and economic importance of Iran's geopolitics. European countries attempted to curry favor and privileges from the Qajars as an expansionist Imperial Russia seized territories in the Caucasus during the reign of Fath 'Ali Shah and made further advances in Central Asia during the reign of Nasir al-Din Shah. The years in between showed signs of steady economic penetration and growing indebtedness to foreign creditors, and yet despite these travails the Qajars managed to hold onto the bulk of their territories through a highly centralized government apparatus. Heightened exchange with Europe—especially Britain and France—led to the dissemination of knowledge about conditions and developments there, which in turn stimulated internal reforms to the Qajar military and its government institutions, particularly during the early years of Nasir al-Din Shah's reign.[3]

The most complete foreign account of nearly all aspects of life in late 19th-century Iran under the rule of the Qajar dynasty was written by Lord George Curzon (1859–1925).[4] Curzon visited Iran for a period of four months, from September 1889 to January 1890, in the early years of his political career.[5] He traveled widely and published an expansive, two-volume narrative of his journey in 1892. *Persia and the Persian Question*—exceeding 1,300 pages in length—offered a detailed description of Iran, which Curzon considered a crucial buffer bordering India, Britain's largest and wealthiest colonial possession.[6]

India's border and security—and British control—was threatened by Russian expansion into Central Asia beginning with the conquest of Turkestan in 1865 and the capture of Tashkent, quickly followed by the annexation of Khodzhent, Samarqand, and Bukhara by 1868, and the Khanates of Khiva and Khokand in 1873 and 1876, respectively. Further Russian expansion in Central Asia continued in subsequent years to form a region, Turkestan, under the jurisdiction of its own Governor-Generalship. The first Governor-General, Konstantin Petrovich von Kaufman (1818–1882), initiated construction of the Trans-Caspian Railway in 1879 at Uzan-Uda on the Caspian Sea. The tracks reached the city of Samarqand in 1888 and Tashkent in 1898. Earlier in the century, during the reign of the Qajar ruler Fath 'Ali Shah, Persia had lost its once

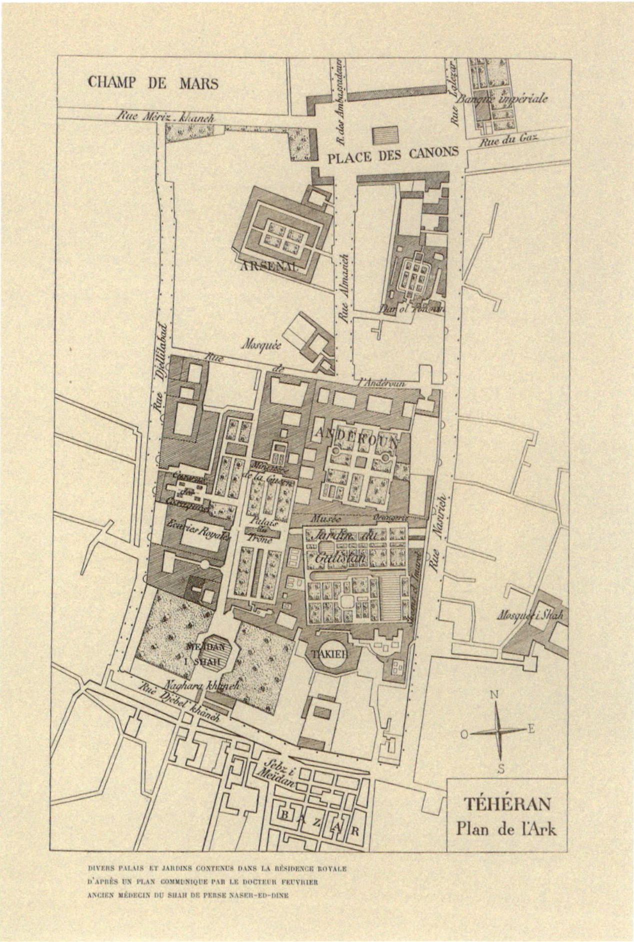

1 *Plan of the Citadel, Tehran*, c. 1900. After Henry-René d'Allemagne, *Du Khorassan au pays des Backhtiaris trois mois de voyage en Perse* (Paris: Hachette, 1911). Harry Elkins Widener Memorial Library, Harvard University, Asia 3219.11.5 F v.3.

expansive territories in the Caucasus to Russia through two wars in 1813 and 1826–28. The Caucasus was permanently lost after the latter Russo-Persian War and the Treaty of Turkmenchay. This earlier history of Iran's military weakness, together with contemporary events to the east in Turkestan, fueled a mounting British anxiety about the safety of India and increased the urgency of securing Persia's borders, enhancing its economic strength, and maintaining British sea trade routes throughout the Persian Gulf and the Indian Ocean.[7] The dedication that Curzon included in *Persia and the Persian Question*—"To the Officials, Civil and Military, in India whose hands uphold the noblest fabric yet reared by the genius of a conquering Nation"—was a transparent, and forceful, statement of Persia's importance to India and British interests there.

In the course of his four-month visit, Curzon described an Iran still stuck in the throes of what he regarded to be an incipient and incomplete modernization process then led by Qajar ruler Nasir al-Din Shah and his ministers, many of whom were members of an expansive royal family. Nasir al-Din Shah, initially a reformist monarch, had already grown wary of, and had become dissatisfied by, the social effects and political implications of modernization several years before Curzon's visit.[8] Radical juxtapositions between the old and the new—equivalent in Curzon's mind to "East" and "West"—were writ large in the urban fabric of Tehran, the city selected as capital in 1786 by Qajar leader Aqa Muhammad Khan.[9]

During Nasir al-Din Shah's reign, the Gulistan Palace complex, the residential and administrative seat of Qajar power (then located to the north of the city), underwent a series of demolitions, repairs, and new construction spanning the years 1867 to 1892 and divided into three main phases (1867–73, 1873–82, and 1882–92) (Fig. 1).[10] The redevelopment of Tehran had already commenced in 1851 with work on the citadel, bazaar, and the royal square. Major changes to the urban landscape occurred in 1867 with the demolition of the old city walls and the subsequent rebuilding of them at a perimeter that circumscribed an area quadruple the previous size. Featuring 12 gates and an octagonal plan, the walls were modeled after those of Paris built from 1840 onward. The larger urban footprint was intended to alleviate high population density—Tehran's former congestion caused by rapid population growth and the concomitant loss of its open space, much of it orchards, to residential and commercial infill. A network of broad avenues and streets, many radiating from large, open squares (including the *Maydān-i Tūp-khāna* [Artillery

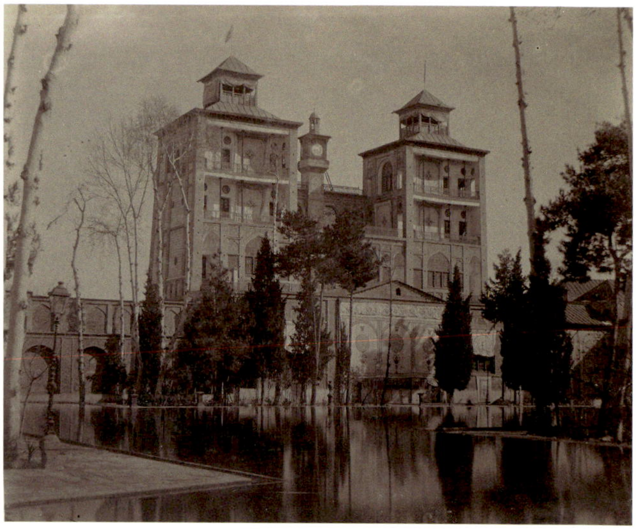

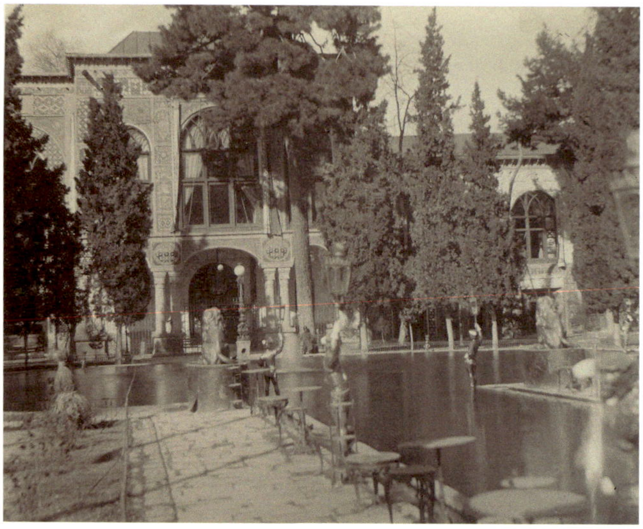

2 *Shams al-ʿImara, Gulistan Palace, Tehran,* detail of page 286 from the *Album of Photographs by ʿAli Khan Vali,* 1862–1900. For full information about the album, see cat. 24, p. 140.

3 *Facade of the Talar-i Salam, Gulistan Palace, Tehran,* detail of page 282 from the *Album of Photographs by ʿAli Khan Vali,* 1862–1900. For full information about the album, see cat. 24, p. 140.

Square] and *Maydān-i Mashq* [Drill Square]), forged new connections and axes across the intramural city. A new residential suburb was established to the north. In addition to these features—redolent of recent urban redevelopments in Paris, Cairo, and Istanbul—Tehran received the modern amenities of horse-drawn trams and street lighting in 1880.[11] Nasir al-Din Shah's first visit to Europe in 1873—including travel to Russia, Germany, Belgium, England, France, Switzerland, Austria, and through the Ottoman Empire to Istanbul on the return—occurred in the midst of these redevelopments and afforded him firsthand experience of conditions in modernizing Europe, although he already had ample access to information through intermediaries.[12] These included a host of Iranians who had traveled to Europe for educational purposes, Europeans who had come to work in Iran, and an array of books that had been translated from European languages into Persian.

During his time in Tehran, Curzon also toured the Gulistan Palace. He was struck by the many buildings then making up the palace and its grounds, and noted their diverse styles, built and decorated in the Persian manner with selective adaptations of European forms and motifs. While scant structures dating to the reign of Fath ʿAli Shah remained—chiefly the *Dīvān-khāna* with its prominent throne set inside an open columned porch (*tālār*) and a building with four wind towers at the corners (*ʿimārāt-i bādgīr*)—Curzon offered equal attention to describing their features as he did to the more recent additions sponsored by Nasir al-Din Shah, chiefly the five-story *Shams al-ʿImara* (Fig. 2), a royal residence towering over the royal square and the bazaar beyond, and the *Takiya Dawla*, a circular theater for the performance of the Shiʿi passion play (*taʿzīya* or *rawża-khvānī*), which commemorated the martyrdom of Imam Husayn during the feast of *ʿāshūrā* on 10 Muharram in the lunar Islamic calendar. One of Curzon's lengthiest descriptions is given to the Talar-i Salam, a reception hall whose primary function was to serve as a museum that safeguarded royal treasure and the gifts given by foreign potentates to the Qajar kings. The two-story structure featured a facade decorated with glazed tile revetment in the "seven colored" (*haft rangī*) technique punctuated by rounded windows and a porch supported by fluted columns with capitals (Fig. 3).[13] A broad carpeted staircase led up to the second floor, with the new museum located on the left, "a great hall or gallery, constructed after the return of the Shah from his first visit to Europe in 1873" (Fig. 4).[14] Underglaze-painted tiles, whose monochrome schemes and graphic techniques reflected the impact of photographic and lithographic models, lined the dadoes of the antechambers of the main reception hall.[15]

Curzon's impression of Tehran's inchoate urban fabric continues in his narration of the museum's contents, arrangement, and means of display:

> This extraordinary chamber, which with its contents alternately resembles an Aladdin's palace, an old curiosity shop, a prince's wardrobe, and a municipal museum, consists of a long parallelogram, crowned by a series of low domes, with plaster decorations in white, blue, and gold, there

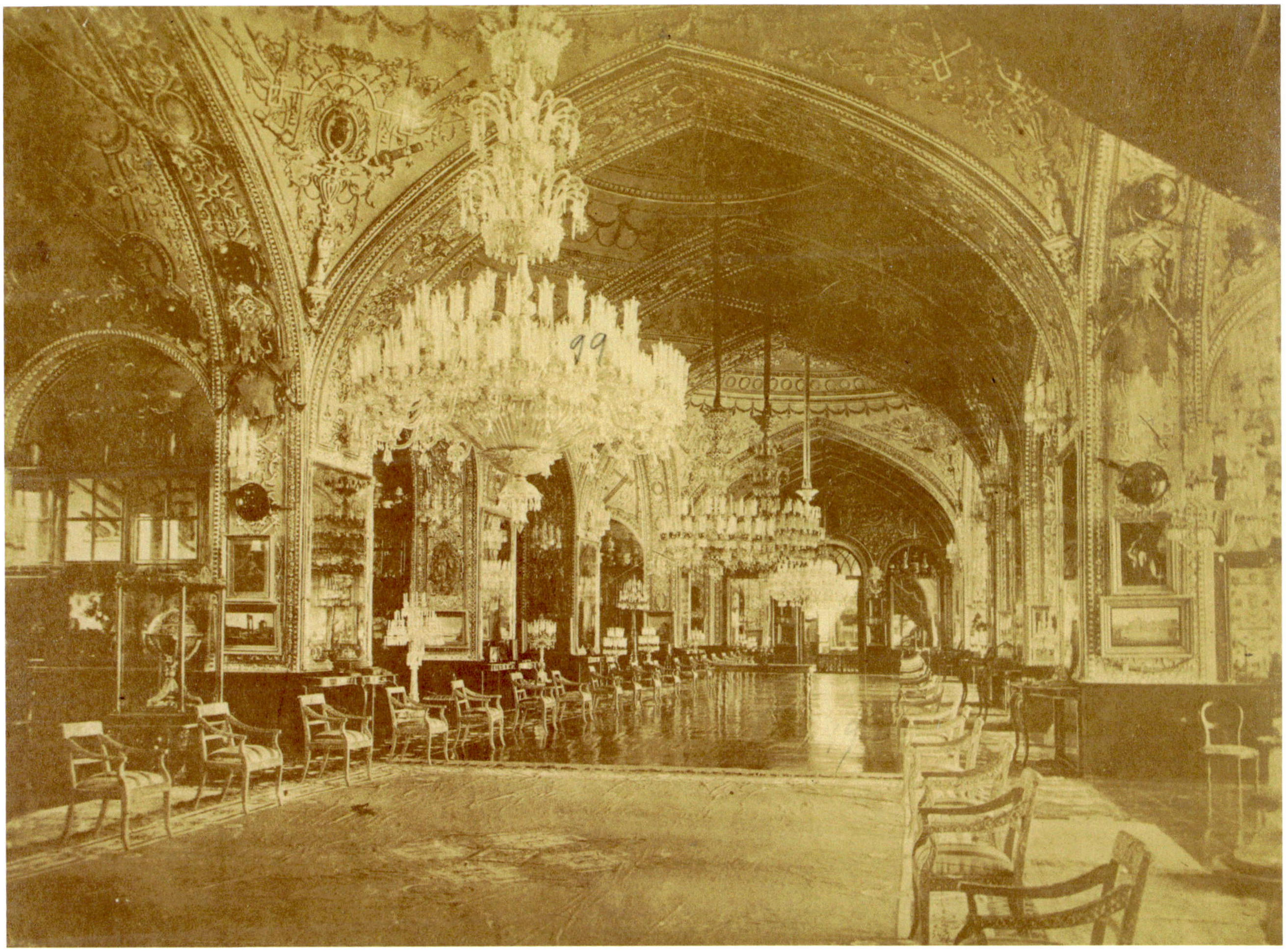

4 *Audience Hall (the Museum) in the Talar-i Salam, Gulistan Palace, Tehran*, Antoin Sevruguin, 1880–90. Albumen print, 21.3 × 15.5 cm (8⅜ × 6⅛ in.). Stephen Arpee Collection of Sevruguin Photographs, Freer Gallery of Art and Arthur M. Sackler Gallery Archives, Smithsonian Institution, Washington, D.C., FSA A2011.03 A.60a.

> being a number of deep recesses, terminating in windows along one side; while the partition between these recesses, and the remaining walls of the room, are fitted with glass cases, in which are displayed, side by side, treasuries of priceless value and the most unutterable rubbish. The central part of the chamber, which is, in part, tile-paved, contains a number of immense porcelain vases, mostly from Europe, candelabra, lustres, armchairs covered with a thin plating of real gold, etc., whilst upon tables or under glass cases are disposed with some slight effort at arrangement, but in ludicrous juxtaposition, Swiss musical boxes, Persian antiquities and specimens, meteorolites, European purchases or presents, and heads of game shot by His Majesty.[16]

In his comprehensive narration—made possible by three separate visits to the Talar-i Salam—Curzon oscillates between outright awe and judgmental dismay. Impressed by countless jewels, pearls, armor and swords, and a vast collection of European porcelains from Sèvres, Dresden, and Worcester, he found the oil paintings "mediocre or execrable."[17] After the vaulted hall of the museum, Curzon passed through a series of chambers that he considered to offer a "farcical contrast of the Oriental and European":

> Illustrations, snipped from the English illustrated newspapers, appear side by side upon the walls with photographs of the Shah and his little boy favourite, the Aziz-es-Sultan, and with inferior copies of Italian oil-paintings. Here is a picture of the Paris exhibition and the Eiffel Tower; there is a deplorable oleograph of an Alpine village, both hung in a room adorned with Persian plaster-work and spread with Persian carpets. I noticed here, what I observed in other palaces that I visited, that the Oriental intellect seems to derive particular gratification from the display of duplicates. Thus, the King's son, the Zil-es-Sultan, has, in his town residence, a long row of facsimile portraits of himself hanging upon a single wall. Similarly, in the royal abode, I noticed in one place two large copies of a semi-nude Venus or Magdalen of the later Italian school, absolutely identical, hanging on either side of a doorway; and the same phenomenon was constantly repeated. The impression left upon me by an inspection of many modern Persian residences of size and magnificence, was this: that whereas the Persian taste, if restricted to its native art or to the employment of native styles, seldom errs, the moment it is turned adrift into a new world, all sense of perspective, proportion, or beauty, all aesthetic perception, in fact, appears to vanish; and in proportion as its choices will have been correct and refined amid native materials, so does it become vulgar and degraded abroad.[18]

Such judgments offered by European visitors to Iran were entirely conventional and frequently repeated.[19] In his memoir published in 1867, Comte Julien de Rochechouart—in Iran from 1863 as successor to Joseph Arthur, comte de Gobineau, at the French Legation in Tehran—had already seized upon what he held to be strange and unwelcome trends in the arts of the Qajar period. In a chapter devoted to "Boarding [bookbinding] and painting," he observed:

> The Persians have no idea about painting as we think of it, and what is more, they do not understand it. Persian rulers have been heard speaking many times about the value we attach to this art and have requested paintings and sent students to study in Rome. But the paintings that they bring them are loathsome and the students sent to Europe learn nothing and return saying—to explain their ignorance—that we have nothing in painting that is remarkable and that the last street-sweeper of Tehran knows better how to hold a brush than Raphael or Titian. Although the "Seated Madonna" has found grace before Raphael and Titian, the Persian artist Persianized it before reproducing it, at first she was not so *décolletée*, then changed the palette; it takes a lot of good will to identify the model.[20]

Elsewhere, Rochechouart dismisses the Persians "as ornamentalists," noting that their "painting is an utterly industrial art form entirely outside the aesthetic norms to which we are accustomed"; he further asserts that their traditional art is in decline and observes that artists "have as their models images of Lorraine that garnish the shop-windows of our village wig-makers or lithographs that decorate the rooms in taverns: Asia, Africa, Nina, 'Matilda's Smile,' 'A Fire in the New World,' and even worse, lewd engravings of the sort only sold in the backstreet shops of certain neighborhoods."[21] The subjects identified here reflect the types found in lithographs and chromolithographs made by such popular print factories as Jean-Charles Pellerin at Épinal, France. A broad range of materials reached Iran from Europe and Russia during the 1800s, including printed works on paper—comprising newspapers, books, postcards, and prints—as well as cotton.[22]

Separated by two decades, Curzon and Rochechouart were struck by what they deemed to be the harmful effects of European art on the national, indigenous, and traditional arts of Iran, as well as the Persians' general failure to draw—or perhaps even understand—the kinds of distinctions Europeans would commonly make between elite and popular art forms, their different mediums, and characteristic means and manners of execution. Across social ranks, Qajar artists and patrons alike freely embraced the products of the newest technologies of representation—lithography, chromolithography, and photography—and the capacities of the mass-produced image, which they held in equal esteem to the conventional and historical mediums of drawing and painting (encompassing watercolor, oil painting, and lacquer) made directly

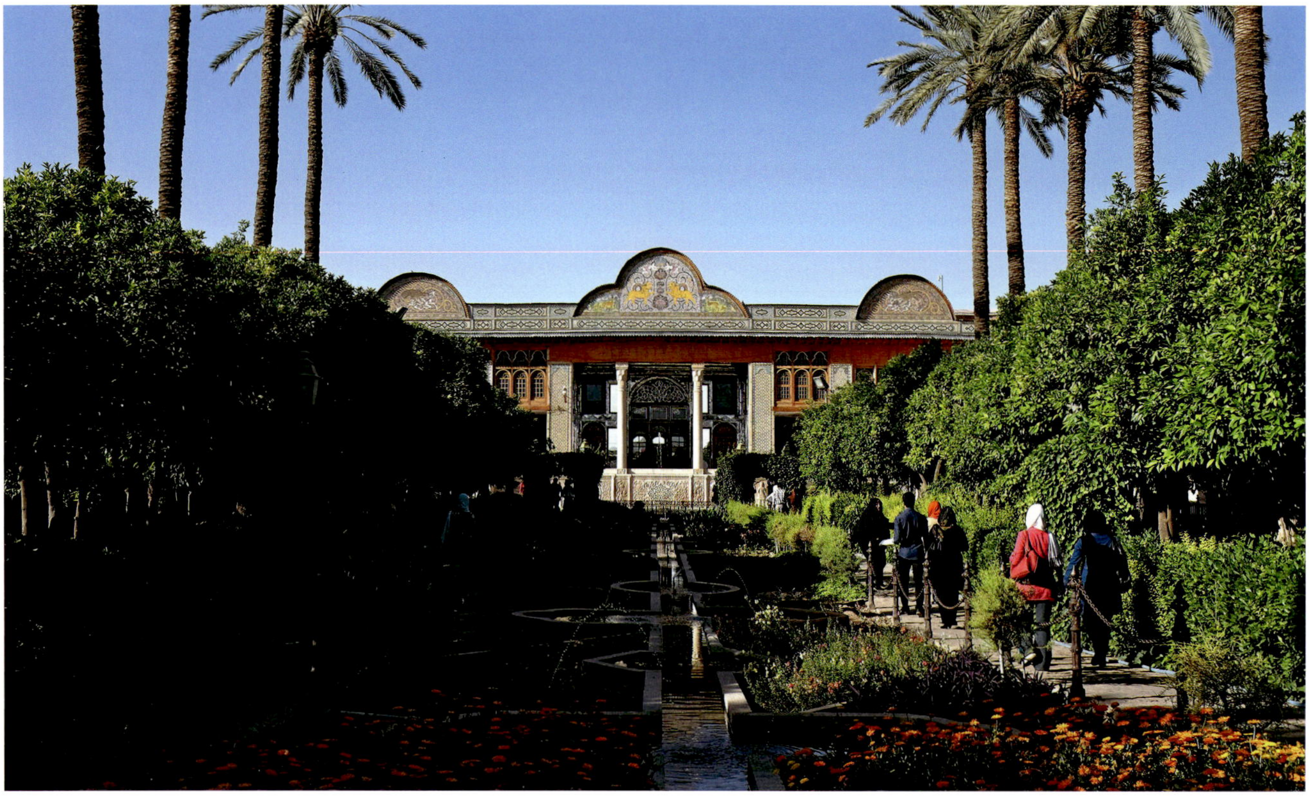

5 *Reception Hall in the Public Area* (bīrūnī), Naranjistan, Shiraz.

by the human hand. But even more than that, Qajar artists—whether working under court patronage or in the bazaars—engaged in a process of artistic creation that elided differences between discrete mediums, translating (in the sense of moving something from one place or condition to another), recycling, and repurposing images and subject matters in a wholly fluid and elastic way. The repeated image and the utter preponderance of duplication perplexed Curzon: he could not fathom what he considered to be inherent redundancy in the frequent "display of duplicates," perhaps because it challenged his cultural expectations of artistry, mastery, originality, good taste, and the exercise of judgment. Whether willfully or not, his opinion depended on a suspension of history, seeing in the Persian exposure and reaction to European art and newly developed technologies of representation a stark rupture rather than a continuity of artistic attitudes and procedures. In fact, the history of art in Iran, especially since the era of the Safavids, had been characterized by receptivity to exogenous traditions (especially European ones) and a manner of conceiving of creativity—and originality—always through relational models. Images of whatever type, format, and medium had always been about images, a *modus operandi* that remained constant throughout the Qajar period.

The form of eclecticism and its many effects witnessed in the art and architecture of the ruler's Tehran Gulistan Palace extended to the private homes of Qajar royals and nobles throughout Iran, and into the realm of those citizens with sufficient resources to acquire objects for their personal use.[23] A prominent example is offered by the Naranjistan (Orangery) of Shiraz, a townhouse built between 1879 and 1886 for Mirza ʿAli Muhammad Khan Qavam al-Mulk, who governed the city under Nasir al-Din Shah's rule. The public area (*bīrūnī*)—used by the owner to receive and entertain male guests—was bounded by an arcaded courtyard that enclosed gardens with trees and featured a water channel interconnected to small pools (Fig. 5). An entrance vestibule and grand reception hall stood at opposite ends of the courtyard on axis with the water feature. The interior facades of the vestibule and court featured "seven-colored" ceramic revetments—depicting courtiers, hunting scenes, immediately recognizable stories from Persian literary classics, and floral compositions—with marble dadoes carved in relief depicting scenes modeled after the Achaemenid sculptures at Persepolis.[24] The reception hall, rising from an elevated stone platform—with stone reliefs of lions again modeled after Persepolitan examples and images of Qajar courtiers, floral and vegetal scrolls, and a stalactite (*muqarnas*) cornice—comprised a rectangular building opened at the front with a deep porch (*tālār*) enclosed on several floors by a number of interconnecting chambers (Figs. 6, 7).

The exterior facade and interior rooms of the reception hall were richly decorated in mirror work, some of it layered beneath colored and painted glass; stained glass as well as polychrome and gold *fixé sous verre*; wood, carved and inlaid with walnut, Indian teak, and mother-of-pearl from the Persian Gulf; painted and gilded wood; plaster, plain, carved, and painted; glazed tiles arranged in continuous surfaces or punctuating brick courses; and marble, sourced from Tabriz and Yazd, used for dadoes and a fireplace. The relief lintel of the green marble fireplace combined a figural scene styled after a Persepolitan image of the Achaemenid ruler Darius (r. 522–486 BCE) receiving tribute

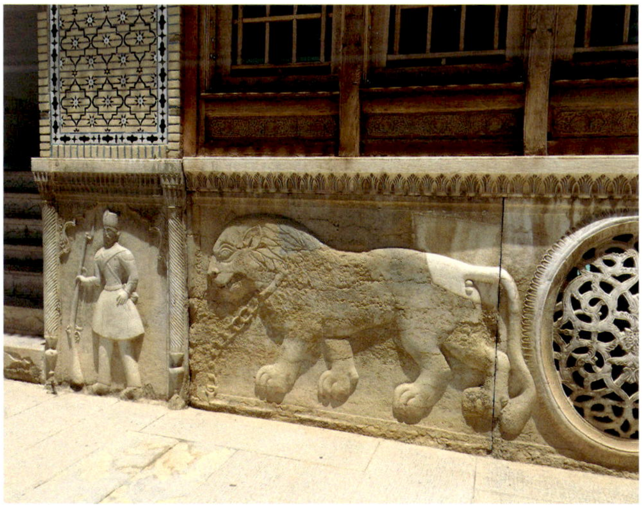

6 *Qajar Guard with Chained Lion*, marble dado of the reception hall, Naranjistan, Shiraz.

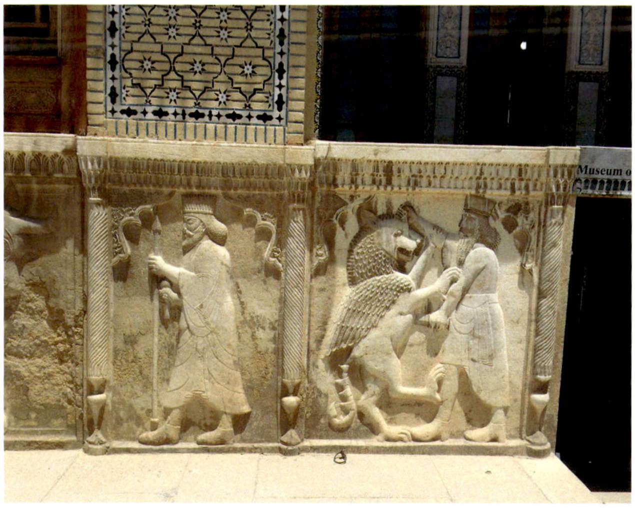

7 *Persepolitan Style Reliefs*, marble dado of the reception hall, Naranjistan, Shiraz.

and portraits of the seated Qavam made after recent photographs (Fig. 8).[25] This broad repertoire of materials and techniques combined naturalistic representation with abstract and geometric modes. While some of the female portrait busts and vignettes of architecturescapes were painted in emulation of European sources, other portraits as well as scenes of seasonal outdoor human activity—fly fishing and ice-skating in British, French, and Dutch landscapes—were attached to the ceilings as polychrome prints, mostly chromolithographs, trimmed to fit inside ornamental painted frames (Figs. 9, 10).[26] Photographs of the Qavam and his family members were also embedded in the mirror-work surfaces enveloping the porch of the reception hall. The opulent, mixed-media decorative program of the Naranjistan reflected the same brand of cosmopolitanism evident at the Gulistan Palace in Tehran, a modernity signaled by the juxtaposition and blending of Persian and European art traditions—their motifs, subject matters, and stylistic manners—both present and past.

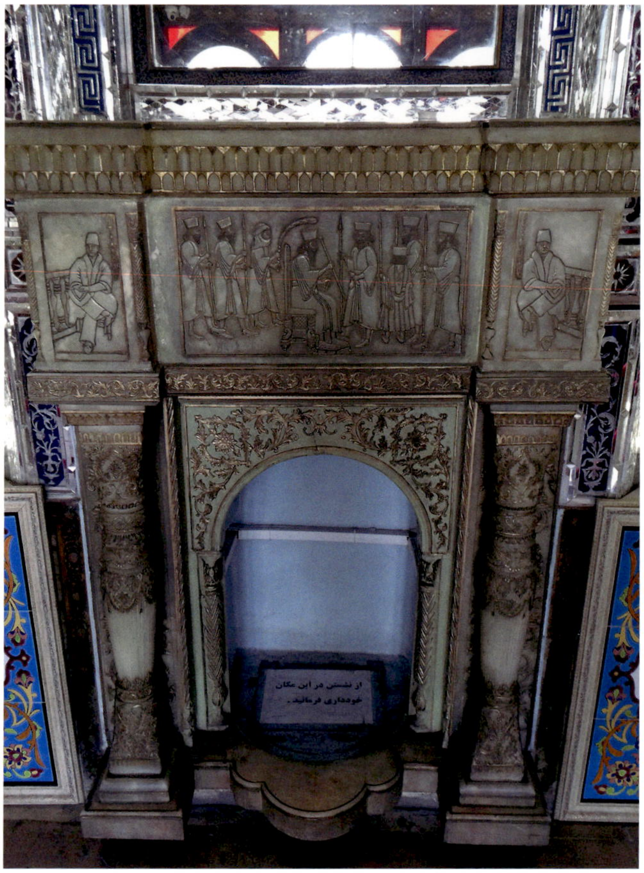

8 *Persepolitan Style Enthronement and Images of the Qavam*, Tabriz green marble fireplace, gilded, reception hall, Naranjistan, Shiraz.

A comparable process of appropriation and adaptation of old and modern materials, foreign and Persian, and their techniques of representation is evident in another major commission of Nasir al-Din Shah, a rock relief at Tang-i Band Burida on the Haraz Road completed in 1878–79 (Fig. 11).[27] In 1873, Nasir al-Din Shah ordered his vizier Husayn ʿAli Khan and an Austrian engineer to supervise the repair and widening of the route connecting the province of Mazandaran on the southern littoral of the Caspian Sea to the inner plain northeast of Tehran. The monumental relief, measuring 8 meters in length and 4 meters in height, commemorated the ruler's successful completion of the roadwork, a difficult feat extolled in an epigraphic border of Persian poetry framing the rectangular composition. The sculptured field presents a frontal equestrian portrait of Nasir al-Din Shah—labeled "portrait of [his] incomparable majesty" (*timsāl-i bī-misāl-i humāyūnī*) in a cursive *nastaʿlīq* script—flanked by ten courtiers and officers who are dressed in formal costume (*sardārī*) and divided in two groups. Each man is identified by name, office, and honorific titles, including court photographer Riza Khan (1843–1889) ("intimate of the emperor, private aide-de-camp, Riza Khan, good fortune of the sultanate, the chief photographer" [*muqarrab al-khāqān ājūdān-i makhṣūṣ Riżā Khān iqbāl al-salṭana ʿakkās-bāshī*]). Riza Khan accompanied Nasir al-Din Shah on his second European tour, in 1878. One final inscription, positioned below the horse's hooves, records the sculptor's name, ʿAli Akbar ("work of the lowly ʿAli Akbar in the year 1878" [*ʿamal-i kamtarīn ʿAlī Akbar fī sana 1295*]). The radical frontal pose of Nasir al-Din Shah, the

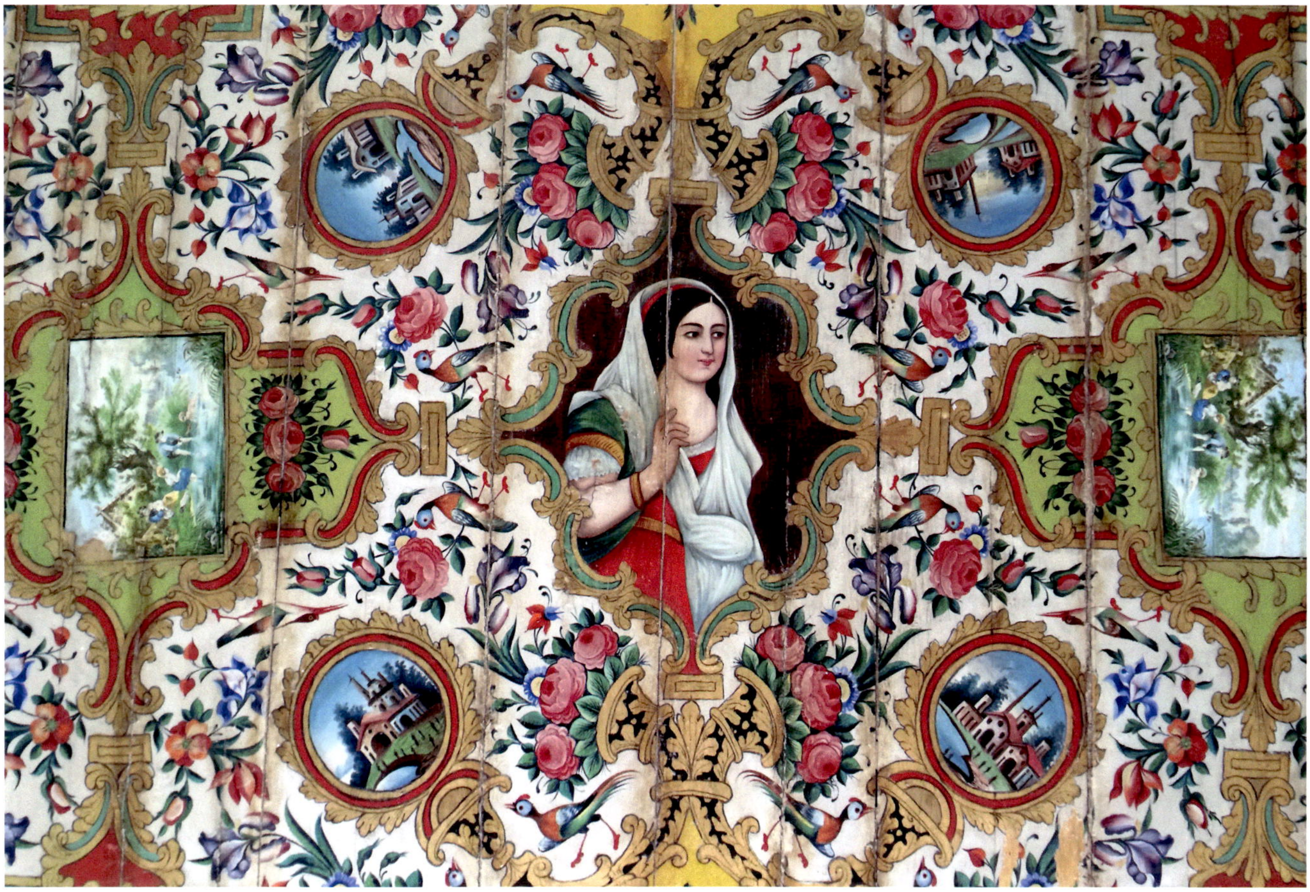

9 *Ceiling Painting Featuring Painted Portrait Busts and Applied Chromolithographs of Landscape Scenes*, private chambers of the reception hall, Naranjistan, Shiraz.

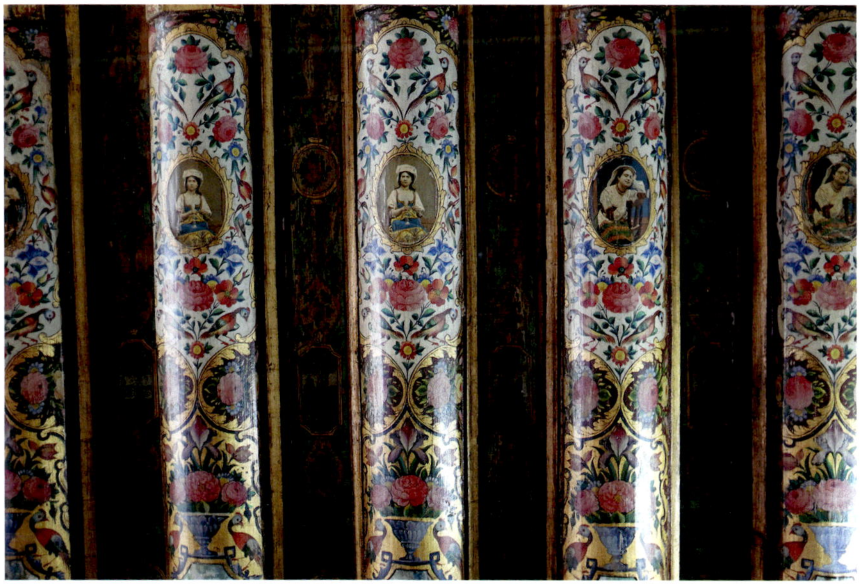

10 *Ceiling Painting Featuring Painted Decoration of Landscape Vignettes and Florals and Applied Chromolithographs of Female Portraits*, private chambers of the reception hall, Naranjistan, Shiraz.

receding lines of the forward-facing slightly overlapping courtiers, and the sense of infinite space conveyed by the blank field and the figures' apparent suspension in it differ from the conventions of earlier monumental sculpture in Iran and suggest the impact of an image mediated through photography.[28] The sense of space is further developed by the various levels of projection that 'Ali Akbar achieved through his carving technique.

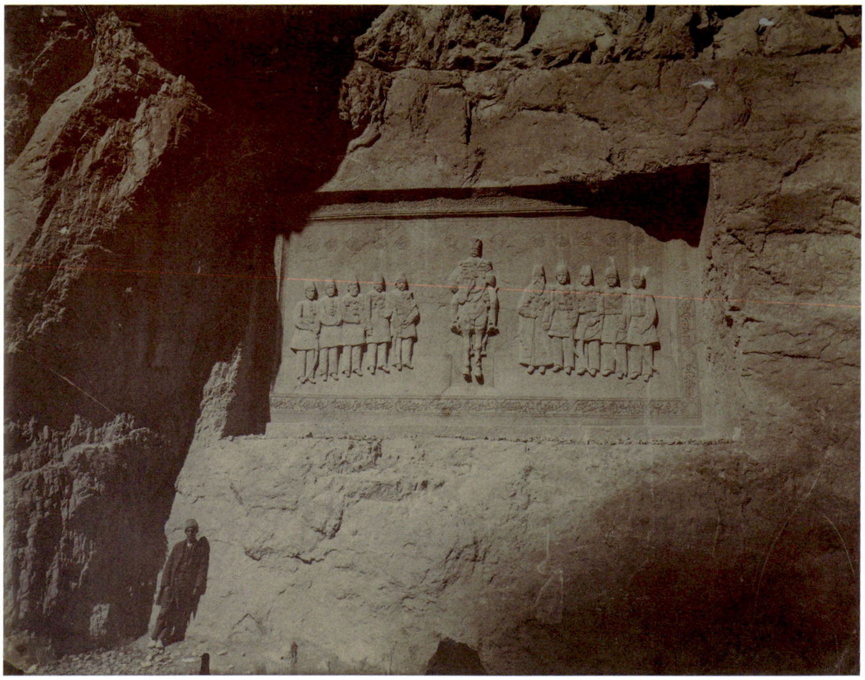

11 *Rock Relief of Nasir al-Din Shah Commemorating the Reconstruction of the Old Road to Mazandaran,* photograph c. 1880s–90s. For full information, see cat. 35, p. 142.

In its subject matter and effect, Nasir al-Din Shah's single monumental relief departed from earlier Qajar-era rock reliefs, all of which were made during the reign of Fath 'Ali Shah in the 1820s and 1830s. Seven reliefs were made during Fath 'Ali Shah's reign: five commissioned by the king, the other two sponsored by his son Muhammad 'Ali and grandson Timur Mirza (Fig. 12).[29] The themes—hunting, feasting, enthronement—and spatial conception of relief sculpture from Fath 'Ali Shah's time are much closer to their direct models, namely, the pre-Islamic Sasanian reliefs concentrated at various sites in southern Iran in the province of Fars (Fig. 13). The chief difference between the Sasanian examples and those of the Qajar period is that figures in the latter wear contemporary clothing. The Sasanians, who

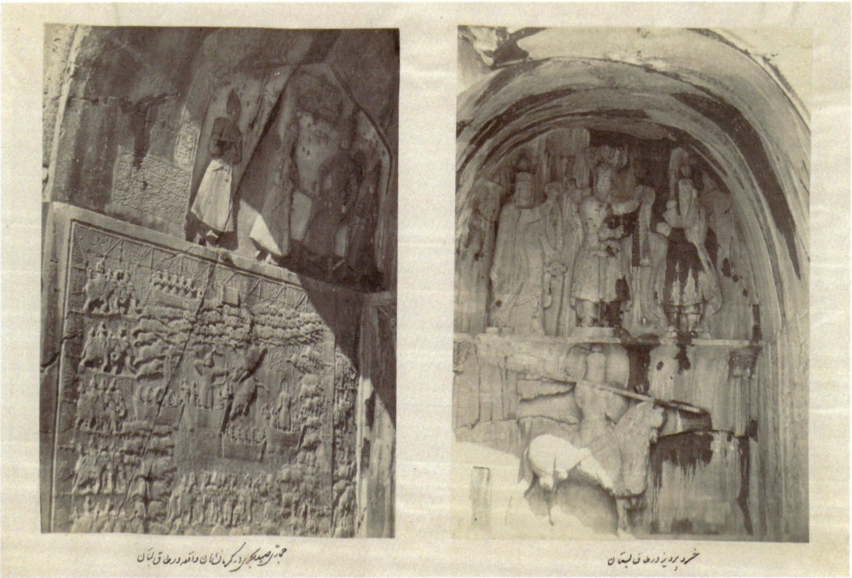

12 Left: *Muhammad 'Ali, Son of Fath 'Ali Shah, in Audience with Two Sons and His Chief Chamberlain, 1820s* (top); *Great Boar Hunt* (bottom), *Dating to the Reign of Sasanian King Khusraw II, Taq-i Bustan, Iran.* Right: *Large Vault with the Investiture of Sasanian King Khusraw I (r. 591–628), Taq-i Bustan, Iran.* Page 266 from the *Album of Photographs by 'Ali Khan Vali, 1862–1900.* For full information about the album, see cat. 24, p. 140.

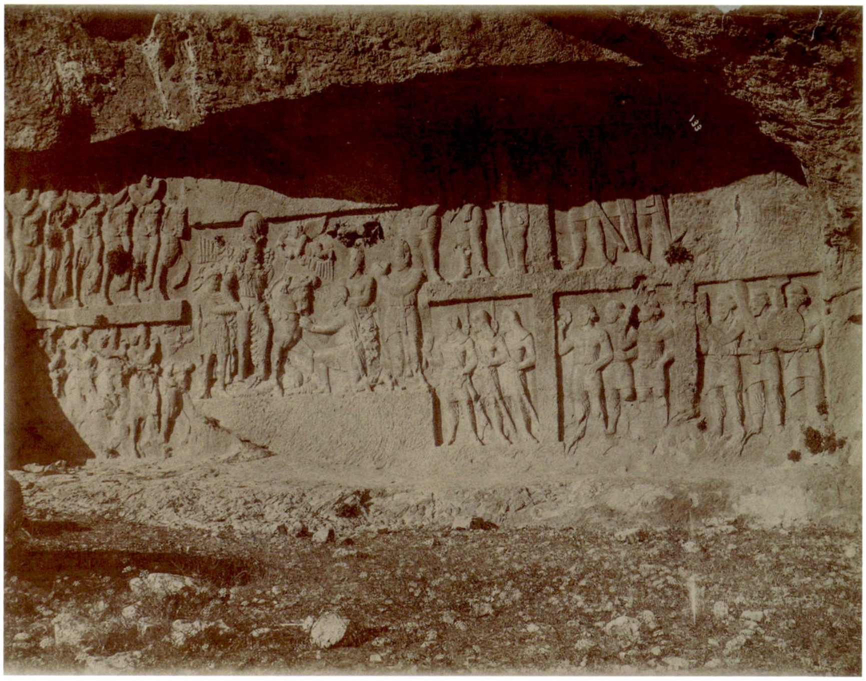

13 *Rock Relief of the Triumph of Shapur I over Valerian*, photograph c. 1880s–1930s. For full information, see cat. 36, p. 142.

ruled Iran from 224 to 651, had added monumental reliefs to sites already developed by the Achaemenids, chiefly in the vicinity of Persepolis (at the Achaemenid royal necropolis of Naqsh-i Rustam and, still closer to Persepolis, at Naqsh-i Rajab). A major Sasanian city, Istakhr, had also been built in proximity to Persepolis and was briefly the capital between 224 and 226. The material layerings enacted by the Sasanians on a historical landscape were clearly actions viewed as of equal political advantage to the Qajar ruler Fath ʿAli Shah.

Fath ʿAli Shah's rock relief commissions were symptomatic of a broad program in which his image proliferated through various fixed and portable objects in dialogue with a deep Iranian past whose traces were evident in the topography of the land, but that also responded to the royal propaganda then being generated for European monarchy.[30] One example is a large lidded box decorated with scenes of enthronement, hunting, and rows of male and female portrait busts (Fig. 14). The scene on the lid depicts an enthroned Fath ʿAli Shah—sitting on the famous "sun throne" (*takht-i khurshīd*)—in audience with officials attended by a prince and courtiers who have gathered under a porch (*tālār*) overlooking an open square.[31] The panels on each side portray the king and princes hunting boar, leopards, lions, and deer. The images of feasting and fighting that appear on the lacquer box recall a general iconography of kingship in pre-Islamic Iran, but more directly reflect the refashioning of those themes in the art and literature of Iran's Islamic period. Traces of history in Iran's landscape had also inspired poets who wrote works about the ethical dimensions of kingship, Nizami Ganjavi (1141–1209) chief among them. His *Khamsa* (Quintet) included a section devoted to the romance between the ruler Khusraw and his beloved Armenian princess Shirin. A major subplot of the story concerned Shirin's relationship to the sculptor Farhad, who famously carved her portrait in one of his rock reliefs (Fig. 15). Such stories about the lives and deeds of kings in Persian poetry of the Islamic period, as well as concepts related to the ruler's prerogatives and responsibilities, offered a rich resource for patrons and artists of the Qajar period as they had under earlier dynastic periods.

While Nasir al-Din Shah's intervention in Iran's landscape at Haraz can clearly be understood as an emulation of the landmarks established by his

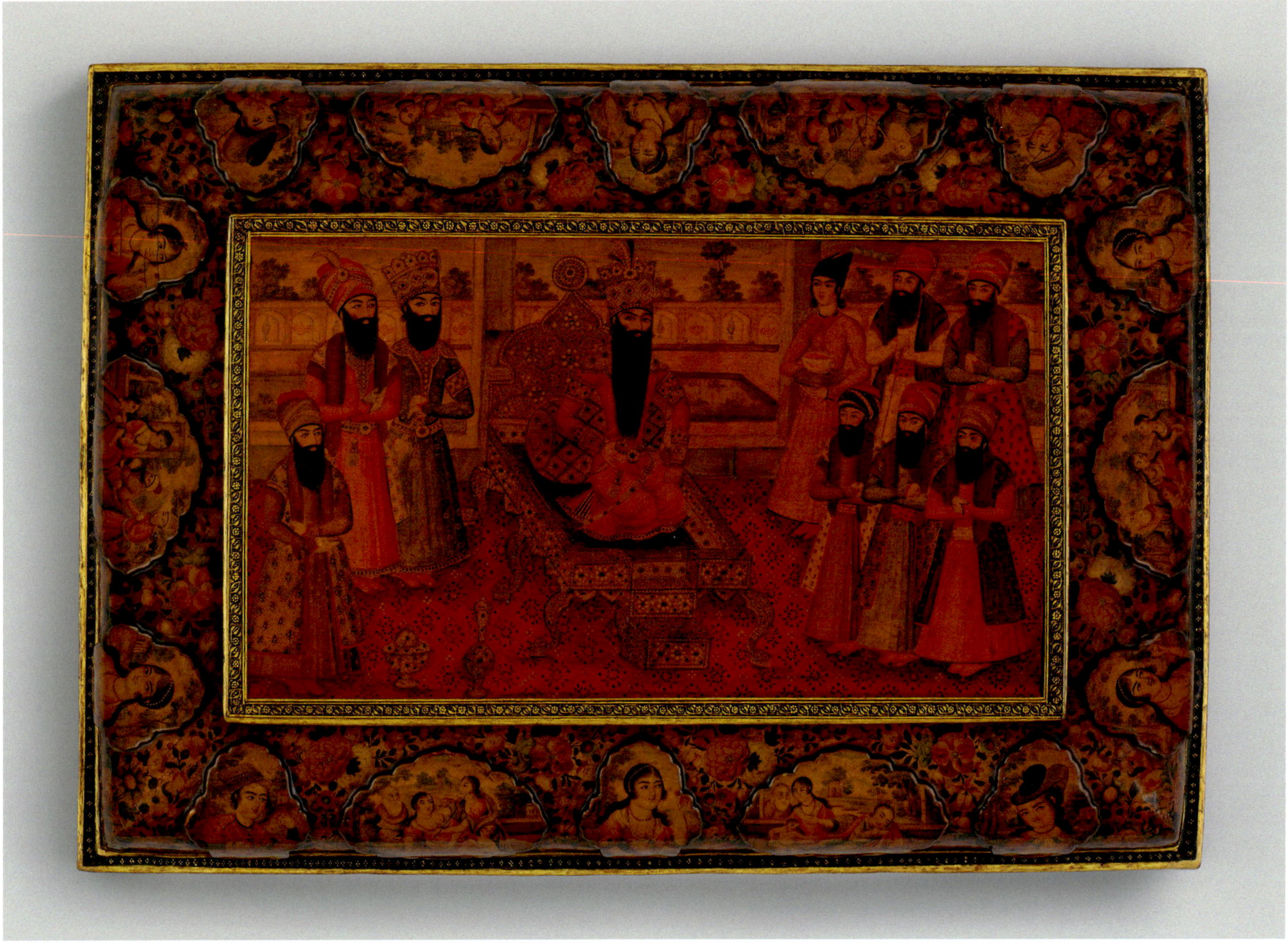

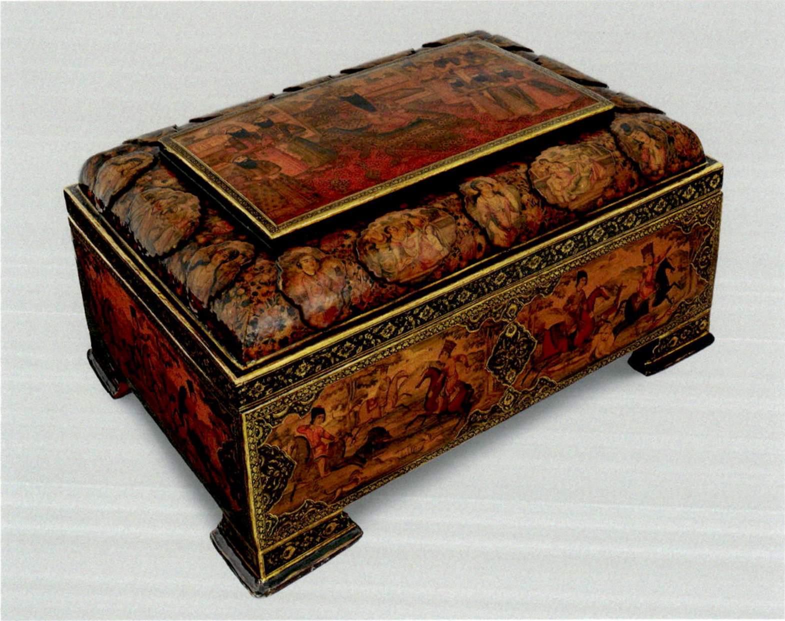

14 *Large Box with Fath 'Ali Shah Seated on the Sun Throne* (Takht-i khurshīd), 1820s–30s. For full information, see cat. 51, p. 148.

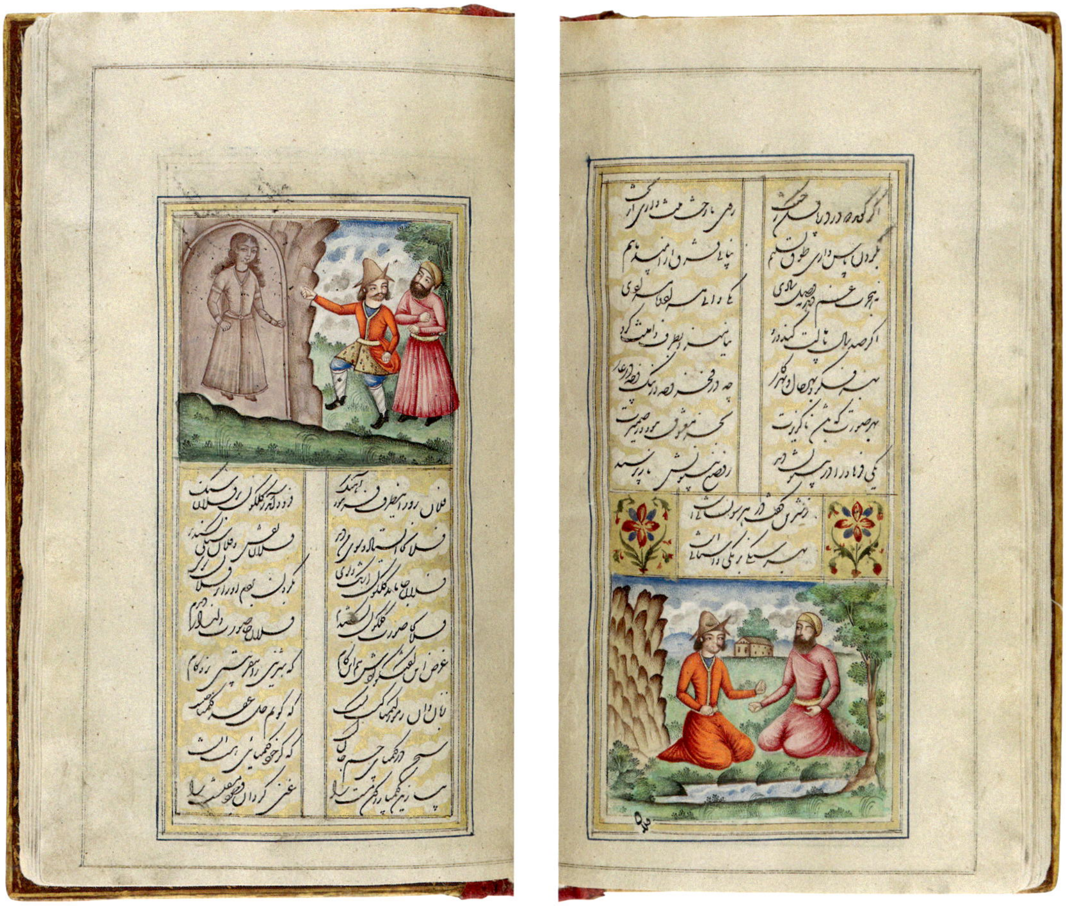

15 *Farhad Receives a Visitor at Mount Bisutun* (right page); *Farhad Shows the Rock Relief of Shirin to His Visitor* (left page), dated January 8, 1838. For full information, see cat. 7, p. 134.

dynastic forebear Fath ʿAli Shah—thereby evoking the history of the ruler's image since pre-Islamic times—it also signaled a new form of intermediality by its adoption of compositional traits redolent of the photograph (a modern reality signaled by the presence of Riza Khan, chief photographer to the court and intimate of the ruler). The relief on the Haraz Road, like the contemporary Naranjistan palace, implied multiple temporal registers as it negotiated a relation between traditions and practices across time.

This characteristic points toward another fundamental feature of Qajar art across mediums: its insistent contemporaneity in dialogue with a broad spectrum of objects whose chronology extended from the immediate past, to the Safavid period of the 1600s and 1700s, and still further back in time.[32] Qajar artists made selective use of a number of existing forms, constructed chronological references that were simultaneously past and present, and referenced aesthetic coordinates both local and international.

David J. Roxburgh is the Prince Alwaleed Bin Talal Professor of Islamic Art History and Chair of the Department of History of Art and Architecture at Harvard University.

Notes

1 Attitudes about Qajar art, how they have shaped its study, as well as some of the new approaches advanced in recent times are reviewed in David J. Roxburgh, "The Harvard Qajar Album—From Cover to Cover," in *An Album of Artists' Drawings from Qajar Iran*, ed. David J. Roxburgh (Cambridge, Mass.: Harvard Art Museums, 2017).

2 The processes and consequences of remediation are discussed in Jay David Bolter and Richard Grusin, *Remediation: Understanding New Media* (Cambridge, Mass.: MIT Press, 1999).

3 From a very large and rich literature, the following works can be identified as key introductions to Qajar history: Peter Avery, G. R. G. Hambly, and Charles Melville, eds., *The Cambridge History of Iran*, vol. 7, *From Nadir Shah to the Islamic Republic* (Cambridge: Cambridge University Press, 1991); Abbas Amanat, *Pivot of the Universe: Nasir al-Din Shah and the Iranian Monarchy 1831–1896* (London: I. B. Tauris, 2008); Edmond Bosworth and Carole Hillenbrand, eds., *Qajar Iran: Political, Social, and Cultural Change, 1800–1925* (Costa Mesa, Calif.: Mazda, 1983); Monica M. Ringer, *Education, Religion, and the Discourse of Cultural Reform in Qajar Iran* (Costa Mesa, Calif.: Mazda, 2001); and Nikki R. Keddie, *Qajar Iran and the Rise of Reza Khan 1796–1925* (Costa Mesa, Calif.: Mazda, 1999).

4 For introductions to 19th-century travel accounts published by Britons who visited Iran, with observations about their various points of emphasis and purpose, see Jennifer M. Scarce, "Persian Art through the Eyes of Nineteenth-Century British Travellers," *British Society for Middle Eastern Studies Bulletin* 8 (1) (1981); and David Blow, "Persia through Writers' Eyes," *Asian Affairs* 39 (3) (2008).

5 A few years later, he became Viceroy of India, a position he held from 1899 to 1905.

6 George N. Curzon, *Persia and the Persian Question*, 2 vols. (London: Longmans, Green, and Co., 1892).

7 The diplomatic and political confrontation between Britain and Russia ensued throughout the 19th century, beginning in 1830, when the British attempted to create a new trade route to Bukhara and to make Afghanistan a protectorate. The common term given to this rivalry is "The Great Game," attributed to British captain Arthur Conolly (d. 1842) and made popular through Rudyard Kipling in his novel *Kim* (1901). For a highly readable historical account, see Peter Hopkirk, *The Great Game: On Secret Service in High Asia* (London: Murray, 1990).

8 For Curzon's attitudes to the signs of reform, see Blow, "Persia through Writers' Eyes," 410. Shifts in Nasir al-Din Shah's attitudes to reformation and modernization are discussed in Maryam Ekhtiar, "Nasir al-Din Shah and the Dar al-Funun: The Evolution of an Institution," *Iranian Studies* 34 (1–4) (2001).

9 Blow quotes a passage from Curzon (*Persia and the Persian Question*, 1:306) that identifies the points of contrast between what he saw as "features of the East and West"; see "Persia through Writers' Eyes," 410.

10 Jennifer M. Scarce, "The Architecture and Decoration of the Gulistan Palace: The Aims and Achievements of Fath ʿAli Shah (1797–1834) and Nasir al-Din Shah (1848–1896)," *Iranian Studies* 34 (1–4) (2001).

11 Tehran's redevelopment is discussed in ibid.; David Blow, "From Islamic Small Town to Westernised Metropolis: The Development of Tehran under the Qajars and the Pahlavis," *The Court Historian* 15 (1) (2010): 5–16; John S. Gurney, "The Transformation of Tehran in the Later Nineteenth Century," in *Téhéran: Capitale bicentenaire*, ed. Chahryar Adle and Bernard Hourcade (Paris: Institut français de recherche en Iran, 1992); and Jennifer M. Scarce, "The Role of Architecture in the Creation of Tehran," in Adle and Hourcade, *Téhéran: Capitale bicentenaire*.

12 Nasir al-Din Shah made trips to Europe in 1873, 1878, and 1889 and produced written records of them. See Naghmeh Sohrabi, *Taken for Wonder:*

Nineteenth-Century Travel Accounts from Iran to Europe (Oxford: Oxford University Press, 2012), chap. 4.

13 The "seven-colored" technique enabled polychrome tiles to be produced without the risk of separate colors bleeding into each other during firing. The technique and its dramatic expansion under the Qajars are discussed in Yves Porter and Arthur Thévenart, *Palaces and Gardens of Persia* (Paris: Flammarion, 2003), 190–94. Numerous examples from the Qajar period are discussed and illustrated in Hadi Seif, *Persian Painted Tile Work from the 18th and 19th Centuries: The Shiraz School* (Stuttgart, Germany: Arnoldsche, 2014).

14 Curzon, *Persia and the Persian Question*, 1:314.

15 The underglaze-painted tiles, done in two series dated 1887 and 1899, are discussed in Jennifer M. Scarce, "Ancestral Themes in the Art of Qajar Iran, 1785–1925," in *Islamic Art in the 19th Century: Tradition, Innovation, and Eclecticism*, ed. Doris Behrens-Abouseif and Stephen Vernoit (Leiden, The Netherlands: Brill, 2006), 244–45. Curzon does not mention the tile series from 1887 in his description. Also see Scarce, "The Role of Architecture in the Creation of Tehran," 87, 90.

16 Curzon, *Persia and the Persian Question*, 1:314. I would like to thank Sarah Mirseyedi for sharing with me a paper that she wrote in a graduate seminar at Harvard University ("Tracing a Genealogy of Eclecticism and Display for the Late-Nineteenth-Century Gulistan Palace"). Mirseyedi offers a critical study of the European reception of Qajar architecture and the new museum in the Talar-i Salam. Through photographs, she reconstructs a history of the mutating display of objects in the main reception hall and discusses the forms of cultural bias exhibited by Europeans who described it.

17 Ibid., 1:314–22.

18 Ibid., 1:322–23.

19 An equally comprehensive description of the Gulistan Palace, especially the Talar-i Salam and its museum, was recorded by Arnold Henry Savage Landor after a visit he made in 1901; see his *Across Coveted Lands: Or, A Journey from Flushing (Holland) to Calcutta, Overland*, 2 vols. (New York: Scribner's Sons, 1903). Landor writes of "glass cases all around crammed full of things arranged with no regard to their value, merit, shape, size, colour or origin," and the vexing proximity of "costly jade and cheap prints," one of many instances of objects combined in groupings that he considered to violate (European) norms of display and taxonomy, divisions between the fine and decorative arts, inherent aesthetic worth versus monetary value, and significance (1:227–37). Another visitor to Iran, C. J. Wills, voiced his concern for the demise of traditional art forms, failures to emulate European techniques of representation (chiefly perspective), and the Persian taste for collecting and copying "doubtful European works." See C. J. Wills, *In the Land of the Lion and Sun, or Modern Persia: Being Experiences of Life in Persia from 1866 to 1881* (London: Ward, Lock and Co., 1891), 113–14, 331, 333.

20 Julien de Rochechouart, *Souvenirs d'un voyage en Perse* (Paris: Challamel Aîné, 1867), 260.

21 Ibid., 261, 264.

22 A recent study focused on images of European women has identified the sources and usages of imported printed materials in the private homes of the Qajar elite, especially in the city of Isfahan. See Parviz Tanavoli, *European Women in Persian Houses: Western Images in Safavid and Qajar Iran*, ed. Sarah B. Sherrill and Moya Carey (London: I. B. Tauris, 2015). Tanavoli describes the profusion and wide dissemination of printed materials throughout Iran (pp. 29–32).

23 Several scholars have characterized the gamut of cultural and artistic practices under the Qajars as a mode of eclecticism shared by other societies in the 1800s. Examples include Layla S. Diba, "An Encounter between Qajar Iran and the West: The Rashtrapati Bhavan Painting of Fath ʿAli Shah at the Hunt," in Behrens-Abouseif and Vernoit, *Islamic Art in the 19th Century*, 287; Oleg Grabar, "Reflections on Qajar Art and Its Significance," *Iranian Studies* 34 (1–4) (2001); Maryam Ekhtiar, "Innovation and Revivalism in Later Persian Calligraphy: The Visal Family of Shiraz," in Behrens-Abouseif and Vernoit, *Islamic Art in the 19th Century*; and J. P. Luft, "The Qajar Rock Reliefs," *Iranian Studies* 34 (1–4) (2001).

24 The Achaemenid Empire (550–330 BCE) was founded by Cyrus the Great. Persepolis, known in Persian as "The Throne of Jamshid" (*Takht-i Jamshīd*), was established by Darius I, c. 518, as the ceremonial center of the empire.

25 Lerner proposed the use of photographs in light of the "Qavam's informal posture, the attention given to his physiognomy, and the overall composition." See Judith A. Lerner, "A Case of Synchronicity: Photography and Qajar Iran's Rediscovery of Its Ancient Past," in *The Eye of the Shah: Qajar Court Photography and the Persian Past*, ed. Jennifer Y. Chi (New York: Institute for the Study of the Ancient World at New York University, 2015), 165. Lerner further suggests that the Persepolitan reliefs at the Naranjistan do not reflect direct study of the Achaemenid site but rather the mediation of photographs. For other remarks on the Naranjistan's reliefs, see Scarce, "Ancestral Themes in the Art of Qajar Iran, 1785–1925," 244.

26 For descriptions of the Naranjistan, see Terence O'Donnell, *The Narenjestan: A Brief History and Interpretation of the House* (Shiraz, Iran: Asia Institute, Pahlavi University, 1970); Marie-France Boyer, "Pizzazz in Shiraz," *The World of Interiors* (February 2016); and Lerner,

"A Case of Synchronicity," 163–66. The European female portrait busts are discussed in Tanavoli, *European Women in Persian Houses*, esp. 27–32. Willem Floor has surveyed the royal palaces and private homes featuring European images. See Willem Floor, *Wall Paintings and Other Figurative Mural Art in Qajar Iran* (Costa Meza, Calif.: Mazda, 2005), esp. 43–208.

27 Nasir al-Din Shah's relief is discussed in Lerner, "A Case of Synchronicity," 167–68; Manūchihr Sutūdah, *Az Āstārā tā Astārbād*, vol. 3 (Tehran: Anjuman-i Āsār-i Millī, 1349 H [1970]), 451–54; and Meisam Fallah and Hosein Sabri, "The Last Iranian Bas-Relief: The Depiction of Naser al-Din Shah Qajar on the Harāz Road," *Antiquity* 87 (337) (2013), http://antiquity.ac.uk/projgall/fallah337 (accessed on October 11, 2016). Sutudah provides a complete reading of the poetic inscription, the sculptor's signature, and dimensions. Fallah and Sabri offer readings of the labels identifying the figures in the relief.

28 These aspects of the relief are described in Lerner, "A Case of Synchronicity," 167–68. Lerner also proposes that the relief results from the collaboration between the sculptor ('Ali Akbar), the photographer (Riza Khan), and a painter, Ja'far. I have not been able to confirm the appearance of Ja'far's name on the Haraz Relief; it is not mentioned in Fallah and Sabri's reading of the labels. Lerner cites Luft as the source of the idea that the relief is based on a painting by Ja'far, which may in turn have been based on a photograph (176n44).

29 For the reliefs of Fath 'Ali Shah, see Judith Lerner, "A Rock Relief for Fath 'Ali Shah in Shiraz," *Ars Orientalis* 21 (1991); and Luft, "The Qajar Rock Reliefs."

30 See Abbas Amanat, "The Kayanid Crown and Qajar Reclaiming of Royal Authority," *Iranian Studies* 34 (1–4) (2001); Layla S. Diba, "Images of Power and the Power of Images: Intention and Response in Early Qajar Painting (1785–1834)," in *Royal Persian Paintings: The Qajar Epoch, 1785–1925*, ed. Layla S. Diba with Maryam Ekhtiar (London: I. B. Tauris Publishers in association with Brooklyn Museum of Art, 1998); Diba, "An Encounter between Qajar Iran and the West"; Priscilla Soucek, "Coinage of the Qajars: A System in Continual Transition," *Iranian Studies* 34 (1–4) (2001); and Priscilla Soucek, "The Visual Language of Qajar Medals," in Behrens-Abouseif and Vernoit, *Islamic Art in the 19th Century*.

31 The *takht-i khurshīd*, fashioned from gold and adorned with precious stones, was ordered by Mirza Husayn Sadr al-Isfahani for Fath 'Ali Shah. It was used by Nasir al-Din Shah for formal audiences and installed in the main reception hall of the Talar-i Salam. For these and other details about Qajar regalia and royal furniture, as well as bibliography, see Veronika Poier, "Cross-Cultural Modernity: Military Reform and the Image of the Shah," in *An Album of Artists' Drawings from Qajar Iran*, ed. David J. Roxburgh (Cambridge, Mass.: Harvard Art Museums, 2017).

32 An example includes imitation of Safavid art in the medium of Qajar lacquer. See Iván Szántó, "Qajar Lacquerware and the Related Art Forms," in *Artisans at the Crossroads: Persian Arts of the Qajar Period (1796–1925)*, ed. Béla Kelényi and Iván Szántó (Budapest: Ferenc Hopp Museum of Eastern Asiatic Arts, 2010), 51; and B. W. Robinson, "Qajar Lacquer," *Muqarnas* 6 (1989): 143. For other examples, see Nasser D. Khalili, B. W. Robinson, and Tim Stanley, *Lacquer of the Islamic Lands*, 2 pts. The Nasser D. Khalili Collection of Islamic Art, vol. 22 (London: Nour Foundation in association with Azimuth Editions and Oxford University Press, c. 1996–97), 2:314–20. In her study of the working album of drawings owned by lacquer artist Lutf 'Ali Khan Suratgar, Diba identified works from the Safavid through Fath 'Ali Shah periods. See Layla S. Diba, "Persian Painting in the Eighteenth Century: Tradition and Transmission," *Muqarnas* 6 (1989): 157–59.

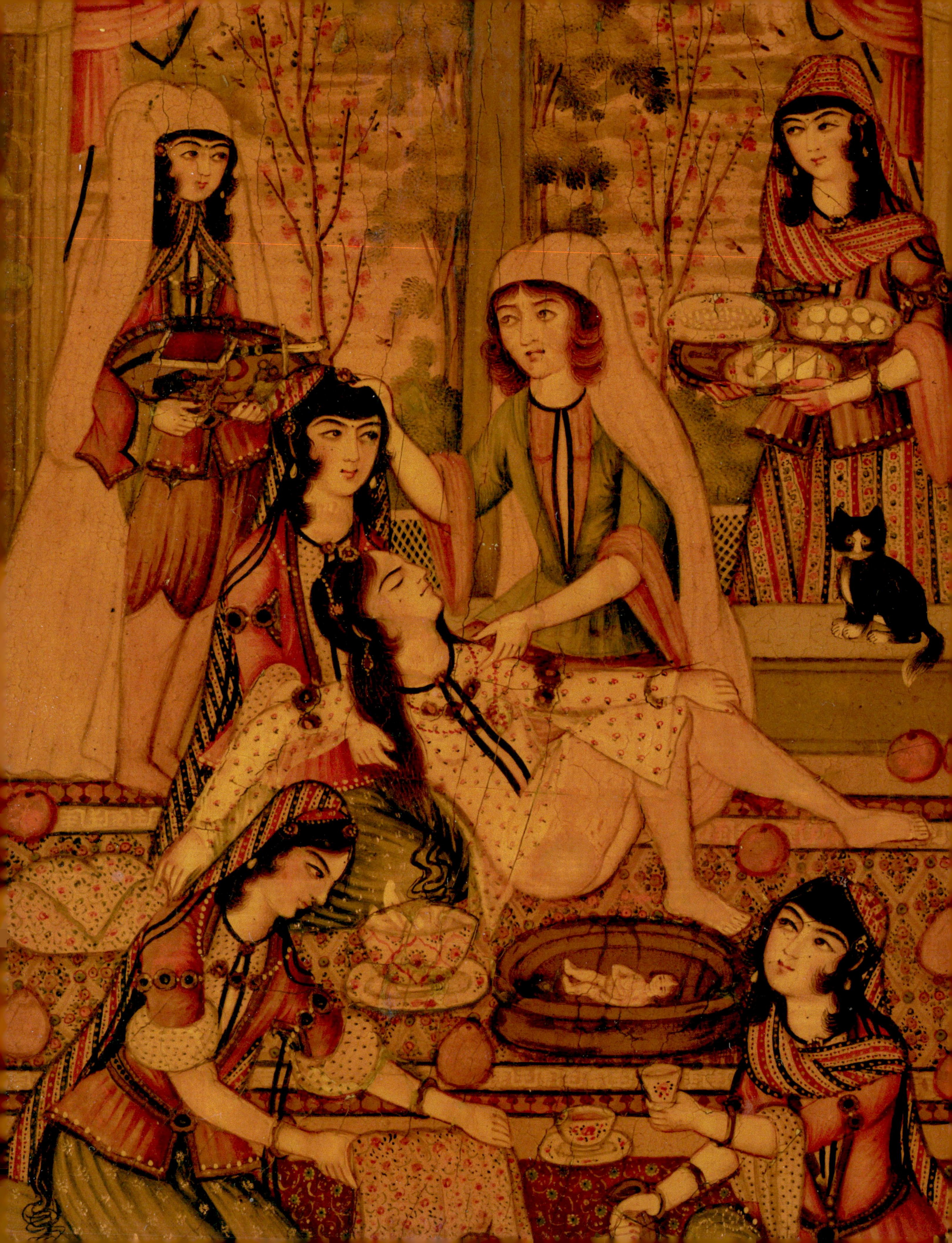

2 Qajar Lacquer as a Medium of Exchange

Mary McWilliams

The powerful and wealthy official Dust ʿAli Khan Muʿayyir al-Mamalik, master of the mint and head of the treasury, commissioned a work of lacquer to represent his country at the 1867 International Exposition in Paris; that he chose this art form reveals the esteem it enjoyed in the Qajar era.[1] Lacquer's high quality of execution was admired by European visitors as well, even as they frequently disparaged other arts and crafts of Qajar Iran. Sir Robert Murdoch Smith, who purchased Persian decorative arts for the South Kensington Museum while serving as director of the Indo-European Telegraph Company, noted in 1875, "The best paintings in Persia are those on a miniature scale on papier-mâché writing cases, (Kalemdans), and book-cases, and small wooden boxes."[2] Although reserving his praise for lacquer objects with floral designs, the usually caustic Comte Julien de Rochechouart, who served as French consul in Iran from 1863 to 1866, was also captivated by these small, intimate works of art:

> To describe the taste with which these flowers are assembled, to convey the harmony of tone and the brilliance of the colors would require a pen more trained than mine; but what I must say, at the risk of attracting the wrath of our porcelain painters, is that they should procure at any price and study carefully some of these boxes; perhaps they would find through this work the secret of giving life to compositions.[3]

Detail: *Rectangular Mirror Case with Scenes of a Baby Boy's Birth and Circumcision*, 1830–50. For full information, see cat. 54, p. 150.

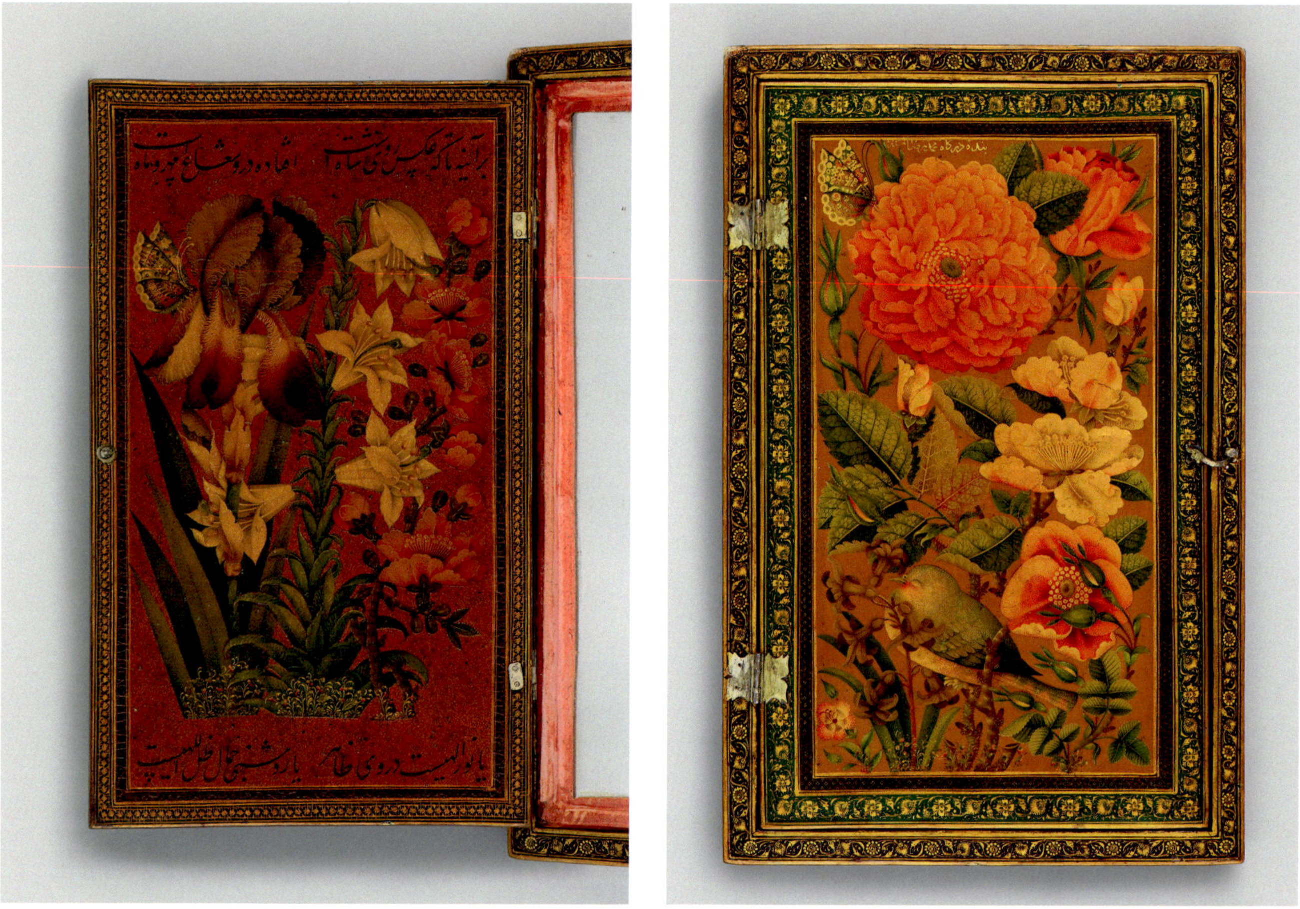

1 *Rectangular Mirror Case with Flowers, Butterfly, and Sleeping Bird* (exterior, right); *Flowers and Butterfly* (interior, left), dated 1263 H (1847–48). For full information, see cat. 57, p. 150.

Persian artists excelled at floral studies and in creating floral compositions (cats. 11, 21). The qualities admired by Rochechouart are evident in a mirror case painted in 1263 H (1847–48) by Muhammad Riza al-Imami (Fig. 1), the artist who later created the mirror case for the Paris Exposition. Muhammad Riza's mirror case demonstrates the essential elements of the rose and nightingale (*gul u bulbul*) repertoire: a prunus branch crosses over rose stems with single and double blossoms ranging from tightly budded to full blown. As it is here, the composition is often enriched with butterflies, songbirds, and contrasting flowers, and the surface filled with vibrantly colored petals and leaves that curve and turn as if moved by a breeze. Rochechouart's advice to French porcelain painters notwithstanding, the life of these compositions cannot be captured from close visual study alone, for their animating spirit derives from a deeply loved literary tradition that fashions complex sensual and spiritual metaphors from the spring garden. In the most common trope, the plaintive nightingale singing to the indifferent rose suggests human love and longing as well as the soul's yearning for mystical union with the divine. In the words of the lyric poet Hafiz of Shiraz (1325–1389): "Now like the zephyr breathing love-tales in roses' hearing, / Now from the yearning bulbul love's myst'ry apprehending."[4]

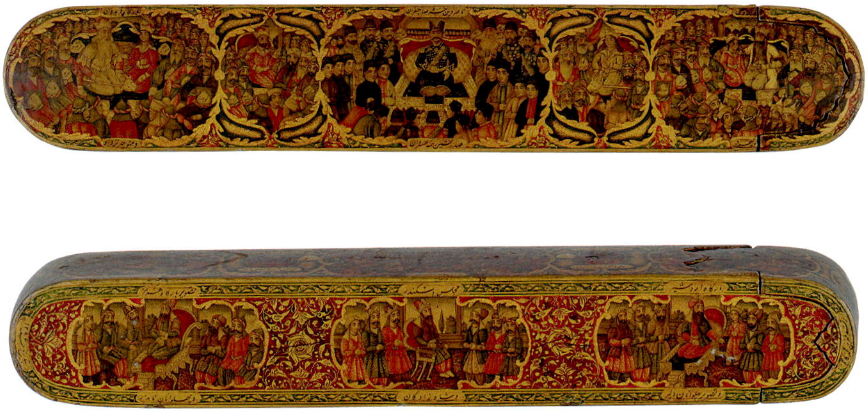

2 *Pen Box with Portraits of Nasir al-Din Shah and Legendary Rulers from the* Shāhnāma (top and base), dated 1296 H (1879–80). For full information, see cat. 72, p. 156.

In addition to floral ornament, Qajar lacquer objects feature decoration as varied as the functions they served and the audiences they reached. The pen box bearing scenes of enthroned rulers probably served as an official gift or a presentation piece (Fig. 2).[5] Minute but recognizable portraits of Nasir al-Din Shah, his sons, and officials fill the top center medallion, while rulers from Persian literature populate the rest of the exterior. In contrast, the snuff box with a humorous scene of lovers discovered *in flagrante delicto* was surely intended for private enjoyment (Fig. 3).[6] At their most elaborate, lacquer objects became handheld picture galleries, with decoration covering every surface, inside and out. Appreciation of their decorative programs requires rotating the objects in the hand, lifting lids, turning covers, and opening drawers.

Calligraphy and illumination form the primary or exclusive decoration for many Qajar lacquer wares, reflecting the enduring importance of the book arts in Persian culture. This essay, however, focuses on pictorial designs to examine the lacquer artists' enthusiasm for combining traditional art forms with content and visual effects from new sources. In the Qajar era, lacquer served as a medium of exchange, crossing boundaries of time, culture, and materials.

Historically, Islamic lacquer has proved an inherently flexible and assimilative medium. It was developed for luxury book covers in the late 15th century at the court of the Timurid dynasty in Herat during the reign of Sultan Husayn (d. 1506).[7] In this formative period, as also centuries later in the Qajar era,

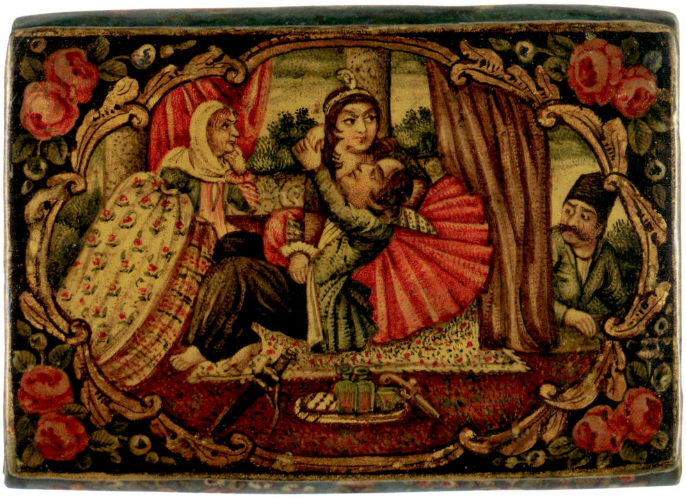

3 *Snuff Box with Lovers Discovered*, mid-19th century. For full information, see cat. 64, p. 154.

artists worked across mediums and appropriated decorative regimes and visual effects from indigenous traditions as well as from East Asian lacquer wares.[8]

Given their wider renown, it is important to note that the Chinese and Japanese traditions, in which objects are covered with the treated sap (*urushi*) of the lacquer tree, are technically distinct from Islamic lacquer. In the Islamic medium, the substrate was usually constructed of pasteboard or papier-mâché. Following coats of a white ground layer, decoration was applied through the interplay of water-based paint, metallic substances, and oil-and-resin-based lacquer. A detail from the inner cover of a small Qur'an shows the delicacy with which the watercolor and metallic pigments could be applied, both opaquely and translucently (Fig. 4). The technique could be further elaborated with multiple layers of tinted lacquers and particles of various metals, as seen in the photomicrograph from the inner lid of Muhammad Riza's mirror case (Fig. 5). Here, particles of brass were sprinkled onto a brass layer, over which an orange-tinted lacquer had already been applied. The design was then painted onto the sparkling surface in water-based paints, after which a final yellow-tinted lacquer completed the work.[9]

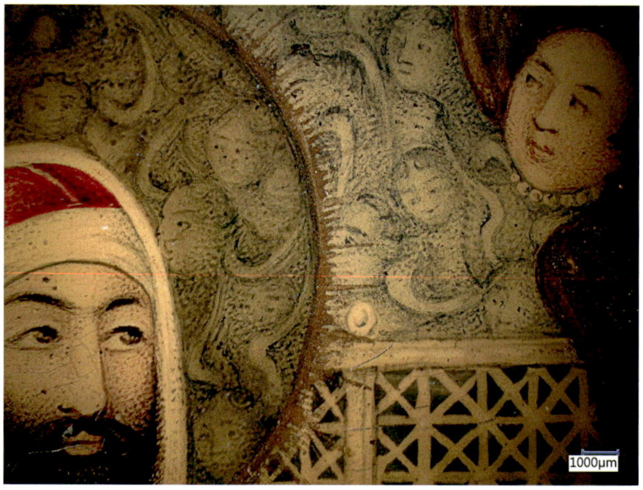

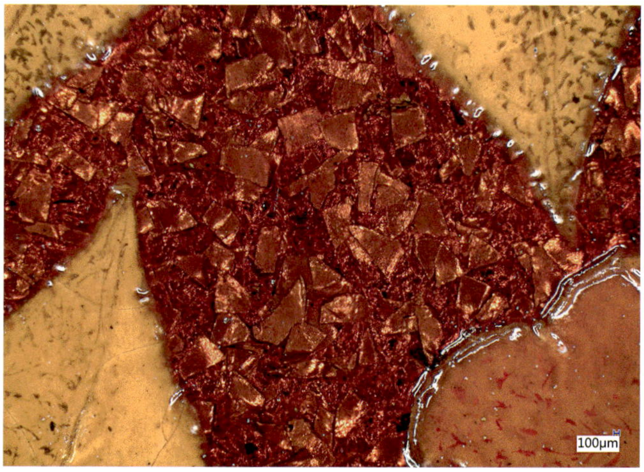

4 Photomicrograph of *Cover for a Small Qur'an* (interior), dated 1279 H (1862–63). For full information, see cat. 67, p. 154.

5 Photomicrograph of *Rectangular Mirror Case with Flowers, Butterfly, and Sleeping Bird* (lid, interior), dated 1263 H (1847–48). For full information, see cat. 57, p. 150.

Because of their exquisite quality and high cost, East Asian lacquers served the Portuguese and Dutch trading networks as prestige gifts to secure the good will of Mughal and Safavid authorities in the 16th and 17th centuries.[10] These portable wares transmitted forms, designs, and decorative effects across Asia and into Europe. Because the earliest known lacquer mirror cases—a form that would become a staple of Qajar production—were decorated by Mughal painters in the early 17th century, it has been suggested that the initial diversification of Islamic lacquer beyond book covers onto a wider range of objects took place in South Asia.[11]

How, then, does Qajar lacquer differ from that of earlier periods in serving as a medium of exchange? The difference is largely one of degree, driven by multiple factors. Those of interest to this essay concern volume: an exponential increase in the quantity of foreign images crossing into Iran in the 19th century and a rise in lacquer production within Iran. At the close of the 18th century, Iran emerged from decades of turbulence and isolation to become enmeshed in the broader world, due largely to the expansionist ambitions and technological advances of European powers.[12] Innovations in travel, communication, and industrial products brought Westerners—primarily the British and

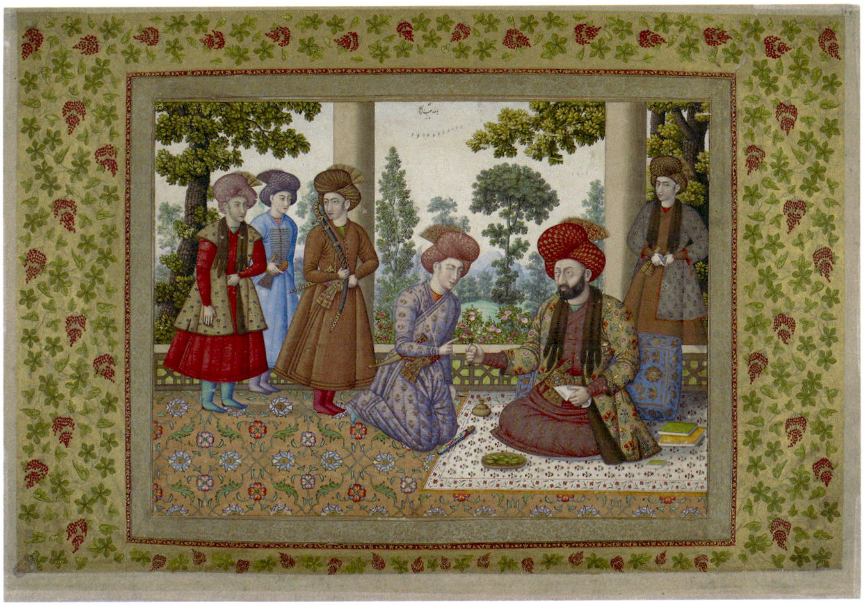

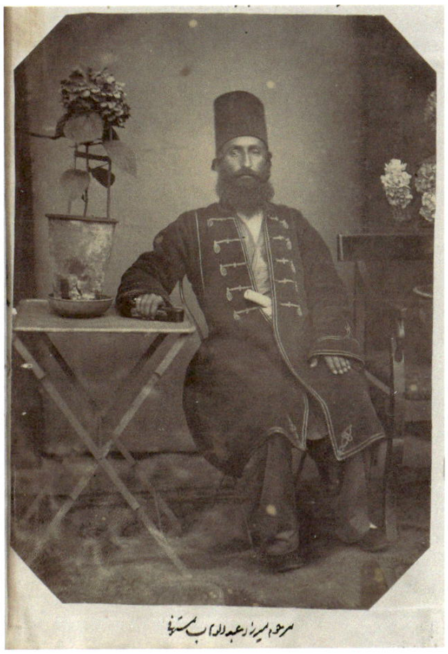

6 *The Grand Vizier Shah Quli Khan Presents a Ring*, attributed to Muhammad Sultani, Iran, Isfahan, dated 1106 H (1694–95). Image: 22.2 × 30 cm ($8\frac{3}{4} \times 11\frac{13}{16}$ in.). Institute of Oriental Manuscripts, Russian Academy of Sciences, St. Petersburg, E-14, fol. 97r.

7 *Portrait of Mirza ʿAbd al-Vahhab Mustawfi*, detail of page 340 from the *Album of Photographs by ʿAli Khan Vali*, 1862–1900. For full information, see cat. 24, p. 140.

Russians—to Iran and, to a later and lesser extent, brought Iranians to the West. The high point of lacquer production in Iran coincided with that of the European reproductive print industry.[13] In addition to their own traditions, Qajar artists suddenly had an unprecedented range of exotica to draw on as source material—from official to popular art forms, from state portraits to fashion plates.

In the Qajar era, lacquer production increased in volume and in range of quality. That the country's ruling officials patronized this medium was as true in the Qajar period as it had been during the reign of the Safavid dynasty (1501–1722), as reflected in the prominent display of lacquer pen boxes in the late 17th-century painting of *The Grand Vizier Shah Quli Khan Presents a Ring* (Fig. 6), and in the late 19th-century studio photograph of Mirza ʿAbd al-Vahhab Mustawfi (a financial comptroller) from the *Album of Photographs by ʿAli Khan Vali* (Fig. 7).[14] We can, however, discern a broadening of the consumer base for lacquer during the Qajar era from the surviving objects' greater volume, repetition of patterns, and range in quality.

European visitors offer hints of the production and price levels over the course of the 19th century. During his voyage of 1811–12, Sir William Ouseley purchased 30 pen boxes in the Isfahan bazaar to bring home as gifts. Noting that Isfahan was the country's largest producer of lacquer and "supplied most provinces of the Kingdome," he was delighted by the quality and selection of book covers, small boxes, mirror cases, and especially pen boxes at his disposal and reported that "of these [pen] cases may be seen, in one shop, parcels three or four feet high, comprising many hundred, of various patterns, and of all prices from a shilling or half-*rial* to three or four guineas or *tomans*."[15]

A half-century later, Rochechouart also remarked on the quantity and range of lacquer produced in Isfahan, and noted the existence of a lower level created for the international export market:

> According to the skill of the painter, he sells his products from 2 francs or less up to 200 francs; to have a suitable inkstand requires 20 francs, and 50 or 60 francs for a book cover or a mirror case. The bazars of Constantinople are encumbered with these products, which sell readily; but the objects exported from Persia are in general of a low price, and I swear that if I had not been informed, I would never have supposed that the Constantinople boxes had the same provenance as those that I saw afterwards in Persia.[16]

Finally, the French collector and specialist in decorative arts Henry-René d'Allemagne noted in 1907:

> The pen box is an object of great luxury, and all but the poorest examples are decorated with a real aesthetic concern. Those pen boxes destined for the wealthy have an altogether extraordinary richness of decoration. . . . The Persians are very fond of beautiful pen boxes and pieces that cost from 500 to 1000 francs are not very rare. They come, naturally, in all prices, and for the moderate sum of one *kran* [*qirān*], one can get a good idea of this kind of work.[17]

The astute observer Rochechouart grasped another critical factor concerning painting in Qajar Iran: that it was primarily a decorative tradition to embellish functional objects.[18] Although lacquer artists certainly produced unique masterpieces for elite patrons, this essay is concerned mainly with the subroyal object that may have been produced in multiples, for it is presumably through repeated patterns that imagery reached the greatest number of consumers. We will examine mechanisms by which Qajar artists achieved this level of production and explore a sampling of their subject matter.

The Qajar era opens on the cusp of mechanical reproduction. As the 19th century progressed, Iranians engaged with lithography and photography, but for lacquer wares, each object of which was traditionally painted by hand, image replication relied on well-worn workshop practices. Willem Floor discerns the existence of two not entirely separate classes of lacquer artists in Qajar Iran: one working on commission for elite patrons including the royal court; and another producing wares on speculation for the market. The second class functioned as a recruiting ground for the first, and apprentices to both groups comprised a third class.[19]

A window into the artists' working methods is offered by some two dozen drawings gathered in a scrapbook now in the Harvard Art Museums, *An Album of Artists' Drawings from Qajar Iran* (hereafter, Harvard Qajar Album).[20] These drawings include preparatory sketches, *aides-mémoire*, and fully developed

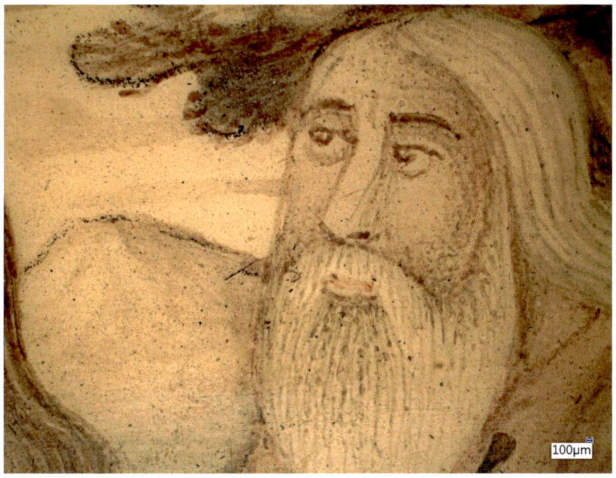

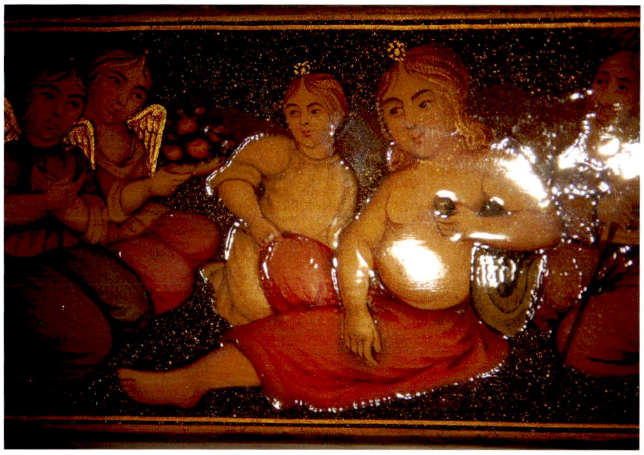

8 Photomicrograph of *Pen Box with Reclining Women and Female Portraits in Medallions*, dated 1287 H (1870–71). For full information, see cat. 69, p. 154.

9 Photomicrograph of *Pen Box with Reclining Women and Female Portraits in Medallions*, 1850–75. For full information, see cat. 70, p. 156.

compositions pricked for transfer to another surface. Most of the album's lacquer-related drawings can be linked to objects produced in Isfahan, and many are by artists working in what are believed to have been two groups active throughout most of the 19th century: the multigenerational Najaf circle, formed by the artist Aqa Najaf ʿAli, and the so-called Imami circle.

Focusing on Isfahan production probably biases this study toward artistic continuity, for the city was the last and grandest capital of the Safavid dynasty. After the tumultuous 18th century, the Safavid era shone in collective memory as a golden age. If Aqa Muhammad Khan, founder of the Qajar dynasty, presented himself as the rightful successor to the Safavids, the artists of Isfahan were no less aware of their city's artistic heritage.[21] Because Isfahan artists out-produced any other lacquer center in Qajar Iran and supplied both domestic and international export markets, it may be argued that their designs had more than a regional importance and probably created a multiplier effect on artists elsewhere.

Creating a work of lacquer was a time-consuming, multistage process.[22] To produce in volume for the market required multiple hands, a ready supply of designs, and versatile compositions that could be reused and updated. Qajar artists had immensely rich sources to draw upon to develop design portfolios that could support this production level, beginning with their own heritage.

In Iran, as elsewhere, copying the work of past masters was an encouraged practice for calligraphers and painters. A double page opening in an album of Persian paintings juxtaposes two closely related studies of a Rose Balsam (cat. 9); the painting on the left side of the album opening is ascribed to Muhammad Hadi, probably the famous flower-painter who flourished in Shiraz in the late 18th century. A certain fluency combined with kinetic memory undoubtedly developed from duplicating traditional favorites, and a relatively free underdrawing in dry media or lighter inks can sometimes be detected (Fig. 8).[23] A more deliberate method to replicate stock patterns employed a template on which the essential outlines were pricked with tiny

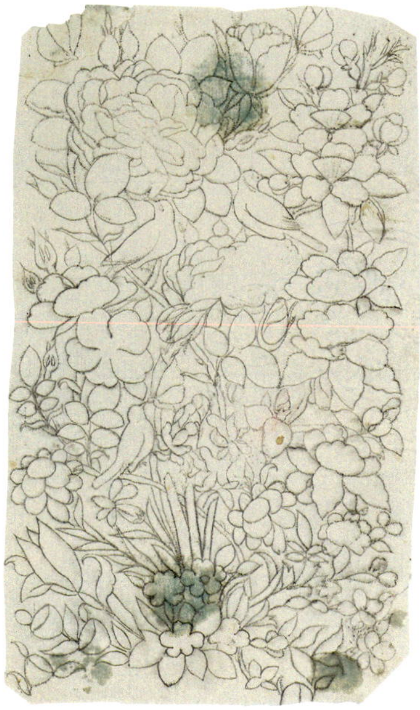

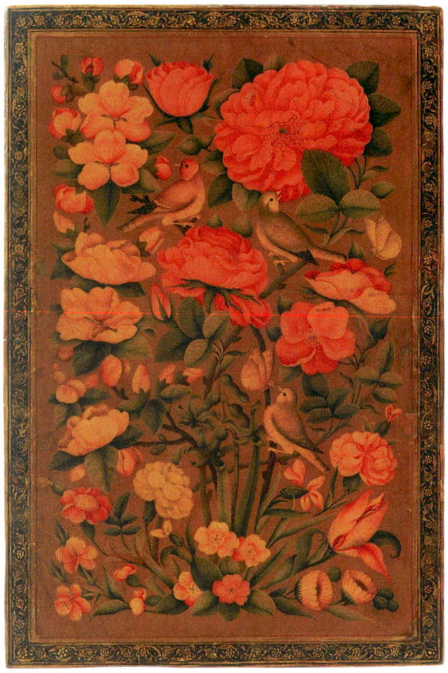

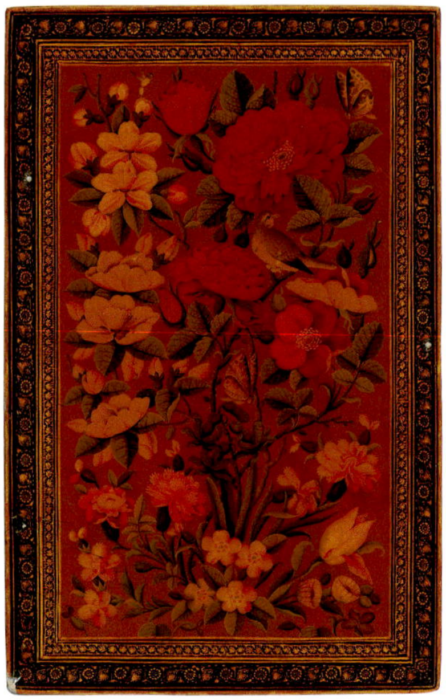

holes. Presumably the design could then be transferred to another surface through pouncing or rubbing with powdered charcoal or chalk.[24] For sparkling or dark backgrounds, the designs were sometimes transferred by pricking the outlines directly into the lacquer surface (Fig. 9).

Despite such copying aides, we rarely find a single design repeated precisely. More commonly, compositions or motif clusters are found to be reworked, rescaled, and remixed with other elements. If recombining and paraphrasing were normative practices, what then does it mean to find a particular composition or vignette duplicated closely? In many cases, it probably represents the work of apprentices obediently reproducing stock patterns, but in other instances, the careful replication may have served as a deliberate "quotation." We will examine a few such direct quotes from sources internal and external to Iran's artistic tradition.[25]

10 *Birds, Flowers, and Butterflies*, c. 1775–1850. For full information, see cat. 10, p. 134.

11 *Mirror Case with Birds and Flowers*, signed by Muhammad Sadiq, Iran, probably Isfahan, dated 1204 H (1789–90). Frame: 20 × 13.7 cm (7⅞ × 5⅜ in.). The Nasser D. Khalili Collection of Islamic Art, London, LAQ 12. (Image after Nasser D. Khalili, B. W. Robinson, and Tim Stanley, *Lacquer of the Islamic Lands*, pt. 1, The Nasser D. Khalili Collection of Islamic Art, vol. 22 [London; New York: Nour Foundation in association with Azimuth Editions and Oxford University Press, 1996–97], cat. 68, p. 103.)

12 *Rectangular Mirror Case with Bird, Flowers, and Two Butterflies* (back), first half 19th century. For full information, see cat. 58, p. 152.

Direct Quotes

If kaleidoscopic variations on the bird-and-flower theme were endemic in Qajar art, then the faithful repetition of one particular composition preserved in a pricked drawing in the Harvard Qajar Album may be meaningful (Fig. 10). This well-balanced yet lively composition is more legible when rendered in multiple colors on a contrasting ground, as on a mirror case of 1204 H (1789–90) bearing the cryptic signature of the artist Muhammad Sadiq (Fig. 11).[26] Although reversed from the drawing, the lacquer painting more clearly reveals the typical crossing of prunus and rose branches, an armature further enriched by three birds, a butterfly, and a mixed floral array.

Unfortunately, little is known of Muhammad Sadiq's life. His signed works appear in multiple mediums, and his likely *floruit* (1740s–90s) forms a critical bridge between the lingering Safavid style of the early 18th century and the dawn of Qajar patronage. He is posited to have been the most celebrated pupil of ʿAli Ashraf, a lacquer painter accomplished in floral designs who had been trained by the last generation of Safavid artists in Isfahan.[27] Muhammad Sadiq is in turn said to have been the master of Aqa Najaf ʿAli, founder of the prolific circle of lacquer artists. Artists from both the Najaf and Imami circles in Isfahan made unambiguous use of Muhammad Sadiq's bird-and-flower composition.[28] Although unsigned, the mirror case in Figure 12 is likely the work of the Najaf circle.[29] On the back of the case, the artist has faithfully employed this cherished composition (except for the omission of two birds), perhaps to pay homage to Muhammad Sadiq's artistry and to advertise an impressive master-pupil chain of transmission (*silsila*). As will be seen below, Muhammad Sadiq's influence over Qajar painters also included figural compositions.[30]

Another example of a direct quote is found on the inner lid of a mirror case (Fig. 13). The languidly reclining nude and wide-eyed cherubs originated in a watercolor by British artist Richard Westall (1765–1836) that inspired three reproductive engravings.[31] The second of these, by British printmaker George Kellaway (fl. 1820–1826), bears the title *The Bower of Venus* and offers the pleasingly ominous subtext: "Hither the laughing loves resort / Hence wing their mystic darts" (Fig. 14).

The third reproductive image appeared in George Hamilton's 1831–32 publication on "the most approved" British artists of the day. From Hamilton's

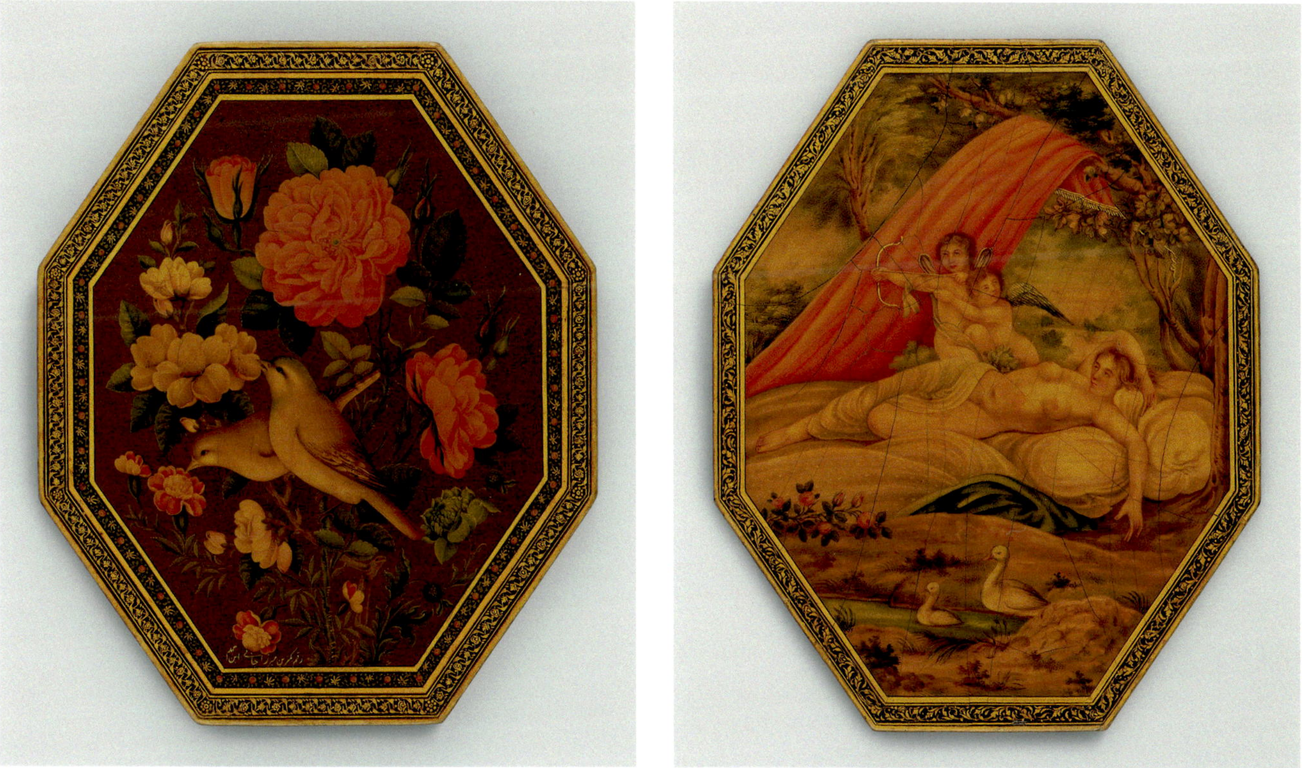

13 *Octagonal Mirror Case with Birds and Flowers* (back, exterior); and *The Bower of Venus* (lid interior), 1825–50. For full information, see cat. 59, p. 152.

description we can gauge the contemporary reception of Westall's painting:

> The painter has represented the Cytherean Goddess, in all the majesty of irresistible beauty, reposing in the umbrageous shelter of her bower; two attendant loves obsequiously watch the glances of her eye, and eagerly await her commands; one of them appears to direct her attention towards an object out of the picture, and the second prepares the mystic dart for him, who, whether mortal or immortal, dares rashly intrude on the seclusion of Venus. This graceful composition is executed in Water colours, and in richness, depth, and brilliancy, is among the most splendid examples of that department of art.[32]

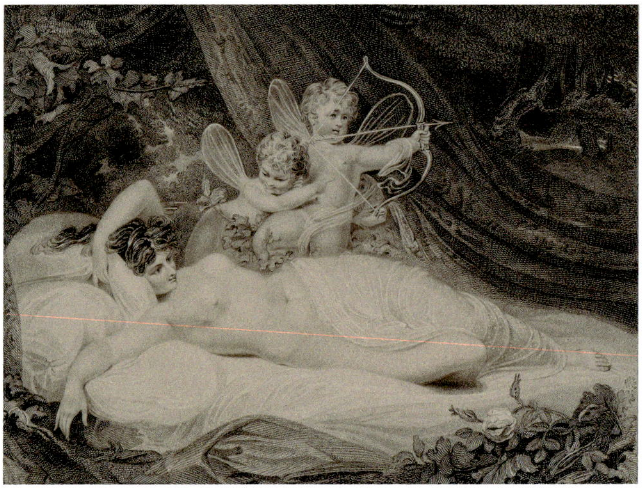

14 *The Bower of Venus* (detail), 1825. For full information, see cat. 42, p. 146.

The outer surfaces of the mirror case bear an elegant bird-and-flower composition, identical but mirror-imaged, set against a shimmering ground (see Fig. 13). The back is signed by an otherwise unknown artist, Mirza Jani b. Ahmad. While both Westall's and Mirza Jani's compositions may be said to express the potential torments of love, their juxtaposition is a rich study in cultural contrasts: one dramatically embodied through overt nudity, the other depersonalized and sublimated into metaphor. Given the high standing enjoyed by Westall and his painting, it seems likely that the lacquer artist, and perhaps his patron, wished to showcase this specific composition.

A different possible motive—"scientific" accuracy—may have inspired the close copying of animal vignettes on a pen box of 1295 H (1878–79) signed by ʿAbbas Shirazi (Fig. 15). The source for the animal studies are found in *The Naturalist's Library*, a 40-volume series edited by Scotsman Sir William Jardine (1800–1874).[33] This popular series served both academic and amateur audiences, and appeared in multiple editions over six decades (1833–96). It featured some 1,300 line engravings, which were often hand-colored (Fig. 16). On the top of the pen box, ʿAbbas Shirazi has reproduced the *Golden Eagle* and the *White-tailed Eagle* from volume 9 of Jardine's study, published in 1838.[34] On the sides, he has reproduced four species of ruminants from Europe and Africa from volume 21, published in 1866.[35] As Bronwen Gulkis has discovered,

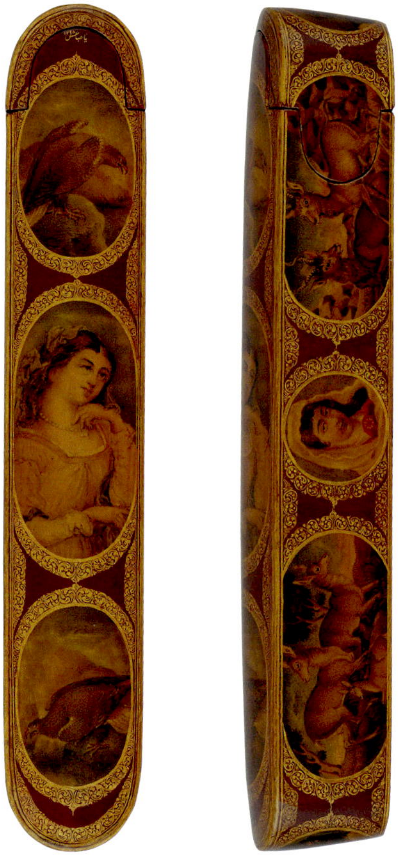

15 *Pen Box with European Woman and Eagles* (top and front), dated 1295 H (1878–79). For full information, see cat. 71, p. 156.

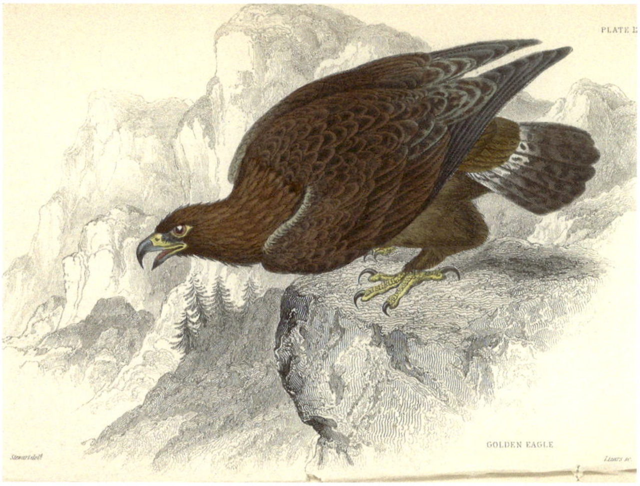

16 *Golden Eagle*, 1838. For full information, see cat. 43, p. 146.

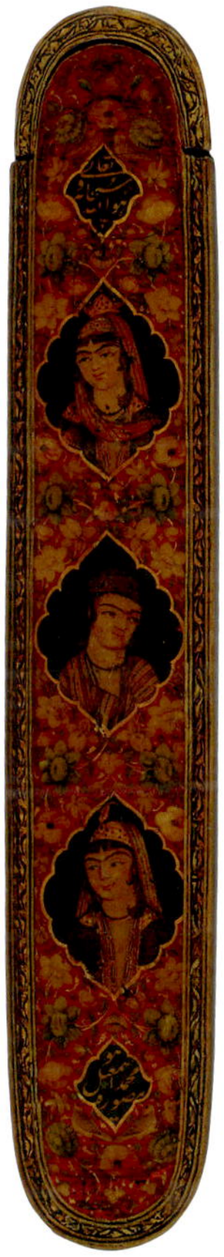

17 *Pen Box with Medallions on Floral Ground*, mid-19th century. For full information, see cat. 56, p. 150.

ʿAbbas was one of several Shiraz artists to draw on *The Naturalist's Library* in the last quarter of the 19th century.[36] How and why Shiraz painters gained access to this publication is a subject for future research, but it seems likely that they wished for their careful copies to point to a popular and well-respected source.

The next example of artistic homage is a pen box signed by Muhammad Ismaʿil (fl. 1840–1872), one of the Qajar era's most interesting lacquer painters (Fig. 17).[37] The overall layout of his pen box with lobed and anchor medallions in vertical orientation directly evokes late Safavid lacquer wares, represented, for instance, on a pen box dated 1102 H (1692–93) and signed by the Isfahan artist Haji Muhammad (fl. 1673–1713) (Fig. 18). On both pen boxes, the lobed medallions contain bust-length portraits of young beauties, and the anchor medallions hold the artist's signature and a pious inscription. The unusual sparkling background of Ismaʿil's pen box, in which tinted lacquer covers parallel lines of flattened copper wire set against a brass layer (Fig. 19), also finds precedent in a pen box by Haji Muhammad, dated 1116 H (1704–5).[38]

In a similar spirit, Zayn al-ʿAbidin of the Imami circle in Isfahan (fl. 1850s–1870s) produced a superb medallion pen box in 1270 H (1853–54) (Fig. 20) that closely echoes the works of the celebrated 18th-century master ʿAli Ashraf.[39] In these two Qajar pen boxes, Zayn al-ʿAbidin and Muhammad Ismaʿil have sensitively evoked a past era. Qajar artists' accomplished reuse of archaic compositions and effects demonstrates the challenge of assigning production dates to unsigned works of lacquer.

Versatile Compositions

The medallion format served Qajar artists far beyond simply being a means to cite Safavid precedents. The long, narrow surface of a pen box presented a design challenge—particularly for figural compositions—which could be eased by subdivision into smaller units. As seen on ʿAbbas Shirazi's pen box above, the medallion composition could be deployed vertically or horizontally, and it created convenient placeholders into which artists could insert fashion updates or juxtapose contrasting imagery.[40]

The value of this compositional strategy can be seen in a drawing in the Harvard Qajar Album and on two pen boxes in which portrait medallions segment the surface for figural vignettes (Figs. 21–23). On their tops, the two pen boxes employ nearly identical designs, probably produced from the same template. As seen in the photomicrographs above (Figs. 8, 9), the design was sketched onto the light background and pricked onto the sparkling background. To accommodate the different sizes of the boxes, the artists made minute adjustments: adding or subtracting a tree or a bit of sky at the margins, or widening a face or two.

These three works can be linked to artists working in Isfahan. Only the pen box with the light background bears an inscription: the punning signature of Najaf ʿAli (*yā shāh-i Najaf*, O King of Najaf!) and the date 1287 H (1870–71). Since this date falls after the accepted death of the artist (c. 1855), this pen box, as well as its sparkling twin, is probably a product of the Najaf workshop. While no exact copy of the Harvard Qajar Album drawing has yet been discovered in the lacquer medium, a few of the individual figures link to pen boxes signed by Najaf ʿAli's master, Muhammad Sadiq, confirming again the chain of transmission and demonstrating the workshop practice of excerpting from and reworking compositions.[41] A considerable number of Qajar lacquer objects bear very similar pastoral scenes with reclining women. The male and female attendants are variously aged and sometimes winged, but the focus is held by the reclining female figures, who are seminude or dressed in generically European gowns.

Female beauty is a nearly universal theme in the visual arts, and over the centuries Persian art has furnished innumerable examples of moon-faced, dark-eyed beauties with black tresses. It is, however, the European woman—clothed or unclothed, bust-length or full-figure—who populates Qajar lacquer wares to a startling degree. Persian painters had long depicted semi-clad women to illustrate stories familiar from classical Persian poetry, most often that of Khusraw spying the bathing Shirin. In contrast to the spare Persian offerings, the European tradition, particularly from the 16th century onward, generated a torrent of bathing nudes—most grandly Venus, Diana, Bathsheba, and Susanna, but also myriad allegorical figures and anonymous nymphs. The prolific portrayal of European women of even royal birth with bared heads, shoulders, and arms must have astonished Iranians, long accustomed to shielding women from any but family eyes.[42]

The influx of such imagery into Safavid Iran, primarily through reproductive prints, helped lay the groundwork for attitudes toward, and representations of, European women, and it is no accident that the word "stereotype"

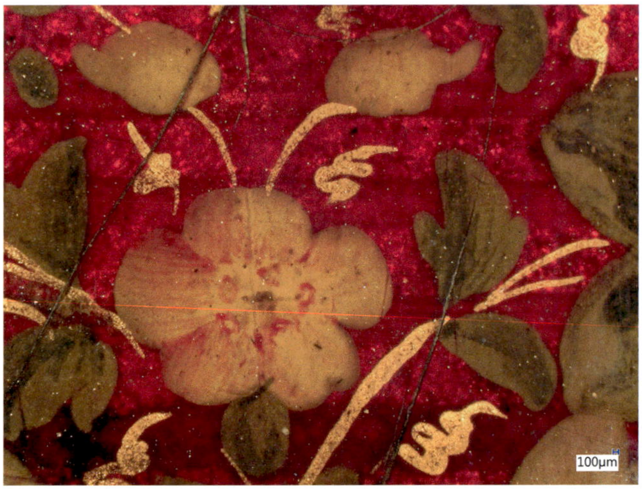

19 Photomicrograph of *Pen Box with Medallions on Floral Ground*, mid-19th century. For full information, see cat. 56, p. 150.

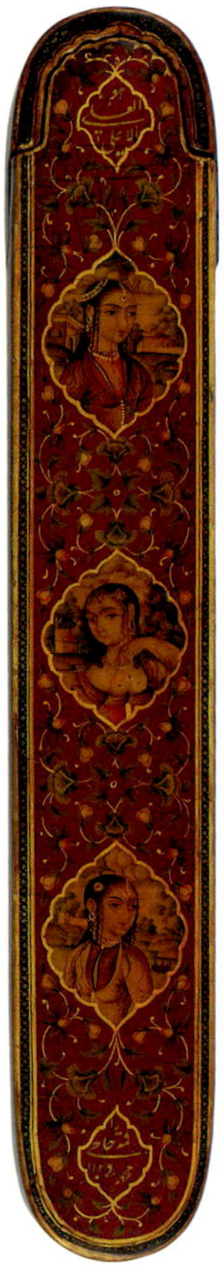

18 *Pen Box with Medallions on Floral Ground*, dated 1102 H (1692–93). For full information, see cat. 50, p. 148.

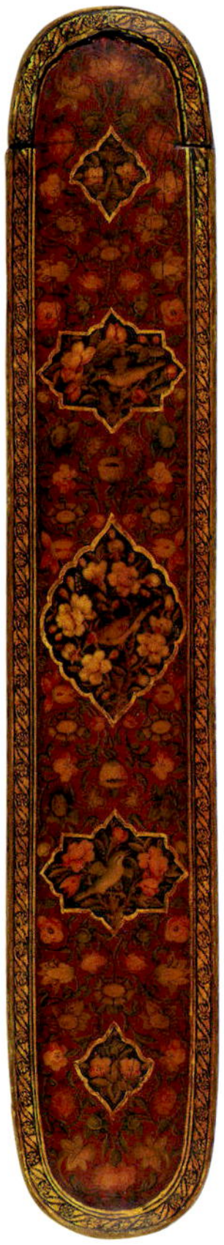

20 *Pen Box with Medallions on Floral Ground*, dated 1270 H (1853–54). For full information, see cat. 62, p. 152.

21 *Design for a Pen Box Organized as Three Scenes around a Reclining Female with Angels and Male and Female Figures*, 1780–1860. For full information, see cat. 19, p. 138.

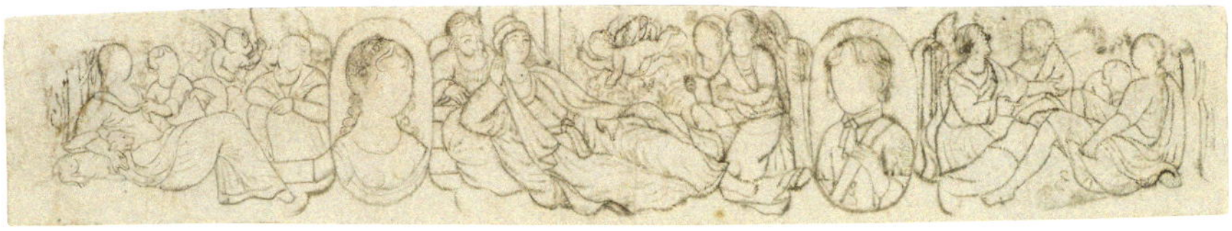

22 *Pen Box with Reclining Women and Female Portraits in Medallions*, dated 1287 H (1870–71). For full information, see cat. 69, p. 154.

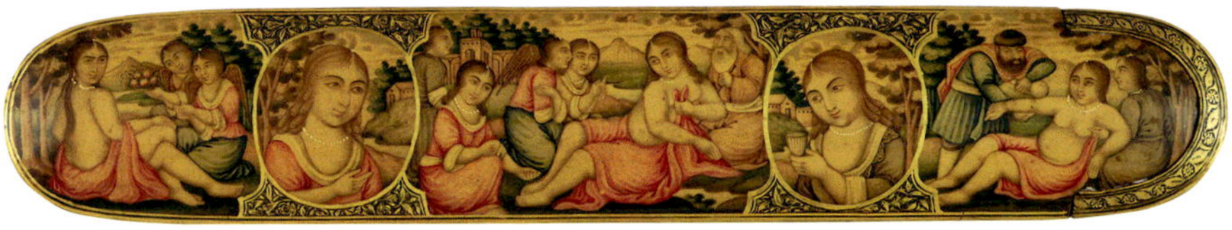

23 *Pen Box with Reclining Women and Female Portraits in Medallions*, 1850–75. For full information, see cat. 70, p. 156.

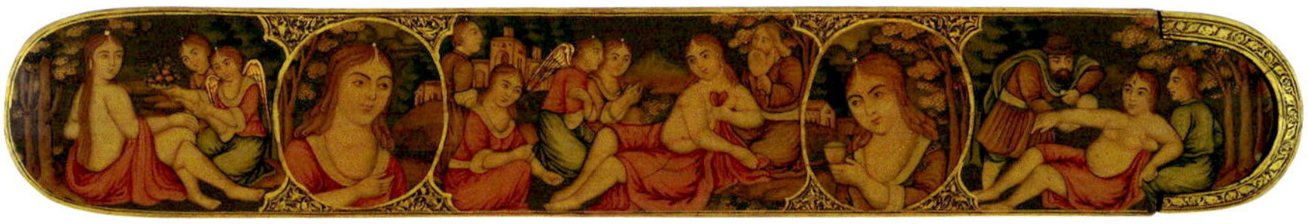

originated in the printing industry. As Amy Landau has shown, the European (*farangī*) came to represent the dangerous lover in Safavid poetry and painting, and the reclining female nude became emblematic of sexual availability.[43] Centuries before opportunities arose for personal contact with Western women, Iranians had eroticized them as the exotic and dangerous "other." As their travel narratives demonstrate, these preconceptions often accompanied Qajar travelers to Europe, coloring their perceptions of women's behavior and place in society.[44]

In Qajar art, the starring role for the dangerous European beauty is held by the Christian maiden whose siren charms bring to near ruin the devout and learned Muslim Shaykh San'an. A medallion-formatted pen box signed by Ja'far b. Najaf 'Ali represents this theme (Fig. 24). As narrated in the 13th-century poem *Manṭiq al-ṭayr* (Conference of the Birds) by Farid al-Din 'Attar, the elderly shaykh journeys to Rome searching for a beautiful maiden, whom he has glimpsed in his dreams. He becomes besotted by love upon finding her, to the dismay of his companions. At her command, he foreswears Islam, drinks wine, bows down before idols, and even becomes a swineherd. After suffering numerous humiliations, the shaykh eventually regains his senses and returns to his original faith. Inspired by his example, the maiden converts to Islam shortly before expiring.

Ja'far's painting is based ultimately on an earlier work by one of the most influential artists of Safavid Isfahan, Muhammad Zaman b. Haji Yusuf

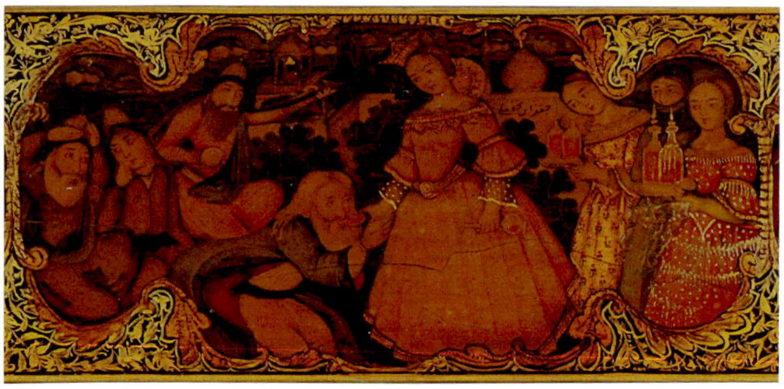

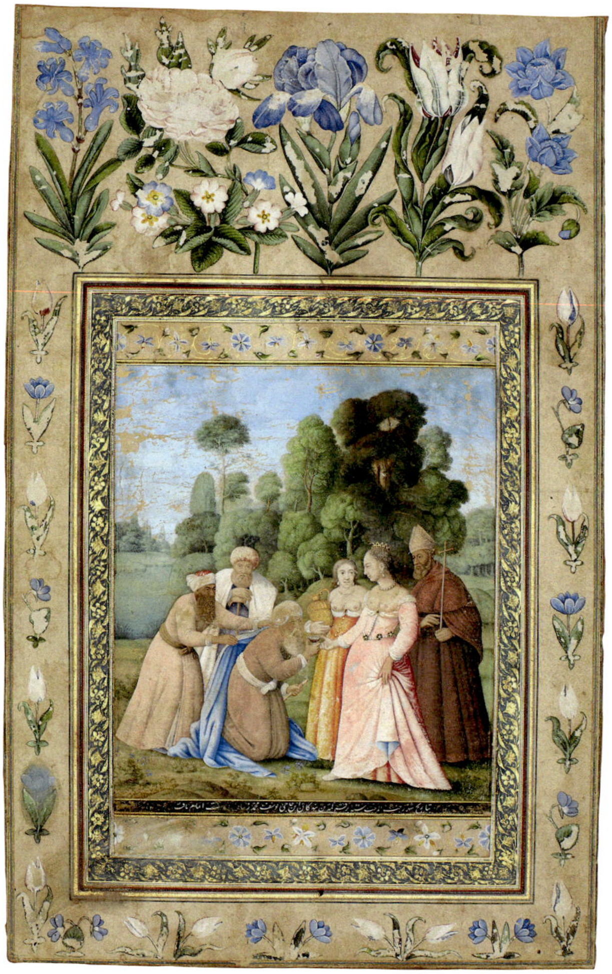

(fl. 1640s–c. 1700), a pioneering figure of the Europeanizing style (*farangī-sāzī*) of painting that would become the predominant visual mode in the 18th century.[45] The Safavid painting illustrates the moment of capitulation, when the kneeling shaykh accepts a cup of wine from the maiden's hand (Fig. 25). Their dangerous charms on full display, the maiden and her wine-bearing attendant are flanked by distraught Muslims at left and a Christian bishop at right.

Jaʿfar's pen box is one of at least nine lacquer works of the Qajar era that resurrect the two main figures in Muhammad Zaman's painting. None is dated and most are unsigned, but the few with signatures name Najaf ʿAli (*yā shāh-i Najaf*), Muhammad Ismaʿil, Muhammad Kazim, and Jaʿfar b. Najaf ʿAli.[46] Stylistically, they are datable to the third quarter of the 19th century.[47] For use on a pen box, the Najaf artists reformatted Muhammad Zaman's composition and updated some of the details. To signal the Christian faith, the bishop has been replaced by the bell tower of an Armenian church, an architectural form that would have been familiar to Isfahan artists from the nearby Armenian community in New Julfa.[48] The Christian maiden and wine-bearing attendants are coiffed and garbed for the early Victorian era, and the wine bearers reflect representations of serving girls with decanters on trays in Victorian prints.[49]

The most interesting changes appear in the depiction of the Christian maiden. Although she is not a princess in ʿAttar's poem, Jaʿfar has exaggerated her crown. On her gown, prominent lace extensions (*engageantes*) issue from mid-length sleeves, and the lace scallops of the low neckline bear a gold band. Her parted hair frames a broad forehead, before looping back over the ears. While none of these elements is unique, all occur in official portraits of Queen Victoria's coronation and oath-taking ceremonies produced by Sir George Hayter (1792–1871), Principal Painter in Ordinary to the Queen.[50] These ceremonies took place in 1838, but Hayter's images had long lives and enjoyed

24 *Pen Box with Scenes of Shaykh Sanʿan and the Christian Maiden, Khusraw and Shirin, and Shirin and Farhad* (detail), 1850–75. For full information, see cat. 65, p. 154.

25 *Shaykh Sanʿan and the Christian Maiden*, Muhammad Zaman, Iran, probably Isfahan, dated 1087 H (1676–77). Watercolor and gold on paper; painting: 14.5 × 13 cm (5 11/16 × 5 1/8 in.); folio: 32 × 20.3 cm (12 5/8 × 8 in.). Sotheby's, London, *Arts of Islamic World*, April 20, 2016, Sale 16220, lot 261.

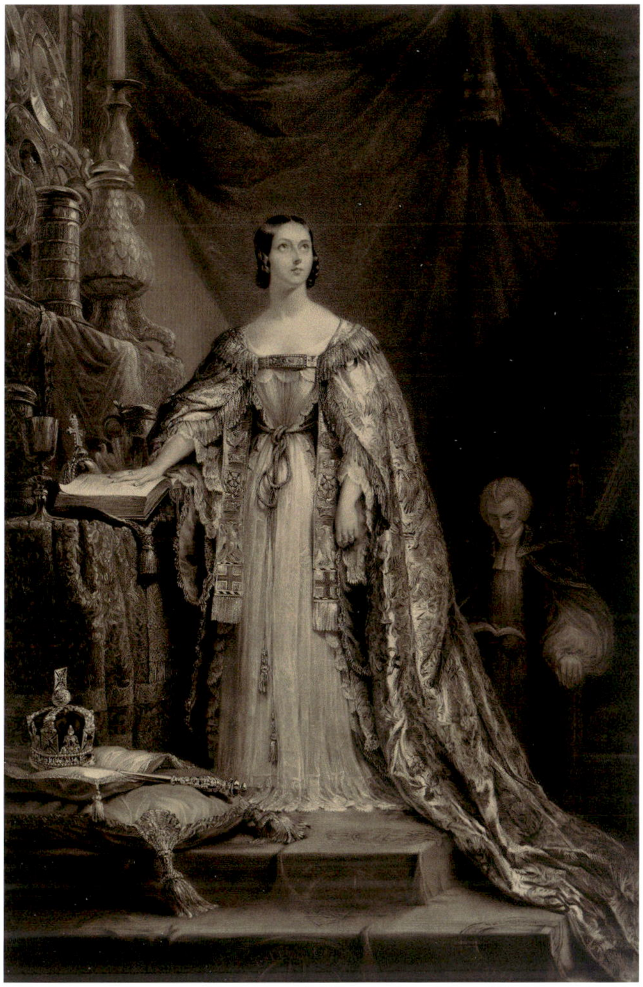

26 W. H. Egleton, after Sir George Hayter, *Queen Victoria Taking the Oath to Maintain the Protestant Faith*, 1853. Mixed method on chine collé, 87.5 × 60.2 cm (34⁷⁄₁₆ × 23¹¹⁄₁₆ in.). The British Museum, London, Acquired with the assistance of the National Heritage Memorial Fund, the Friends of the British Museum, the Art Fund, Mrs. Charles Wrightsman, the Michael Marks Charitable Trust, and numerous individual donors, 2010,7081.6473.

wide circulation through reproductive prints (Fig. 26).[51] In 1853, a new edition of Victoria's oath-taking was issued, with the quotation: "I will to the utmost in my power maintain the Protestant Reformed religion established by law, and will maintain inviolably by settlement of the United Church of England and Ireland."[52] Who better to represent the Christian maiden than the famous "maiden monarch" crowned to uphold Christianity?

Admittedly, this interpretation is a heavy weight to lay on the delicate shoulders of Jaʿfar's tiny figure, but it is supported by contemporary events. Relations between Iran and Great Britain had reached a dangerous low by the mid-1850s. The deteriorating state of affairs found vivid expression in a dream related by the young Nasir al-Din Shah to his prime minister in 1855:

> In a dream I saw a garden with a tall, massive pine tree in the middle. I was viewing it from a distance and the name of the tree was Victoria. Indeed that tree was the country and the monarchy of England. I ordered the pine tree called Victoria to be uprooted and replanted in another location and said: Call it Muhammad. Victoria is bad.[53]

Hostilities finally broke out over Iran's conquest of Herat in 1856. Bitterly resisting British pressure to relinquish this prize, Nasir al-Din Shah called for jihad, rousing the Iranian people to intense anger and resentment against Great Britain. That the shah's very name meant "defender of the faith" made his eventual capitulation to the demands of the Christian nation all the more humiliating.[54]

If the medallion-format facilitated decoration by dividing a large or awkward surface into more manageable units, it also multiplied the number of compositions needed. One formula that readily organized even tiny spaces into a legible setting was the terrace (*tālār*) structure. As seen on the base of the pen box depicting Nasir al-Din Shah (Fig. 2), a few horizontal and vertical elements—balustrade and pillars—separate foreground from background, providing a platform for the figures and framing a view over distant treetops. Muhammad Kazim employed this thumbnail setting in three medallions to depict Hurmuz, Iskandar (Alexander the Great), and Ardashir granting audience to their courtiers. As seen in the painting of Shah Quli Khan (Fig. 6), this terrace formulation had crystallized as the venue for official meetings in paintings of the late Safavid period.[55] Examples of Safavid terraces survive in Isfahan on a few palace structures; typically, the terrace projects from an enclosed

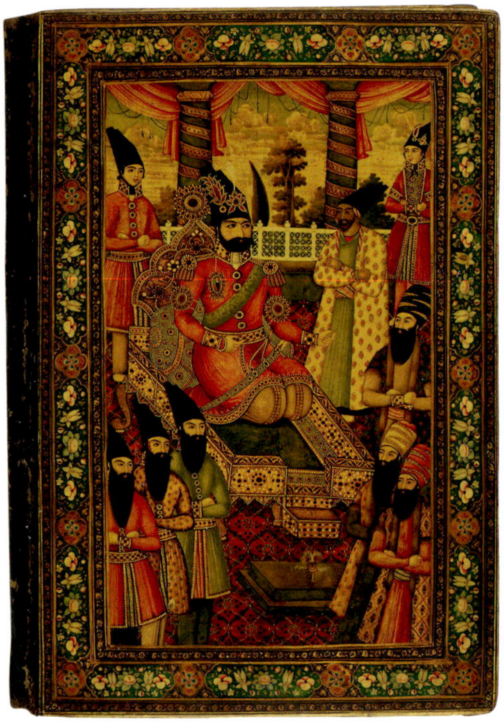

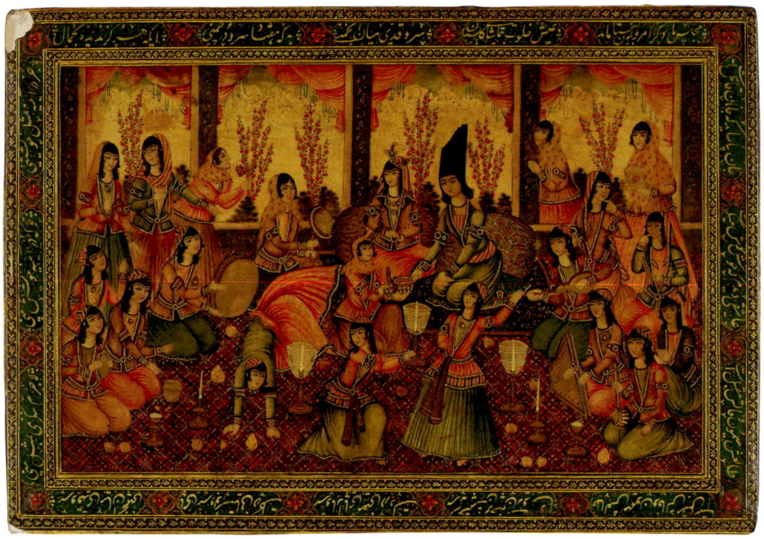

27 *Large Book Cover with Enthronement Scene of Muhammad Shah* (back), 1830s–40s. For full information, see cat. 53, p. 150.

28 *Large Book Cover with Entertainment Scene on a Terrace* (back), 1820s–40s. For full information, see cat. 52, p. 148.

pavilion; it is shaded by a high ceiling supported by pillars or columns, and bordered by a low balustrade, which may have an openwork geometric pattern.

The lacquer book covers that feature enthronements of the second and third Qajar rulers, Fath ʿAli Shah and Muhammad Shah, employ the terrace composition, but their larger scale permits greater detail (Fig. 27). The crimson drapery, curtain cords, and spiraling columns are again based on Safavid precedents as indicators of a palace setting.[56] By the early Qajar period, however, the purposes for which the terrace setting could serve had generalized well beyond the royal audience or official gathering. Two large book covers employ the essential elements of the terrace as the setting for festivities in the women's quarter, with refreshments, musicians, and dancers (Fig. 28). Comparison of the book cover with two drawings from the Harvard Qajar Album (Figs. 29, 30) reveals how effectively Qajar artists constructed lively compositions by juggling stock elements, such as the flowering and evergreen trees glimpsed beyond the draperies and the acrobatic dancers and servants bearing trays and water pipes.

These two drawings reflect a further codification of the terrace formula. Both feature a double row of balustrades: one joined to the columns at the back of the terrace, as usual, plus an additional one in the front that functions as a *repoussoir*. The treatment of the balustrades, particularly with a gap in the front and finials atop posts, departs from the Safavid paradigm. The source for this variant was probably Indian painting, as seen in the miniature from the *Small Clive Album* featuring lovers on a terrace (Fig. 31).[57] By the 18th century,

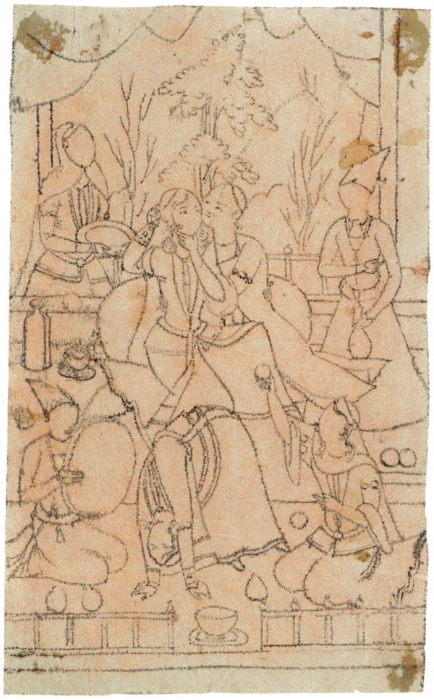

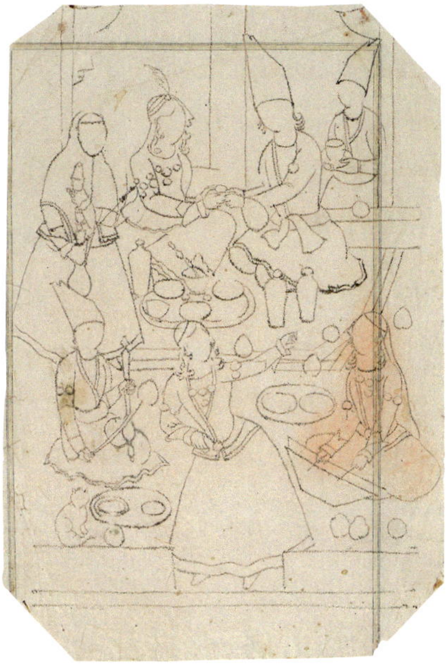

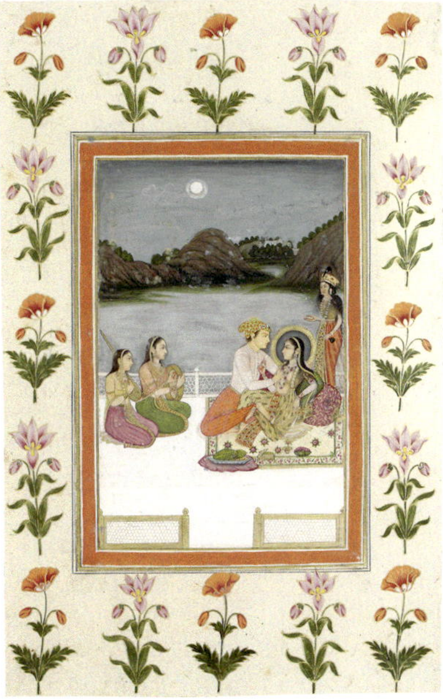

29 *Embracing Couple on a Terrace, Attended by Male and Female Servants, a Musician, and a Dancer*, 1820s–50s. For full information, see cat. 13, p. 136.

30 *Couple with Male and Female Attendants Entertained by Musicians and a Dancer*, 1820s–50s. For full information, see cat. 15, p. 136.

31 *Lovers on a Moonlit Lakeside Terrace*, folio from the *Small Clive Album*, India, first half 18th century. Watercolor and gold on paper; painting: 18.5 × 12.3 cm (7¼ × 4¹³⁄₁₆ in.). Victoria and Albert Museum, London, Gift of Mr. John Goelet, IS.48:47/B-1956.

the roofless terrace enclosed by lattice work balustrades had become a staple composition in Indian painting, serving a wide range of subjects, including enthronements, formal audiences, amorous couples, Hindu divinities, and *rāgamālās* (visual representations of modes in classical Indian music).

Shorn of official or royal connotations, the terrace setting was used for an equally broad range of subjects in Qajar art. On a mirror case that probably served as a wedding gift (Fig. 32), Indian-style balustrades enclose two intimate scenes in the women's quarters. On the lid, a midwife attends to an exhausted new mother at the center of the composition. The newborn lies naked in a large basin, while attendants wrap the afterbirth.[58] On the back of the case, all eyes focus on the baby's circumcision. In both scenes, the figures are arranged in a quincunx (a configuration like the five-side of a die), with the key players positioned in the center, as also seen in the enthronement scene on the book cover and the Harvard Qajar Album drawing (Figs. 27, 29).

The formula joining quincunx and double-balustrade terrace was used for a gathering of a markedly different character on a mirror case in the Museum für Lackkunst, Münster (Fig. 33). The lid depicts an assembly of philosophers and students, including Mir Findiriski and Shaykh Baha'i, two revered philosophers of the Safavid "School of Isfahan." The key to identifying the popular episode is the centrally located lion, at whose sudden and unexpected appearance the Isfahan scholars reacted according to the philosophies they espoused. Initially startled, Shaykh Baha'i calmed himself through the power of rational thinking. Through the powers of self-control and inner serenity

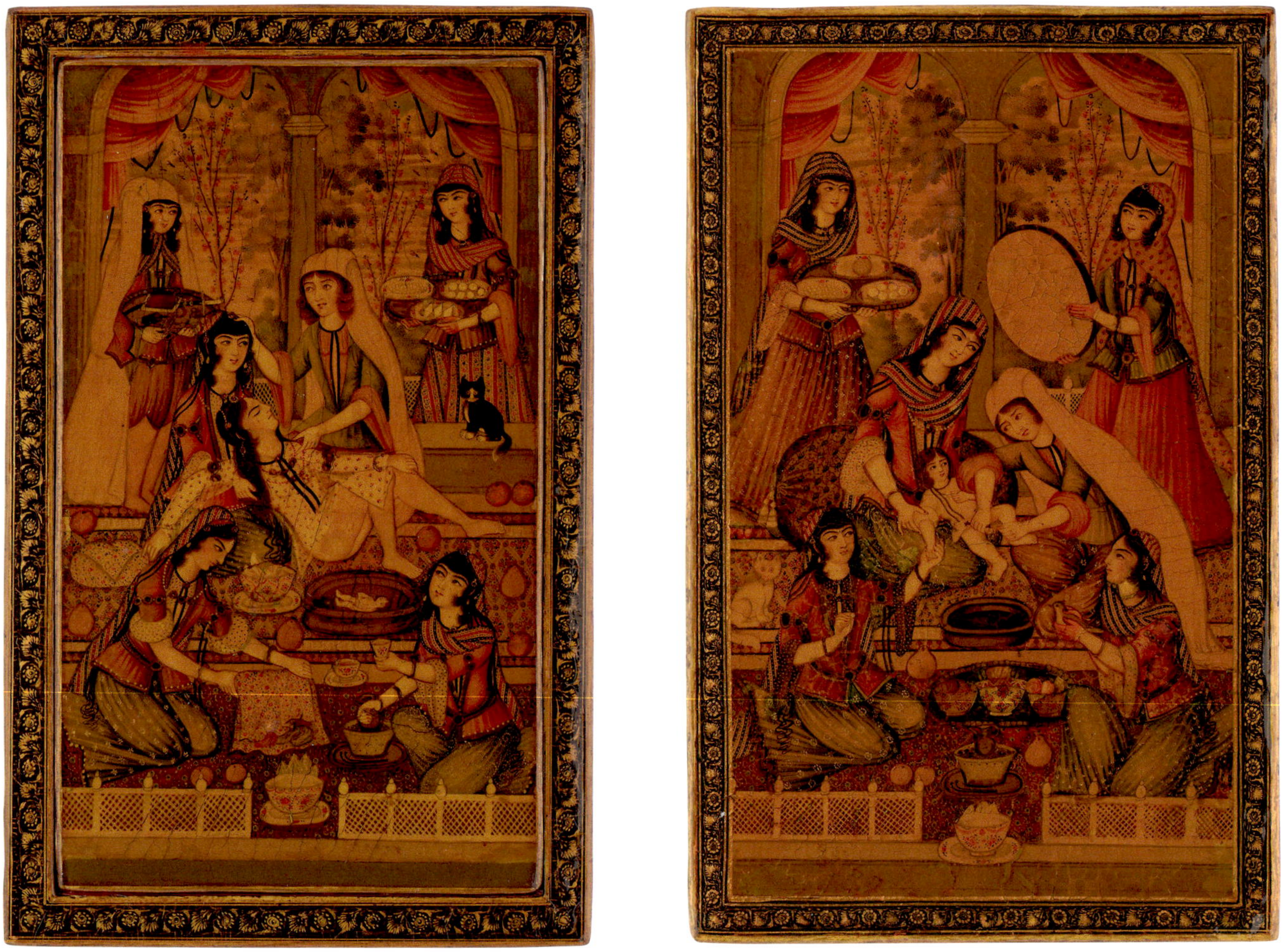

32 *Rectangular Mirror Case with Scenes of a Baby Boy's Birth and Circumcision* (front and back), 1830s–40s. For full information, see cat. 54, p. 150.

gained from mysticism, Mir Findiriski mastered the wild beast itself.[59] The middle ground of this composition—the two shaykhs and the lion—closely follows the representation found in a wall painting in Mir Findiriski's mausoleum in Isfahan.[60]

Persian lacquer painters made frequent use of the shorthand terrace composition in the second quarter of the 19th century.[61] As the examples above show, the schematized compositional device was deracinated from its original architectural and iconographic contexts.

Fluid Forms and Mobile Figures

Equally removed from their original context are some of the figures who populate these scenes. The circumcision scene on the mirror case above offers telling examples (Fig. 32). The attendant kneeling at left, grasping the baby's hand, reappears in two Harvard Qajar Album drawings of lovers on a terrace.[62] With minor adjustments to poses, costumes, and props, the mother, baby, and the kneeling attendant lifting a bird at right served in many depictions of the Virgin and Child.

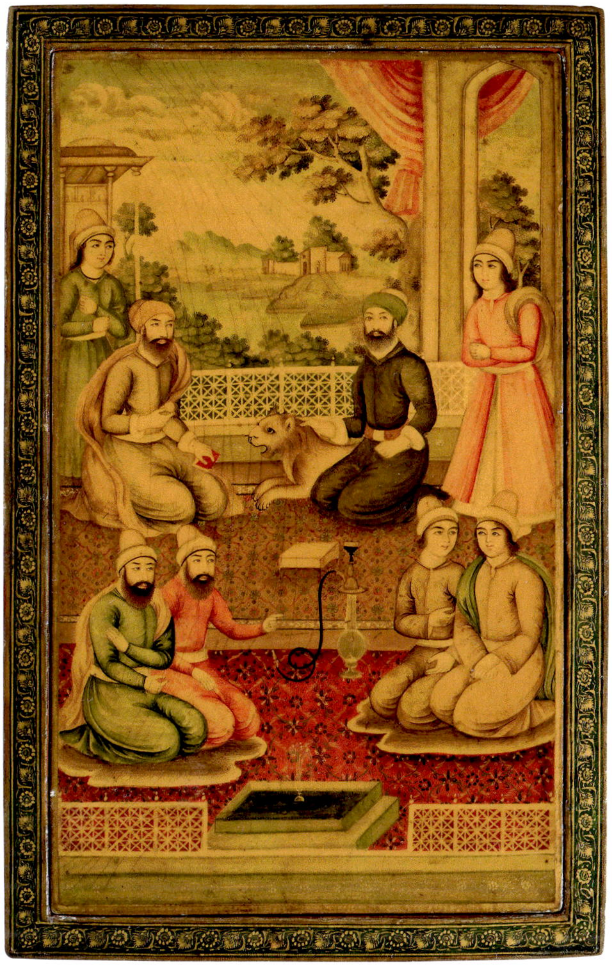

33 *Rectangular Mirror Case with Mir Findiriski, Shaykh Baha'i, Companions, and a Lion*, 1830s–40s. For full information, see cat. 55, p. 150.

Borrowings from Christian imagery appear frequently in Qajar art, although the figures appear untethered from iconographic content and, as noted by Rochechouart, have usually evolved considerably from their sources.[63] Particularly prevalent in lacquer is a composition based on the "Virgin of the Chair," usually set on a terrace overlooking architecture of a vaguely European character. An especially popular version that can be linked to the Najaf circle shows the mother and child with the bird-lifting attendant, as seen in one Harvard Qajar Album drawing and on two mirror cases (Figs. 34–36).[64]

A bird-bearing attendant plays a tangential role at best at a circumcision ceremony, and in representations of the Virgin and Child, this figure signals an iconographic conflation. Mosaic Law laid three requirements on the parents of a firstborn son: that the child be circumcised, that the mother offer an animal sacrifice for her purification after childbirth, and that the child be presented to the priest in the temple for redemption. Pictorially, the Christian tradition sometimes telescopes two of these events into a single image: the mother's offering of sacrificial birds for her purification and the presentation of the child in the temple.[65]

The lid of the mirror case in Figure 36 draws on a second popular composition that also occurs in the Harvard Qajar Album (Fig. 37). Here, three elderly men surround the Virgin and Child on a terrace. The figure kneeling at the baby's feet suggests the Adoration of the Magi, while the figure pointing to an open book suggests images of the Virgin and Saints. It is not surprising that the Najaf artists once again inherited this repertoire from Muhammad Sadiq, in whose signed works can be found closely related figures and architectural elements from both compositions.[66]

If European sources exist for these specific Christian compositions and individual figures, they have proven elusive. Murdoch Smith noted that Christian imagery was "to be found in the paintings in the palaces of Ispahan, by Dutch and Italian artists in the time of Shah Abbas."[67] Palaces of the Qajar era in Tehran and Shiraz also contained paintings of the Virgin and Child, and many European travelers commented on the Persian fashion of pasting an eclectic array of European prints onto the ceilings and walls of the finer houses (examples of which are discussed in the introductory essay to this volume).[68] Whatever the ultimate sources, the Persian workshop practices of reusing and repurposing eventually deconstructed compositions into autonomous elements. Figures could be repositioned and their poses and costumes altered as

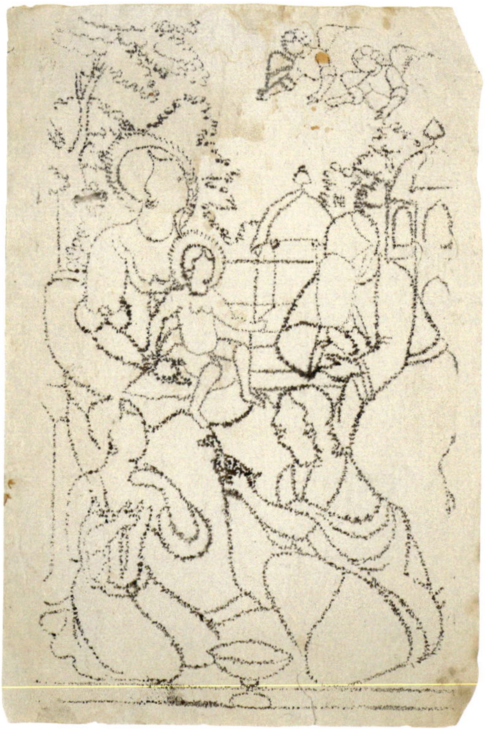
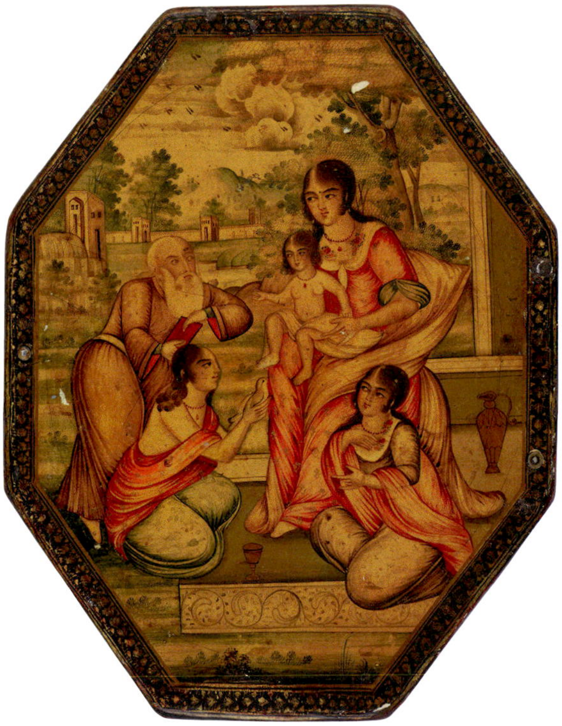
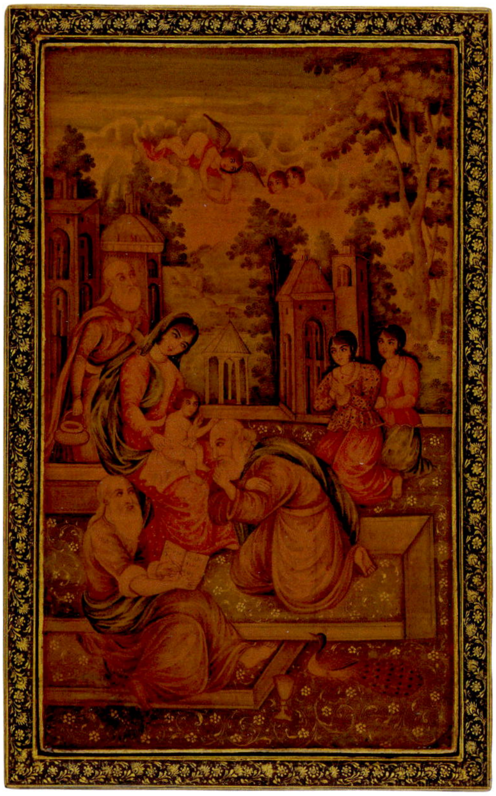
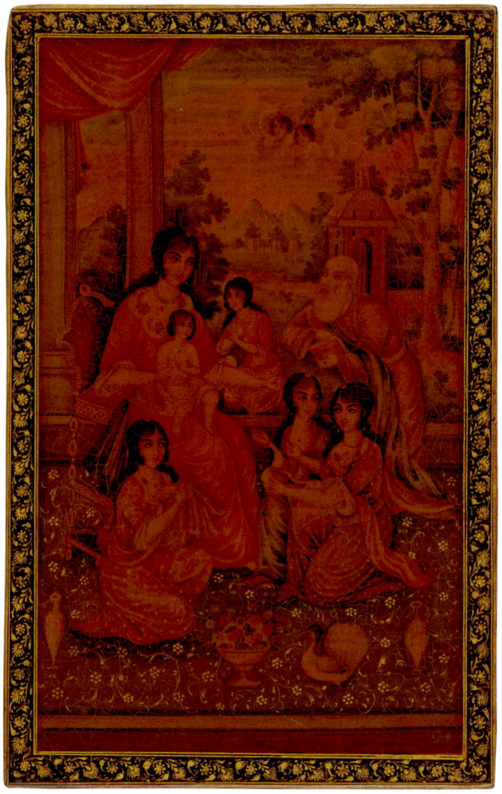

34 *Virgin and Child with Attendants*, 1780s–1870s. For full information, see cat. 14, p. 136.

35 *Octagonal Mirror Case with Virgin and Child*, first half 19th century. For full information, see cat. 61, p. 152.

36 *Rectangular Mirror Case with Virgin and Child* (front and back), first half 19th century. For full information, see cat. 60, p. 152.

freely as the paper dolls (*Poupées à habiller*) or *Constructions* produced for the *Images d'Épinal*.[69]

The next Qajar lacquer object to be examined, a medallion-format pen box of 1281 H (1864–65) in Figure 38, brings together many of the preceding themes, reveals the lacquer artist engaged in a wider network of social, artistic, and commercial exchanges, and opens avenues for further research. The larger medallions on the top and sides of the pen box feature doll-like figures of Persian and European men enjoying the company and favors of Persian women in what are probably brothel scenes.[70] It is, however, the smaller medallions and the connecting strapwork that interest us here.

On a far larger scale, foliate and floral strapwork was employed to frame and link medallions on the walls and ceilings of reception halls in some of the finer residences of the Qajar era, as for example, the Naranjistan in Shiraz (see Figs. 9 and 10 in David Roxburgh's introduction). Paintings, photographs, or European prints usually filled the medallions, and as demonstrated by Parviz Tanavoli, images of Western women, particularly bust-length portraits taken from reproductive prints, proved the most popular fillers.[71]

The smaller medallions on the pen box contain bust portraits of European beauties rather generally resembling those found in lacquer wares, with one exception: the right-most medallion on the top of the pen box holds the signature of the artist, Ahmad b. Najaf ʿAli, together with the image of a young woman who glances over her shoulder toward the viewer, her chin balanced on the finger of one hand and her elbow cupped by the other. The same figure occurs on two drawings in the Harvard Qajar Album (Fig. 39) and in a print pasted in the mirror room of the Zavelian house in the Armenian suburb of New Julfa, Isfahan.[72] The print (Fig. 40) is a chromolithograph by the multi-talented French artist Bernard-Romain Julien (1802–1871), published in both Paris and London.[73]

The Zavelian house preserves a treasury of lithographs, many the work of French commercial lithographers who flourished in the second and third quarters of the 19th century by reproducing the paintings of contemporary French and British artists. Tanavoli has documented that until the 1870s, the Zavelian house belonged to the Nurian family, who had been employed by various English trading companies.[74] Close connections can be found between Najaf lacquer wares and at least three prints in the Zavelian house and one in the nearby Shahshahani house.[75] Given the wide circulation of European prints in Qajar Iran, these connections may be purely coincidental, but it seems likely that the houses and the social and professional exchanges they embodied served as resources for Persian artists.[76]

Julien and Ahmad's young woman reveals yet another commercial network that joined Iran to the wider world and influenced lacquer artists. She appears again on a fine Russian pen box from about 1880 produced by the prestigious Lukutin manufactory in Danilkovo (Fig. 41). As Monika Kopplin has noted, the Lukutin factory increased production of lacquer for the Persian market in the later 19th century, reflecting the Russian Empire's strong interest in Iran and growing ambitions in the region.[77] The form and decoration of the pen box demonstrate how skillfully the Lukutin firm targeted Persian consumers. Late Qajar artists in turn incorporated certain aspects of Russian lacquer into their own work. To take one example, Muhammad Baqir from the village of Samirum, near Isfahan, successfully adopted the Russian technique of using oil- rather than water-based paint and appropriated the overall layout of Lukutin pen boxes, with gold filigree ends flanking oblong medallions containing a figure on the top and luminous, Western-style landscapes on the sides (cat. 77).

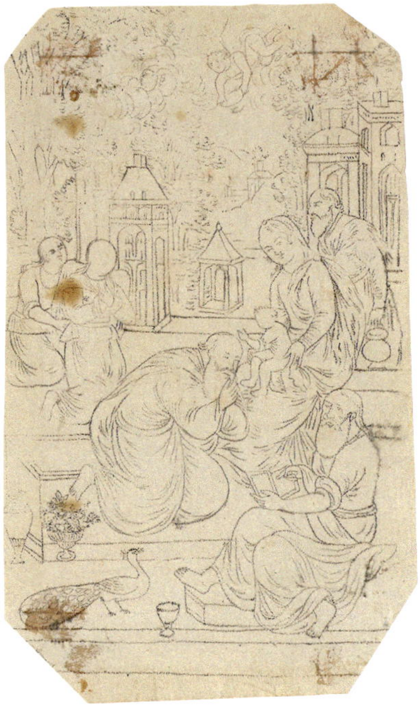

37 *Virgin and Child with Three Old Men, Angel, Female Companion, and Putto in the Sky*, 1780–1850. For full information, see cat. 12, p. 134.

Conclusion

Through well-established workshop practices, inventive adaptation of source material, and high volume of production, Persian artists transformed lacquer into one of the most characteristic and compelling visual expressions of the Qajar era. Connected to a larger world of trade, Qajar artists developed design portfolios with versatile compositions that could seamlessly combine stock motifs and new fashions. Working at the high point of their industry, they used this flexible medium as an experimental arena. They combined their traditional cultural heritage—for example, the classics of Persian literature or Safavid painting—with new forms and visual effects adapted not only from traditional trading partners, such as India, but also from Russia and Europe.

An indirect but critical driver of the lacquer artists' visual repertoire were the technical advances in the European printing industry that generated an explosion of French and British reproductive prints in the 18th and 19th centuries.[78] Available in the market but also through social and professional contacts, reproductive prints connected Persian artists with the Armenian and European communities in Iran. Lacquer artists incorporated and often reformulated Western imagery for their own purposes, creating new contexts for, and new content from, the foreign material, but also providing an alternative mode for its consumption within Iran. As noted by Farshid Emami, Mira Xenia Schwerda, and David J. Roxburgh in this volume, lacquer artists also readily adapted the visual properties and subject matter of photography and lithography. In 1903, for example, the artist Mubarraz al-Shuʿara employed the medallion format to juxtapose a near-photographic portrayal of men gathered in a courtyard with the conventional theme of beautiful reclining women (cat. 76). The beauties, however, now wear updated fashions of the late Qajar era.

Judging from the range in quality and market prices, Qajar lacquer reached a relatively broad spectrum of consumers. Representations of Shaykh Sanʿan or the family of Imam ʿAli (cat. 67) reflected both the interests of the court and popular sentiment. Perhaps it would be fair to say that in its heyday, Qajar lacquer functioned something like the medium of American television in its early years; both innovative and imitative, it pulled and recombined material

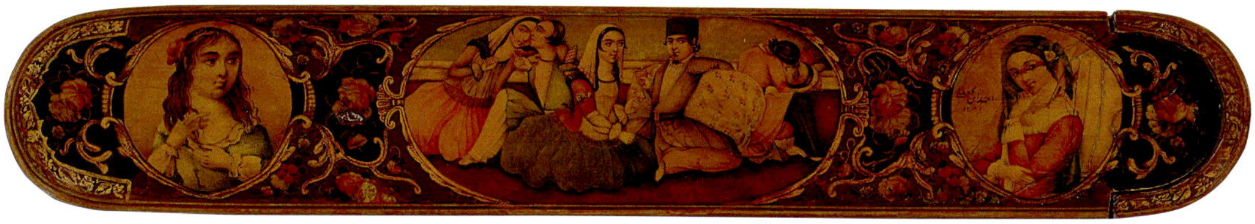

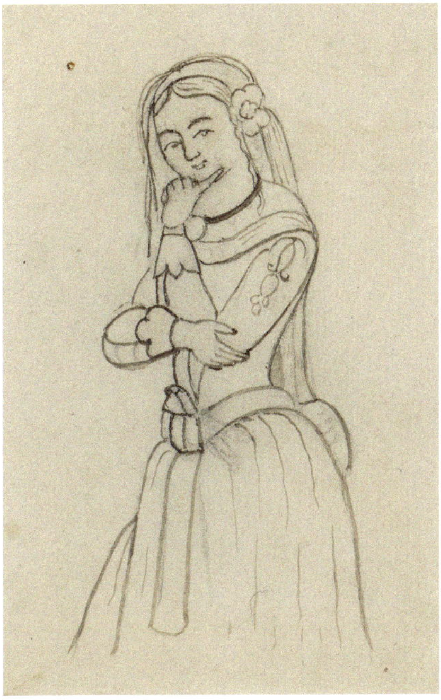

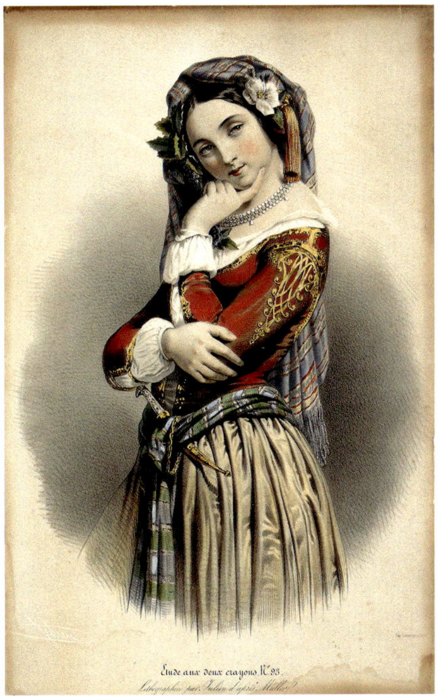

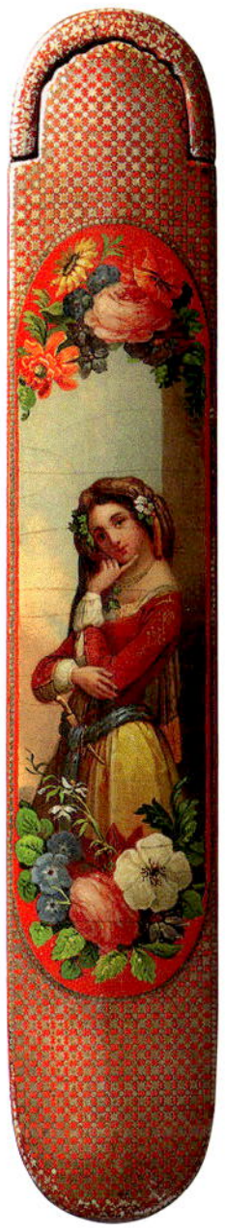

38 *Pen Box with Amorous Couples and Female Portraits in Medallions*, dated 1281 H (1864–65). For full information, see cat. 68, p. 154.

39 *Study Sheet with Flowers and Female Portraits and Figures* (detail), 1850–75. For full information, see cat. 17, p. 136.

40 Bernard-Romain Julien, *Portrait of a Young Woman (Etude aux deux crayons No. 93)*, c. 1838. Chromolithograph on paper, 35 × 15 cm (13¾ × 5 15/16 in.). Benaki Museum, Athens, ΓΕ_38238.

41 *Pen Box with Young Woman*, c. 1880. For full information, see cat. 73, p. 156.

from sources foreign and domestic, contemporary and historical, and high-, middle-, and low-brow. It served varied tastes and purposes, from pious to humorous, official to personal, and aspirational to inspirational. Any impact—accidental or indirect—that Qajar lacquer may have had on its enthusiastic consumers remains largely unknown, but it generated a steady supply of spinoffs and reruns.

Mary McWilliams is the Norma Jean Calderwood Curator of Islamic and Later Indian Art at the Harvard Art Museums.

Notes

1 The lacquer object created for the Paris Exposition is a mirror case painted by Isfahan artist Riza al-Imami, now in the Victoria and Albert Museum, London, 922–1869; it is described as "the finest piece of lacquer in the Victoria and Albert Museum collection," in B. W. Robinson, "Persian Painting under the Zand and Qājār Dynasties," in *The Cambridge History of Iran*, vol. 7, *From Nadir Shah to the Islamic Republic*, ed. P. Avery, G. R. G. Hambly, and Charles Melville (Cambridge: Cambridge University Press, 1991), 888, pl. 68. An important patron of art and architecture, Dust 'Ali Khan (1820–1873) held numerous offices in the Qajar government and enriched himself by extending monopolies over the state treasury and the royal mint during the 1860s. See Abbas Amanat, *Pivot of the Universe: Nasir al-Din Shah Qajar and the Iranian Monarchy, 1831–1896* (Berkeley: University of California Press, 1997), 388, 499n67.

2 Sir Robert Murdoch Smith, *Persian Art* (New York: Scribner, Welford, and Armstrong, 1877), 41. He served as director of the Telegraph Company in Tehran for 20 years, and from 1873 to 1885 acted as an agent of the Department of Science and Art of the South Kensington Museum (later the Victoria and Albert Museum). See Jennifer Scarce, "Persian Art through the Eyes of Nineteenth-Century British Travellers," *Bulletin of the British Society for Middle Eastern Studies* 8 (1) (1981); Jennifer Scarce, "Major-General Sir Robert Murdoch Smith KCMG and Anglo-Iranian Relations in Art and Culture," in *Anglo-Iranian Relations Since 1800*, ed. Vanessa Martin (New York: Routledge, 2005); and http://www.vam.ac.uk/content/articles/m/sir-robert-j-murdoch-smith.

3 Julien de Rochechouart, *Souvenirs d'un Voyage en Perse* (Paris: Challamel Aîné, 1867), 271.

4 Translated in A. J. Arberry, *Fifty Poems of Hafiz* (Cambridge: Cambridge University Press, 1947), 122. Also see William L. Hanaway, Jr., "Paradise on Earth: The Terrestrial Garden in Persian Literature," in *The Islamic Garden*, ed. Elisabeth B. MacDougall and Richard Ettinghausen (Washington, D.C.: Dumbarton Oaks, Trustees for Harvard University, 1976); Julie Scott Meisami, "Allegorical Gardens in the Persian Poetic Tradition: Nezami, Rumi, Hafez," *International Journal of Middle East Studies* 17 (2) (May 1985); and "*'Zur Rose sprach die Nachtigall . . .' Bilder von Rose und Nachtigall (gul-u-bulbul) in der islamischen Lackmalerei*," in *Aus 1001 Nacht: Islamische Lackkunst in deutschen Museen and Bibliotheken*, ed. Reingard Neumann (Münster, Germany: Museum für Lackkunst, 2009).

5 For a description of a similarly decorated "royal pen box" (*qalamdān-i kayānī*) and references to Henry-René d'Allemagne's account of a pen box created as a presentation piece for Nasir al-Din Shah by his poet laureate, see B. W. Robinson, "Lacquer, Oil-Paintings and Later Arts of the Book," in *Treasures of Islam*, ed. Toby Falk (Geneva: Musée d'art et d'histoire, 1985), 187. For the original, see Henry-René d'Allemagne, *Du Khorassan au pays des Backhtiaris: Trois mois de voyage en Perse*, vol. 1 (Paris: Hachette et Cie, 1911), 82–84.

6 For a drawing of the same scene, see cat. 20, p. 138.

7 For a history of Islamic lacquer, see Tim Stanley, "Lacquer in the Islamic World," in *The World of Lacquer: 2000 Years of History*, ed. Pedro de Moura Carvalho (Lisbon: Calouste Gulbenkian Museum, c. 2001); Tim Stanley, "The Rise of the Lacquer Binding," in *Hunt for Paradise: Court Arts of Safavid Iran, 1501–1576*, ed. Jon Thompson and Sheila R. Canby (New York: Rizzoli, 2003); Nasser D. Khalili, B. W. Robinson, and Tim Stanley, *Lacquer of the Islamic Lands*, pt. 1, The Nasser D. Khalili Collection of Islamic Art, vol. 22 (London: Nour Foundation in association with Azimuth Editions and Oxford University Press, c. 1996–97), 10–29; B. W. Robinson, *An Exhibition of 50 Pieces of Persian, Indian, and Turkish Lacquer at Bernheimer Fine Arts Ltd. from 10 June to 27 June 1986* (London:

Bernheimer Fine Arts Ltd., 1986); and Layla S. Diba, "Lacquerwork," in *The Arts of Persia*, ed. R. W. Ferrier (New Haven, Conn.: Yale University Press, 1989).

8 Layla S. Diba, "Lacquerwork of Safavid Persia and Its Relationship to Persian Painting," Ph.D. dissertation, New York University, 1994, esp. "Lacquerwork in Persia in the Timurid Period (1371–1507)," vol. 1, 54–108; and Khalili, Robinson, and Stanley, *Lacquer of the Islamic Lands*, 1:10–19.

9 For in-depth analyses, see Ina Sahl and Barbara Springmann, "Ausgesprochen vielschichtig—Islamische Lackarbeiten aus technologischer Sicht," in Neumann, *Aus 1001 Nacht*; Erika Neumann-Henneberg, "Technologische Untersuchungen an Lackarbeiten aus Persien," *Zeitschrift für Kunsttechnologie und Konservierung* 18 (2004); and Katherine Eremin and Claire Grech, "Materials and Techniques of Persian Lacquerwork," in *A Collector's Passion: Ezzat-Malek Soudavar and Persian Lacquer*, ed. Massumeh Farhad and Mary McWilliams (Washington, D.C.: Smithsonian Institution, 2017).

10 The Portuguese and later the Dutch trading companies included East Asian, especially Japanese, lacquer in their inter-Asian trade from the mid-16th through the 17th century. See Oliver Impey and Christiaan Jörg, *Japanese Export Lacquer: 1580–1850* (Amsterdam: Hotei Publishing, 2005), 19–29, 34, 46, 252–54, 262.

11 Stanley, "Lacquer in the Islamic World," 167–68; and Neumann, *Aus 1001 Nacht*, 141–42.

12 Firuz Kazemzadeh, *Russia and Britain in Persia: Imperial Ambitions in Qajar Iran* (New York: I. B. Tauris, 2013), 3–99. See also G. R. G. Hambly, "Iran during the Reigns of Fath ʿAli Shah and Muhammad Shah," in Avery, Hambly, and Melville, *The Cambridge History of Iran*, vol. 7, *From Nadir Shah to the Islamic Republic*.

13 Thomas M. Bayer and John R. Page, *The Development of the Art Market in England: Money as Muse, 1730–1900* (London: Pickering & Chatto, 2011); and Linda C. Hults, *The Print in the Western World: An Introductory History* (Madison: University of Wisconsin Press, 1996). For an illuminating picture of the American market for European reproductive prints, see DeCourcy E. McIntosh, "New York's Favorite Pictures in the 1870s," *Magazine Antiques* (April 1, 2004).

14 D'Allemagne (*Du Khorassan au pays des Backhtiaris*, 1:81) noted on his travels in 1907 that all the banks, stores, government offices, and Persian nobles employed "mirzas," who functioned as professional secretaries, clerks, or accountants. As can be observed in this photograph from the *Album of Photographs by ʿAli Khan Vali*, their attributes consisted of a scroll of paper and a pen box, which, to paraphrase D'Allemagne, contained everything necessary for writing: pens, pencils, pen knife, scissors, and a minuscule ink holder, which held a few pinches of powdered ink dissolved in the water of a sponge made of a wad of floss.

15 Sir William Ouseley, *Travels in Various Countries of the East, More Particularly Persia*, vol. 3 (London: Rodwell and Martin, 1819–23), 62ff.

16 Rochechouart, *Souvenirs d'un Voyage en Perse*, 273.

17 D'Allemagne, *Du Khorassan au pays des Backhtiaris*, 1:81–84.

18 Rochechouart, *Souvenirs d'un Voyage en Perse*, 262, 265.

19 Willem Floor, "Art (*Naqqashi*) and Artists (*Naqqashan*) in Qajar Persia," *Muqarnas* 16 (1999): 130.

20 Mary McWilliams, "Reflections of the Najaf Circle in Isfahan," in *An Album of Artists' Drawings from Qajar Iran*, ed. David J. Roxburgh (Cambridge, Mass.: Harvard Art Museums, 2017).

21 Roger Savory, "Last of the Qezelbāš," in *Society and Culture in Qajar Iran: Studies in Honor of Hafez Farmayan*, ed. Elton L. Daniel (Costa Mesa, Calif.: Mazda Publishers, Inc., 2002).

22 Floor, "Art (*Naqqashi*) and Artists (*Naqqashan*) in Qajar Persia," 127.

23 Eremin and Grech, "Materials and Techniques of Persian Lacquerwork."

24 I have yet to find an incontrovertible example of pounced (dotted) outlines on a work of Persian lacquer. This may be due to the fact that the dotted outlines would have been blurred by the artist retracing the outline with a wet or dry medium, or by the application of a finishing coat of lacquer.

25 For similar processes in 18th-century Indian painting, see Molly Emma Aitken, "Parataxis and the Practice of Reuse, from Mughal Margins to Mir Kalān Khān," *Archives of Asian Art* 59 (2009).

26 The phrase *yā ṣādiq al-waʿd* (O You who are true to your promise!) is one of the inscriptions believed to have been used by Muhammad Sadiq as a punning signature. Khalili, Robinson, and Stanley, *Lacquer of the Islamic Lands*, 1:74–75.

27 For information on ʿAli Ashraf, see ibid., 1:72–74.

28 For example, see an undated mirror case with the crypto-signature of Najaf ʿAli or his workshop, *yā shāh-i Najaf* (O Lord of Najaf!), in Sotheby's, London, April 25, 2002, lot 59; and a mirror case dated 1206 H (1844–45) signed by Zayn al-ʿAbidin (al-Imami), Metropolitan Museum of Art, New York, 2009.170.

29 The attribution is suggested by the decoration on the interior of the lid—dervishes seated by a stream—which appears often on works by the Najaf circle; see, for example, the front of a pen box signed by Najaf ʿAli dated 1269 H (1852–53), Harvard Art Museums, 2014.316.

30 Khalili, Robinson, and Stanley, *Lacquer of the Islamic Lands*, 1:75. For a discussion of the transmission of the Safavid artistic legacy through the 18th century, see Layla S. Diba, "Persian Painting in

the Eighteenth Century: Tradition and Transmission," *Muqarnas* 6 (1989).

31 A Royal Academician, Westall taught drawing to Princess (later Queen) Victoria for eight years. The first reproductive print of the painting is by British printmaker R. M. Meadows (1780–1812). Stipple printed in color, it bears the caption "Venus and Cupids / From the original Drawing in the Possession of John Julius Augustus Esq." The British Museum, London, 1934,0113.5.

32 George Hamilton, *The English School: A Series of the Most Approved Productions in Painting and Sculpture, Executed by British Artists from the Days of Hogarth to the Present Time* (London: C. Tilt, 1831–32), 994.

33 The first edition was published by Jardine's brother-in-law, Edinburgh printer and engraver William Home Lizars. It featured four main sections: Ornithology, Mammalia, Entomology, and Ichthyology, each prepared by a leading naturalist. Lizars engraved the illustrations, which were produced by various artists. For further information, see Christine Elisabeth Jackson and Peter Davis, *Sir William Jardine: A Life in Natural History* (New York: Leicester University Press), 2001.

34 Sir William Jardine, *Birds of Great Britain and Ireland, Part I: Birds of Prey*, The Naturalist's Library, vol. 9 (Edinburgh: W. H. Lizars, 1838), pls. 12, 13.

35 ʿAbbas Shirazi has closely followed the plates for Salt's Antelope, the Addax, the Common Roebuck, and the Fallow Deer from Sir William Jardine, *Mammalia. Ruminating Animals, Part I: Deer, Antelopes, Camels, & C.*, The Naturalist's Library, vol. 22 (Edinburgh: W. H. Lizars, 1866), pls. 33, 25, 15, 7, respectively.

36 Bronwen Gulkis, in Farhad and McWilliams, *A Collector's Passion*.

37 Whether Muhammad Ismaʿil should be associated with the Imami or Najaf circle of lacquer artists in Isfahan is contested. He is associated with the Najaf circle in Khalili, Robinson, and Stanley, *Lacquer of the Islamic Lands*, 2:46; and with the Imami circle in Floor, "Art (*Naqqashi*) and Artists (*Naqqashan*) in Qajar Persia," 140–41. His compositions appear in works signed by artists in both groups.

38 The Nasser D. Khalili Collection of Islamic Art, London, LAQ 297, in Khalili, Robinson, and Stanley, *Lacquer of the Islamic Lands*, 1:68–70, cat. 37. See also Eremin and Grech, "Materials and Techniques of Persian Lacquerwork."

39 The pen box by ʿAli Ashraf is dated 1160 H (1747–48); The Nasser D. Khalili Collection of Islamic Art, London, LAQ 224, in Khalili, Robinson, and Stanley, *Lacquer of the Islamic Lands*, 1:78–79, cat. 43.

40 The connection between the contents of medallions on a given pen box is sometimes elusive. ʿAbbas Shirazi's animal studies and European beauties seem linked only by their status as exotica.

41 For examples, see an undated pen box in Robinson, "Persian Painting under the Zand and Qājār Dynasties," 873, pl. 8; and an undated pen box in Christie's, London, October 11, 2005, lot 124.

42 Parviz Tanavoli, *European Women in Persian Houses: Western Images in Safavid and Qajar Iran*, ed. Sarah B. Sherrill and Moya Carey (London: I. B. Tauris, 2015).

43 Amy S. Landau, "Visibly Foreign, Visibly Female: The Eroticization of *Zan-i Farangi* in Seventeenth-Century Persian Painting," in *Eros and Sexuality in Islamic Art*, ed. Francesca Leoni and Mika Natif (Burlington, Vt.: Ashgate, 2013). Also see Axel Langer, "European Influences on Seventeenth-Century Persian Painting: Of Handsome Europeans, Naked Ladies, and Parisian Timepieces," in *The Fascination of Persia: The Persian-European Dialogue in Seventeenth-Century Art and Contemporary Art of Teheran*, ed. Axel Langer (Zurich: Museum Rietberg, 2013).

44 Mohammad Tavakoli-Targhi, "Eroticizing Europe," in *Society and Culture in Qajar Iran: Studies in Honor of Hafez Farmayan*, ed. Elton L. Daniel (Costa Mesa, Calif.: Mazda Publishers, 2002); and Mohammad Tavakoli-Targhi, "Women of the West Imagined: The *Farangi* Other and the Emergence of the Women Question in Iran," in *Identity Politics and Women: Cultural Reassertions and Feminisms in International Perspective*, ed. Valentine Moghadam (Boulder, Col.: Westview Press, 1994).

45 Amy S. Landau, "Man, Mode, and Myth: Muhammad Zaman ibn Haji Yusuf," in *Pearls on a String: Artists, Patrons, and Poets at the Great Islamic Courts*, ed. Amy S. Landau (Seattle: University of Washington Press, 2015); and Langer, "European Influences on Seventeenth-Century Persian Painting."

46 McWilliams, "Reflections of the Najaf Circle." Earlier examples of lacquer artists employing this composition have survived: for instance, a pen box in Muḥammad ʿAlī Karīmzāda Tabrīzī, *Aḥvāl va āṣār-i naqqāshān-i qadīm-i Īran va barkhī az mashāhīr-i nigārgar-i Hind va ʿUṣmānī*, vol. 2 (London: Interlink Longraph, 1985–91), 792, 1020–21, Figs. 108, 110; and two mirror cases in Neumann, *Aus 1001 Nacht*, 104, 121. Also see a discussion of this composition in Diba, "Persian Painting in the Eighteenth Century," 159.

47 The composition also survives in a pricked drawing in the Harvard Qajar Album, although its lozenge format and larger scale were not likely intended for a pen box (see object number 1960.161.18 [a]). A drawing that is even closer to the composition of Jaʿfar's pen box, and that is formatted for the top of a pen box, is reproduced in Karīmzāda Tabrīzī, *Aḥvāl va āṣār-i naqqāshān*, 1:457, Fig. 14.

48 John Carswell, *New Julfa: The Armenian Churches and Other Buildings* (Oxford: Clarendon Press, 1968).

49 For example, two reproductive prints of the mid-19th century after works by English painter William Powell Frith (1819–1909): *Miss Lucy B* and *Sherry, Sir?*, The British Museum, London, 1865,1014.633, 1914,1009.13.

50 In Hayter's painting, it can be seen that Ja'far's gold band is actually a buckle that joins the edges of a heavy robe and the Queen's hair is braided at the ears before looping back behind them.

51 Although plausible, it is not necessary for the Najaf artists to have seen the 1853 reproductive print. Victoria's reign (1837–1901) saw a tremendous expansion in the market for newspapers, books, periodicals, and prints; thus, her likeness was constantly available through a diverse assortment of mediums. See John Plunkett, *Queen Victoria: First Media Monarch* (Oxford: Oxford University Press, 2003). The young Victoria's signature hairstyle can be better understood in Franz Xaver Winterhalter's 1842 portrait of the queen wearing regalia of the Order of the Garter. Many copies of this popular painting exist, and it was reproduced in prints, as can be seen pasted onto the vaulted ceiling of the Shahshahani house in Isfahan; see Tanavoli, *European Women in Persian Houses*, 109, 118, pls. 40c, 46. Tanavoli's caption is "Portrait of young woman, chromolithograph."

52 British Museum Collections Online, object number 2010,7081.6473 (accessed August 2016).

53 Amanat, *Pivot of the Universe*, 265.

54 Ibid., 277–303. For the reactions of "ordinary" Iranians to the varied aspects of European culture they encountered in their own country, see Morteza Nouraei, "Ordinary People and the Reception of British Culture in Iran, 1906–41," in *Anglo-Iranian Relations since 1800*, ed. Vanessa Martin (New York: Routledge, 2005).

55 Langer, "European Influences on Seventeenth-Century Persian Painting," 218.

56 As seen, for example, in two paintings: 'Ali Quli Jabadar (fl. 1657–c. 1716), *Shah Sulayman with Courtiers on a Veranda*, c. 1670–75, Institute of Oriental Manuscripts, Russian Academy of Sciences, St. Petersburg, E–14, fol. 98A; and Muhammad Zaman, *Judith with the Severed Head of Holofernes*, c. 1680, The Nasser D. Khalili Collection of Islamic Art, London, MSS 1005.

57 The *Small Clive Album* is thought to have been given by Shuja' al-Dawla, the Nawab of Avadh, to Robert Clive (1725–1774), Commander in Chief of British India, during his last stay in India, from 1765 to 1767.

58 Gulkis, in *A Collector's Passion*.

59 There are usually three philosophers in the story, as recounted in Muhammad Kamal, *Mulla Sadra's Transcendent Philosophy* (Aldershot, U.K.: Ashgate, 2006), 30.

60 *Encyclopaedia Iranica*, s.v. "Mir Fendereski," Sajad H. Rizvi, http://www.iranicaonline.org/articles/mir-fendereski-sayyed-amir-abul-qasem. This subject occurs in a drawing in the Harvard Qajar Album (object number 1960.161.24 [a]). See Farhad Dokhani, "Religious Subjects and Themes: Shi'i Islam and the Revival of Iranian Sufism and Dervishes," in Roxburgh, *An Album of Artists' Drawings*. The fresco in the mausoleum is described in Willem Floor, *Wall Paintings and Other Figurative Mural Art in Qajar Iran* (Costa Mesa, Calif.: Mazda Publishers, 2005), 152–53n69. The lid of the Münster lacquer mirror case offers a partial view of a Safavid roofed terrace. The back of the case depicts a similar gathering of scholars and students, perhaps the famous confrontation between Shams Tabrizi and Jalal al-Din Rumi, as recounted in Haci Bektaş Veli's *Maqālāt* (Conversations).

61 The terrace with an Indian-style front balustrade appears widely in Qajar lacquer, but few objects are dated. Exceptions include a pen box of 1258 H (1842–43) signed by Abu al-Hasan Isfahani, Harvard Art Museums, 2014.312; and two works in The Nasser D. Khalili Collection of Islamic Art: book covers of 1262 H (1845–46) attributed to Zayn al-'Abidin (LAQ 29) and a pen box of 1256 H (1840–41) by Abu al-Hasan Isfahani (LAQ 151); see Khalili, Robinson, and Stanley, *Lacquer of the Islamic Lands*, 1:172–75, cats. 128, 129.

62 On folio 7a (Fig. 29), her hand lifts a piece of fruit; in another drawing, on folio 6b, her hand is empty; see Roxburgh, *An Album of Artists' Drawings*.

63 Rochechouart, *Souvenirs d'un Voyage en Perse*, 260.

64 See McWilliams, "Reflections of the Najaf Circle in Isfahan."

65 By some interpretations, the sacrificial offering of the two birds and the presentation in the temple are fused in the Christian tradition as early as the Gospel of Luke (2:22–24), where they are mentioned together. In Luke's account, Mary and Joseph offered two birds for the sacrifice, rather than the preferred bird and lamb, presumably because of their poverty. An example of the presentation in the temple in which the sacrificial birds appear is the drawing by Carlo Ridolfi (1602–1658), *The Presentation of Christ in the Temple*, Harvard Art Museums, 1957.128.7. The white-bearded figure holding a book and facing the Virgin in the Qajar compositions may represent the priest or possibly Joseph.

66 For example, an oval mirror case dated 1195 H (1780–81), in Sotheby's, London, April 22, 2015, lot 160; and a rectangular mirror case dated 1210 H (1795) in Bernisches Historisches Museum, Bern, 1913.620.0072. Another rectangular mirror case with Sadiq's punning signature employs many of the same figures on a double-balustrade terrace, but the inscription is probably a later addition; Christie's, London, April 27, 2012, lot 984. Muhammad Sadiq's figures and compositions were also employed by the Isfahan artist Sayyid

Mirza on a mirror case dated 1231 H (1815–16), in Chester Beatty Library, Dublin, Is X014. A lacquer instrument case in the Ashmolean Museum, Oxford, EA1955.1, offers three figural scenes that combine elements from the two compositions of the seated Virgin and Child and a scene of Indian women on a double-balustraded terrace. Although the case is undated and unsigned, B. W. Robinson suggested it may be an early work by Najaf ʿAli; see Robinson, "Lacquer in the University of Oxford," in *Islamic Art in the Ashmolean Museum*, ed. James Allan (Oxford: Oxford University Press, 1995), 45–47, Figs. 1–3. It is tempting to link these lacquer objects depicting the Virgin seated in a chair to the account given by Joseph Arthur, comte de Gobineau, a French diplomat posted in Iran from 1855 to 1858, who stated that a Qajar artist returned from Italy with a Virgin of the Chair (*Vièrge à la chaise*) composition that subsequently proved very popular (see Roxburgh, "Painting after Photography," in this volume). According to Gobineau, the Qajar artist had been dispatched to Italy by Muhammad Shah Qajar (r. 1834–1848). As the examples by Muhammad Sadiq and Sayyid Mirza mentioned above demonstrate, however, the two compositions featuring the seated Virgin that are of concern in this essay were in use by Persian artists well before the reign of Muhammad Shah.

67 Smith, *Persian Art*, 41.

68 Floor, *Wall Paintings and Other Figurative Mural Art in Qajar Iran*, 52, 53, 105.

69 The Pellerin family of Épinal, France, began making popular prints known as *Images d'Épinal* in the mid-18th century. By the latter half of the 19th century, much of the firm's business was in the creation of inexpensive paper toys for children, including toy theaters, jumping jacks, and construction models of many kinds. Because of their fragility, few have survived. See Henri George, *La belle histoire des images d'Épinal* (Paris: Cherche midi éditeur, c. 1996).

70 For European sources on prostitution in Qajar Iran and a less charming picture of the status of women, see Gavin R. G. Hambly, "The Traditional Iranian City in the Qajar Period," in Avery, Hambly, and Melville, *The Cambridge History of Iran*, vol. 7, *From Nadir Shah to the Islamic Republic*, 587–88; and Mansureh Ettehadieh (Nezam Mafi), "The Social Condition of Women in Qajar Society," in *Society and Culture in Qajar Iran: Studies in Honor of Hafez Farmayan*, ed. Elton L. Daniel (Costa Mesa, Calif.: Mazda Publishers, 2002).

71 Tanavoli, *European Women in Persian Houses*, 27.

72 Ibid., 162, 176, pls. 85, 97. The second drawing of the maiden appears on folio 21b in the Harvard Qajar Album; see McWilliams, "Reflections of the Najaf Circle."

73 Julien's lithograph may be after a painting by British artist William James Müller (1812–1845), according to an inscription on the chromolithograph in the Benaki Museum, Athens, which reads: "Lithographié par Julien d'après Müller." Benaki Museum, Athens. For information on Müller, see Cyril George Edward Bunt, *The Life and Art of William James Müller of Bristol* (Leigh-on-Sea, U.K.: F. Lewis, 1948). I have been unable to confirm Müller's authorship of this figure, which was probably copied by other artists. A nearly identical image appears in an oil painting titled *Estrella en Reflexion*, attributed to the circle of Constant-Joseph Brochart (1816–1899) in Lawrence Auctioneers of Crewkerne, Somerset, U.K., *Fine Art Sale: Pictures, Furniture, Clocks, & Rugs*, October 16, 2015, lot 1464. For this reference, I am grateful to Elizabeth Rudy, the Carl A. Weyerhaeuser Associate Curator of Prints at the Harvard Art Museums.

74 Tanavoli, *European Women in Persian Houses*, 37.

75 There are many general similarities between the pasted prints and the figures found in the Harvard Qajar Album and on lacquer wares. In addition to Julien's figure with finger on chin, the closest matches are listed below (plate numbers are from Tanavoli, *European Women in Persian Houses*). "A woman toying with her beaded necklace" (probably Bernard Chiapory): Zavelian House, pl. 88; and a pen box by Haydar ʿAli b. Najaf ʿAli, Harvard Art Museums, 2014.329. "A woman with a fan": Zavelian House, pl. 91; a pen box of 1329 H (1911–12) by ʿAbd al-Husayn Saniʿ Humayun, The Nasser D. Khalili Collection of Islamic Art, London, LAQ 107; and Harvard Qajar Album folio 1960.161.43 (b, top). "A lute player" (Josephine Ducollet after Brochart): Shahshahani House, pl. 36; and Harvard Qajar Album folio 1960.161.22(a).

76 In the Safavid era, the Armenian community in New Julfa provided a meeting point for Persian, European, and Armenian artists. See Landau, *Pearls on a String*, 180, 186–88; and Gary Schwartz, "Between Court and Company: Dutch Artists in Persia," in Langer, *The Fascination of Persia*, 164–66.

77 Monika Kopplin, *Russian Lacquer: The Collection at the Museum für Lackkunst* (Munich: Hirmer Publishers, 2015), 14, 24–25, 172–77, cats. 92–97. See also Kazemzadeh, *Russia and Britain in Persia*, esp. 1–99.

78 By the end of the 19th century, further technological developments diminished the livelihoods of both reproductive printmakers and lacquer painters. The costly and time-consuming processes of the printmakers could not compete with advances in photographic reproductive techniques. Persian lacquer artists saw one of the staple products of their trade—the pen box—become outmoded due to advances in the technology of writing tools and text reproduction.

همیگشت گودرز بر گرد کوه
بنودش بد و راه و آمد ستوه
پیاده ببود و سپر برگرفت
چو نخچیر جویان که اندر گرفت

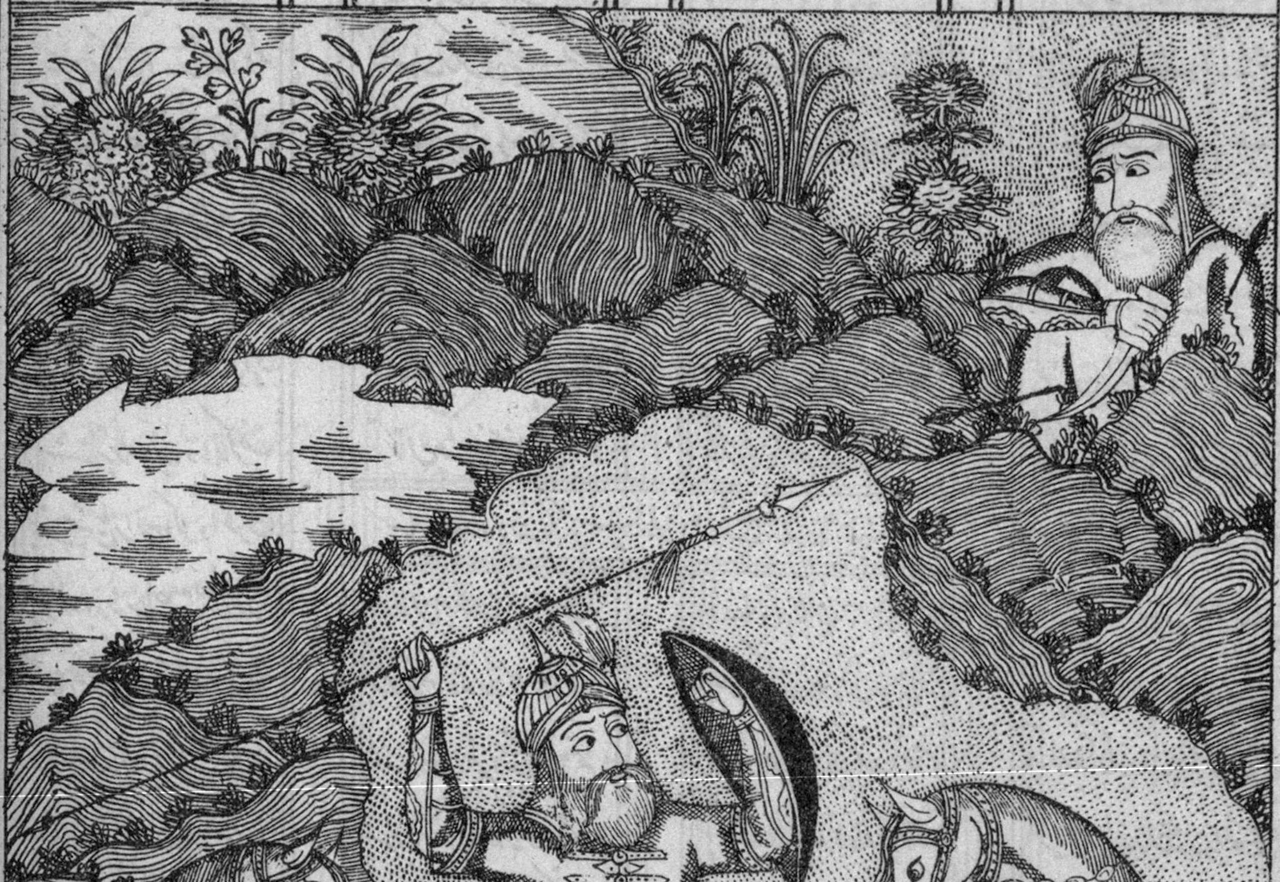

گرفته سپر پیش و زوبین بدست
ببالا نهاده سر از جای پست
همی دید پیران مر او را ز دور
بجست از سر سنگ سالار تور

بینداخت زوبین بگردار تیر
برآمد ببازوی سالار پیر
چو گودرز شد خسته بر دست اوی
ز کینه بخشم اندر آورد روی

بینداخت زوبین به پیران رسید
زره در برش سر بسر بردرید
ز پشت اندر آمد براه جگر
بغلطید و آسیمه برگشت سر

برآمدش خون جگر از دهان
روانش همی رفت زی همرهان
چو شیر ژیان اندر آمد بسر
بزوبین پولاد خسته جگر

بر آن کوه خارا زمانی طپید
پس از کین و آوردگه آرمید
زمانه بزهر آب داده است چنگ
بدرد دل شیر و چرم پلنگ

چنین است خود کردش روزگار
نگه دار همی پند آموزگار
چو گودرز بر شد بر آن کوهسار
بدیدش بدانگونه افکنده خوار

3 The Lithographic Image and Its Audiences

Farshid Emami

Detail: *Battle of Gudarz and Piran*, from the *Shāhnāma* (Book of Kings) by Firdawsi, dated 1265–67 H (1848–50). For full information, see cat. 45, p. 146.

Lithography emerged as a popular mode of bookmaking in Iran in the early 1800s, not long after its invention by Alois Senefelder (d. 1834) in the closing years of the 18th century. The first known book printed by means of lithography is a copy of the Qur'an published in the northwestern city of Tabriz in 1248 H (1832–33), although the first lithographic press in Iran had probably been established in the 1820s.[1] In 1821, the Crown Prince ʿAbbas Mirza had requested that the equipment for lithographic printing be sent from Tiflis to Tabriz.[2] Three years later, in 1824, a certain Jaʿfar Khan reportedly imported lithography equipment from Moscow, where he had received instructions in printing techniques.[3]

When situated within the broader trajectory of endeavors to institute a printing press in the Arabic script, the relatively swift adoption of lithography contrasts with the fairly long history of failed attempts to establish a typographic printing press. Indeed, 17th-century experiments notwithstanding, it was only in the 1810s that printing from movable type acquired widespread use in Iran.[4] Yet after a period of printing in both movable type and lithography, which lasted until around 1852, typography ceased to be practiced in the following two decades, during which lithography was the sole printing technique employed in book production.[5]

The positive reception of lithography arose primarily from its potential to perpetuate longstanding art forms and practices associated with handmade manuscripts. In contrast to typography, lithographic printing allowed for the re-creation of the layout and aesthetic appearance of a fine codex-format book, complete with the cursive script, illuminated title-pieces, and illustrated leaves.[6] Also contributing to the success of lithography was the relative cheapness of its equipment compared to the apparatus required for movable type printing.[7]

Following its success in book production in the 1840s and 1850s, the purview of lithography expanded beyond the printed codex to journals, single-sheet portraits, and posters—each with its distinctive format and entirely novel in 19th-century Iran. Hailed as the image-making technique of the new age, lithography was appreciated as an art form in its own right, with artists specializing in the craft and signing their printed drawings. In the meantime, the lithographic image—whether produced in local workshops or imported from abroad—pervaded Qajar visual culture, affecting established artistic practices in mediums ranging from polychrome tiles to paintings and lacquer objects. Illustrating mass-produced historical accounts and mythical narratives, the lithographic image was instrumental in visualizing, authenticating, and propagating the emerging conceptions of the past and in fashioning new national subjectivities in the age of colonial expansion and the rise of nation states. Depicting religious themes and narratives, it played a central role in the formation and dissemination of new expressions of popular piety in the nascent mass culture of Qajar Iran.

The Lithographed Book: Between Manuscript and Print

One might assume that the advent of the printed book marks a radical departure from manuscript tradition. Yet, as in other contexts, in mid-19th-century Iran the distinction between the two mediums was far more blurred; not only did lithographed books emulate the layout of the handwritten codex, but several types of mixed-media books were also produced. A copy of the *Mukhtār-nāma* (Book of Mukhtar) printed from movable type in 1845, for instance, featured drawings made by the woodcut technique that were then painted.[8] Another interesting case is a typographic edition of the *Khamsa* (Quintet) by the 12th-century poet Nizami, in which blank spaces were provided for illustrations to be completed by a painter.[9]

The 1847–48 edition of the *ʿAjāʾib al-makhlūqāt wa gharāʾib al-mawjūdāt* (The Wonders of Creation and Oddities of Existence) epitomizes the earliest corpus of Persian lithographed books (cat. 44).[10] An encyclopedic compendium penned by the late 13th-century author Zakariya b. Muhammad al-Qazwini, the *ʿAjāʾib* was written in Arabic and translated into Persian and Turkish and had been among the most frequently illustrated manuscripts. The lithographic edition perpetuates key features of these handmade precedents; written in the cursive hanging script named *nastaʿlīq*, it opens with an illuminated title page (*sarlawḥ*), as was the norm in such manuscripts.[11]

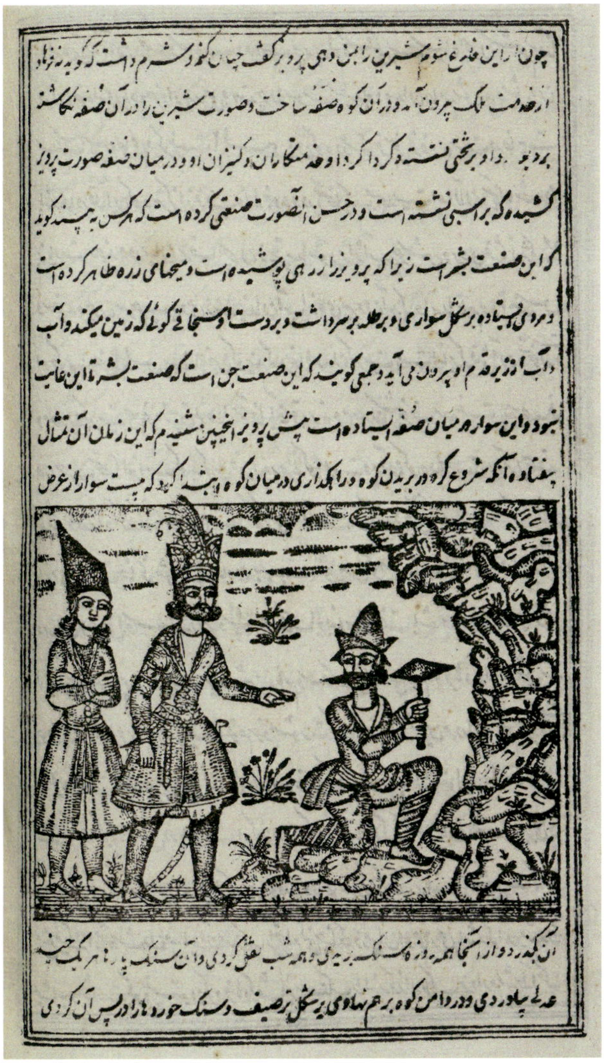

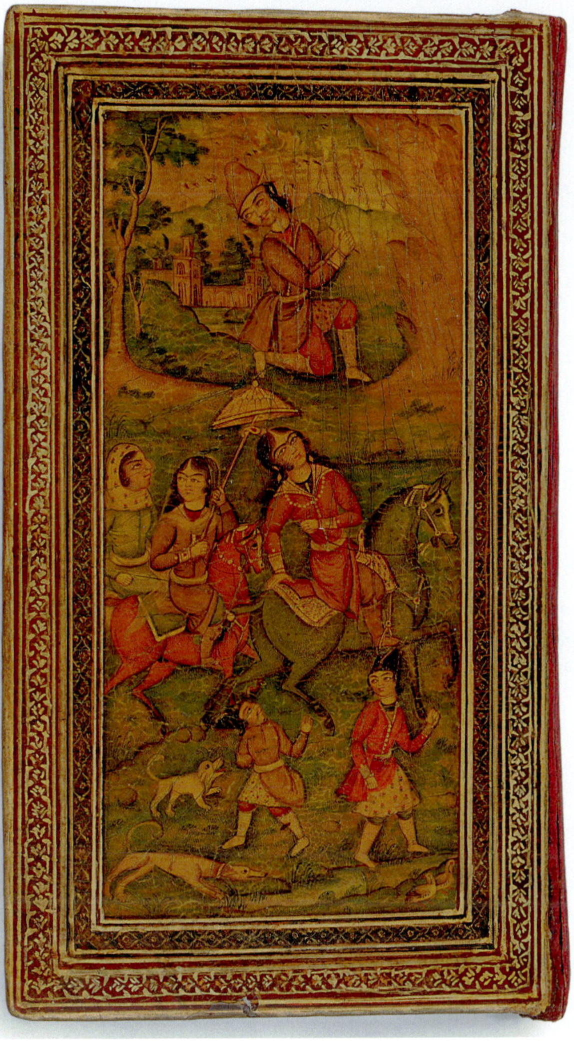

1 *Farhad at Mount Bisutun*, 1264 H (1847–48). For full information, see cat. 44, p. 146.

2 *Shirin Visits Farhad at Mount Bisutun*, cover of the manuscript, dated 22 Shawwal 1254 H (January 8, 1838). For full information, see cat. 7, p. 134.

The following pages are illustrated with three hundred or so images depicting wondrous plants, exotic creatures, signs of the Zodiac, and humorous anecdotes. The drawings were, at least in part, the work of Mirza ʿAli Quli Khawʾi (fl. 1846–1855), who was among the first artists to specialize in making lithographic images.[12]

Like its overall format, the illustrations of the *ʿAjāʾib* also draw on established models. For instance, in the description of Mount Bisutun—which appears in a section on the world's mountains—the author refers to the romance of Shirin and Farhad; it was at Mount Bisutun that the legendary stone-carver Farhad was forced to toil in order to reach his beloved Shirin, an Armenian princess. This digression from the main narrative provides the basis for the accompanying illustration (Fig. 1), which depicts the familiar scene of Farhad at Mount Bisutun, visited by the Sasanian king Khusraw, who seeks Shirin's love. Several other illustrations of the *ʿAjāʾib* are marked by a similarly tangential relation to the text. It is as if the book is conceived as a container for a set of amusing pictures, tenuously connected to the text but conjuring up a broader world of fables known to the reader-viewer, as the ubiquity of the scene in various mediums suggests (Fig. 2). Indeed, given the relatively high rate of illiteracy in 19th-century Iran, it is not unreasonable to assume that such illustrated printed books were not solely intended for individual reading; they might also have been recited by one person for larger groups, with images engaging a wider audience.

Along with well-known literary works, the early years of printing also saw a profusion of religious books, particularly on popular Shiʿi themes and narratives.[13] One of the most popular books was *Ṭūfān al-bukāʾ* (Deluge of Tears), written in 1250 H (1834) by Muhammad Ibrahim b. Muhammad Baqir Jawhari (d. 1837). A recent study has shown that at least 58 illustrated editions of the book were published in the Qajar period, making it one of the most popular books of its time.[14] Its popularity, however, did not lie solely in its appeal to individual readers. Written in a combination of prose and verse, the book narrates the lives and deeds of the saints of Shiʿism, and was widely used during mourning assemblies (*rawżа-khvānī*), where the text was employed by narrators to recite the lives and sufferings of the Shiʿi imams.

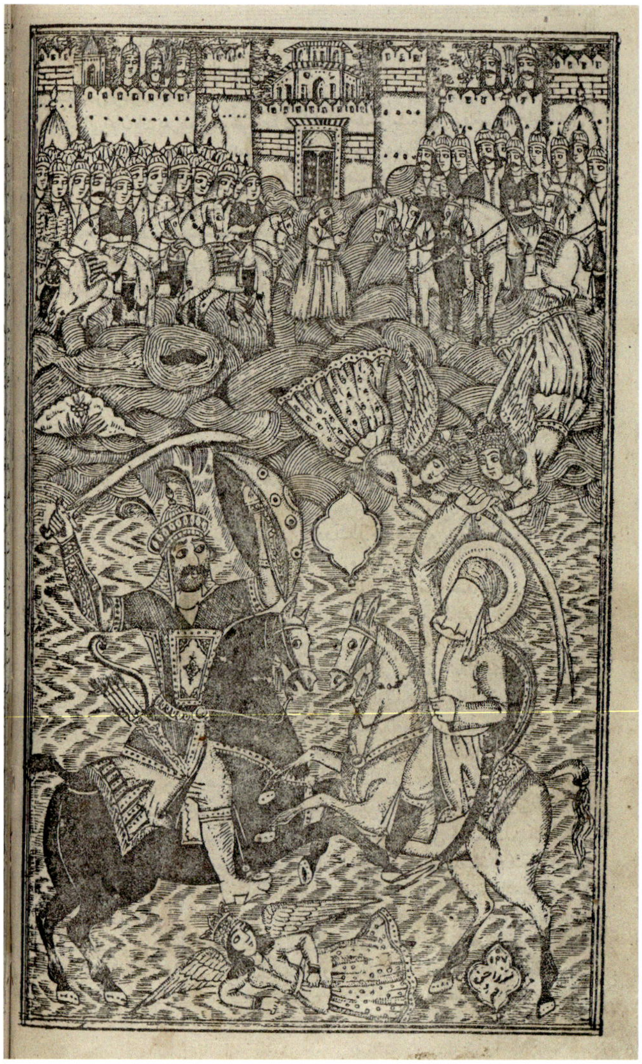

3 *Battle of Imam ʿAli and Marhab*, page from a lithographed copy of *Ṭūfān al-bukāʾ* (Deluge of Tears) by Muhammad Ibrahim b. Muhammad Baqir Jawhari, Iran, Tehran, 1275 H (1858). Illustration by Mirza Hasan. Folio: 20.5 × 33 cm (8 1/16 × 13 in.). Harry Elkins Widener Memorial Library, Harvard University, OL 39328.20 F.

Just as narrators drew on Jawhari's text to enliven their verbal recitations, artists devised new formulas to visualize the expanding repertoire of religious themes that the book offered. One of the most elaborate scenes, included in an 1858 edition of the *Ṭūfān al-bukāʾ*, depicts the confrontation between Marhab and ʿAli b. Abi Talib, the son-in-law and cousin of the Prophet Muhammad and the first Shiʿi imam, during the battle (*ghazva*) of Khaybar, which occurred in the time of the Prophet (Fig. 3). Holding his famed double-edged sword, Imam ʿAli is depicted as a haloed figure, his face covered with a veil. Hovering above the imam are angels Michael (*Mīkāʾīl*) and Raphael (*Isrāfīl*), with Gabriel (*Jibraʾīl*) lying on the ground. According to Jawhari, these angels were sent by God to aid the imam in battle.[15]

As the examples of the *ʿAjāʾib* and *Ṭūfān al-bukāʾ* show, the printed book and its images were implicated in a broader web of social and religious practices. Yet one also needs to consider the perceptions and uses of the lithographed book as a mass-produced item available for sale. Indeed, unlike manuscript production, which mostly relied on personal commissions, publishing a lithographed book was primarily a market-driven undertaking. As mentioned

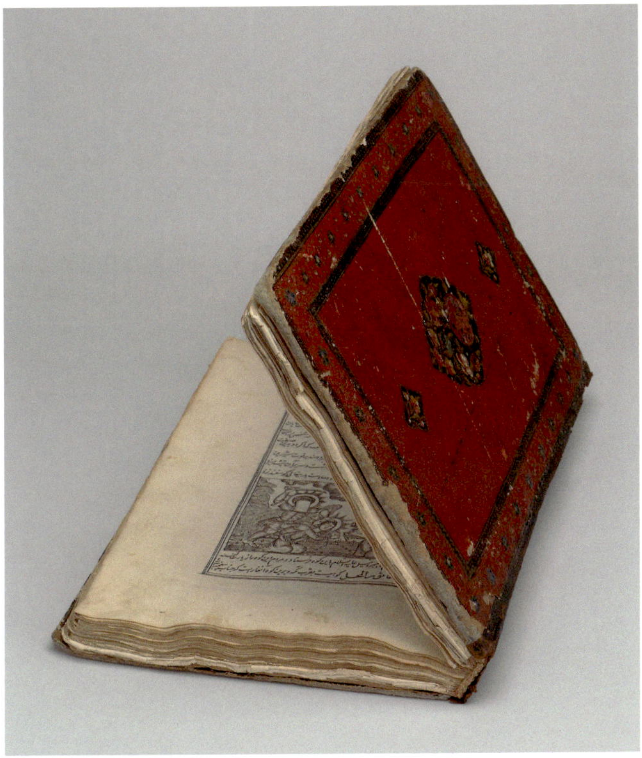

4 *Cover with Medallions*, for a lithographed copy of *ʿAjāʾib al-makhlūqāt va gharāʾib al-mawjūdāt* (Wonders of Creation) by al-Qazwini, Iran, Tehran, 1264 H (1848). Watercolor and lacquer on pasteboard; overall: 31.5 × 21 × 4.4 cm (12⅜ × 8¼ × 1¾ in.); folio: 30.8 × 18.8 cm (12⅛ × 7⅜ in.). Harry Elkins Widener Memorial Library, Harvard University, OL 37702.2 F (6W).

above, the success of the illustrated lithographed book to a large extent stemmed from its capacity to expand upon the already established clientele of artistically elaborated manuscripts. As with handwritten codices, features such as binding would have allowed customers to personalize their printed books relative to their taste, social standing, and pocketbook. While the copy of the *ʿAjāʾib* in the present exhibition has a leather binding, another copy of the same edition, owned by the Widener Library at Harvard University, features a relatively fine lacquer binding. In this case, the lithographed book was wrapped in an attire known in the traditional book market (Fig. 4).[16]

Not surprisingly, the first generation of Persian lithographed books was produced, marketed, and perceived in terms akin to handmade manuscripts. One need only consider the sensory experience of a person holding a lithographed copy of Qazwini's *ʿAjāʾib* with a leather or lacquer binding and leafing through its illustrated pages: the book clearly projected a sense of the artisanal quality of the traditional book and its visual, tactile, and olfactory traits. Nevertheless, the printed sheets bound between the covers could bear only a semblance to the painted manuscript; gone was not just the polychromatic display of organic and mineral pigments, but also the very quality that made an illustrated book a truly unique object. Indeed, this in-between type of book did not live long. As a reproducible medium, lithography soon began to alter traditional conceptions of the illustrated book along with its patterns of production and consumption.

Printing the Book of Kings

The transformations that the advent of lithography brought about in the imagery, readership, and social significance of the illustrated book is particularly evident in the earliest lithographic editions of Firdawsi's *Shāhnāma* (Book of Kings).[17] The first known edition of the *Shāhnāma* printed by means of lithography was published in Bombay in 1262 H (1846), and was patronized by Muhammad Mahdi Arbab (d. 1896), an expatriate Iranian merchant from Isfahan.[18] This lithographic publication was in turn inspired by the first typographical edition of the *Shāhnāma*, which had been published in Calcutta in 1829 by British Major Turner Macan. Judging from his introduction, the primary attraction of Macan's edition for Muhammad Mahdi was its attempt to prepare an authentic version of Firdawsi's work, pruned of later accretions and interpolations. And yet the factor that had propelled Muhammad Mahdi to sponsor a lithographic version of Macan's *Shāhnāma* was the latter's aesthetic appearance: as with earlier books printed in the Arabic script, the text of Macan's *Shāhnāma* was penned in *naskh*, the script that was most useful for movable type printing, yet regarded as less refined than *nastaʿlīq*—particularly by audiences in the Persianate cultural sphere.[19] The 1846 lithographic edition was not only written in *nastaʿlīq*, but also featured illuminated title pages and 57 illustrations by an unknown artist.

The text and illustrative program of the "Bombay *Shāhnāma*" served as the model for all subsequent lithographed editions that were published in Iran.[20] The earliest of these appeared in Tehran in 1265–67 H (1848–50), and was likewise patronized by a merchant called Haji Muhammad Husayn of Tehran (cat. 45). Known as the *Shāhnāma-yi Kajūrī* (after its calligrapher, Mustafa Quli b. Muhammad Hadi Sultan Kajuri), the Tehran *Shāhnāma* also featured 57 illustrations, several of which bear the signature of ʿAli Quli Khawʾi.

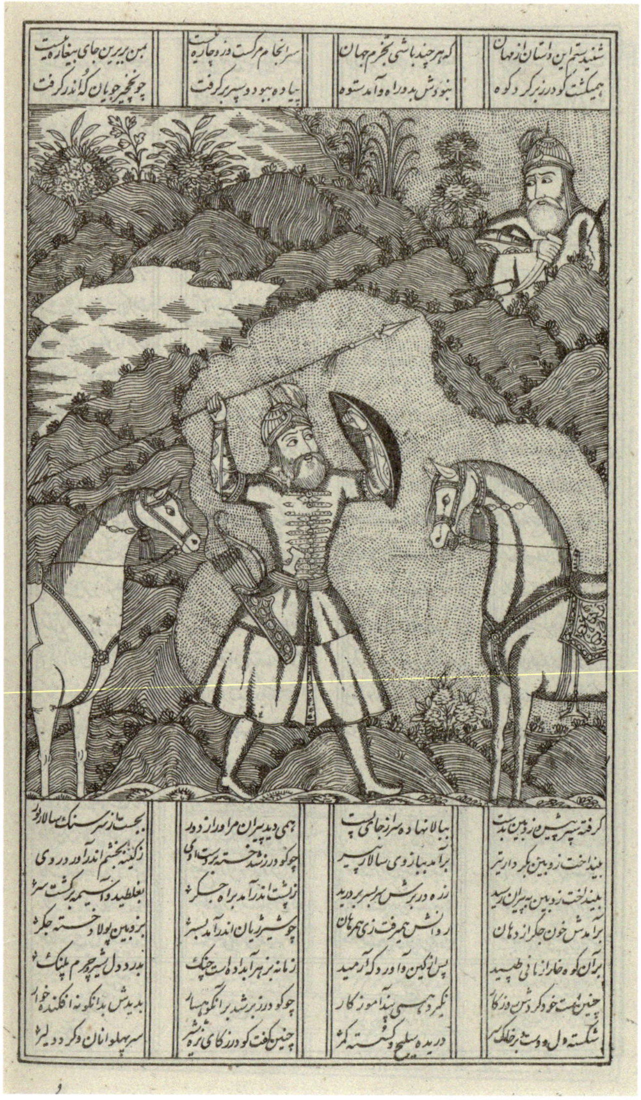

5 *Battle of Gudarz and Piran*, from the *Shāhnāma* (Book of Kings) by Firdawsi, dated 1265–67 H (1848–50). For full information, see cat. 45, p. 146.

With multiple pictures depicting enthroned rulers and heroic battles, the illustrative program of the *Shāhnāma-yi Kajūrī* (and the earlier Indian version, for that matter) appears to follow the dominant models and themes of 19th-century Qajar art. Several illustrations, however, evince a quality peculiar to the lithographic medium. Consider, for instance, the use of hatching and stippling in the *Battle of Gudarz and Piran* (Fig. 5). One of the frequently illustrated scenes in the manuscripts of the *Shāhnāma*, it depicts the last episode at the end of one of the recurrent battles between Iran and Turan. Standing at the center of the composition is the Iranian commander Gudarz, whose lance stretches diagonally toward the Turanian vizier Piran, who is tucked behind rocks. While undulating lines give a sense of volume to the rocks, stippling further demarcates the spaces where the main characters of the scene appear. These differing textures accentuate the sense of confrontation between the two characters and echo the sense of anguish expressed on their faces. Comparing ʿAli Quli's drawing with a late 15th-century painted rendition of the same episode (Fig. 6) demonstrates how patterns created through hatching and stippling have taken the role of colors in articulating the picture plane. In this work, ʿAli Quli has invested an established iconography with a new visual dynamism derived from the medium of line drawing, and of lithographic printing in particular.

As Ulrich Marzolph has pointed out, the scribes of lithographed books in Qajar Iran were likely familiar with the "transfer system" recommended by Senefelder, for otherwise texts would have appeared in reverse on the printed

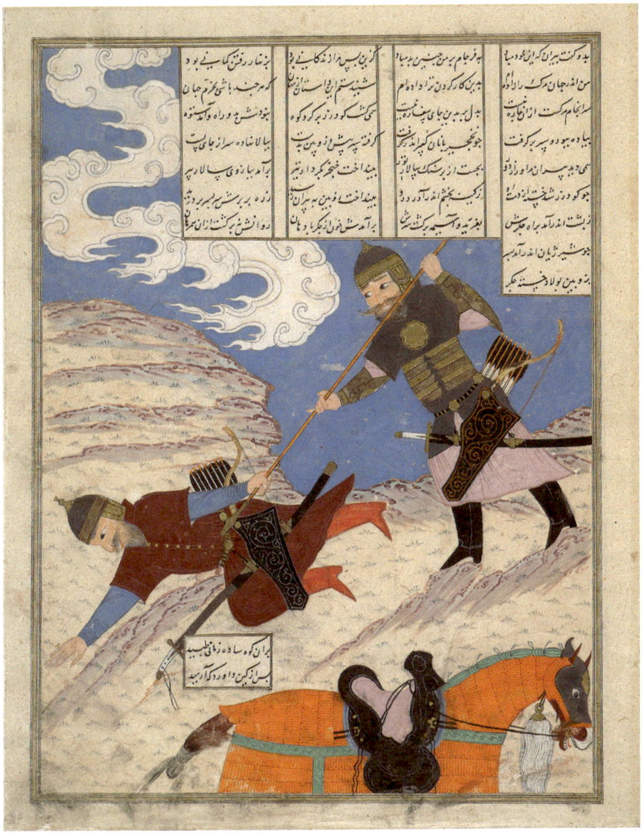

6 *Battle of Gudarz and Piran*, folio from a manuscript of the *Shāhnāma* (Book of Kings) by Firdawsi, Iran, c. 1490. Ink, watercolor, and gold on paper; folio: 34 × 24.9 cm (13 3/8 × 9 13/16 in.). Harvard Art Museums / Arthur M. Sackler Museum, The Edwin Binney, 3rd Collection of Turkish Art at the Harvard Art Museums, 1985.264.

page.[21] According to this method, the text or drawing is first made with "chemical transfer ink" on paper. Once the paper is dry, one wets the reverse side of the paper with nitric acid (aquafortis), places it face-down on the stone slab, and "make[s] the transfer print with a moderately swift motion of the press." The stone is then treated with a chemical compound and water, allowing for the creation of a master copy yielding multiple impressions.[22] While a variation of this method was probably used in the printing houses of Qajar Iran, particularly for printing texts, evidence suggests that for transferring a drawing to the lithographic slab, other established artistic methods were also employed. A working sketch paper by ʿAli Quli, for instance, shows that the artist had used the technique of pouncing: that is, pinholes were pricked through the original sheet of paper carrying the drawing so that it could be transferred to another surface.[23] As such, the charcoal powder, sprinkled on the back side of the transfer paper, provided a reverse trace of the intended design, which had to be inked again directly on the stone plate. Moreover, several drawings by ʿAli Quli in the Tehran *Shāhnāma* (including the *Battle of Gudarz and Piran*) are the reverse of the illustrations in the Bombay *Shāhnāma*, tipping us off to the possibility that the artist drew on the stone itself while beholding the Bombay *Shāhnāma* for inspiration.[24]

The *Shāhnāma-yi Kajūrī* also shows novel characteristics in terms of imagery and subject matter. A peculiar case is the scene of *Zoroaster Offering the Eternal Fire to Gushtasb* (Fig. 7). Unprecedented in the illustrated manuscripts of the *Shāhnāma*, the scene belongs to a section of the book that deals with the emergence of Zoroastrianism during the reign of legendary Kayanid king Gushtasb.[25] Standing on the left side of the picture is Zoroaster, rendered with a radiating halo, offering the eternal fire from paradise (an emblem of Zoroastrian faith) to Gushtasb. The addition of this scene was surely propelled by the presence of Parsi and Irani Zoroastrians in India, communities whose ancestors had emigrated from Iran, fleeing recurrent waves of persecution (between the 10th and 19th centuries). Equally remarkable is the pictorial model used for the portrayal of Zoroaster: it was based on a Sasanian rock relief at Taq-i Bustan (an ancient site located in Kermanshah, western Iran), which shows the investiture of the Sasanian ruler Ardashir (r. 224–241). Given that the Bombay *Shāhnāma* was published in 1846, it is unlikely that a photograph of the rock relief was available in India at the time, so the drawing was probably based on a European print. One possible source is the travel book of English artist Sir Robert Ker Porter (published 1821–22), which featured several detailed drawings

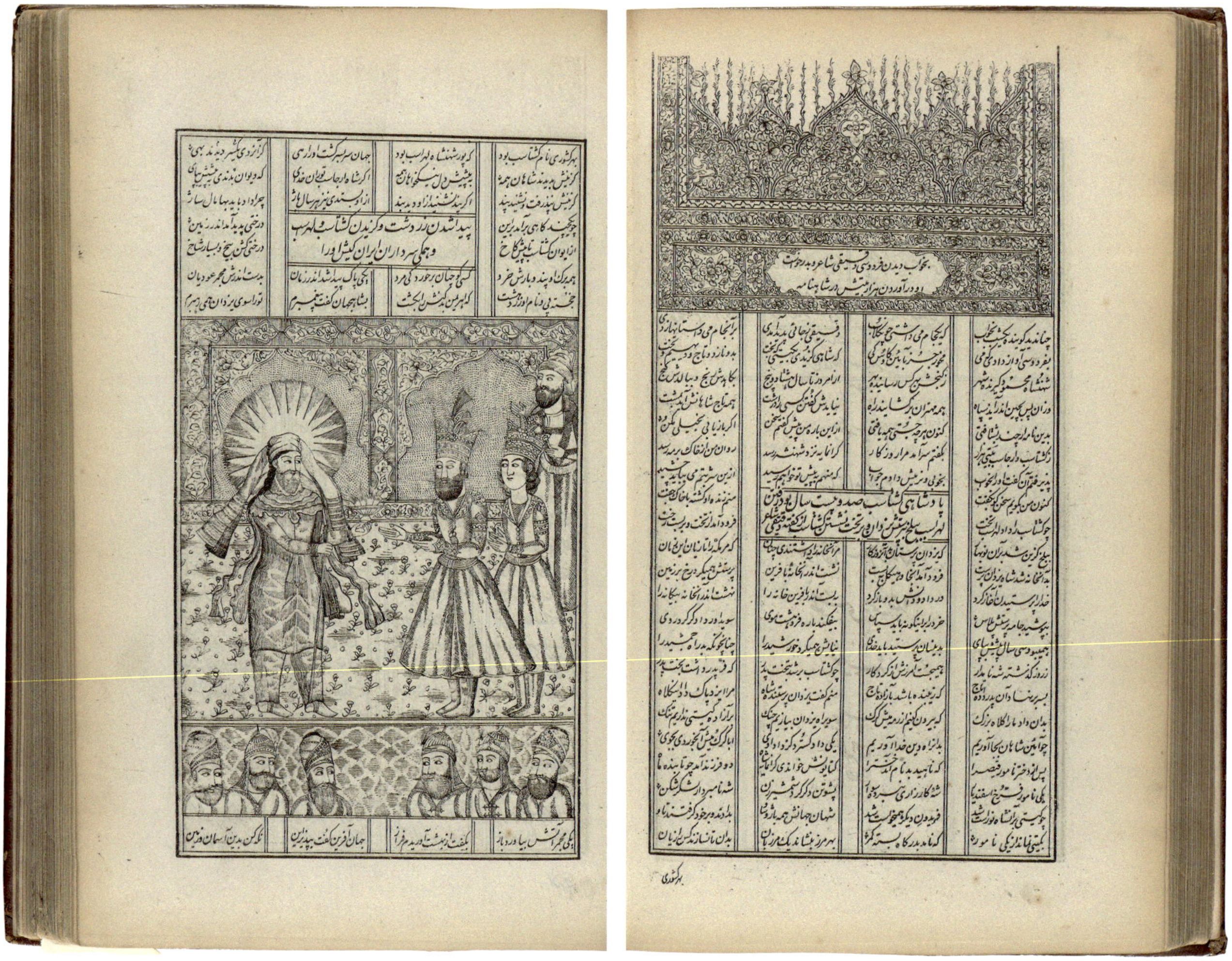

7 *Title Page* (right); *Zoroaster Offering the Eternal Fire to Gushtasb* (left), dated 1265–67 H (1848–50). For full information, see cat. 45, p. 146.

of ancient Iranian rock reliefs, including the one at Taq-i Bustan (Fig. 8). In his accompanying description, Porter suggested that the figure represents Mithra (an ancient Iranian deity), but added that it "may be meant for the glorified Zoroaster himself."[26] The depiction of Zoroaster in the *Shāhnāma-yi Kajūrī* thus represents one of the earliest effects of the mobilization of images set forth by the global dissemination of prints: a drawing of a Sasanian rock relief, published in England, is adopted as the image of Zoroaster in India, where it finds its way into a copy of the *Shāhnāma*. This image, in turn, serves as a model in Tehran, where it is incorporated into the first illustrated *Shāhnāma* printed in Iran.[27]

By replicating the quintessential traits of a deluxe, handwritten, painted codex—with illustrated pages, illuminated headpieces, and calligraphic penmanship—the lithographed editions of the *Shāhnāma* surely demonstrate a measure of continuity with the manuscript tradition. That a printed book was known after its calligrapher, Kajuri, reflects the enduring significance of the art of writing as the most esteemed aesthetic form, and suggests how it was possible to retain a semblance of calligraphic excellence in lithographic reproduction. Nevertheless, there can be no doubt that the emergence of printing led to a fundamental shift in patterns of patronage and perceptions of the *Shāhnāma*. The sponsorship of merchants indicates that the production of a majestic copy of "The Book of Kings" was no longer a princely prerogative; until this point, the masses' encounter with the stories from the *Shāhnāma* was through the oral performances of storytellers, but with the advent of print, a broader public could now possess an illustrated copy of Firdawsi's work and become private, silent readers. This transformation did not occur only in the number of readers but also in their understanding of the text. Following Macan's edition, all printed editions of the *Shāhnāma* were accompanied by a glossary, facilitating its comprehension for a reading public assumed to be less conversant in literature. The *Shāhnāma* was now a reproducible book, engaging a new class of audiences. It retained the appearance of a manuscript but lost much of its former mythical aura as both text and object.

Beyond Printed Codex: Lithographic Image as a Public Medium

The *Shāhnāma-yi Kajūrī* was probably published by one of the several lithographic printing houses that were set up in Tehran in the 1840s.[28] It was indeed only from this period onward that the Qajar capital became the locus of new technologies; during the first half of the 19th century, the primary hub of modernizing impulses and technical innovations was Tabriz, where the first printing presses (both in movable type and lithography) had been established.

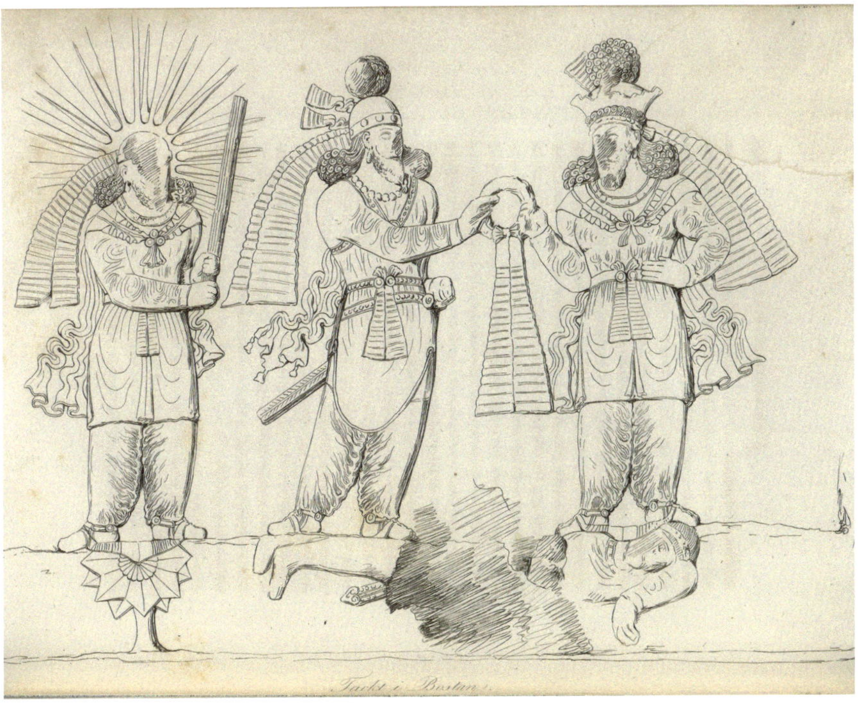

8 *Drawing of the Rock Relief at Taq-i Bustan, Iran, Showing the Investiture of the Sasanian Ruler Ardashir*, after Sir Robert Ker Porter, *Travels in Georgia, Persia, Armenia, Ancient Babylonia, &c. &c. during the Years 1817, 1818, 1819, and 1820*, vol. 2 (London: Longman, Hurst, Rees, Orme, and Brown, 1821–22), 191. Houghton Library, Harvard University, Arc 400.3*.

Printing activity in Tehran accelerated after 1848, when Nasir al-Din Shah (r. 1848–1896) ascended the Qajar throne and moved from Tabriz (residence of Qajar crown princes) to the capital. Through the initiative of the young shah's ill-fated prime minister Mirza Taqi Khan Amir Kabir (in office 1848–51), the early years of Nasir al-Din Shah's reign also saw the establishment of two new state institutions: the Dar al-Funun (Abode of the Sciences), founded in 1851 and dedicated to the teaching of military and technical subjects, and the Majma' al-Sanayi' (Assembly of Arts), which was inaugurated around the same time and consisted of a set of workshops dedicated to the manufacture of new artifacts, some of them modeled after traditional examples.[29] In addition to a photography studio, the Dar al-Funun was equipped with a lithographic press for printing textbooks. Over the course of the second half of the 19th century, the expansion of printing gradually led to the formation of a new reading public in the Qajar capital.

The emergence of a public domain in Tehran was further bolstered by the physical transformation and expansion of the city.[30] Beginning in the 1850s, the moats surrounding the citadel (*arg*) were replaced with broad avenues, and subsequently, a new plan was drawn up for the expansion of the capital, whereby the city developed beyond its former confines and was surrounded by new walls and gates. Although erected on the palace grounds, the buildings that housed institutions like the Dar al-Funun and Majma' al-Sanayi'—sites of new technologies and artistic endeavors—were no longer hidden behind the citadel's walls, but rather were accessible through the capital's new avenues. Provided with lamps, paved with stones, and lined with coffeehouses, Tehran's transformed urban spaces not only defined a new interface between the palace and the city, but also shaped and accommodated a novel terrain of social life where printed items came to be consumed. In the meantime, the architecture of Tehran's new public buildings, gates, royal palaces, and elite mansions shifted toward a more flamboyant style that mixed elements adapted from European sources with established local forms (Fig. 9). Some architects drew inspiration from photographic or lithographic representations of European buildings. The decorations of elite mansions were inspired, in part, by lithographic images of European or local origin.[31] The result was a hybrid visual identity that embodied and represented the cosmopolitan cultural outlook of the court and elites in the late Qajar era.

The readership of the earliest lithographed books largely overlapped with and expanded upon that of illustrated manuscripts; it was only with the advent of official newspapers that the medium reached a broader public. The earliest newspaper of the country, the *Kāghaẕ-i akhbār* (literally, "news paper"), was first published by way of lithography in 1837 during the reign of Muhammad Shah (r. 1834–1848). But neither this journal nor its successor, the *Vaqāyi'-i ittifāqīya* (literally, "happenings"), featured pictures. Lithographic illustration

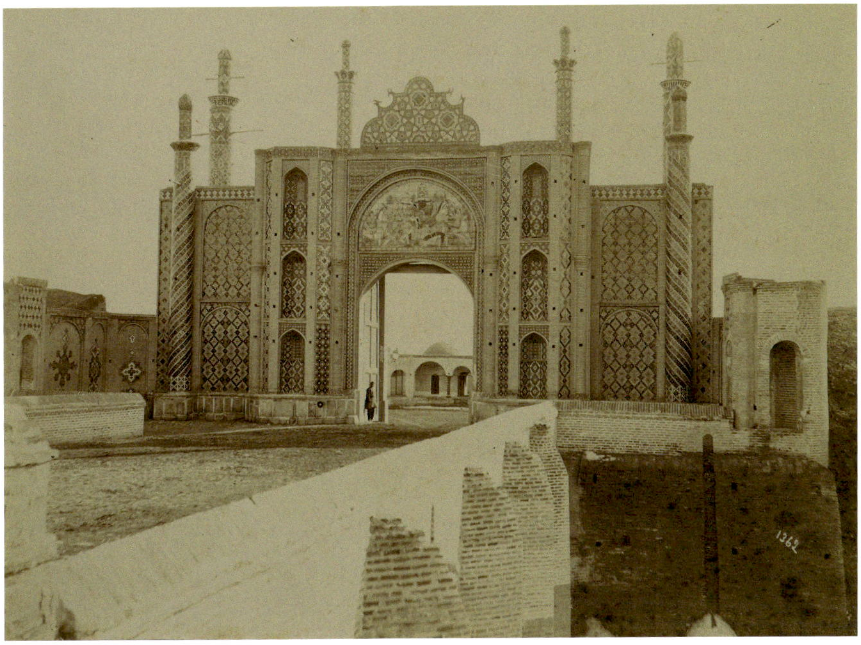

9 *Dawlat Gate*, attributed to Antoin Sevruguin, late 19th century. Albumen silver print; photograph: 22.4 × 15.1 cm (8 13/16 × 5 15/16 in.). Collection of Azita Bina and Elmar W. Seibel.

began to play a more prominent role in the *Rūznāma-yi dawlat-i ʿalīya-yi Īrān* (The Journal of the Sublime State of Iran), the official gazette of the Qajar state in the 1860s.

The greater role of images was primarily due to the leadership of Abu al-Hasan Ghaffari Kashani (d. 1866), the chief painter (*naqqāsh-bāshī*) of the Qajar court, who was appointed as editor of the *Rūznāma* in 1861 by Nasir al-Din Shah.[32] In his appointment edict, the shah referred to Abu al-Hasan's mastery in making lithographic images (*bāsma-yi taṣvīr*), "one of the greatest arts" (*funūn-i muʿaẓẓama*) and "difficult deeds" (*umūr-i muʿżala*). Wishing that this "novel and noble art" (*fann-i badīʿ-i sharīf*) would become common in Iran, he decreed that Abu al-Hasan be put in charge of the capital's newspaper and that, "in each issue, based on circumstances, a couple of illustrations (*majlis-i taṣvīr*) be printed."[33] It was along the same lines, in pursuit of making more public use of images, that the shah gave orders for the founding of a royal art school (*nāqqāsh-khāna-yi dawlatī*) one year later. Also headed by Abu al-Hasan, who had been given the title Artisan of the Kingdom (*Ṣānīʿ al-Mulk*) in 1861, the school also comprised a lithographic workshop (*kār-khāna-yi bāsma-yi taṣvīr*) equipped with four printing presses. While the primary function of the workshop was publishing government newspapers and announcements, it also produced copies "after the works of famous [European] masters" for sale and accepted individual commissions for reproducing portraits.[34]

It was on the pages of the *Rūznāma*—and in the single-sheet copies printed in the Royal Art School—that the modes of realistic image-making practiced by the chief court painter in oils and watercolors became publicly accessible in the form of mechanically reproduced lithographic images. In addition to portraits of the shah and courtiers, Abu al-Hasan's drawings for the journal included representations of the inner spaces of the palace complex on ceremonial occasions, visualizing the hitherto inaccessible faces and spaces of monarchy for the masses. The phrase *majlis-i taṣvīr* (literally, "depiction of assembly"), which had long referred to illustrations of age-old narratives of Persian literature or idealized courtly scenes, was now used to designate periodically published pictures of the day-to-day deeds of a living monarch. A lithographic depiction of, say, the latest hunting activity of Nasir al-Din Shah (Fig. 10) operated in dual temporal domains: it represented the shah at once as a ruler partaking of an ancient ethos of kingship, and as a monarch in the age of the mechanical reproduction of images, seeking to establish a new relationship with his subjects.

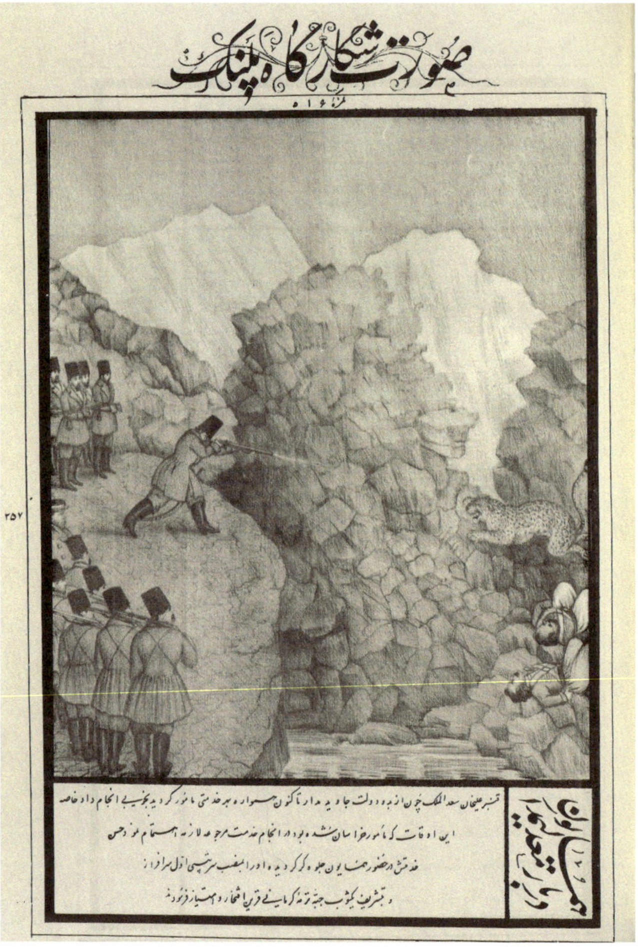

10 *Nasir al-Din Shah Shooting a Leopard*, Abu al-Hasan Ghaffari Saniʿ al-Mulk, lithographic drawing from the *Rūznāma-yi dawlat-i ʿalīya-yi Īrān* (The Journal of the Sublime State of Iran) 516 (5 Ramadan 1278 H [March 6, 1862]). Harry Elkins Widener Memorial Library, Harvard University, DS307 .R89 F 1:472–550 (1277–1280).

Such blending of artistic themes and methods originating in different periods is evident in the full gamut of Abu al-Hasan Ghaffari's artistic production in the 1860s. In this period, he continued to be active in the medium of the lacquered pen box, as one example in the Harvard Art Museums suggests (cat. 63). If in the drawings of the *Rūznāma* he combined old and new models to depict a contemporary moment, in lacquer he injected new pictorial conventions derived from European sources into established prototypes and subject matters. Indeed, despite their entirely different origins, both lithography and lacquer can be considered as more "public" mediums; lacquer objects, particularly in the 19th century, were also mass-produced and functioned as portable objects, appealing to new audiences and catering to the increasingly diversified market of the later Qajar era.

From the 1860s onward, with the dissemination of images through newspapers, the impact of mechanically reproduced pictures became more pronounced in other mediums. A vignette on the top of a pen box, produced in Isfahan in 1296 H (1878–79) and signed by the artist Muhammad Kazim reveals the effects of this profusion of images (Fig. 11).[35] The outer surfaces of the pen box are decorated with multiple scenes depicting legendary and historical Persian kings, except for the central scene on the top, which portrays Nasir al-Din Shah seated on the throne and attended by princes, courtiers, and pages. Six figures are identified by labels: immediately to Nasir al-Din Shah's right is Masʿud Mirza, "The Shadow of the Sultan" (*Ẓill al-Sulṭān*), the king's eldest son and, since 1873, the governor of Isfahan and Iran's southern provinces. To the left of Zill al-Sultan is his younger brother prince Kamran Mirza, labeled "the heir apparent" (*Nā'ib al-Salṭana*), who succeeded his father as Muzaffar al-Din Shah (r. 1896–1907). Other courtiers are depicted to the left of the shah, including the prime minister (*ṣadr*) and the comptroller general (*mustawfī*).

The overall illustrative program of the pen box was not novel; indeed, several examples of these so-called Kayani royal pen boxes, produced by members of the Najaf circle in Isfahan, exist in private and public collections.[36] (The Najaf circle is discussed in the essay by Mary McWilliams in this volume.) What sets the scene on the 1878–79 pen box apart from its precedents is a new sense of realism in the individualized rendition of princes and courtiers. Indeed, even without the labels, a contemporary person likely could have recognized figures such as Zill al-Sultan. This realistic aspect becomes clearer if one compares the scene to an earlier example of the same type of pen box (Fig. 12), produced about six years earlier in 1289 H (1872–73) and signed by Muhammad Isma'il (d. c. 1882–92), another artist of the Najaf circle.[37] While Muhammad Isma'il's work is also characterized by a sense of individualized portraiture, it lacks a photographic quality in the rendering of faces and garments. In Muhammad Kazim's work, by contrast, one can sense the quality of studio portraiture even in the tiny faces. It was the dissemination of photographically produced portraits of the nobility through lithographic publications that allowed artists to infuse established pictorial models with a more pronounced degree of realistic portraiture.

11 *Pen Box with Portraits of Nasir al-Din Shah and Legendary Rulers from the* Shāhnāma (detail), 1296 H (1879–80). For full information, see cat. 72, p. 156.

12 *Pen Box with Portraits of Nasir al-Din Shah Qajar and Legendary Rulers from the* Shāhnāma (detail), Muhammad Isma'il, Iran, Isfahan, 1289 (1872–73). 3.9 × 3.9 × 22.8 cm (1 9/16 × 1 9/16 × 9 in.). Nasser D. Khalili Collection of Islamic Art, London, LAQ 217. (Image after Nasser D. Khalili, B. W. Robinson, and Tim Stanley, *Lacquer of the Islamic Lands*, pt. 2, The Nasser D. Khalilli Collection of Islamic Art, vol. 22 [London; New York: Nour Foundation in association with Azimuth Editions and Oxford University Press, 1996–97], cat. 250, p. 63.)

Representing Kings: From Books to Tiles

The broadening reach of lithography and photography did not just transform established artistic practices; it was also in these mediums that the nascent impulse to revive older discourses—as manifest in the literary movement known as *bāzgasht-i adabī* (literary return)—and to engage with ancient models—as seen in the impact of pre-Islamic rock reliefs in the arts of the Fath 'Ali Shah period—took on new meanings and expressions. A pioneering work with extensive implications for the visual arts was the *Nāma-yi khusravān* (Book of Kings), an illustrated history of Iran from its legendary beginning to the Qajar period.[38] First published in 1868, the book was penned by Jalal al-Din

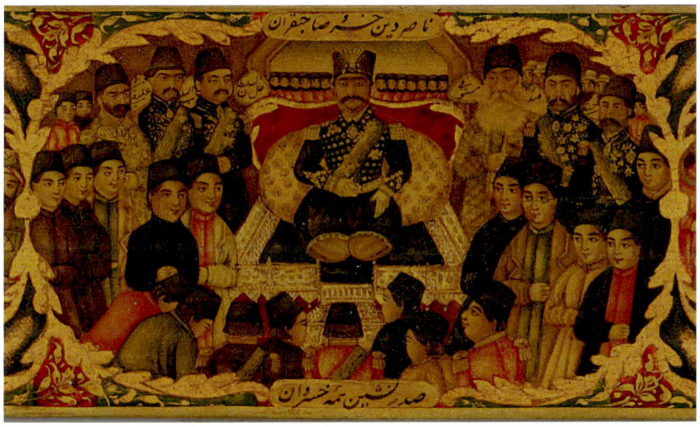

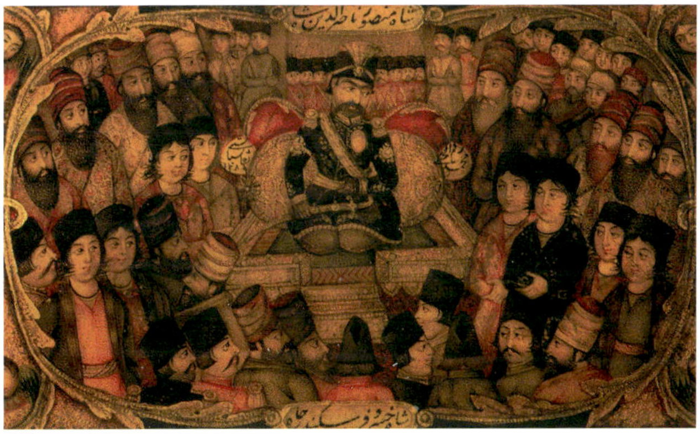

Mirza (d. 1872), a Qajar prince with reformist and antiquarian leanings who was educated at the Dar al-Funun.[39] Written in "pure Persian" (i.e., without any words of Arabic origin) and intended as a textbook for children, the *Nāma-yi khusravān* represented a novel conception of history, as Abbas Amanat has noted. In a radical break from age-old modes of historiography, history did not start with the rise of Islam in seventh-century Arabia, but in a primordial time in ancient Iran.[40] The nationalist conception was surely influenced by European ideas; Jalal al-Din Mirza had been taught French at the Dar al-Funun and was likely familiar with European writings. But this was not his sole source of inspiration: interestingly, his history of Iran does not begin with the Achaemenids, as Europeans would have it, but instead with mythical rulers styled the "Abadian," as narrated by the Zoroastrian priest Azar Kayvan (d. c. 1609–18), who was a native of the Fars region in Iran and was patronized by the Mughal emperor Akbar (r. 1556–1605).[41] This reference is indicative of the multiplicity of sites and sources that contributed to the genesis of a revivalist/modernist movement in the late Qajar era.

A similar interplay among themes and models of diverse origins can be seen in the book's pictures, which were drawn by artist Mirza ʿAbd al-Muttallib (d. 1903).[42] Covering the pre-Islamic history of Iran from its mythical beginnings through the fall of the Sasanian dynasty in the seventh century, the first volume of the book features more than 50 full-page portraits of kings modeled after a wide range of ancient sources. Claimed to be derived from "portraits of the kings possessed by Europeans," the depictions of Sasanian kings were in fact all based on coins, drawings of which were also included in the publication. The inspiration for the portrait of the legendary ruler Jamshid (Fig. 13), however, was a relief at Persepolis, the royal seat of the Achaemenid dynasty, which was known in popular parlance as The Throne of Jamshid (*Takht-i Jamshīd*). When these drawings were being prepared in the mid-1860s, multiple photographs of the ruins of Persepolis were available (Fig. 14).

In the decades that followed the publication of *Nāma-yi khusravān*, its illustrations served as standard portrayals of ancient kings in various mediums. In a late 19th-century manuscript of the *Gulistān* (Rose Garden) composed by 13th-century poet Saʿdi (Fig. 15), the artist used the image of Jamshid published in the *Nāma-yi khusravān* as his model to illustrate an anecdote that alludes to Jamshid. The pictures were also widely used by tilemakers in Tehran and in the provinces. A tile panel at the Gulistan Palace, dated 1899, included the full cycle of kings depicted in the *Nāma-yi khusravān*.[43]

The enduring influence of the illustrations of the *Nāma-yi khusravān* is also evident in the *Shāhnāma-yi bahādurī* (cat. 47), the last lithographic edition of the *Shāhnāma* published in the Qajar era. In the scene depicting Jamshid, the artist has incorporated ʿAbd al-Muttallib's drawing in an expanded setting, which features more reliefs and evokes an audience hall at Persepolis (Fig. 16). Published between 1901 and 1908 during the Constitutional Revolution,

Shāhnāma-yi bahādurī, as Ulrich Marzolph notes, is in fact unprecedented in terms of its size and format, which is closer to that of a newspaper.[44] Rather than being integrated with the text, illustrations cover the entire surface of a page, with the reverse sides left blank. Customers were likely able to order the illustrations separately; the copy in the present exhibition features fewer illustrations than those documented by Marzolph.

With their explicit references to identifiable ancient sites, these illustrations not only gave the stories of the *Shāhnāma* a more pronounced sense of authenticity, but also tied them to a specific territory and temporality. The interchangeable use of illustrations in a purportedly historical book (*Nāma-yi khusravān*) and a mythical narrative (*Shāhnāma*) blurred the boundary between myth and history. These lithographed publications shaped and embodied the process that gradually led to the co-opting of Firdawsi's poem as a national narrative for the fledgling subjectivities of the country, just as the multiethnic territories under Qajar rule were gradually morphing into a modern nation state. One can discern in the succession of these illustrated prints and their sponsorship by late Qajar elites the seeds of the full-fledged appropriation of the *Shāhnāma* into Iranian nationalism in the 20th century.

Lithographic Portraiture

In terms of style, the illustrations of the *Nāma-yi khusravān* depart from those of the earlier lithographed books, such as the ones illustrated by ʿAli Quli. This development was not an individual initiative, however. A newspaper essay published in 1300 H (1882) reveals contemporary perceptions of this

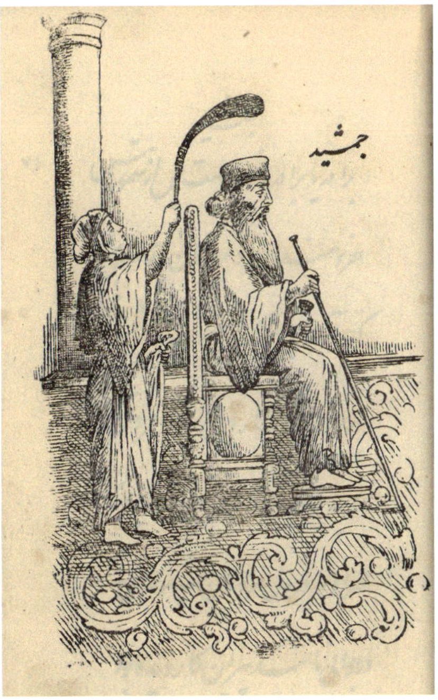

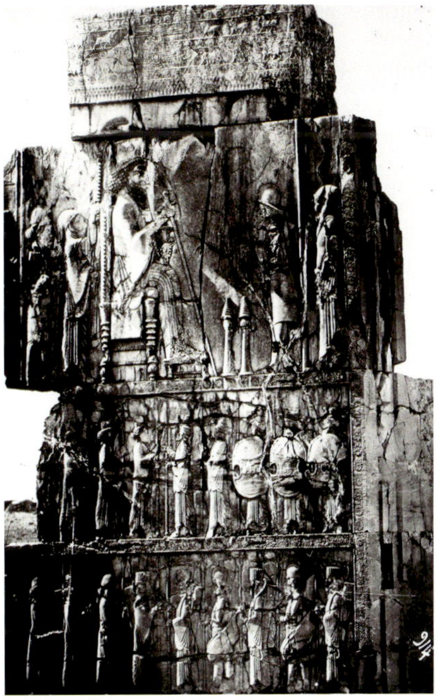

13 *Portrait of the Legendary Ruler Jamshid*, Mirza ʿAbd al-Muttallib. Lithographed illustration after Jalal al-Din Mirza, *Nāma-yi khusravān, dāstān-i pādshāhān-i Pārs*, vol. 1 (Tehran: 1868). Butler Library, Columbia University, 955 J215.

14 *Persepolis (Iran): Throne Hall, Northern Wall, West Jamb of Eastern Doorway: View of Relief Picturing Enthroned King Giving Audience, as well as Registers Picturing Persian and Median Guards* (detail), 1902–5. For full information, see cat. 38, p. 144.

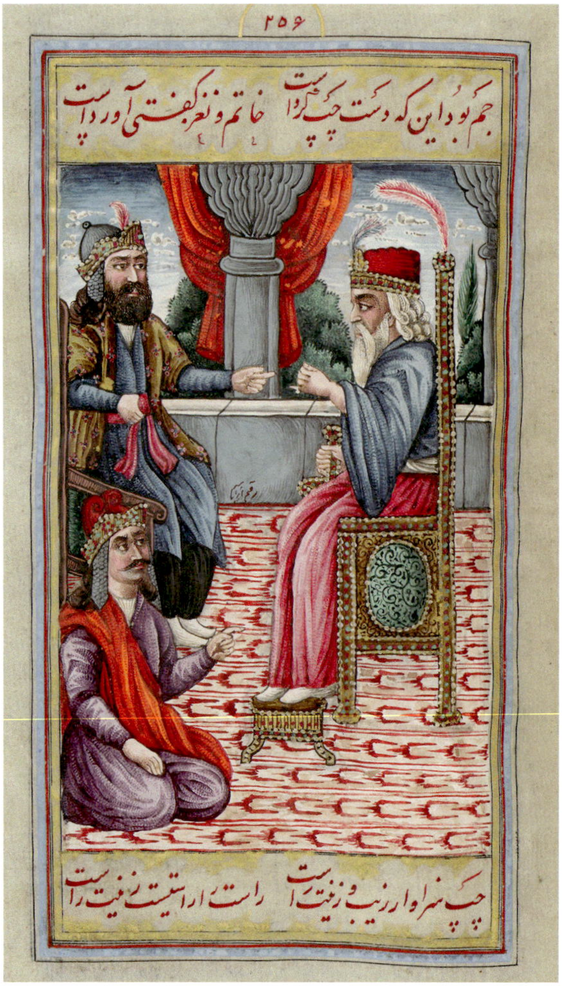

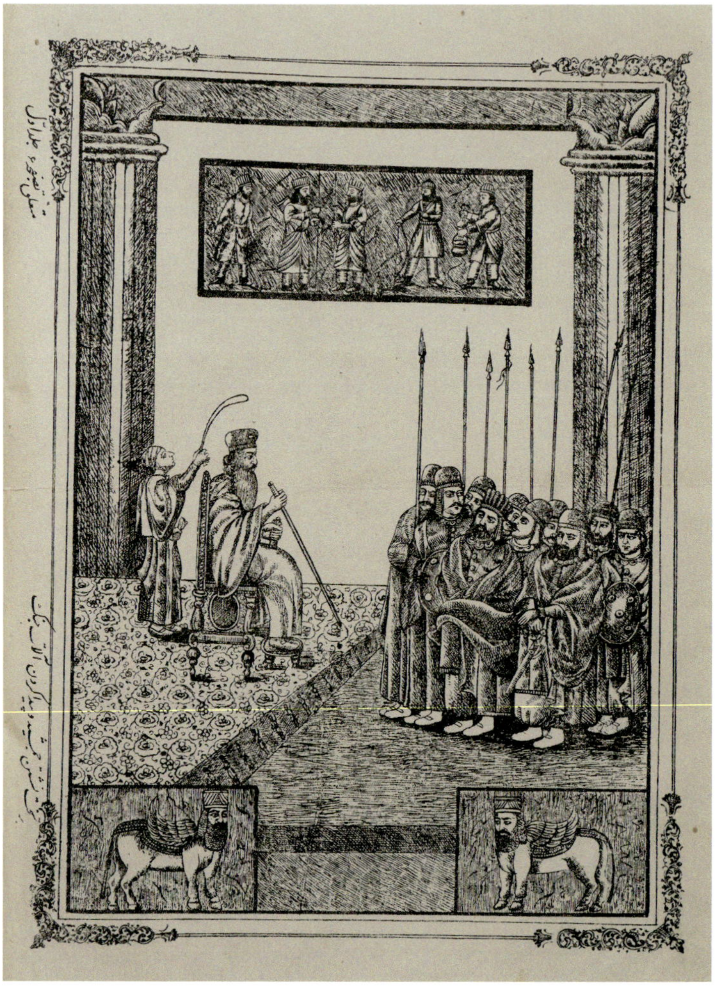

development as well as the continuing interest in lithography as a medium for the public dissemination of portraits:

> One of the fine arts is image printing (*inṭibāʿ-i ṣūrat*) by way of lithography, and it has been a while that in Europe this art has reached a degree of perfection like other arts. Yet in the protected domains [of Iran] although it is now around forty years that printing images has been common, and sometimes the artists of the country have done it well, still due to the lack of knowledge of the nuances and points of this noble art it was not the way it must have been. A few years ago the Chief Painter (*nāqqāsh-bāshī*) Aqa Mirza ʿAbd al-Muttallib of Isfahan travelled to Europe and became the rarity of the age in this craft.[45]

In late 19th-century journals, subtle references to photography characterizing the lithographic works of Abu al-Hasan Ghaffari gave place to more direct borrowing from photographs. This shift was facilitated by the use of a fat crayon in addition to delineating pencils, a technical development that

15 *Jamshid Explains the Wearing of Rings*, late 19th century. For full information, see cat. 8, p. 134.

16 *Jamshid Enthroned*, 1901–4. For full information, see cat. 47, p. 148.

allowed for rendering gradations of light and dark in lithographed pictures.[46] This is particularly evident in the images featured in *Sharaf* and *Sharāfat* (journals published c. 1883–1903), which were dedicated to publishing the lives and portraits of nobles and famous people.[47] It has been shown that a large number of drawings in both journals, whether depicting a figure or a building, were modeled after photographs.[48] But most drawings differed from the original photograph in terms of details and overall composition; often, the head of the represented figure was further tilted and the garments were given a more orderly appearance.[49] Indeed, the transfer of the photographic image to the lithographic slab was far from a straightforward process. According to one contemporary report, Mirza Abu Turab Khan Ghaffari (d. 1890), a pupil of Mirza ʿAbd al-Muttallib and the artist responsible for most of the drawings published in the *Sharaf*, employed a peculiar method: he would place a mirror in front of the photograph, drawing directly onto the lithographic slab while looking at the photograph's reflection in the mirror.[50] The creation of a lithographed drawing after a photograph thus entailed a fairly complex cognitive process.

The painted lithographic portrait of Muzaffar al-Din Shah (Fig. 17) has its origin in the artistic practices associated with the late Qajar journals. It is signed by Mirza Mahdi Khan, who was given the title Illustrator of the Kingdom (*Muṣavvir al-Mulk*) by Muzaffar al-Din Shah, and whose illustrations appeared frequently in *Sharāfat*.[51] Active in oil painting, lithography, and photography, Musavvir al-Mulk epitomizes the late Qajar artist and his wide range of expertise in old and new mediums. Painted in 1896, the year of the new shah's accession to the throne, the portrait of Muzaffar al-Din Shah is subtly tinted and framed with polychrome marginal illumination, offering a more vibrant depiction of the recently enthroned Qajar ruler than the black-and-white drawings regularly published in the journal. The overall effect of the work stems from a peculiar overlaying and mingling of various mediums and techniques of image-making: photography, lithography, painting, and illumination. Even in this final format, one can still sense in the eyes of the shah the peculiar look associated with longer photographic exposures.

Visualizing Piety in the Age of Prints

Informed by top-down processes, the examples discussed above were primarily concerned with the role of lithography in representing the Qajar monarchy and nobility, in incorporating the past into the spaces of the present, and in fabricating a novel sense of historical consciousness. And yet from the outset, these governmental, elite-centered initiatives were accompanied by more popular, bottom-up responses and appropriations. Indeed, the majority of lithographic printing houses set up in the mid-1800s, in Tehran and elsewhere, was private; their publishing activities were primarily driven by the demands of the market, rather than by commissions from the court or aristocracy. As

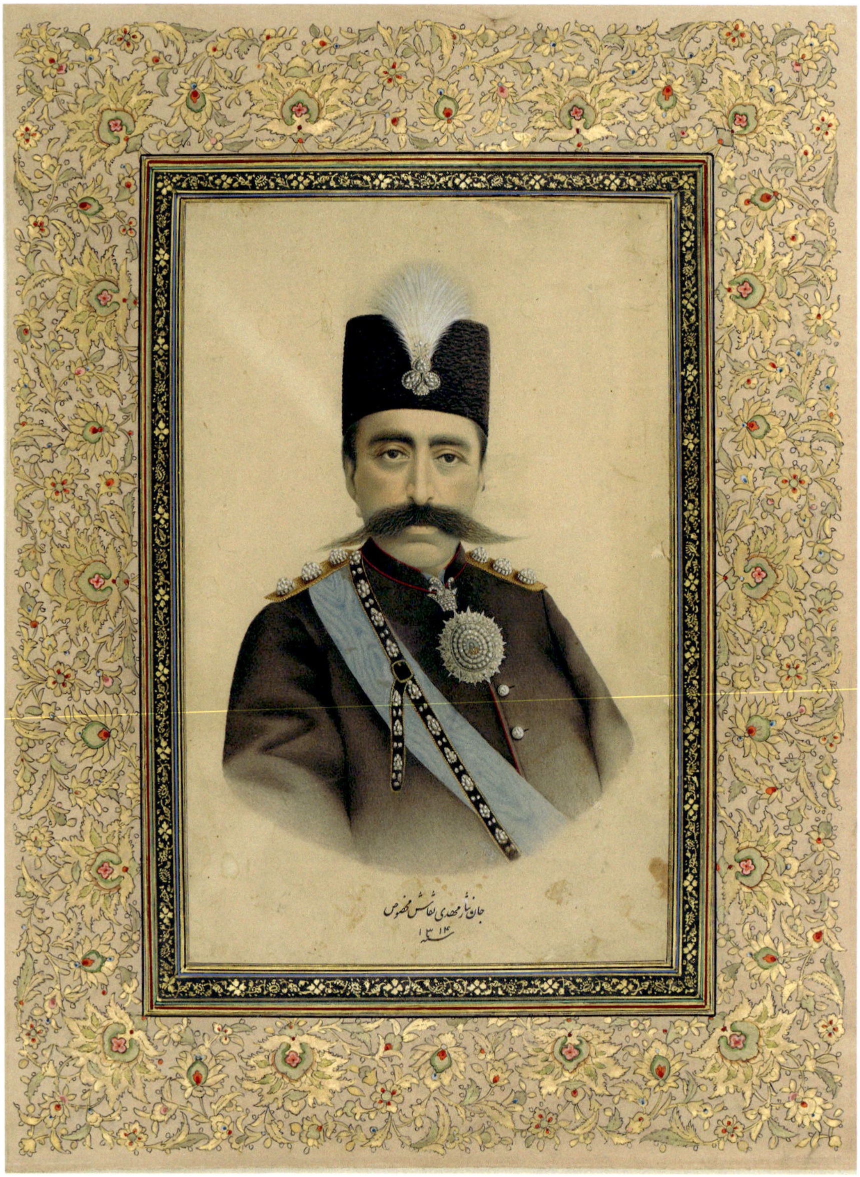

17 *Muzaffar al-Din Shah Qajar*, dated 1314 H (1896–97). For full information, see cat. 46, p. 146.

a truly public medium, lithography and other printing techniques were not exclusively elitist or state-controlled; rather, they functioned in an in-between terrain of social interactions and cultural production.

The effect of new printing technologies on ordinary culture is particularly evident in the realm of popular piety. The Qajar era witnessed a surge in the production of devotional images and religious icons (*shamā'il*) (see, for example, cat. 6). As artists began to infuse old themes with models derived from Western Christian sources (increasingly available through prints), it became more and more common to depict the Prophet Muhammad and imams in a natural manner, without the facial veil favored by more conservative classes (as in the illustrations of the *Ṭūfān al-bukā'*).

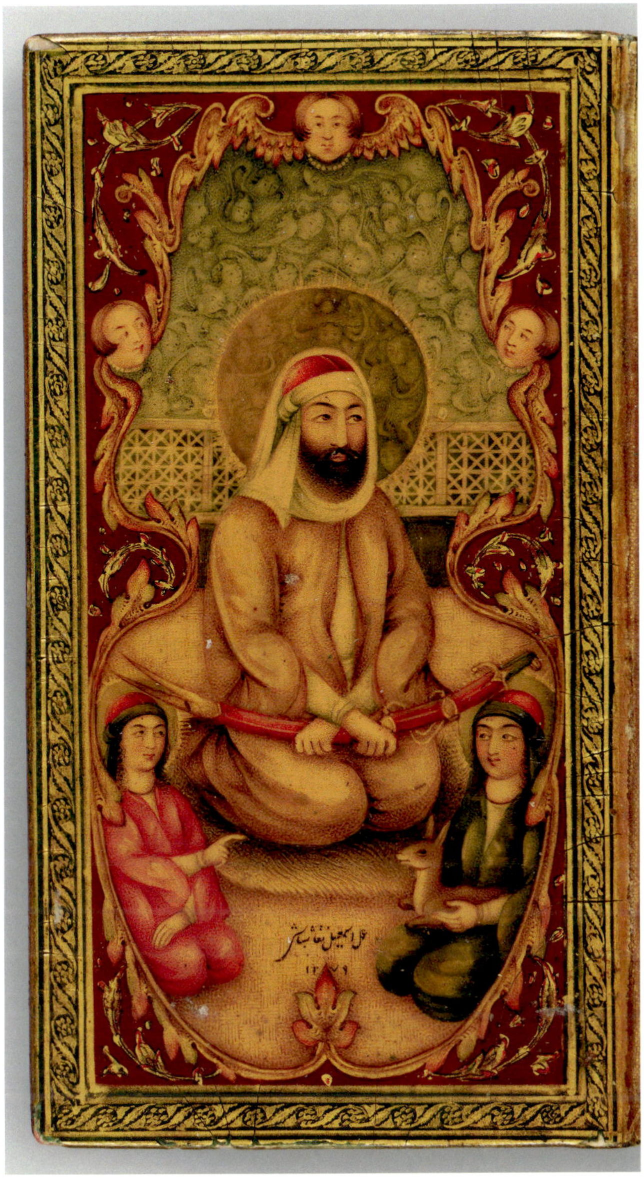

18 *Cover for a Small Qur'an* (interior), dated 1279 H (1862–63). For full information, see cat. 67, p. 154.

A painting on the inner cover of the lacquer binding of a copy of the Qur'an (Fig. 18), signed by Muhammad Isma'il, epitomizes this emerging religious imagery. It depicts Imam 'Ali b. Abi Talib attended by his sons Hasan and Husayn, the second and third imams of Twelver Shi'ism, respectively. The haloed face of Imam 'Ali and the use of modeling are suggestive of the influence of European pictorial sources. The image is also embedded in longstanding notions of religious figures and imams as terrestrial manifestation of the divine; a poem inscribed on a similar painting by Muhammad Isma'il describes how the face of 'Ali is like a "mirror reflecting the beauty of God" and how beholding this beautiful icon brings grace and wards off the evil eye.[52] The small size of the Qur'an suggests that it was meant to be used as a portable object attracting divine protection for the carrier.[53] Adding a religious icon to a copy of the Qur'an accentuated the benedictory function of the words of God, while inflecting the holy scripture of Islam with conspicuous signs of the Shi'i sect.

With the introduction of lithography, the type of pious imagery that appeared on such personal devotional items—or was encountered on the walls of shrines or on the screens used by storytellers—acquired greater public visibility. Further, the uses of printing for devotional purposes were not limited to illustrated religious books; pilgrimage scrolls and amulets, for instance, were also made by way of lithography.[54] Printing normalized the naturalistic depiction of religious figures. Gradually, in the domain of pious imagery, a reciprocal relation was formed between lithography and other mediums, as printed pictures began to serve as models for painters and tilemakers. The result was a distinctive Shi'i popular culture, wherein mechanically produced images occupied a central position.

By the early 20th century, these popular image-making practices reached a zenith in the school of painting known as "coffeehouse painting" (*naqqāshī-yi qahva-khānaī*).[55] A half-century later, thanks to the arrival of advanced printing machinery, single-sheet lithographic prints of the 19th century gave way to polychromatic posters. A set of pious posters published by the Adabiyya bookstore in Tehran around the 1950s is a later example of such developments.[56] One of the posters (Fig. 19) reproduces an early 20th-century painting by Husayn Zaydi Latifi, better known as Sayyid 'Arab, one of the key practitioners of coffeehouse painting. Composed of multiple vignettes, the painting illustrates

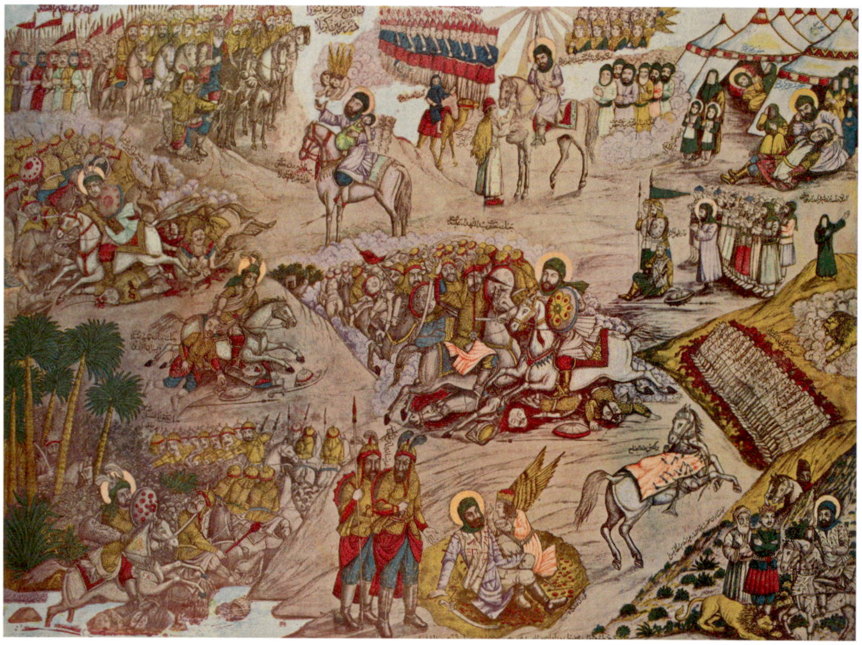

19 *Battle of Karbala* (detail), c. 1950. For full information, see cat. 48, p. 148.

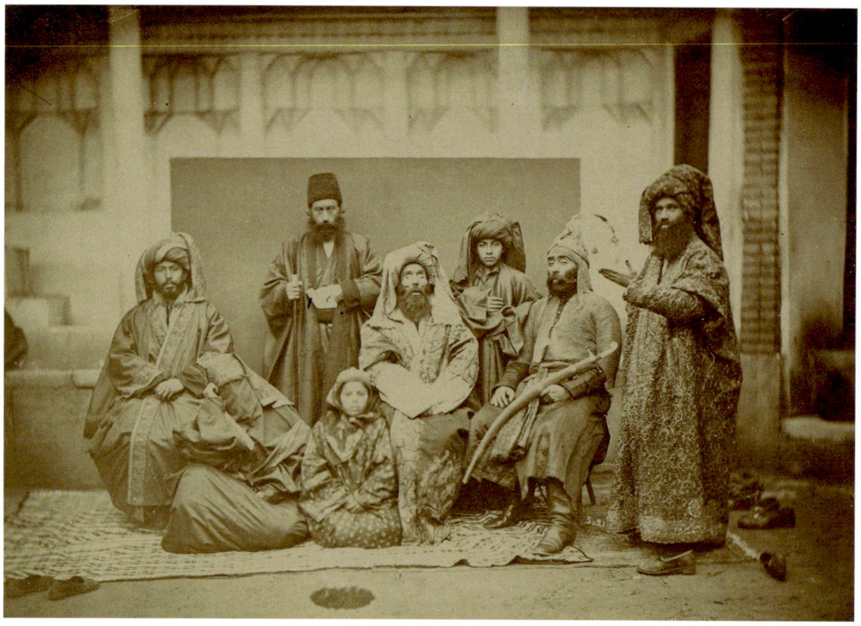

20 *Taʿzīya Performers*, late 19th century. For full information, see cat. 34, p. 142.

the various events of the battle of Karbala in 680, during which Husayn b. ʿAli, the third Shiʿi imam and a grandson of the Prophet Muhammad, was martyred along with a number of his family members and companions. Visualizing the single most historic event in Shiʿi Islam, the painting is connected with the practice of *parda-khvānī* (literally, "reciting from a curtain"), whereby storytellers used such detailed renditions of the battle of Karbala, painted on large textile screens, to narrate the sufferings of Imam Husayn and his companions. It was also related to the tradition of *taʿzīya*, a theater-like performance in which

21 *Ibrahim's Sacrifice* (detail), c. 1950. For full information, see cat. 49, p. 148.

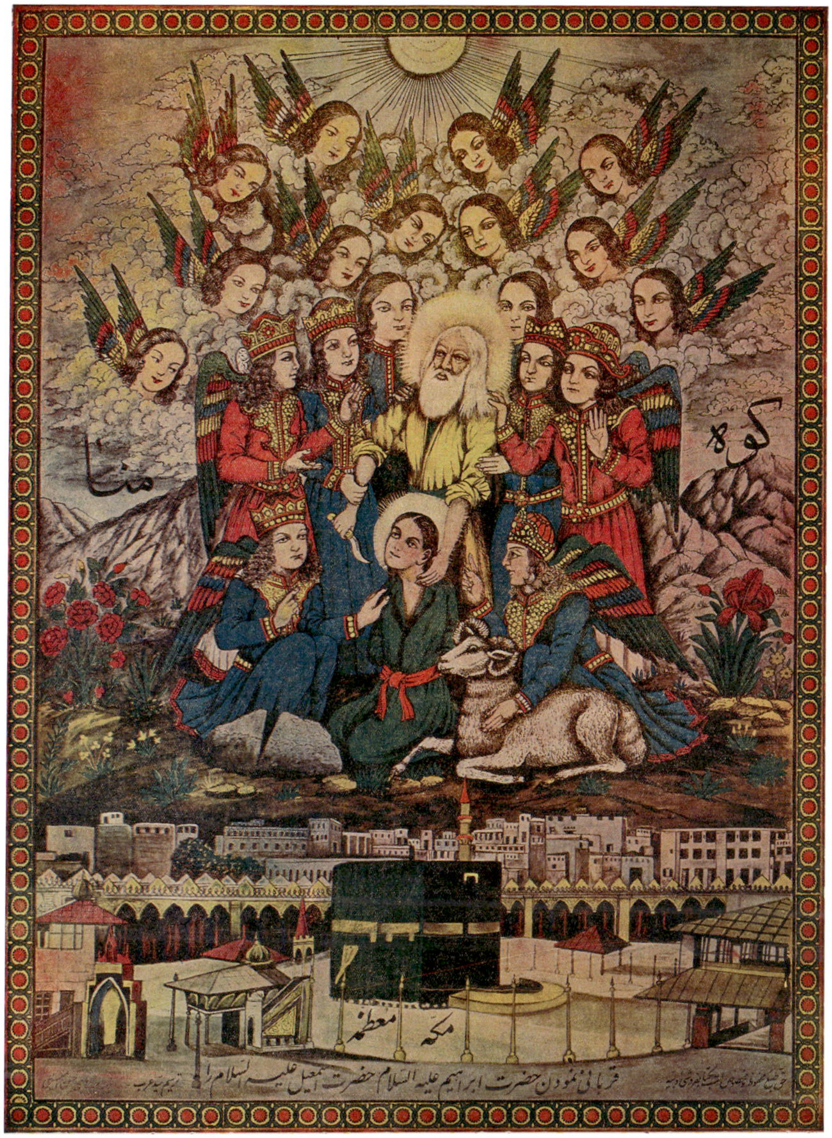

the Karbala events were reenacted (Fig. 20).[57] For the person purchasing such a poster in the early 1900s, it was surely reminiscent of the aural, performative function of the original large screen during the performance of a narrator at a coffeehouse or a reenactment of the Karbala events in a public square. On the other hand, one can also discern in these posters how the reincarnation of the painting as a reproducible image—as an individual poster exhibited on a wall—altered its original perception as a unique communal experience. Indeed, one might argue that the multiplication of such images through mechanical reproduction contributed to the demise of *parda-khvānī*.

Another interesting poster, also based on a painting by Sayyid ʿArab, depicts the sacrifice of Ismaʿil by Ibrahim (Fig. 21). Dressed in a yellow garment and rendered with long white hair and beard, Ibrahim stands in the middle of the picture, holding a knife in his right hand while his left hand touches Isma'il's neck. Depicted in three-quarter profile, Isma'il's head tilts slightly upward, his tranquil face reflecting the Qur'anic narrative of his willingness to be sacrificed. The prophet and his son are surrounded by 19 winged angels, standing on the ground or hovering above in a swirl of clouds topped by a sunburst. At the bottom, the Ka'ba is depicted within the arcaded courtyard of the Masjid al-Haram (the Sacred Mosque) in Mecca, above which extends the Mountain of Mina (*kūh-i Minā*). The Qur'an claims that Ibrahim's sacrifice took place near this site (37:102–7).

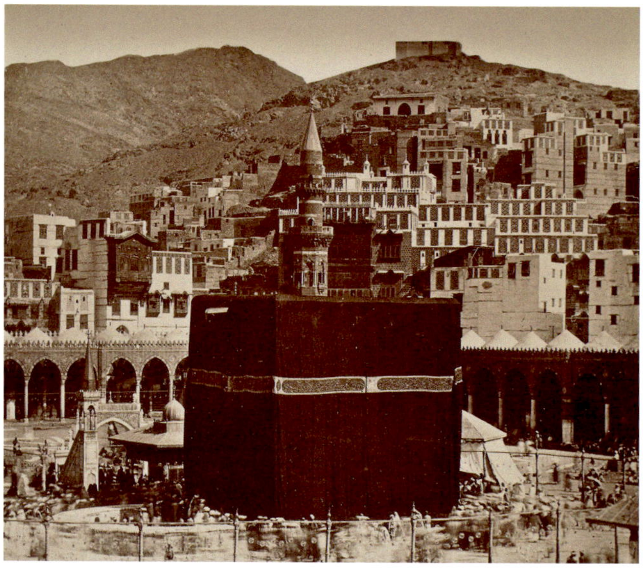

22 *Mecca. View of the Ka'ba and the Sacred Enclosure* (Hijr) *and Its Surroundings*, 1880–81. For full information, see cat. 25, p. 140.

Depictions of Mecca have a long history in Islamic visual culture. Indeed, the overall composition of Sayyid 'Arab's painting can be traced back to illustrations of the Prophet Muhammad's night journey (*isrā'*) from Mecca to Jerusalem and his subsequent ascension (*mi'rāj*) to the heavens of Islamic cosmology. Painted representations of the *mi'rāj* in manuscripts commonly depict Mecca and the Masjid al-Haram in the lower register, topped with a portrait of the Prophet Muhammad riding on his celestial steed into skies filled with angels. What differentiates our painting from these earlier models should come as no surprise to the reader: the depiction of the Ka'ba was clearly based on a photograph (Fig. 22). This photographic reference authenticated the picture, adapting it to the expectations of audiences who were by now more accustomed to evidentiary photographic depictions of the holiest site of Islam.

In all, these works are emblematic of the ways in which late Qajar art was informed by the circulation of images in various media—old and new, mechanically produced or handmade. Printed items, and the lithographic image in particular, occupied a central position in this circuit of pictures. Lithography was deeply implicated in established sociocultural practices and also penetrated new domains such as popular piety and the historical imagination, altering notions of myth, religion, and history in a fundamental way. The lithographic image mediated not only between established and novel modes of image-making, but also between new notions of the past and the exigencies of the present, between elitist initiatives and popular beliefs and practices. It was simultaneously a primary artistic expression of a visual culture and a source of its transformation.

Farshid Emami is a Ph.D. candidate in the Department of History of Art and Architecture at Harvard University.

Notes

1 Saʿīd Nafīsī, "Ṣanʿat-i chāp-i muṣavvar dar Īrān," *Payām-i naw* 2 (5) (1945–46).

2 *Encyclopaedia Iranica*, s.v. "Lithography, i. In Persia," by Olimpiada P. Shcheglova.

3 See Peter Avery, "Printing, the Press, and Literature in Modern Iran," in *The Cambridge History of Iran*, vol. 7, *From Nadir Shah to the Islamic Republic*, ed. P. Avery, G. R. G. Hambly, and Charles Melville (Cambridge: Cambridge University Press, 1991), 815–22.

4 There is a fairly large literature on the history of printing in Iran. For an overview, see *Encyclopaedia Iranica*, s.v. "Čāp," by Willem Floor. For a bibliography, see ʿAlī Būẕarī and Muḥammad Āzādī, *Ma'khaz-shināsī-i kitāb'hā-yi chāp-i sangī va surbī* (Tehran: Kitābdār, 1390 H [2011–12]). A survey of the earliest published books is provided in Shahlā Bābāzāda, *Tārīkh-i chāp dar Īrān* (Tehran: Ṭahūrī, 1999). On the history of printing and printing houses, also see Ḥusayn Mīrzā Gulpāyagānī, *Tārīkh-i chāp va chāp-khāna dar Īrān: (1050 Qamarī tā 1320 Shamsī)* (Tehran: Nashr-i Gulshān, 1378 H [1999]). For a survey and study of the earliest illustrated lithographed books, see Ulrich Marzolph, *Narrative Illustration in Persian Lithographed Books* (Leiden, The Netherlands: Brill, 2001). Also see Nile Green, "Stone from Bavaria: Iranian Lithography in Its Global Context," *Iranian Studies* 43 (3) (2010). As Green has shown, the industrialization of printing in the early 19th century played a key role in the genesis of Arabic-script typography.

5 See Bābāzāda, *Tārīkh-i chāp dar Īrān*. As Marzolph points out, since Babazada's study was based on the holdings of the National Library of Iran (*Kitāb khāna-yi Millī*), the dates given may not be entirely accurate. Nevertheless, there is consensus that typography was abandoned for about two decades.

6 Lithography also resonated with the method of printing from wooden blocks, which had long been used in textile production. See *Encyclopaedia Iranica*, s.v. "Čāp," by Willem Floor and "Čīt," by Jennifer M. Scarce. The Persian term *bāsma* (initially used for printing in general and later for lithography in particular) originally referred to woodblock printing on textiles. For the first generation of Qajar artists, the process of transferring a design to the hard surface of the stone block and printing multiple copies was likely reminiscent of the *bāsma* process.

7 Both Marzolph and Shcheglova cite aesthetic and economic factors as the causes for the success of lithography, although Marzolph prioritizes economic reasons over cultural ones. While cultural perceptions of calligraphy as an artistic form were definitely a significant factor in retaining the manuscript-based elements, it is also important to consider aspects of production, and particularly the ways in which lithography allowed for simulating calligraphic writing using ink on paper.

8 Bābāzāda, *Tārīkh-i chāp dar Īrān*, 102; and Marzolph, *Narrative Illustration in Persian Lithographed Books*, 21.

9 Marzolph, *Narrative Illustration in Persian Lithographed Books*, 19–20.

10 The earliest known illustrated lithographed book was a copy of Maktabi's *Layla va Majnūn*, which appeared in 1843. For a list of titles in chronological order, see Marzolph, ibid., 270–74.

11 For a study focused on al-Qazwini and his text, see Persis Berlekamp, *Wonder, Image, and Cosmos in Medieval Islam* (New Haven, Conn.: Yale University Press, 2011).

12 See Ulrich Marzolph, "Mirzā ʿAli-Qoli Xu'i: Master of Lithograph Illustration," *Annali (Istituto Orientale di Napoli)* 57 (1–2) (1997). The signature of ʿAli Quli Khaw'i appears on only one of the drawings, but it is reasonable to assume that he was responsible for other illustrations as well.

13 Books on religious topics were indeed among the earliest published in a typographic medium, but these publications primarily appealed to the students (*ṭullab*) of religious seminaries (sing., *madrasa*).

14 ʿAlī Būẕarī, *Chihil ṭūfān: barrasī-yi taṣāvīr-i chāp-i sangī-i Ṭūfān al-bukā' fī maqātil al-shuhadā* (Tehran: Kitābkhāna, Mūzih va Markaz-i Asnād-i Majlis-i Shūrā-yi Islāmī, 2011).

15 For Jawhari's text and other renditions of the scene, see ibid., 166–95. Signed by Mirza Hasan and dated 1275 H (1858), the drawing is based on

an original composition by ʿAli Quli Khaw'i published in 1852.

16 Bookbinding emerged as a specific craft in the early centuries of Islam. In the traditional market, bookbinders (sing., *ṣaḥḥāf*) had their own separate shops, and the same practice continued into the early years of the introduction of lithography.

17 For studies of lithographed editions of the *Shāhnāma*, see Ulrich Marzolph, "The *Shahnama* in Print: Lithographed Editions of the Persian National Epic," in *Heroic Times: A Thousand Years of the Persian Book of Kings*, ed. Julia Gonnella and Christoph Rauch (Munich: Edition Minerva, 2012); Ulrich Marzolph, "Illustrated Persian Lithographic Editions of the *Shânâme*," *Edebiyât* 13 (2) (2003); and Marjolijn van Zutphen, "Lithographed Editions of Firdawsī's *Shāhnāma*: A Comparative Study," *Oriens* 37 (2009).

18 Aside from his introduction to the *Shāhnāma*, there is limited biographical information about Muhammad Mahdi. The only other source known to me is a book that he wrote about his hometown, Isfahan, after returning from India. See Muḥammad Mahdī b. Muḥammad Riżā al-Iṣfahānī, *Niṣf-i jahān fī taʿrīf al-Isfahān*, ed. Manūchihr Sutūdah (Isfahan: Ta'yīd, 1340 H [1961]).

19 The primacy of aesthetic factors for Muhammad Mahdi does not mean that one can draw a binary opposition between the approaches of 19th-century Western Orientalist and Iranian elites, as Marzolph assumes. As his introduction shows, Arbab was genuinely interested in preparing an authentic edition of the *Shāhnāma*. His views were formed in the context of an indigenous literary movement known as "literary return" (*bāzgasht-i adabī*), which rejected the innovations of the Safavid period and sought to "return" to classical forms of Persian poetry.

20 For a comparative study of the illustrations of the lithographic editions of the *Shāhnāma* published in late Qajar Iran, see Ulrich Marzolph and Muḥammad Hādī Muḥammadī, *Ālbūm-i Shāhnāma: taṣvīr'hā-yi chāp-yi sangī-yi Shāhnāma-yi Firdawsī* (Tehran: Chīstā, 1384 H [2005–6]).

21 Marzolph, *Narrative Illustration in Persian Lithographed Books*, 15–16.

22 See Alois Senefelder, *The Invention of Lithography*, trans. J. W. Muller (New York: The Fuchs & Lang Manufacturing Company, 1911), 190–93.

23 The drawing is now in the private collection of Muhammad ʿAli Karimzade Tabrizi. For a study, see ʿAlī Būzarī, "Sketching and Copying in the Niello-Prints of the Qajar Period," *Nāma-yi bahāristān* 10 (15) (2009). As Buzari has shown, the pounced drawing closely matches an image in the lithographed copy of the *Ṭūfān al-bukā'* (The Deluge of Tears), also illustrated by Mirza ʿAli Quli Khaw'i.

24 See below for a textual description of this practice in a slightly later period.

25 This section was not composed by Firdawsi, but rather by the Zoroastrian poet Daqiqi and was later incorporated by Firdawsi into his own *Shāhnāma*.

26 Sir Robert Ker Porter, *Travels in Georgia, Persia, Armenia, Ancient Babylonia, &c. &c. during the Years 1817, 1818, 1819, and 1820*, vol. 2 (London: Longman, Hurst, Rees, Orme, and Brown, 1821–22), 193.

27 Engagement with ancient rock reliefs of course began earlier, during the reign of Fath ʿAli Shah. In 1821, a new rock relief was appended to the original Sasanian ones by Muhammad ʿAli Mirza Dawlatshah, who was a Qajar prince and a son of Fath ʿAli Shah.

28 By the late 1840s, according to Shcheglova (*Encyclopaedia Iranica*, s.v. "Lithography i. In Persia"), there were at least six active lithographic presses in the Qajar capital.

29 On the Dar al-Funun, see Maryam Ekhtiar, "Nasir al-Din Shah and the Dar al-Funun: The Evolution of an Institution," *Iranian Studies* 34 (1–4) (2001). For a study of the Majma' al-Sanayiʿ, see Shahrām Yūsufīfar, "Majmaʿ al-ṣanāyiʿ (tajrubī-yi nawgarā'ī dar mashāghil-i kārgāh'hā-yi salṭanatī-yi dawra-yi Qājār)," *Ganjīna-yi asnād* 21 (3) (2011).

30 Jennifer M. Scarce, "The Role of Architecture in the Creation of Tehran," in *Téhéran: Capitale bicentenaire*, ed. Chahryar Adle and Bernard Hourcade (Paris: Institut français de recherche en Iran, 1992).

31 See Parviz Tanavoli, *European Women in Persian Houses: Western Images in Safavid and Qajar Iran*, ed. Sarah B. Sherrill and Moya Carey (London: I. B. Tauris, 2015).

32 For a study of Abu al-Hasan Ghaffari's career, see Yaḥyā Ẕukā', *Zindagī va āṣār-i ustād Ṣanīʿ al-Mulk Abū al-Ḥasan Ghaffārī (1229–83 Q.)* (Tehran: Markaz-i Nashr-i Dānishgāhī, 1382 H [2003–4]). Abu al-Hasan had probably mastered this mode of spatial rendition while working on the manuscript of the *Hazār va yak shab* (1,001 Nights). Also see Mansureh Ettehadieh (Nezam Mafi) and Bahman Farman Farmaian, "The Beginnings of Illustrated Journals during the Reign of Nasser ed-Din Shah, and the Work of Sani ol-Molk," *Qajar Studies: Journal of the International Qajar Studies Association* 6 (2006).

33 *Rūznāma-yi dawlat-i ʿalīya-yi Īrān* 472 (19 Safar, 1277), 7; cited in Farīd Qāsimī, ed., *Sarguzasht-i matbūʿāt-i Īrān: Rūzgār-i Muḥammad Shāh va Nāṣir al-Dīn Shāh* (Tehran: Sāzmān-i Chāp va Intishārāt, Vizarāt-i Farhang va Irshād-i Islāmī, 1380 H [2001]), 708.

34 Abbas Amanat, "Court Patronage and Public Space: Abu'l-Hasan Saniʿ al-Mulk and the Art of Persianizing the Other in Qajar Iran," in *Court Cultures in the Muslim World: Seventh to Nineteenth Centuries*, ed. Albrecht Fuess and Jan-Peter Hartung (New York: Routledge, 2011), 433.

35 The pen box is illustrated with multiple scenes depicting legendary rulers of the Kayani and Sasanian dynasties, the tales of which are narrated in Firdawsi's *Shāhnāma*, among other sources. In decorating the pen box, Muhammad Kazim, who was a son of the renowned

lacquer artist Aqa Najaf, followed an established model. See Nasser D. Khalili, B. W. Robinson, and Tim Stanley, *Lacquer of the Islamic Lands,* pt. 2, The Nasser D. Khalili Collection of Islamic Art, vol. 22 (London: Nour Foundation in association with Azimuth Editions and Oxford University Press, 1996–97), 60–63.

36 On the Najaf circle of painters, see Willem Floor, "Art (*Naqqashi*) and Artists (*Naqqashan*) in Qajar Persia," *Muqarnas* 16 (1999).

37 See Maryam Ekhtiar, "Muhammad Isma'il Isfahani: Master Lacquer Painter," in *Persian Masters: Five Centuries of Painting*, ed. Sheila Canby (Bombay: Marg Publications, 1990).

38 Jalāl al-Dīn Mīrzā, *Nāma-yi khusravān: dāstān-i pādshāhān-i Pārs*, 3 vols. (Tehran: n.p., 1868–72). Jalal al-Din Mirza had initially envisioned the book in four volumes, but the fourth volume, which was to cover the Qajars, never appeared.

39 For a study of the book and its author, see *Encyclopaedia Iranica*, s.v. "Jalāl-al-Dīn Mīrzā," by Abbas Amanat and Farzin Vejdani. Also see Abbas Amanat, "Pūr-i khāqān va andīsha-yi bāzyābī-yi tārīkh-i millī-yi Īrān: Jalāl al-Dīn Mīrzā va *Nāma-yi Khusravān*," *Īrān-nāma* 17 (1) (1999).

40 In this respect, *Nāma-yi khusravān* is of course similar to the narrative of Firdawsi's *Shāhnāma*, which likewise begins in a mythical time. What sets Jalal al-Din Mirza's work apart is that its history extends beyond the pre-Islamic period and into the present. In this grand scheme, the rise of Islam is sidelined as a minor event. There is also a more pronounced emphasis on historical authenticity in the *Nāma-yi khusravān*, which is particularly achieved through the use of images drawn from ancient sites.

41 *Encyclopaedia Iranica*, s.v. "Āẕar Kayvān," Henry Corbin. For an analysis of the movement led by Azar Kayvan and its repercussions, see Mohamad Tavakoli-Targhi, "Contested Memories: Narrative Structures and Allegorical Meanings of Iran's Pre-Islamic History," *Iranian Studies* 29 (1–2) (1996).

42 On the life and works of Mirza 'Abd al-Muttallib, see Muḥammad 'Alī Karīmzāda Tabrīzī, *Aḥvāl va āṡār-i naqqāshān-i qadīm-i Īran va barkhī az mashāhīr-i nigārgar-i Hind va 'Uṡmānī*, vol. 1 (London: Interlink Longraph, 1363 H [1985]), 344–34; and Marzolph, *Narrative Illustration in Persian Lithographed Books*, 39–40.

43 Jennifer M. Scarce, "Ancestral Themes in the Art of Qajar Iran, 1785–1925," in *Islamic Art in the 19th Century: Tradition, Innovation, and Eclecticism*, ed. Doris Behrens-Abouseif and Stephen Vernoit (Leiden, The Netherlands: Brill, 2006), 245.

44 For a study, see Ulrich Marzolph, "The Last Great *Shahnama*: The *Shahnama-yi Bahaduri* (1319–26/1901–8)," in *Shahnama Studies I*, ed. Charles Melville (Cambridge: Cambridge University Press, 2006).

45 *Ittilā'*, 23 Jumada II, 1300. Quoted in Suhaylā Raīsī Mubāraka and Mahbūba Bābāī, *Muṭāla'ātī dar tārīkh-i chāp dar Īrān* (Tehran: Gulshan-i Rāz, 1378 H [1999]), 111.

46 The change is discussed by Floor, who dates it to the late 1860s and links the emergence of the fat crayon to the development of photography. See Floor, "Art (*Naqqash*) and Artists (*Naqqashan*) in Qajar Persia," 133.

47 For facsimiles of these journals, see Javād Ṣafīnizhād, ed., *Dawra-yi rūznāma-i Sharaf va Sharāfat* (Tehran: Yasāvulī, 1363 H [1984]).

48 Mohammad Sattari and Houshang Salamat, "Photography and the Illustrated Journals *Sharaf* and *Sharāfat*," *History of Photography* 37 (1) (2013).

49 Ibid.

50 Cited in ibid., 76. For a biography and study of the works of Abu Turab Khan, see Muḥammad Gulbun, *Sarguẕasht va āṡār-i taṣvīrgar-i buzurg, Mīrzā Abū Turāb Khān Ghaffārī Kāshānī, 1263–1307, H. Q.* (Tehran: Anjuman-i Āṡār va Mafākhir-i Farhangī, 1386 H [2007–8]).

51 For a biography and list of his works, see Karīmzāda Tabrīzī, *Aḥvāl va āṡār-i naqqāshān-i qadīm-i Īran va barkhī az mashāhīr-i nigārgar-i Hind va 'Uṡmānī*, 3:1247–51. According to Karimzada Tabrizi, it was common to make extra copies of the lithographic drawings printed in the journal.

52 For a discussion and reproduction, see Ekhtiar, "Muhammad Isma'il Isfahani," 139–41.

53 Mohammad Ali Amir-Moezzi, "Icon and Meditation: Between Popular Art and Sufism in Imami Shi'ism," in *The Art and Material Culture of Iranian Shi'ism: Iconography and Religious Devotion in Shi'i Islam*, ed. Pedram Khosronejad (London: I. B. Tauris, 2012). As Amir-Moezzi notes, there is some evidence to suggest that such portraits were likely used for Sufi devotional practices.

54 Ulrich Marzolph, "From Mecca to Mashhad: The Narrative of an Illustrated Shi'i Pilgrimage Scroll from the Qajar Period," *Muqarnas* 31 (2014); and Ulrich Marzolph, "The Pictorial Representation of Shi'i Themes in Lithographed Books of the Qajar Period," in Khosronejad, *The Art and Material Culture of Iranian Shi'ism.*

55 For a survey of some of the paintings preserved in Iranian institutions, see Hādī Sayf, *Naqqāshī-yi qahva-khāna* (Tehran: Vizārat-i Farhang va Āmūzish-i 'Ālī, 1369 H [1990]). On the reemergence of the coffeehouse as a social institution and the development of a public sphere in this period, see Rudi Matthee, *The Pursuit of Pleasure: Drugs and Stimulants in Iranian History, 1500–1900* (Princeton, N.J.: Princeton University Press, 2005), chap. 10.

56 Although published under the Pahlavi dynasty (1924–79), the posters reproduce early 20th-century paintings and thus can be considered as later manifestations of Qajar visual culture. Religious posters as single-leaf prints were first introduced in the 19th century.

57 Peter J. Chelkowski, ed., *Eternal Performance: Ta'ziyeh and Other Shiite Rituals* (London: Seagull, 2010).

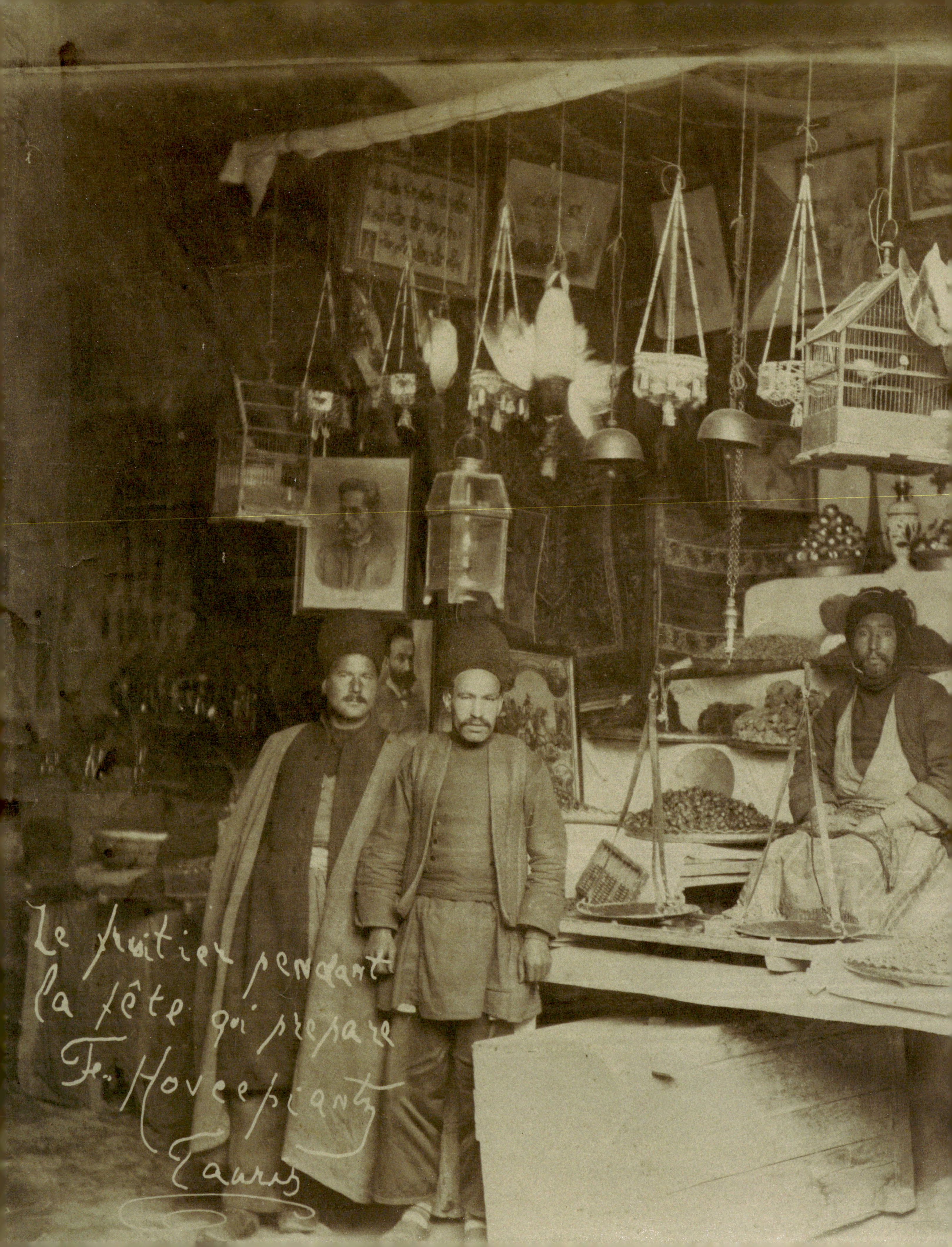
Le fruitier pendant
la fête qui prepare
Fr. Hoveepiantz
Tauris

4 Iranian Photography

FROM THE COURT, TO THE STUDIO, TO THE STREET

Mira Xenia Schwerda

This essay focuses on Iran's vibrant history of photography, from its beginning in royal palaces, to the establishment of the first commercial photography studios, to its role in documenting political events during the Constitutional Revolution in the early 1900s. Iranian photography was never isolated from the global history of the medium and was continually shaped by the effects of polyglotism, travel, developments in technology and printing, and changes in audience and demand. Photographers living in Iran closely followed changes throughout Europe, Russia, and the Ottoman Empire; indeed, photographic images traveled around the globe, and their mobility throughout the 19th century is a recurring theme of the essays in this volume. In examining photography in the Qajar era, this essay shifts a common scholarly focus from the ruler as tastemaker to examine non-royal photographers and their audiences. While images taken by the "photographer king" Nasir al-Din Shah (r. 1848–1896) were confined to the Gulistan Palace in Tehran—and never produced for circulation beyond its walls—photographs made and acquired by sub- or non-royal agents were intended to be seen and shared. The emerging study of Iranian photography has so far emphasized the Qajar court, at the expense of non-royal sources, agents, audiences, and their influence.

Detail: *Fruit Sellers Preparing for Festivities,* late 19th century. For full information, see cat. 33, p. 142.

The Language of Innovation: Polyglotism and the Beginnings of Photography in Iran

In 1295 H (1878–79), Qajar statesman and prolific writer Muhammad Hasan Khan I'timad al-Saltana Sani' al-Dawla (1843–1896) discussed the beginning of photography in Iran in his book *Mir'āt al-buldān* (Mirror of Cities): "Towards the end of the reign of . . . Muhammad Shah . . . Monsieur Richard Khan who at present teaches English and other languages at the Dar al-Funun used, with much toil, to take pictures on silver plate."[1]

The daguerreotype, a photographic process named after one of its inventors, Jacques Daguerre, had been officially presented at the Academy of Sciences in Paris in January 1839.[2] The process captured and fixed the photographic image for the first time. In a darkroom, a copper plate would be coated in silver, sensitized with iodine flakes, and then transferred to the camera without exposure to light. In order for the picture to be taken, the lens cap was removed until the correct exposure had been reached. The plate was treated with mercury vapor to develop the image, which was then made permanent by bathing the plate in a solution of salt. This process removed the sensitized chemicals from the plate and stopped further chemical reactions. The fixed image was a positive, which meant that only one copy existed; unlike a negative it could not be reproduced. Three years later, two daguerreotype cameras were gifted to the court of Muhammad Shah (r. 1834–1848) by Queen Victoria of Great Britain and Tsar Nicholas I of Russia.[3] It appears that these cameras remained unused until 1844, when French photographer Jules Richard (1816–1891) arrived at the court. Fluent in six languages (although not a word of Persian[4]), Richard photographed Crown Prince Nasir al-Din—who would later succeed his father, Muhammad Shah, as ruler—and his sister 'Izzat al-Dawla (1834/5–1905) in Tabriz.[5]

Another pioneering photographer active in Iran during these years was the prince Malik Qasim Mirza (1807–c. 1862), son of Fath 'Ali Shah. Most likely the first Iranian daguerreotypist, he was also a painting enthusiast and lived in the Iranian province of Azerbaijan.[6] In 1840, Eugène Flandin described Malik Qasim Mirza as

> one of the most remarkable men in the Orient, concerning the extent of his ideas, his learning, and . . . his broad knowledge of Europe. He speaks six languages, without counting his own: French, perfectly, English, Russian, Turkish, Arabic, and Hindustani. . . . In prince Malek-kassem Mirza I found one of the greatest amateur painters I have met in this country.[7]

A trait common to early photographers in Iran was the ability to understand foreign languages, which helped them follow developments in the field in other countries. Another commonality between Richard and Malik Qasim Mirza is that little of their original work survives.[8] The few surviving daguerreotypes depicting Qajar sitters seem mostly to have been taken abroad and are now in collections outside Iran.

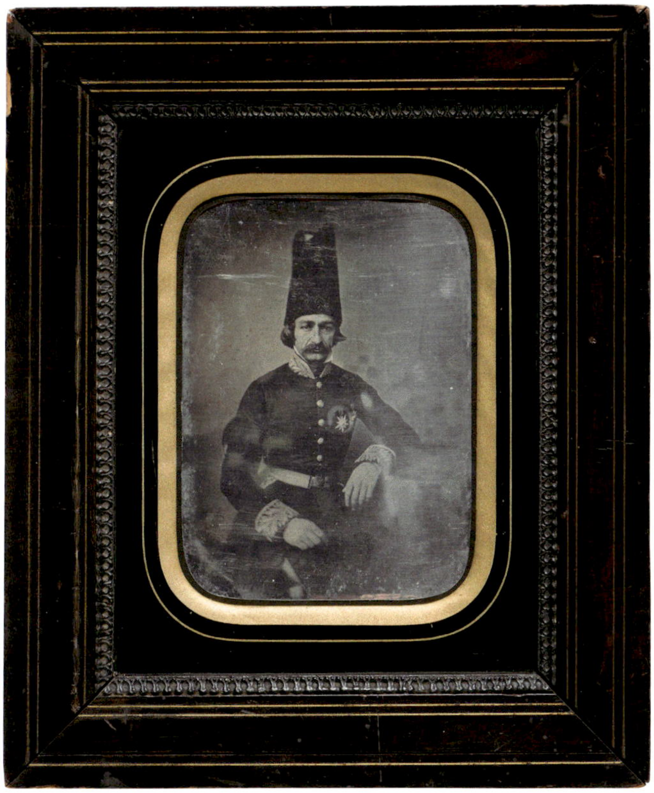

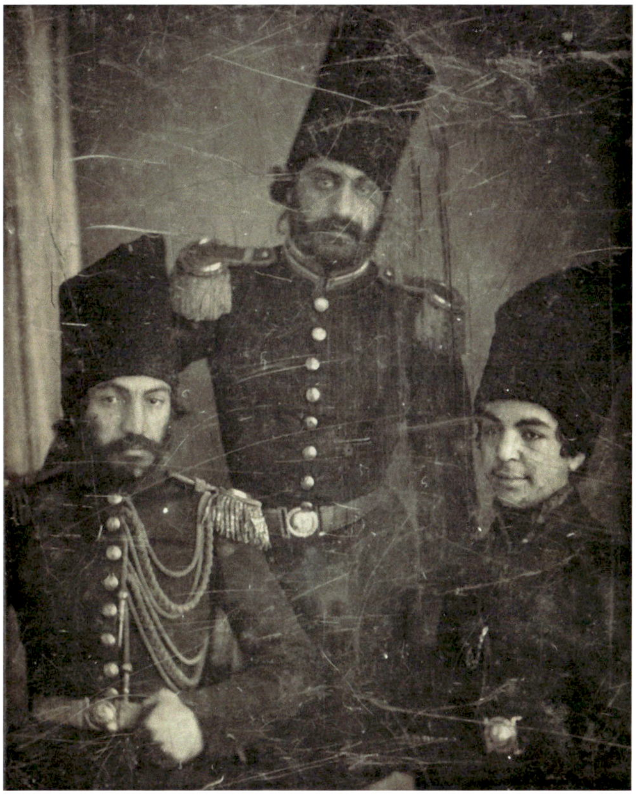

1 *An Unidentified Qajar Gentleman*, 1843–51. For full information, see cat. 22, p. 138.

2 *Portrait of Officers of the Persian Army*, 1840s–50s. Daguerreotype; quarter plate, 7.2 × 5.7 cm (2 13/16 × 2 1/4 in.). State Historical Museum, Moscow, ГИМ 56388 И VII 1279.

The daguerreotype portrait of an unidentified gentleman in Qajar military dress (Fig. 1) was taken by Wilhelm Schönfeld (1810–1887).[9] Like many of Schönfeld's portraits, this daguerreotype was embellished by hand; touches of shell gold and a silver colorant were added to the collar and the medal on the chest. Initially trained in Paris, Schönfeld operated a studio in St. Petersburg, Russia,[10] one of a large number of European photographers residing there in the 1840s and 1850s.[11] St. Petersburg was in these decades a popular destination for the Qajar elite, whether for tourism, work, or education. Many Iranians who would later take up photography spent time in the city. Schönfeld's daguerreotype demonstrates the practice of having one's photograph taken as a souvenir of travel, as does the equally compelling—and equally unidentifiable—daguerreotype of three Qajar military officers (Fig. 2).[12] It was easier in these early years to have a photographic portrait taken outside Iran, for the medium did not yet have a commercial basis in Qajar lands.

In Iran and Russia, the daguerreotype process was utilized longer than in many other parts of the world; elsewhere, the medium was displaced by new processes beginning in the 1850s.[13] Richard produced daguerreotypes in 1853–54, and Malik Qasim Mirza dedicated an album of daguerreotypes to Nasir al-Din Shah in May 1850. In the mid- and late 1850s, there was frequent overlap in photographic practices, as new technology did not completely displace older methods until supplies for the latter became unobtainable. During that gradual transition, one could have a daguerreotype taken in one studio and a *carte de visite* made in another,[14] as Figure 3 reveals. Seated to the right is the same Qajar gentleman whose likeness is captured in Schönfeld's daguerreotype.

In addition to the rise of a few individual professional photographers, the medium became institutionalized in Iran. In 1851, three years after Nasir al-Din Shah had ascended the throne, the polytechnical college Dar al-Funun was founded in Tehran.[15] The initiative was spearheaded not by the shah, but by his grand vizier Amir Kabir, who had risen to power from a relatively humble background. Intended to offer military training, the curriculum was complemented by instruction in the sciences, medicine, history, foreign languages, and photography. Richard was hired as one of the first teachers at the college, but his interest in photography was shared by several members of the faculty, as recorded by I'timad al-Saltana:

> In the early part of the reign of our present Shah [Nasir al-Din] . . . when the Dār al-Funūn was built, Monsieur Krziz the Austrian artillery instructor, made some photographic experiments on paper. Monsieur Focchetti, the biology teacher, was the first person to use the collodion process at the Tehran College; and Monsieur Carlhian, who had accompanied Farrukh-Khān Amīn al-Dawla from Paris to Tehran in order to propagate the science and methods of photography, made the use of the collodion process widespread.[16]

The last individual named here, Farrukh Khan Amin al-Dawla (1812–1871), was a regular fixture at the courts of Muhammad Shah and Nasir al-Din Shah and a proponent of Western education. He is most likely the figure seated at left of the *carte de visite* (Fig. 3).[17]

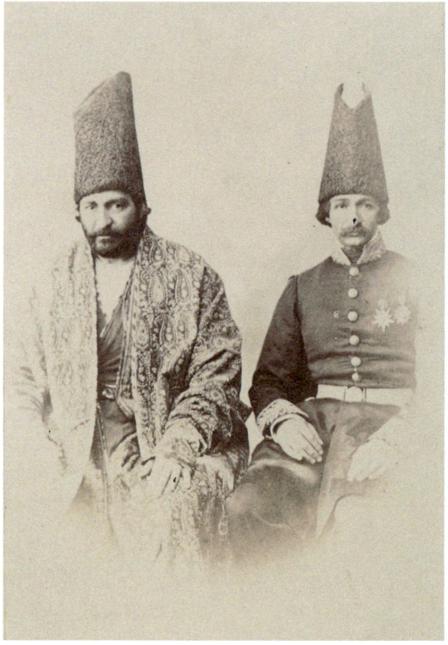

3 Carte de Visite *of Two Qajar Gentlemen*, 1843–51. For full information, see cat. 23, p. 138.

Richard worked not only for the Dar al-Funun, but also for two institutions to which it was connected, the Ministry of Publications (*Vizārat-i Inṭibā'āt*) and the Governmental Office of Translation (*Dār al-Tarjuma-yi Dawlatī*).[18] Among the works produced there were books on photography: for example, *Kitāb-i 'aks* (Book of Photography), translated by Muhammad Kazim b. Ahmad Mahallati in 1863.[19] The inclusion of photography in the curriculum of the Dar al-Funun and the translation of photographic manuals into Persian stimulated the spread of photography in Iran.

The Propagation of Photography in Iran: Technical Change, Urban Studios, and the Armenian Photography Network

An important change in photographic technology occurred around 1851, when the wet collodion process was invented by Frederick Scott Archer in England.[20] Over the next 30 years, it would gradually replace daguerreotype technology. Unlike the daguerreotype, which produced a unique image, the wet collodion process imprinted the negative on a glass plate, from which an unlimited number of copies could be printed onto paper. This process required

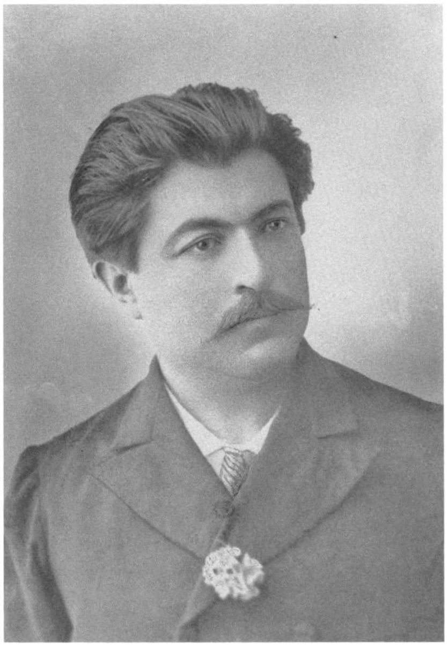

4 *Antoin Sevruguin in Vienna*, before 1880. Modern gelatin silver print from original photograph, 22.5 × 16 cm (8⅞ × 6⁵⁄₁₆ in.). Matenadaran Mesrop Mashtots Institute of Ancient Manuscripts, Yerevan, Armenia.

a portable darkroom, as the glass plates had to be prepared shortly before the exposure was made. The collodion solution, which caused the image to adhere to the plate, lost sensitivity after about 10 minutes.[21] Before the plate dried, it was coated in light-sensitive silver nitrate, covered in a light-proof holder, and placed inside the camera.[22] The plate was developed in the darkroom immediately after exposure.[23] The entire process required about 15 minutes. Images were usually printed on paper coated with an egg white solution (albumen), which gave the print its characteristic glossy texture.

These technical innovations allowed photographers to sell printed copies of their photographs at more affordable prices. Some photographers utilized the collodion process to re-photograph existing daguerreotypes, thereby creating a negative of the daguerreotype positive and enabling copies to be printed. This could explain the relationship between the daguerreotype and *carte de visite* recording the same Qajar gentleman (Figs. 1, 3). Decades after photography's introduction at the royal court[24] and its establishment at the Dar al-Funun, the first public studio opened in Tehran in 1868.[25] By 1888, the number of photographers working in Iran had surged, as observed by I'timad al-Saltana: "Nowadays the very number of photographers and their workshops in the capital Tehran and other major cities of Iran would make their enumeration a most arduous task."[26]

Perhaps the best-known of these new professional photographers was Antoin Sevruguin (late 1830s–1933), who established a studio in Tehran around 1870.[27] Born to a Russian diplomat of Armenian descent and a Georgian mother in the Russian embassy in Tehran, Sevruguin grew up in Iran and Georgia and learned several languages, including Persian, French, and Russian.

The importance of having an aptitude for foreign languages is evidenced by a manuscript written by "Antoin Khan," now in Tehran's National Library.[28] It is a short text on the art of taking photographs, which the author composed based on French manuals and then translated into Persian. He dedicated it to the crown prince Muzaffar al-Din in Tabriz in 1878.[29]

Sevruguin had studied photography with Dimitri Ermakov (1846–1916) in Tiflis before moving to Iran with his brothers, first settling in Tabriz and later in Tehran.[30] During his life, Sevruguin continued to travel throughout Qajar Iran and abroad, as demonstrated by his voluminous corpus of photographs. One of the few works offering visual proof of his travel outside Iran is a studio portrait made in Vienna (Fig. 4), taken at a time when even professional photographers could not always bring their cameras while traveling. During his travels to Austria and elsewhere, he most likely met with other photographers to learn about recent developments in the field. Sevruguin's photographs were well-known abroad: his work was published in newspapers and books,[31] and he had won prizes at the World Fair in Brussels (1897) and in Paris (1900).[32] The back of his photographs feature representations of these medals alongside medallion portraits of three pioneering photographers—Niépce, Daguerre,

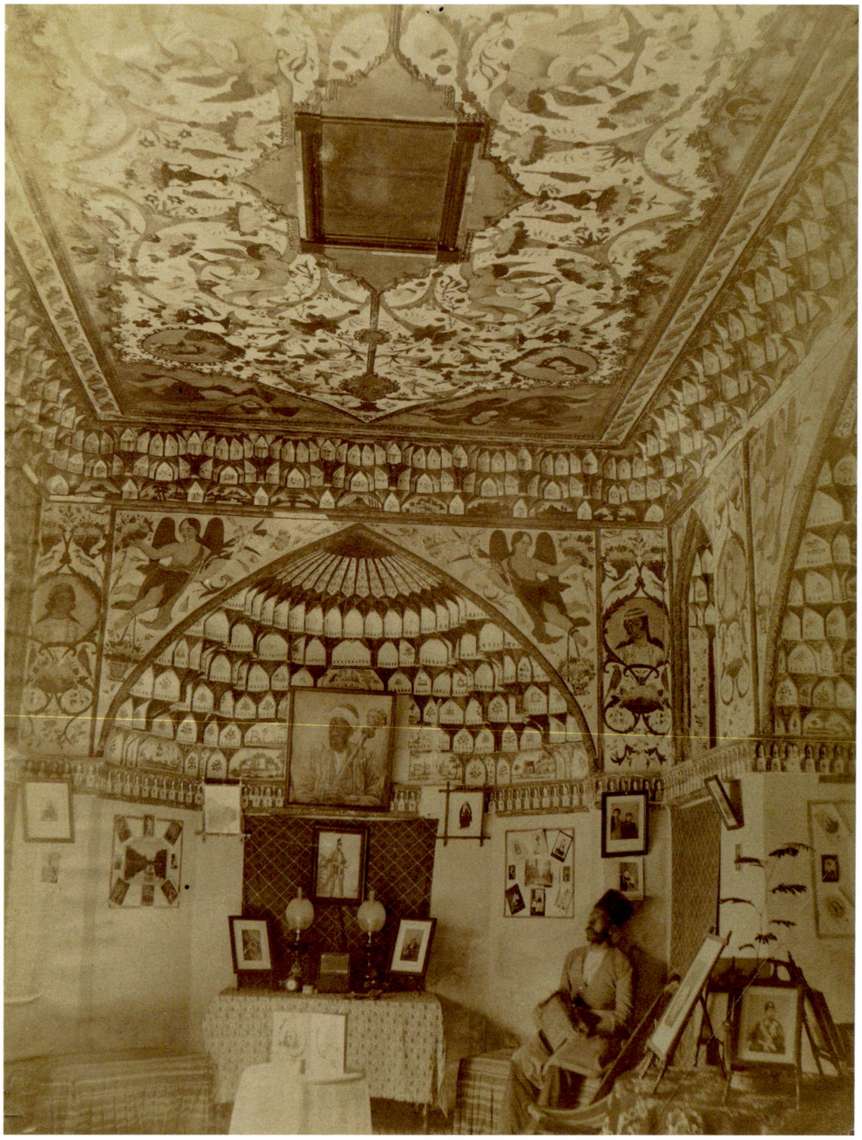

5 *A Photographer's Room*, late 19th century. For full information, see cat. 28, p. 140.

and Talbot—positioning Sevruguin as connected with and indebted to this photographic lineage.[33] Sevruguin also belonged to an influential subgroup of photographers: the informal network of Armenian photographers. Centuries earlier, Armenians had established commercial networks throughout Europe and Asia. Traveling Armenian merchants developed early credit systems across the world and exchanged political news and other information.[34] Benefiting from this exchange and their multilingual upbringing, Armenians learned the photographic trade early and traveled into areas where photography was not yet very well known. The network of Armenian photographers was especially active in Iran, but also throughout Europe, Turkey, and the Caucasus. After photography became established and the number of practitioners had multiplied in cities, photographers then turned to rural areas to open their studios,

6 *Woman Smoking a Water Pipe*, late 19th century. For full information, see cat. 29, p. 140.

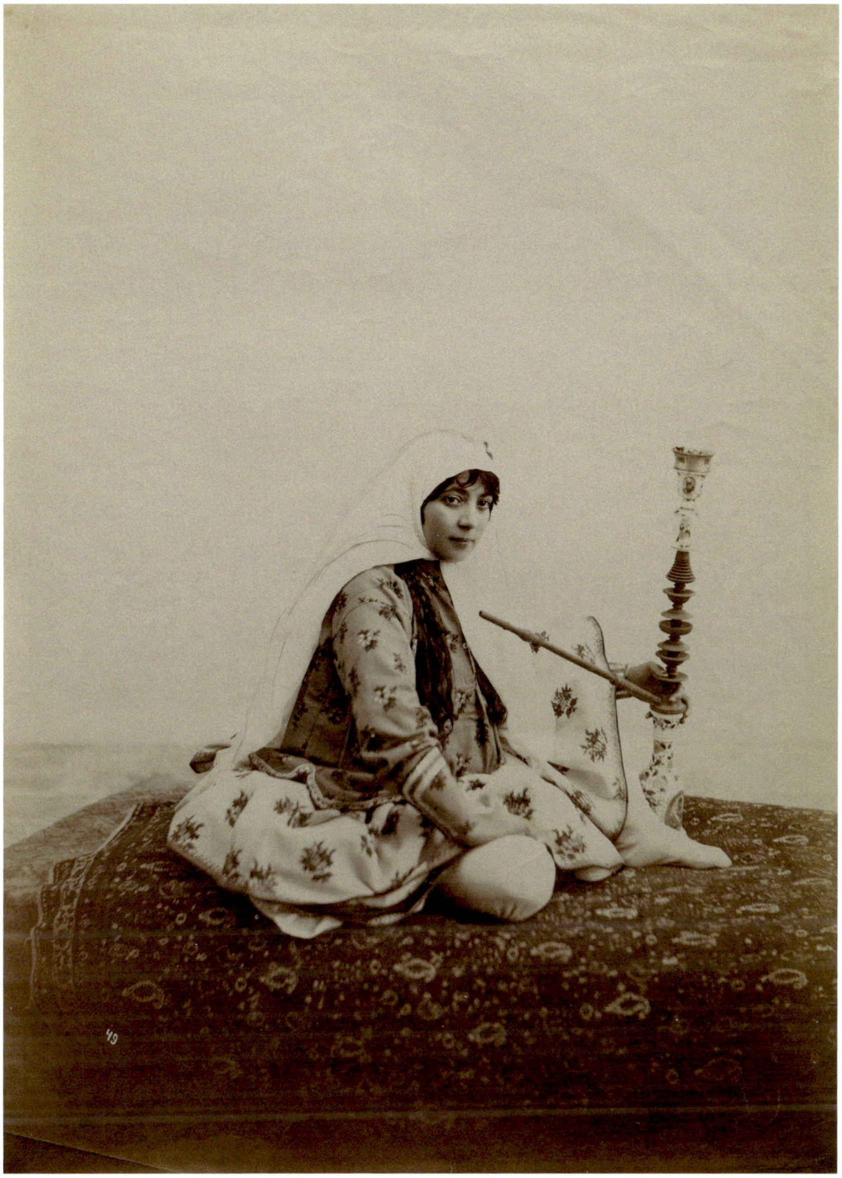

many of which were set up as family businesses. Rural photographers with modest studios, whose names are often forgotten today, were not isolated from developments outside Iran, as prints and photographs crossed borders of country and language.

Prior to his interest in photography, Sevruguin had trained as a painter in Tiflis, apparently showing interest in Rembrandt as well as in the Persian miniature painters Bihzad (d. 1535) and Riza ʿAbbasi (d. 1635).[35] The image of a photographer's room, in which paintings and photographs are juxtaposed, can be attributed to Sevruguin (Fig. 5).[36] His training as an artist is evident in his photographic work. Not only did he have an exceptionally good eye for composition and lighting, but on occasion he also employed draftsmanship in the making of the photographs. Sometimes he scratched and drew directly onto the glass plates to modify the images before printing them. In other instances, he over-painted certain areas of the photograph to simplify the background and to enhance the appearance of the figure or building.[37]

In an image of a woman smoking a water pipe, for example, Sevruguin partially drew her headscarf by hand (Fig. 6). This young woman served as a model for a series of studio photographs composed by Sevruguin.[38] In this image, her hand rests on a decorated water pipe (*qalyān*) while she looks toward the camera.[39] In the Qajar era, tobacco was a common pleasure for both men and women, and many women of the upper classes were addicted to the water pipe.[40] Depictions of female smokers appear repeatedly in Sevruguin's oeuvre and were a popular subject with male and female clients, who collected the images and mounted them in albums.[41]

Unlike the other prints of this series, the photograph in Figure 6 is an oversized print, a format extremely rare for Sevruguin. This points to different audiences for commercial photographs; besides private Iranian and non-Iranian clients, photographs were purchased by institutions (museums, libraries, and schools) and by media or publishing companies. Professional interest in such large prints is further attested by two of Sevruguin's other folios—similar in size to Figure 6—which were in the possession of the Musée de l'Homme, Paris, before being transferred to the Bibliothèque nationale de France.[42] Sevruguin's photographs differed in size and other aspects of their printing due to such factors as the time of production and their target audience. The circulation and reproduction of the prints also varied depending on the purchaser and their intended function.

The Circulation of Images: Photography and Printing in the Late Qajar Era

Compiling albums of photographs was a popular activity in Iran, just as it was elsewhere in the 19th century, and it created a booming market for the work of commercial photographers like Sevruguin. One example is a photography album with a cover of green cloth that appears to have been owned by an American missionary family based in Tabriz or Urmia and was assembled sometime in or after 1896.[43] Judging from the contents of the album, its owner traveled to Tehran at least once and purchased there a large number of photographic prints from Sevruguin's studio. The photographer sold photographs of ancient and contemporary monuments and architecture (cats. 35, 36), as well as his series of portraits of men and women in costume or staged in scenes of daily life (cats. 26, 29, 30, 37).

Sevruguin and other contemporary photographers inside and outside Iran took up the themes of daily life and festivities in domestic settings. These images were often created as studio tableaux, as seen in the water pipe smoker and the *Reclining Woman with Dancer and Musicians* (cat. 37), but were also posed outdoors, as evidenced by the scenes of a bathhouse and a family (discussed below). Iranians and foreign visitors readily purchased such genre scenes for photograph albums.

A number of Iranian photographers produced images of people and life in Qajar Iran, yet Sevruguin had a dominance over the market that is attested by the sheer number of his photographs that survive in albums assembled by Iranians and non-Iranians alike.[44] The album with the green cover, for example, includes the photograph of the photographer's room as its final image (above, Fig. 5), as well as a different photograph of the female smoker in Figure 6.

The photographs of the female smoker are examples of commercial photographs intended to be sold to an eager public, but other photographs of women cannot be categorized so easily. The four photographs of Iranian women in a small album (Fig. 7) at first appear to be private photographs of women posing without veils, yet the captions, which were inscribed on the photographic negative, identify them as a group of performers led by a woman called ʿAziz, who appears in three-quarter profile at lower right. These photographs could have had a promotional or commercial purpose, even though their simplicity sets them apart from the more typical scenes arranged and captured in commercial studios.

Qajar interest in representations of women and their mobility within society can be discerned not only in the albums themselves, but also in the ways that they were displayed in public. In a photograph of a fruit and nut store, for example, diverse prints of men and women hang in the background (Fig. 8).[45] From many written and visual sources we know that photographs and prints, especially prints depicting women, were a popular form of decoration in commercial and domestic spaces throughout Qajar Iran, from the Gulistan Palace to small houses in the countryside. While European travelers like Ella Sykes were surprised that Iranians bought prints of Western women smoking, those same travelers did not find it odd that they themselves acquired photographs of Iranian women smoking (Fig. 6).[46] Even as many European visitors tried to articulate their cultural differences from Iranians, both groups clearly shared an interest in printing and photography. Colored prints were of especial interest, since photography was still a monotone medium.[47] Efforts to add color to photographs included hand-coloring, as seen in the image of men in a public bathhouse (Fig. 9).[48]

In fact, the desire to experience color photography dates back to the inception of the medium, when daguerreotypes were sometimes painted and photographers soon began to ponder how to fully reproduce color through a photographic process.[49] In the West, the hand-colored photograph had been preceded by the hand-colored print; in Iran, where printing was introduced later than elsewhere, photographs and prints came onto the scene at more or less the same time. David J. Roxburgh and Mary McWilliams demonstrate in their essays how monochrome photographic images were adapted and transformed in the mediums of watercolor and painted lacquer wares. An interesting

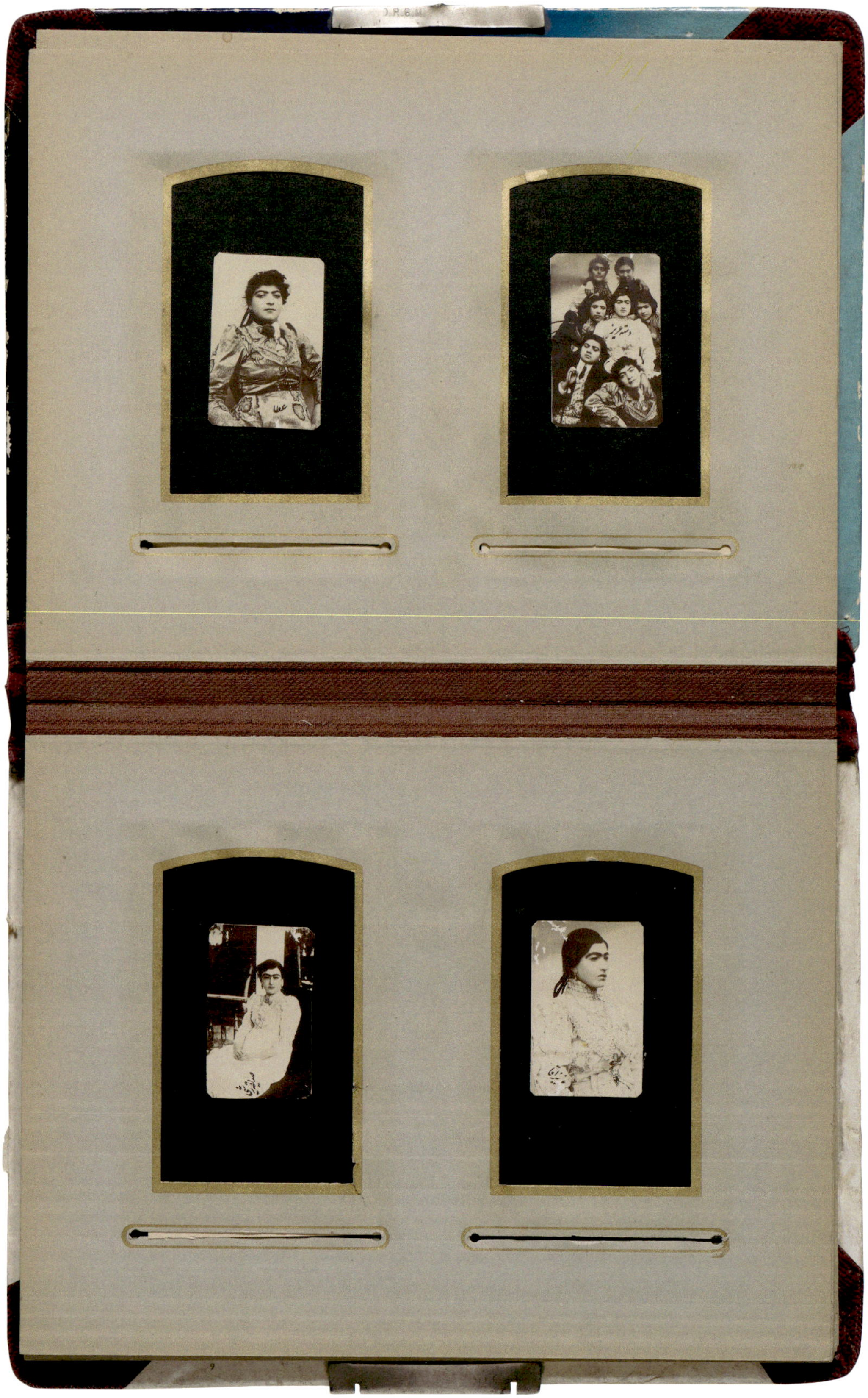

7 *Small Album with Photographs of Women*, late 19th century. For full information, see cat. 27, p. 140.

8 *Fruit Sellers Preparing for Festivities*, late 19th century. For full information, see cat. 33, p. 142.

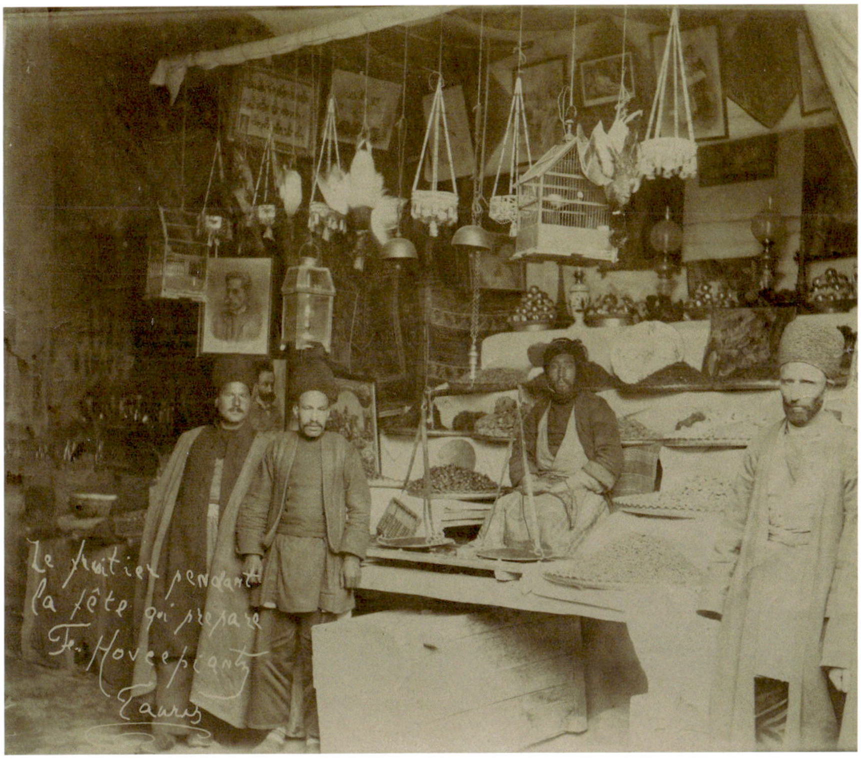

9 *Persian Bath*, late 19th century. For full information, see cat. 26, p. 140.

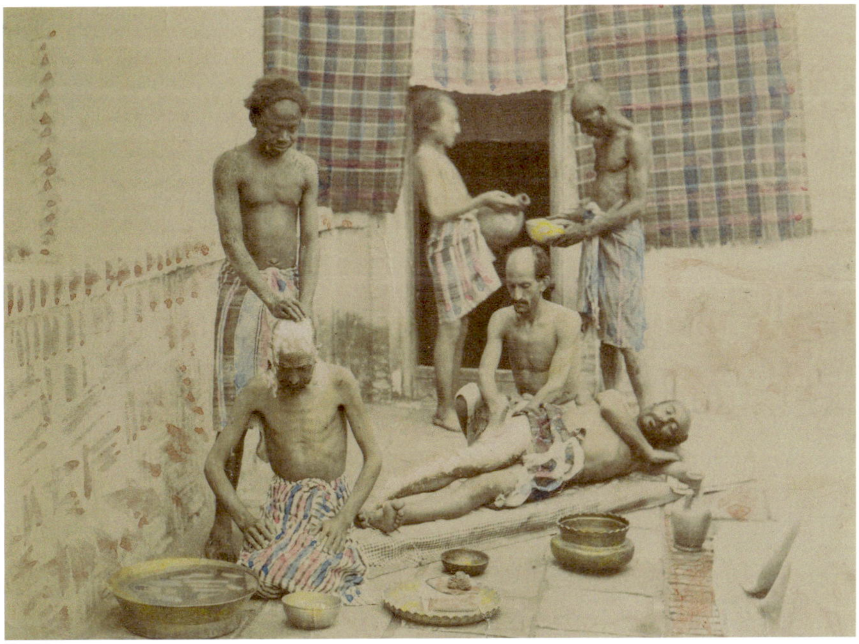

example is a pen box with depictions of seated and reclining women (Fig. 10), which was likely modeled after prints and studio photographs. The depiction of the women in the center of the pen box is reminiscent of staged domestic scenes set in a fictional, exclusive domestic space (*andarūn*) or harem, yet they were actually photographed in the studio.

A comparable image is the colored print of a Persian family (Fig. 11), which was produced on the basis of a photograph (Fig. 12). The print is a so-called photochrome, a version of the chromolithograph.[50] This process was one of the first attempts to print multiple copies in color instead of coloring each copy by hand. In the photochrome process, the photographic negative was inscribed on a lithographic stone and then each color was added to it as a separate layer.[51] Photochromes depicted people and places all over the world, but most were produced in Zurich.[52]

The polychrome version of the Persian family demonstrates yet again the remarkable mobility of images in the 19th century. Photographs and prints moved in and out of Iran and often returned in a different version. A photograph taken and sold in Tehran might have a second life when turned into a print published in a book, included in an illustrated journal, or made into a postcard. The photograph of the Persian family (Fig. 12), for example, discussed above, was also transformed into a postcard[53] and ultimately appeared on the cover of the American newspaper *The New-York Tribune* in 1906 (Fig. 13). Sometimes these images made their way back to Iran, as in illustrated European journals, which were very popular in the country. After their arrival, these printed reproductions could inspire further mediations in other versions and mediums. Such commercial photographs and prints functioned very differently from the photographs taken by Nasir al-Din Shah, which did not leave the confines of the Gulistan Palace during his lifetime and were not intended for viewing outside the royal circle. Because of the many copies of sub-royal images, their constant circulation, and their translation into other mediums, it is not always possible to reconstruct their genesis. All the same, it is important to remember that these images were made and disseminated within a connected, cosmopolitan sphere.

New Technologies, New Audiences, and the Amateur Photographer

During Nasir al-Din Shah's long reign, photography changed from a medium available only to the court to one of broad commercial and public interest. While photography and printing became more affordable than before, it would take several more years before photography studios were open to customers of modest means.[54] Another dimension of these technological developments and their dissemination was the figure of the amateur or photography enthusiast. Most early photographers based in Iran, professional or amateur, had learned how to take photographs and had purchased their equipment outside Iran. At the end of the 19th century, however, specialized stores like the Tehran

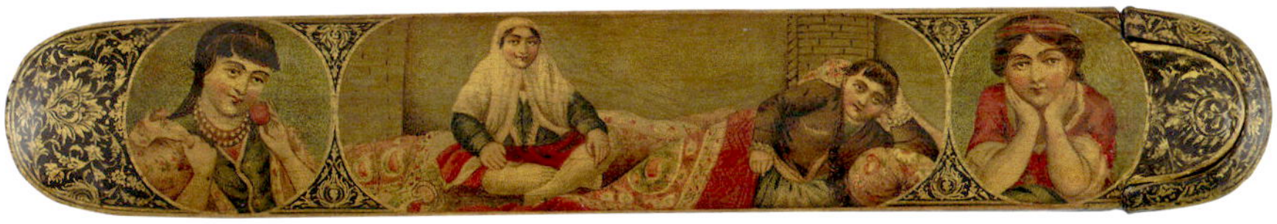

10 *Pen Box with Seated and Reclining Women*, second half 19th century. For full information, see cat. 74, p. 156.

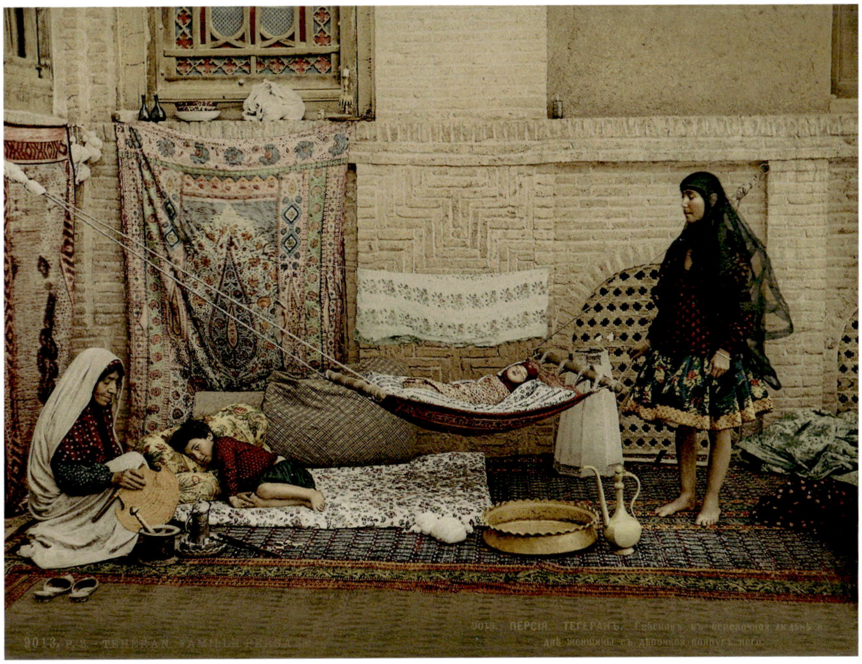

11 *The Persian Family*, 1904–12. For full information, see cat. 31, p. 142.

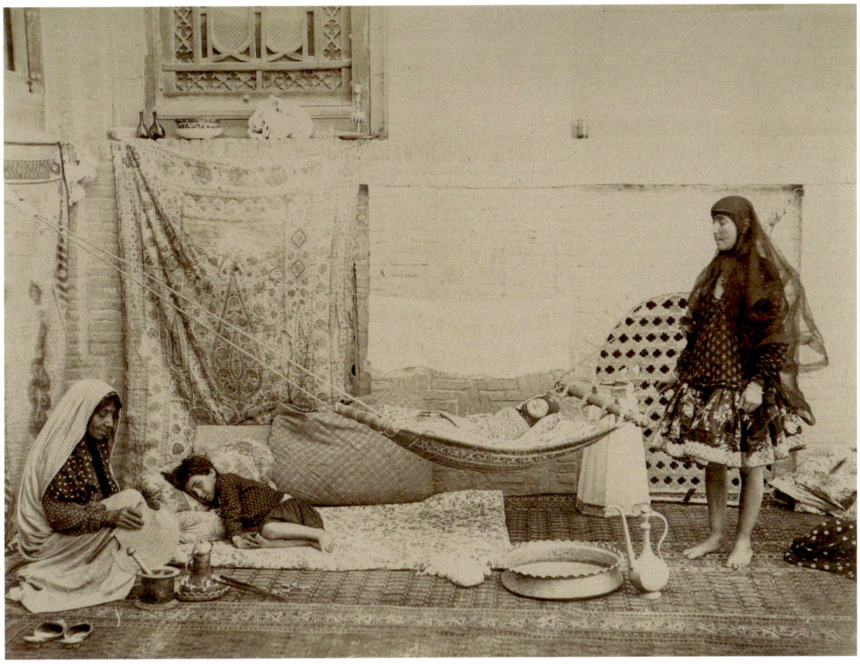

12 *The Persian Family*, late 19th century. For full information, see cat. 30, p. 142.

Toko began to sell photographic equipment. This store, partially owned by Dutch photography enthusiast Albert Hotz (1855–1930), was located on Lalazar Avenue,[55] one of the places symbolizing a new, modern Tehran in the era of Nasir al-Din Shah (Figs. 14, 15).[56]

Hotz's album of photographs (to which Fig. 15 belongs) contains pictures he himself had taken during his travels, as well as others that he had purchased from professional photographers. The photographs that he captured were printed in platinotype by London-based photographer John Thomson. A permanent and expensive process preferred by art photographers, the platinum print process—which, like the albumen print, was achieved through contact-printing—was popular from the late 1870s to 1900 and dominated salon walls at the turn of the 20th century.[57] Not all of the photographs that Hotz purchased can be attributed today, as in the case of the photographs of the Tehran Toko. But in his surviving collection of 15 photographic albums and several portfolios of single photographs now at the Leiden University Library in the Netherlands, one can see that Hotz favored photographs taken by Sevruguin and German photographer Ernst Höltzer, who was based in Isfahan. Hotz's passion for photography accompanied him on all his trips: in addition to the many photographs he took in Iran, he also purchased prints by famous photographers who worked in the Middle East, including Pascal Sébah and Félix Bonfils.

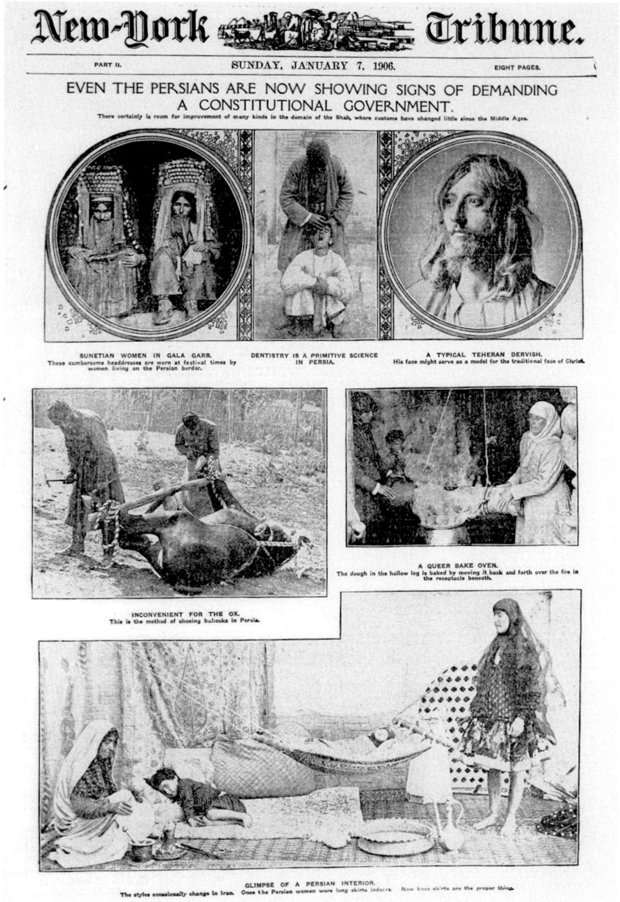
New-York Tribune.

PART II. SUNDAY, JANUARY 7, 1906. EIGHT PAGES.

EVEN THE PERSIANS ARE NOW SHOWING SIGNS OF DEMANDING A CONSTITUTIONAL GOVERNMENT.

There certainly is room for improvement of many kinds in the domain of the Shah, where customs have changed little since the Middle Ages.

SUNETIAN WOMEN IN GALA GARB.
These cumbersome headdresses are worn at festival times by women living on the Persian border.

DENTISTRY IS A PRIMITIVE SCIENCE IN PERSIA.

A TYPICAL TEHERAN DERVISH.
His face might serve as a model for the traditional face of Christ.

A QUEER BAKE OVEN.
The dough in the hollow log is baked by moving it back and forth over the fire in the receptacle beneath.

INCONVENIENT FOR THE OX.
This is the method of shoeing bullocks in Persia.

GLIMPSE OF A PERSIAN INTERIOR.
The styles occasionally change in Iran. Once the Persian women wore long skirts indoors. Now knee skirts are the proper thing.

13 *New-York Tribune*, January 7, 1906. Chronicling America: Historic American Newspapers, Library of Congress, Washington, D.C.

Matching Hotz in his passion for photography, ʿAli Khan Vali (1846–1902), the longtime governor of the province of Azerbaijan in northwestern Iran, was one of the most interesting early enthusiasts of photography in Iran.[58] His masterpiece—an album of enormous dimensions, containing more than 1,400 albumen photographs annotated with detailed handwritten texts across its 440 pages—is being displayed publicly for the first time in the present exhibition.[59] The album chronicles ʿAli Khan Vali's life and his accomplishments; unlike the photographic reports, which he submitted to the king, it functions as his personal archive. It is an object of remembrance, not intended to be circulated or multiplied. Indeed, circulation would not have been possible, as the album is too unwieldy to be carried by a single person.[60]

The album's photographs depict many kinds of people: men and women, old and young, Iranians and foreigners, people of all social classes, from slave to king. Even a large number of the photographs focused on architecture or landscapes include people in those environments (or at least evidence of

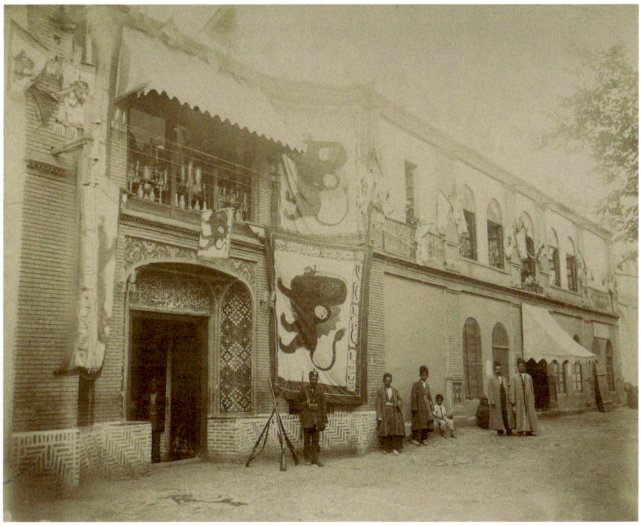

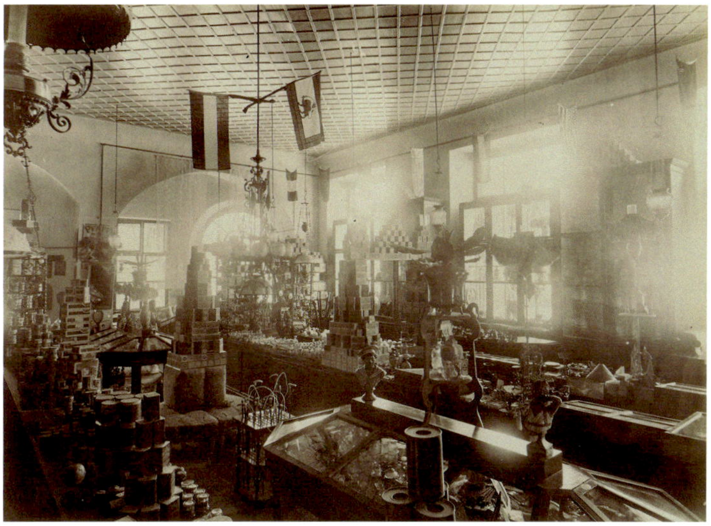

14 *Exterior View of Toko Department Store (Tehran)*, 1893–1903. Albumen print; folio: 40 × 32.2 cm (15¾ × 12¹¹⁄₁₆ in.); photograph: 28.3 × 22 cm (11⅛ × 8¹¹⁄₁₆ in.). Collection of Azita Bina and Elmar W. Seibel.

15 *Interior View of Toko Department Store (Tehran)*, 1893–1903. For full information, see cat. 39, p. 144.

human inhabitation). The album features self-portraits of ʿAli Khan Vali, photographs of close family members—especially children—many friends, and even famous Qajar grandees. The album includes purchased photographs, like the portraits of Nasir al-Din Shah, and photographs taken of photographs, like those of Mirza Riza Kirmani, who assassinated Nasir al-Din Shah in 1896. When ʿAli Khan Vali came across something of interest, he most likely documented it photographically, encompassing everything from people, events, and landscapes to calligraphies, drawings, maps, and other photographs—all manner of things that he wanted to show and preserve in his album. In the service of the Qajar court, ʿAli Khan Vali quelled rebellions, governed cities and provinces, improved infrastructure, and occasionally accompanied Nasir al-Din Shah on his travels. He documented many of these events with photographs dating from 1862 to roughly 1900.

During his childhood, ʿAli Khan Vali spent an extended period of time in St. Petersburg, where he accompanied his father, the diplomat Muhammad Qasim Khan Vali. It was there—a key location for the Qajar elite to have photographs taken, to purchase equipment, and to study the technique—that the young ʿAli Khan Vali acquired his initial training in photography. Besides photography, he also studied French, history, geography, and geometry. After Muhammad Qasim Khan retired in 1850, he took his son on a tour of Berlin, Brussels, Paris, London, and Istanbul. Following his return to Tehran, ʿAli Khan Vali completed his studies at the Dar al-Funun. All this he describes on the first pages of his album in a condensed biography (Fig. 16).[61]

In 1879, ʿAli Khan Vali began his service as governor in the historical city of Maragha, and started to take large numbers of photographs. He also purchased prints from other photographers and incorporated those into the album.[62] The album combines images from his time in Maragha, Tabriz, and Urmia, and also

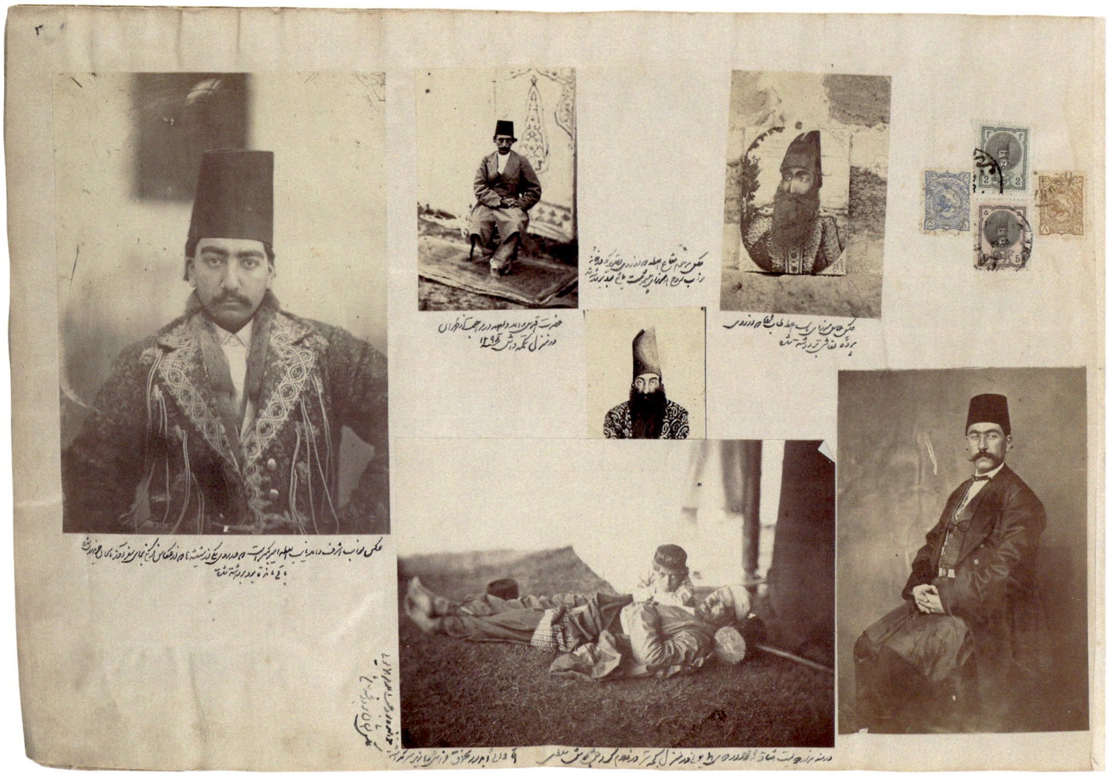

16 Pages 2 (right) and 3 (left) from the *Album of Photographs by ʿAli Khan Vali*, 1862–1900. For full information, see cat. 24, p. 140.

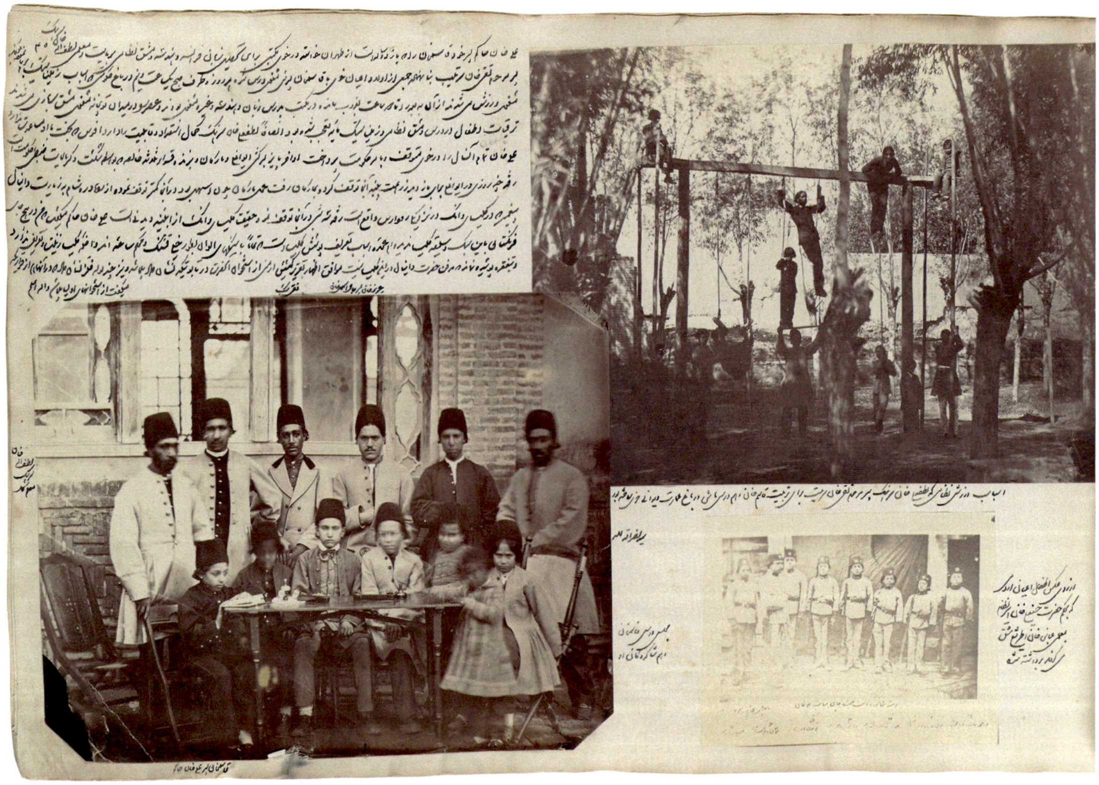

17 Pages 44 (right) and 45 (left) from the *Album of Photographs by ʿAli Khan Vali*, 1862–1900. For full information, see cat. 24, p. 140.

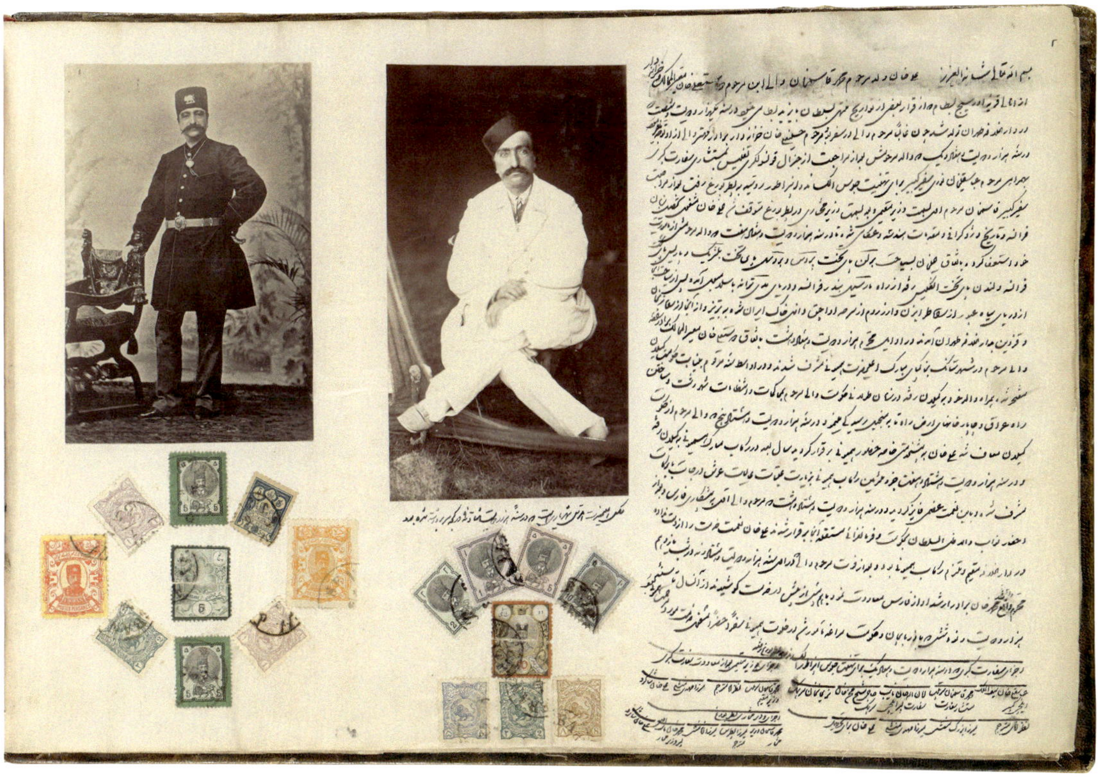

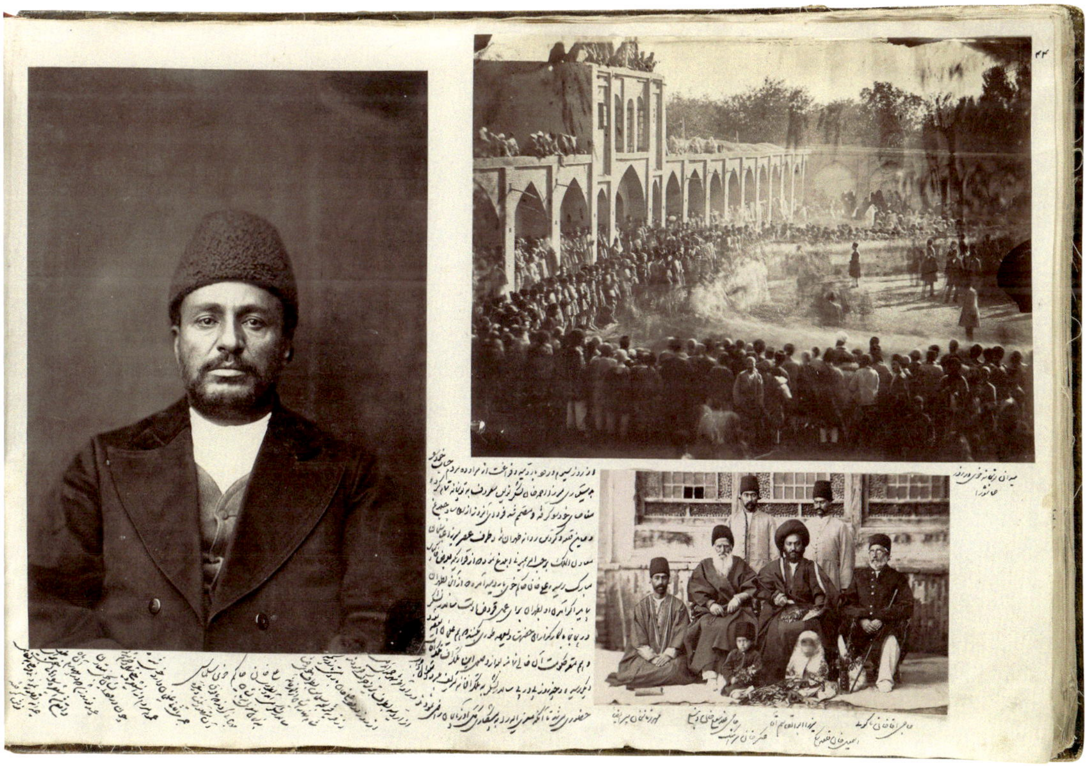

documents his travels throughout Armenia. While governor, ʿAli Khan Vali became a devoted reformer and dedicated his energies to the urbanization of the region and the reform of the school system.[63] He documented those activities with his camera.

On page 44 of the album, a self-portrait of ʿAli Khan Vali captures the viewer's gaze (Fig. 17). To the right of his portrait is a depiction of the *ʿāshūrā* festivities in the *Maydān-i tūp-khāna* (a square for military exercises) in Khoy. The photograph shows the advances and limits of photography at that time. As exposure time decreased and shutter speed increased, it had become possible to take un-posed photographs while outside.[64] The first photographs of the masses, at public events like *ʿāshūrā* festivities, funeral ceremonies, or demonstrations, date to that time. Yet as the blurred images show, the technology was not completely suited for what we would today think of as an action shot. Another example of this change in technology is a photograph featuring a large group of women who are likely participating in an *ʿāshūrā* ceremony and who have clearly not posed for the photographer (Fig. 18).

On the left page of Figure 17, ʿAli Khan Vali has documented the progress of the school he established in Khoy. The school provided lessons in French, geometry, and military exercises.[65] On the lower left, ʿAli Khan Vali's son, Qasim Khan, appears in the center of a group portrait of students at the school.[66] In the photograph to the right, the young students can be seen in Austrian military uniforms. According to ʿAli Khan Vali's notations, the students began each school day with an hour and a half of gymnastics, the equipment for which would have been set up in the government garden and can be seen in the

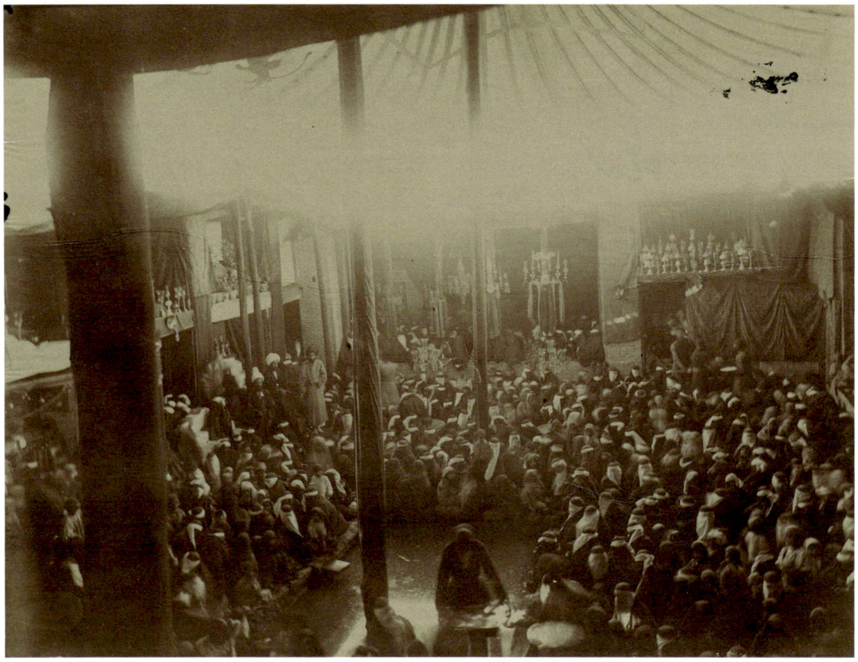

18 *Women Attending a Public Performance*, late 19th century. For full information, see cat. 32, p. 142.

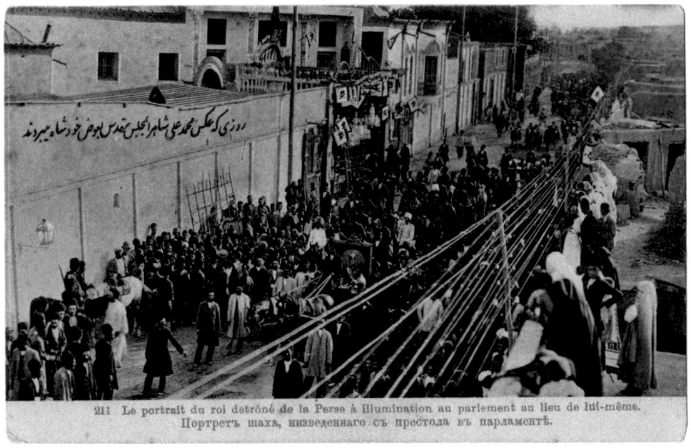

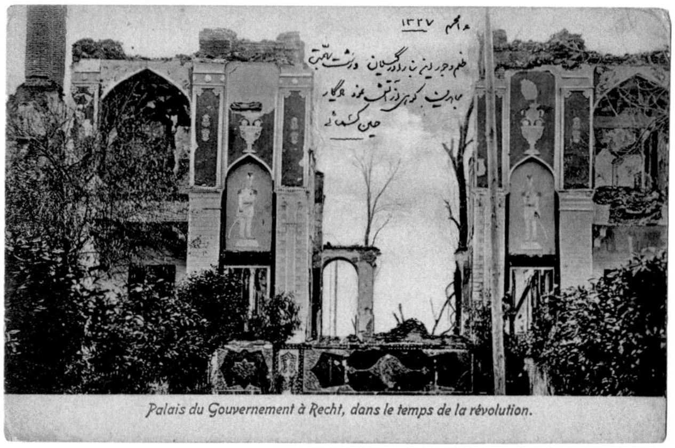

19 *Procession with Portrait of Muhammad ʿAli Shah at the Opening of the Parliament in Tehran*, c. 1907. For full information, see cat. 40, p. 144.

20 *Destroyed Palace in Rasht*, 1906–11. For full information, see cat. 41, p. 144.

photograph on the top right of the page. They then would have been occupied with lessons until their day ended with military exercises in Tupkhana Square.

People of the lower and middle classes appear in the two outdoor images of *ʿāshūrā* festivities (Figs. 17, 18). However, it was not until the Pahlavi period that people with modest incomes would be able to afford a visit to a photographer's studio, much less own a camera themselves.[67] Even so, photography would play an important, and still very much understudied, role in the Constitutional Revolution that brought the Qajar era to its close.

Depicting Change: Photographing Political Events in the Streets

When ʿAli Khan Vali documented his reforms in photographs and writing, he became his own archivist, but he did not plan on a large circulation for these images. For the photographers and publishers active during the Constitutional Revolution, however, a wide circulation of imagery was critical to their goals. The photographic postcard would become the main medium for the circulation of images among the masses during this time, depicting political events—from demonstrations to executions—and introducing the revolutionaries in text and image.[68] Collected by Iranians and non-Iranians, these postcards were sent all over the world; their influence can be gauged by the sheer number that were produced and by the fact that Muhammad ʿAli Shah (r. 1907–1909) imprisoned and executed a photographer for taking portraits of the supporters of the constitution during his crackdown on the Constitutionalists in 1907.[69]

Photographers and publishers documented Muhammad ʿAli Shah's antagonism to the constitutionalist movement. When the Constitutionalists had forced the king to abdicate, thereby rendering him unable to fulfill his ceremonial duties at the parliament, a photographer produced visual evidence of his absence. A photograph reproduced as a postcard (Fig. 19) records how the parliamentarians carried the king's likeness into parliament so that the events could proceed in the king's absence. The Constitutionalists' calculated usage of royal portraiture for their own means was significant, but equally important was the fact that the event was immediately captured photographically and distributed on postcards, circulating evidence both of the Constitutionalist success in forcing Muhammad ʿAli Shah to step down from the throne and of their adherence to customs and traditions despite radical political change. The court was never able to match the Constitutionalists in their adoption of the new medium for political purposes, and accordingly very few postcards printed by royalist publishers exist.

One of the most arresting postcards of this period depicts the ruined palace of Rasht, decorated with paintings of life-sized soldiers in front of a bleak sky (Fig. 20). The French caption briefly notes that this is the governmental palace of Rasht during the time of the revolution. The Persian caption is quite different; besides denoting that this card is "a souvenir of Rasht," we find a poem by the revolutionary poet Husayn Kasmaʾi (1862–1921)[70]: "A mountain of fire turned the injustice and tyranny of this building into a memorial, thanks to the efforts of the Mujahiddin." The card was published in Tehran by Sayyid ʿAbd al-Rahim Kashani, who himself was involved in the Constitutional Revolution as the head of a revolutionary group called the *Anjuman-i Fāṭimīya*.[71] The members of the group claimed to be *sayyids*, or descendants of the Prophet Muhammad. Unlike some of the revolutionary writers of the upper classes, Kashani made sure to represent all strata of society in his depiction of the struggle for political change. Kashani would become a parliamentarian after the revolution, before which he had published political journals and postcards and sold them in his store at the Sirah-i Amir junction in Tehran.[72]

From the photographs taken by and for the king, which never left the palace, to the widely circulated postcards depicting photographs of political events, photography—its technology and its audiences—underwent rapid change and development in Iran in little more than half a century. In the early decades, technical development was often linked to polyglotism and travel, and St. Petersburg initially served Iranians as the major focal point for acquiring photographic knowledge and equipment. The consumer base widened from court circles to the upper and middle classes when the daguerreotype process, which created a unique image, was replaced with the collodion process, which produced several copies of the image at a more affordable price. As increasingly varied methods of photographic reproduction came into play, the arena in which photographs appeared expanded from private spaces to public shops, from personal albums to print publications. In these few decades, photography evolved from a court curiosity to an agent for social and political change.

Mira Xenia Schwerda is a Ph.D. candidate in the Center for Middle Eastern Studies and the Ph.D. program in History of Art and Architecture at Harvard University.

Notes

1 I'timād al-Salṭana, *Mir'āt al-buldān-i nāṣirī*, vol. 3 (Tehran, 1295 H [1878–79]), 20–22. Translation as cited in Iraj Afshar, "Some Remarks on the Early History of Photography in Iran," in *Qajar Iran: Political, Social, and Cultural Change, 1800–1925*, ed. Clifford Edmund Bosworth and Carole Hillenbrand (Costa Mesa, Calif.: Mazda, 1983), 262.

2 The daguerreotype process was invented by Frenchmen Jacques Daguerre (1787–1851) and Nicéphore Niépce (1765–1833). On January 7, 1839, it was introduced to the public through a presentation by François Arago at the Academy of Sciences in Paris. See Geoffrey Batchen, *Burning with Desire: The Conception of Photography* (Cambridge, Mass.: MIT Press, 1997).

3 See Chahryar Adle and Yahya Zoka, "Notes et documents sur la photographie iranienne et son histoire," *Studia Iranica* 12 (2) (1983): 253; and Iraj Afshar, "Some Remarks on the Early History of Photography in Iran," 261–62.

4 On Jules Richard, see Adle and Zoka, "Notes et documents sur la photographie iranienne et son histoire," 252–57; and *Encyclopaedia Iranica*, s.v. "Rishār Khān," by Shireen Mahdavi, http://www.iranicaonline.org/articles/rishar-khan (accessed August 22, 2016).

5 Adle and Zoka, "Notes et documents sur la photographie iranienne et son histoire," 253.

6 On Malik Qasim Mirza, see ibid., 262–75. It is unclear when Malik Qasim Mirza took his first daguerreotypes. See ibid., 251–52, 260.

7 Eugène Flandin, *Voyage en Perse de mm. Eugène Flandin, peintre, et Pascal Coste, architecte*, vol. 1 (Paris: Gide et J. Baudry, 1851), 151–57.

8 While none of Richard's photographs have survived, the painter Kamal al-Mulk made several paintings based on his daguerreotypes. See Adle and Zoka, "Notes et documents sur la photographie iranienne et son histoire," 258–60. A recent photographic copy, which had been taken of a daguerreotype self-portrait of Malik Qasim, exists, but the original was most likely destroyed. The original must have been taken sometime between 1839 and 1847. See Yaḥyā Ẕukā, *Tārīkh-i 'akkāsī va 'akkāsān-i pīshgām dar Īrān* (Tehran: Shirkat-i Intishārāt-i 'Ilmī va Farhangī, 1997), 8–17; Adle and Zoka, "Notes et documents sur la photographie iranienne et son histoire," 271–72; and *Encyclopaedia Iranica*, s.v. "Daguerreotype," by Chahryar Adle, vol. 6, fasc. 6, 577–78. An album of Malik Qasim's daguerreotypes dedicated to Nasir al-Din Shah and dated to 1850, perhaps the oldest Iranian album, is preserved at the *ālbum-khāna*, Gulistan Palace, Tehran. A copy of it has recently been made available to researchers at the Gulistan (inv. no. 1330/1912). Yet, as the original is still inaccessible, I was not able to conduct further research on this potentially important example of early photography for this essay. See Adle and Zoka, "Notes et documents sur la photographie iranienne et son histoire," 267, 273.

9 On the back of the image, the name of the photographer and the location of his studio are inscribed in Russian and French (see cat. 22). The nationality of Schönfeld is unclear, but his name, the spelling of his first name in Cyrillic (Vil'gel'm), his language skills, and his business contacts in Russia suggest that he might have been a German trained in France, like many other photographers of his time. As most researchers have emphasized his training in Paris and the French text on his labels, he has been identified as French, even though documentary evidence for this does not exist. Schönfeld is a perfect example of the cosmopolitan, polyglot, and mobile early pioneers in photography. On this particular daguerreotype, see Muḥammad Riżā Ṭahmāsbpūr, "Kashf-i nakhustīn dāgiru'tīp, az taṣvīr-i yak Irānī," *'Aks* 244 (Khurdād 1388 H [June 2009]): 33–35; and Jennifer Y. Chi, ed., *The Eye of the Shah: Qajar Court Photography and the Persian Past* (New York: Institute for the Study of the

Ancient World at New York University, 2015), 1, 178. Tahmasbpur believes that the sitter might be Amir Nizam Garrusi.

10 On Schönfeld, see [Gosudarstvennyi tsentr fotografii], *Sankt-Peterburg v fotografiiakh serediny XIX–nachala XX veka: katalog vystavki* (St. Petersburg: Rosfoto, 2008), 105; and his studio notices and advertisements published in the Russian photography database "Stereoscop" (https://stereoscop.ru/photograph/шенфельд-вильгельм). I would like to thank Elena Bulat of the Weissman Preservation Center at Harvard Library and Natalia Avetyan of the Hermitage Museum in St. Petersburg for this information. For another example of Schönfeld's work, a hand-colored daguerreotype portrait of a woman, see Jochen Voigt, *Der gefrorene Augenblick: Daguerreotypie in Sachsen 1839–1860. Inkunabeln der Photographie in sächsischen Sammlungen* (Chemnitz, Germany: Edition Mobilis, 2004), 21.

11 Alexei Loginov writes: "The first professional daguerreotype specialists working in Russia came from abroad. All of them had already worked in various cities of Europe." See Alexei Loginov, "Russian Empire," in *Encyclopedia of Nineteenth-Century Photography*, vol. 2, ed. John Hannavy (New York: Routledge, 2007), 1228.

12 See T. G. Saburova, *Dagerotip v Rossii: Sobranie Istoricheskogo muzeia: katalog* (Moscow: Gosudarstvennyi istoricheskii muzei, 2014), cat. 258; and T. G. Saburova, *U istokov fotoiskusstva: sobranie dagereotipov Gosudarstvennogo Istoricheskogo muzeia* (Moscow: Izd-vo Art-Rodnik, 1999), cat. 259. I would like to thank Ludmila Rogova of the Multimedia Art Museum in Moscow and Tatiana Saburova of the National History Museum in Moscow for their efforts to help us acquire the reproduction rights for the image.

13 Saburova lists several daguerreotypes taken between 1850 and 1854 in her catalogue; see Saburova, *Dagerotip v Rossii.*

14 The *carte de visite* was a small photograph (around 9 × 6 cm), usually a portrait, glued to a piece of card, which was often imprinted by the photographer. It had the appearance of a calling or visiting card, but was rarely used for that purpose. It was first mentioned in 1851, but only patented in 1854 by French photographer Disdéri. See John Plunkett, "Carte-de-visite," in *Encyclopedia of Nineteenth-Century Photography*, 1:276–77. Several souvenir photographs depicting Qajar gentlemen in Paris, Tiflis, Moscow, and at many other locations are preserved in the collection of the Brooklyn Museum. For an example of a *carte de visite* from St. Petersburg, see Brooklyn Museum, object number 1997.3.98; viewable online at https://www.brooklynmuseum.org/opencollection/objects/161203 (accessed July 7, 2016).

15 See *Encyclopaedia Iranica*, s.v. "Dār al-Fonūn," by John Gurney and Negin Nabavi; and Maryam Ekhtiar, "Nasir al-Din Shah and the Dar al-Funun: The Evolution of an Institution," *Iranian Studies* 34 (1–4) (2001).

16 I'timād al-Saltana, *Mir'āt al-buldān-i nāṣirī*, 3:20–22. Translation from Afshar, "Some Remarks on the Early History of Photography in Iran," 261.

17 For the *carte de visite*, see Chi, *Eye of the Shah*, 66, 187. On Farrukh Khan Amin al-Dawla, see *Encyclopaedia Iranica*, s.v. "Amīn-al-Dawla, Farrok Khan Gaffārī," by F. Gaffary, available at http://www.iranicaonline.org/articles/amin-al-dawla-abu-taleb-farrok-khan-gaffari-1227-88-1812-71-a-high-ranking-qajar-official (accessed September 11, 2016).

18 See Adle and Zoka, "Notes et documents sur la photographie iranienne et son histoire," 257. On translation in the Qajar era, see Farzin Vejdani, *Making History in Iran: Education, Nationalism, and Print Culture* (Stanford, Calif.: Stanford University Press, 2015), 17–34.

19 Mahallati had been a student of the Dar al-Funun and later studied in France. The manuscript of *Kitāb-i 'aks* is kept at the National Library of Iran, #F/580. See Muhammad Reza Tahmasbpour, "Photography in Iran: A Chronology," *History of Photography* 37 (1) (2013): 7. For other Qajar sources on photography, see 'Abbās Raḥīmī, *Qājārīya va āmūzish-i 'akkāsī* (Tehran: Farzān Rūz, 2012).

20 See Bryan Clark Green, "Wet Collodion Negative," in *Encyclopedia of Nineteenth-Century Photography*, 2:1485–86; and the J. Paul Getty Museum's video *Photography: The Wet Collodion Process*, available at http://www.getty.edu/art/collection/video/142887/photography:-the-wet-collodion-process (accessed July 7, 2016).

21 See the Getty's *Photography* video, at the 40-second mark.

22 See Green, "Wet Collodion Negative," 1486.

23 According to Green, "Exposure times ranged from less than one second to several minutes, depending upon the intensity of the light, and the age and quality of the collodion." Ibid.

24 Aqa Riza had been announced as the official court photographer in 1863, and the Royal Photography Atelier (*'akkās-khāna-yi mubāraka-yi humāyūnī*) had been established at the Gulistan Palace in 1858. See Tahmasbpour, "Photography in Iran," 7–8.

25 The studio was managed by 'Abbas 'Ali Bayk, a student of Aqa Riza. See ibid., 9.

26 Muḥammad Ḥasan Khān I'timād al-Salṭana, *Ma'āthir wa al-āthār: Chihil sāl-i tārīkh-i Īrān: dar dawra-yi Pādishāh-i Nāṣir al-Dīn Shāh*, ed. Īrāj Āfshār, vol. 1 (Tehran: Shirkat-i Intishārāt-i Asāṭīr, 1363– H [1984–]), 94; translation from Afshar, "Some Remarks on the Early History of Photography in Iran," 262.

27 On Sevruguin, see Ẓukā, *Tārīkh-i 'akkāsī va 'akkāsān-i pīshgām dar Īrān*, 136–41; Fredrick N. Bohrer, ed., *Sevruguin and the Persian Image: Photographs of Iran, 1870–1930* (Washington, D.C.:

Arthur M. Sackler Gallery, Smithsonian Institution; Seattle: University of Washington Press, 1999); and L. A. Ferydoun Barjesteh van Waalwijk van Doorn and Gillian M. Vogelsang-Eastwood, eds., *Sevruguin's Iran: Late Nineteenth Century Photographs of Iran from the National Museum of Ethnology in Leiden, the Netherlands* (Tehran: Zaman; Rotterdam: Barjesteh van Waalwijk van Doorn, 1999). The studio was located on the ʿAla al-Dawla street (later called Firdawsi Avenue), Tehran. See Afshar, "Some Remarks on the Early History of Photography in Iran," 272; and Corien J. M. Vuurman, "Antoin Sevruguin (ca. 1840–1933). A Beloved Photographer, in Iran and the West," in Barjesteh van Waalwijk van Doorn and Vogelsang-Eastwood, *Sevruguin's Iran*, 170. Photographs of the exterior of the studio can be found in Ẕukā, *Tārīkh-i ʿakkāsī va ʿakkāsān-i pīshgām dar Īrān*, 139.

28 The name Sevruguin is not mentioned in the manuscript, merely "Antoin Khan," which is how Sevruguin was referred to in Iran. Even though the text has been attributed to Sevruguin, this is not completely certain. Another French speaker with the same first name might have lived in Iran. Multiple references to an Antoin Khan, who was a translator, exist. See also Afshar, "Some Remarks on the Early History of Photography in Iran," 274.

29 On the manuscript, see Raḥīmī, *Qājārīya va āmūzish-i ʿakkāsī*, 221–25. Rahimi believes that the manuscript is by Antoin Sevruguin.

30 On Ermakov, see Lika Mamatsashvili and Herman Maes, *Masters of 19th-Century Photography: Dimitri Ermakov. Photographer and Collector* (Amsterdam: Pegasus, 2014).

31 His photographs were reprinted in countless travelogues but often without his name. Exceptions are Ella C. Sykes, *Through Persia on a Side-Saddle* (Philadelphia: J. B. Lippincott, 1898); and Ella R. Durand, *An Autumn Tour in Western Persia* (Westminster: A. Constable & Co., 1902).

32 See Vuurman, "Antoin Sevruguin (ca. 1840–1933)," 169.

33 For a reproduction of Sevruguin's photographic imprint, see Bohrer, *Sevruguin and the Persian Image*, 35.

34 On Armenian merchants in Iran during the Safavid period and their trading networks, see Ina Baghdiantz McCabe, *The Shah's Silk for Europe's Silver: The Eurasian Trade of the Julfa Armenians in Safavid Iran and India, 1530–1750* (Atlanta: Scholars Press, 1999).

35 See Vuurman, "Antoin Sevruguin (ca. 1840–1933)," 169. Vuurman received her biographical information from an interview with Sevruguin's grandson; it is not based on written documentation.

36 In *Eye of the Shah*, the photograph of the studio was attributed to B. Agaiantz, based on Zuka's identification. However, the photograph is not signed and this attribution is not clear from the album itself. Zuka identified some photographs as by Agaiantz, even though they are signed "Sevruguin" in Cyrillic. See Ẕukā, *Tārīkh-i ʿakkāsī va ʿakkāsān-i pīshgām dar Īrān*, 197–205; and Chi, *Eye of the Shah*, 77, 188. See also notes 44 and 50, below. My thanks to Reza Sheikh for discussions on this matter.

37 Freer and Sackler Archives, Smithsonian Institution, Washington, D.C., "Antoin Sevruguin and Photographic Manipulation," http://www.asia.si.edu/iran-in-photographs/sevruguin-negatives.asp (accessed July 7, 2016).

38 Museum Volkenkunde, Leiden, 3311 and 3315. See reproductions of these photographs in Barjesteh van Waalwijk van Doorn and Vogelsang-Eastwood, *Sevruguin's Iran*, 35–36.

39 On the history and significance of the water pipe, see *Encyclopaedia Iranica*, s.v. "Galyān," by Shahnaz Razpush.

40 *Encyclopaedia Iranica*, s.v. "Tobacco," by Willem Floor, http://www.iranicaonline.org/articles/tobacco (accessed July 7, 2016). Also see Rudi Matthee, *The Pursuit of Pleasure: Drugs and Stimulants in Iranian History, 1500–1900* (Princeton, N.J.: Princeton University Press, 2005), chaps. 5 and 8.

41 There are several photographs featuring female smokers in the collection of the Freer and Sackler Archives, Smithsonian Institution, Washington, D.C.: FSA A.4 2.12.GN.43.10, FSA A.4 2.12.GN.30.03, FSA A. 4 2.12.Up.19, FSA A.4 2.12.GN.42.04, and FSA A.4 2.12.GN.53.03. The photographs of female smokers became a trope and were even taken up by female Western tourists; for example, see FSA A.4 2.12.GN.61.10. Some of the photographs of female smokers also have a distinct erotic connotation. The women's skirts are tucked up and their upper thighs are visible; see in particular FSA A.4 2.12.GN.43.10, FSA A.4 2.12.GN.30.03, and FSA A.4 2.12.Up.19. In contrast, see the distinctively casual and non-erotic qualities of Ernst Höltzer's depictions of female smokers in Ernst Höltzer, *Persien vor 113 Jahren. Text und Bilder*, ed. Mohammad Assemi (Tehran: Kultur und Kunstministeriums, Zentrum für die Persische Ethnologie, 1975), 306–7.

42 Bibliothèque nationale de France, Paris, Eo 967a.

43 The album is depicted in Chi, *Eye of the Shah*, 107, 191.

44 Sevruguin's photographs can be distinguished from other contemporary photographs set in Iran because many of them were numbered in a specific system and signed or stamped with his name; his photographs are also marked by his particular style, technique, and composition. However, in the 19th century, it was common to acquire someone else's photographs and reprint them under one's own name. Therefore, several images exist that have been attributed both to Sevruguin and to his mentor, Ermakov. A detailed study of appropriation and re-appropriation of photographs at this time in Iran and of

the Sevruguin-Ermakov corpus has not been published yet. See note 50, below.

45 On prints of women in Qajar houses, see Pamela Karimi, *Domesticity and Consumer Culture in Iran: Interior Revolutions of the Modern Era* (London: Routledge, 2013), 26–39; and Parviz Tanavoli, *European Women in Persian Houses: Western Images in Safavid and Qajar Iran*, ed. Sarah B. Sherrill and Moya Carey (London: I. B. Tauris, 2015). I would like to thank Megan Sarno for helping me render in English the unidiomatic French captions on the photograph of the fruit sellers and the revolutionary postcards.

46 Sykes regularly noted the many kinds of prints one encountered in Persian houses, including "a series of hideous German prints, representing languishing ladies in evening dress, smoking cigarettes"; see Sykes, *Through Persia on a Side-Saddle*, 73.

47 If one looks closely at photographs from this time, it becomes clear that they are often not "black and white" as they are called, but rather different shades of sepia, brown, or gray.

48 On hand-colored Iranian photographs, see Carmen Pérez González and Reza Sheikh, "From the Inner Sanctum: Men Who Were Trusted by the Kings," in Chi, *Eye of the Shah*, 150–51. An unpainted version of the top photograph in Figure 8 appears in the second Nafisi album in the Freer and Sackler Galleries. See http://www.asia.si.edu/iran-in-photographs/qajar-album-two.asp#page/19 (accessed September 11, 2016).

49 See William R. Alschuler, "Color Theory and Practice. 1800–1860," in *Encyclopedia of Nineteenth-Century Photography*, 2:315–18.

50 The photograph of the Persian family has been wrongly attributed to Ernst Höltzer. See Béla Kelényi and Iván Szántó, eds., *Artisans at the Crossroads: Persians Arts of the Qajar Period* (Budapest: Ferenc Hopp Museum of Eastern Asiatic Arts, 2010), 122, C.9.1.1. My thanks to Iván Szántó for discussing this matter. It is also listed in Ermakov's oeuvre, but this has to be taken with a grain of salt, as this photographer is known for passing off other people's photographs as his own. See Mamatsashvili and Maes, "Masters of 19th-Century Photography," 221.

51 See Peter Kunz and Bruno Weber, "The 19th-Century Photochrom Printing Process," in *Voyage en couleur: Photochromie, 1876–1914*, ed. Sabine Arqué et al. (Paris: Éditions Eyrolles, 2009), 180–87.

52 The company Photoglob, in Zurich, created photochromes of many places of touristic interest, including France, Morocco, and the Holy Land. However, it produced only two images featuring Iran: one is that of the Persian family with a hammock, the other depicts a young Persian woman (9014 P.Z.). The production of photochromes ended when color photography was introduced.

53 For the postcard, see Qāsim Ṣāfī, *Kārt-pustāl'hā-yi tārīkhī-yi Īrān* (Tehran: Mu'asassa-yi Farangī-yi Gustarish-i Hunar, 1989), 121. On the speed of reproduction and circulation of photographs in the late Qajar era, see my article focusing on the photographic documentation of the events after the assassination of Nasir al-Din Shah: Mira Xenia Schwerda, "Death on Display: Mirza Riza Kirmani, Prison Portraiture and the Depiction of Public Executions in Qajar Iran," *Middle East Journal of Culture and Communication* 8 (2–3) (2015).

54 See Reza Sheikh, "The Rise of the Kingly Citizen," in *Portrait Photographs from Isfahan: Faces in Transition, 1920–1950*, ed. Parīsā Damandān Nafīsī (London: Saqi, 2004).

55 On the Tehran Toko, see *Encyclopaedia Iranica*, s.v. "Dutch-Persian Relations," by Willem Floor. On Albert Hotz, see *Encyclopaedia Iranica*, s.v. "Hotz, Albert Paul Herman," by Cyrus Ala'i, http://www.iranicaonline.org/articles/hotz-albert-paul-herman (accessed September 11, 2016); and Theresia H. E. Engelberts, *A Persian from a Distant Land: Albertus Paulus Hermanus Hotz: A Memoir* (The Hague: Ansureß Press, 2000). On Hotz's interest in photography, see Corien Vuurman, *Nineteenth-Century Persia in the Photographs of Albert Hotz: Images from the Hotz Photograph Collection of Leiden University Library, The Netherlands* (Rotterdam: Barjesteh van Waalwijk van Doorn, 2011).

56 The photograph of the exterior of the Tehran Toko shows the store on the right. It has been captioned in German as *Teheran, Regierungshaus, Photographisches Geschäft (ganz rechts außen, das Schild gerade noch leserlich)* (Tehran, governmental building, store for photographic equipment [on the far right, the sign just visible]).

57 The platinotype was a version of the platinum print marketed by the British company Willis. Platinum prints were extremely popular with art photographers. According to Mike Ware, "By the close of the century, more platinotypes could be seen on the salon walls than any other print medium: the process had achieved pre-eminence." See Mike Ware, "Platinum Print," in *Encyclopedia of Nineteenth-Century Photography*, 1136–37.

58 On 'Ali Khan Vali, see Ẕukā, *Tārīkh-i 'akkāsī va 'akkāsān-i pīshgām dar Īrān*, 66–74.

59 The album is on loan to the Special Collections, Fine Arts Library, Harvard University, AliA.0001-0300 AKP111. It has been completely digitized and can be viewed online: http://nrs.harvard.edu/urn-3:FHCL:1125271 (accessed July 7, 2016). The album's text has been transcribed and published in Aṣghar Muḥammad'zāda, ed., *Āẕarbāyjan va Vālī-yi 'akkās: Bar 'asās-i nuskha'hā-yi khaṭṭī va ālbūm-i 'Alī Khān Vālī* (Tehran: Nashr-i Awḥadī, 1390 H [2011]). A more detailed article on the album is forthcoming: Shabnam

Rahimi-Golkhandan, "Ali Khan Vali: The Histories of an Archive," in *Photography's Shifting Terrain. Conference Proceedings*, ed. Shamoon Zamir and Nassar Issam (London: I. B. Tauris, 2017).

60 The albums that ʿAli Khan Vali sent to Nasir al-Din Shah and that are now stored in the *album-khāna* of the Gulistan Palace are of a smaller size. Three albums by ʿAli Khan Vali are in the collection of the Gulistan: album no. 294 (7315) with 69 photographs taken in the years 1304 and 1305 H (1886 and 1887), featuring photographs of the province of Azerbaijan and images of Armenia; album no. 212 (7233), produced in 1307 H (1889), featuring images of Ardabil; and album no. 223 (7264), also dated to 1307 H in Ardabil, featuring additional photographs by Lutf Allah al-Husayni. On the albums in the Gulistan, see Ẕukā, *Tārīkh-i ʿakkāsī va ʿakkāsān-i pīshgām dar Īrān*, 66–74.

61 On ʿAli Khan's life, see Chahryar Adle, "Ṣāḥib-i Nasq, ʿAlī Khān Vālī va sardār-i Humāyūn Vālī," *Bukhārā* 28 (1381 H [2002]).

62 See page 327 of the album, where ʿAli Khan Vali mentions that he uses photographs taken by others next to his own images.

63 Ẕukā, *Tārīkh-i ʿakkāsī va ʿakkāsān-i pīshgām dar Īrān*, 70–71.

64 See note 23, above.

65 Ẕukā, *Tārīkh-i ʿakkāsī va ʿakkāsān-i pīshgām dar Īrān*, 70–71.

66 Qasim Khan, who is depicted in many photographs in the album, became the head of the Tabriz municipality, where he introduced the telephone and founded a gas lamp factory. See ibid.

67 Sheikh, "Rise of the Kingly Citizen."

68 See Sassan Pejhan, "A Picture Postcard View of the Persian Constitutional Revolution," *Journal of Persianate Studies* 3 (2) (2010); and Ṣāfī, *Kārt-pustāl'hā-yi tārīkhī-yi Īrān*. On photography of the Constitutional Revolution, see Reza Sheikh, "National Identity and Photographs of the Constitutional Revolution," in *Iran's Constitutional Revolution: Popular Politics, Cultural Transformations and Transnational Connections* (London: I. B. Tauris, 2010).

69 See Tahmasbpour, "Photography in Iran," 12.

70 See *Encyclopaedia Iranica*, s.v. "Kasmāʾi, Mīrzā Ḥosayn," by Pezhmann Dailami.

71 See Pejhan, "Picture Postcard View of the Persian Constitutional Revolution," 198.

72 See Muʿīn al-Dīn Miḥrābī, "Sayyid ʿAbd al-Raḥīm Kāshānī. Namāvanda-yi Tihrān dar dawra'hā-yi haftum va hashtum-i majlis-i shawrā-yi millī," *Asnād-i bahāristān dawra-yi jadīd* 3 (1392 H [2013–14]).

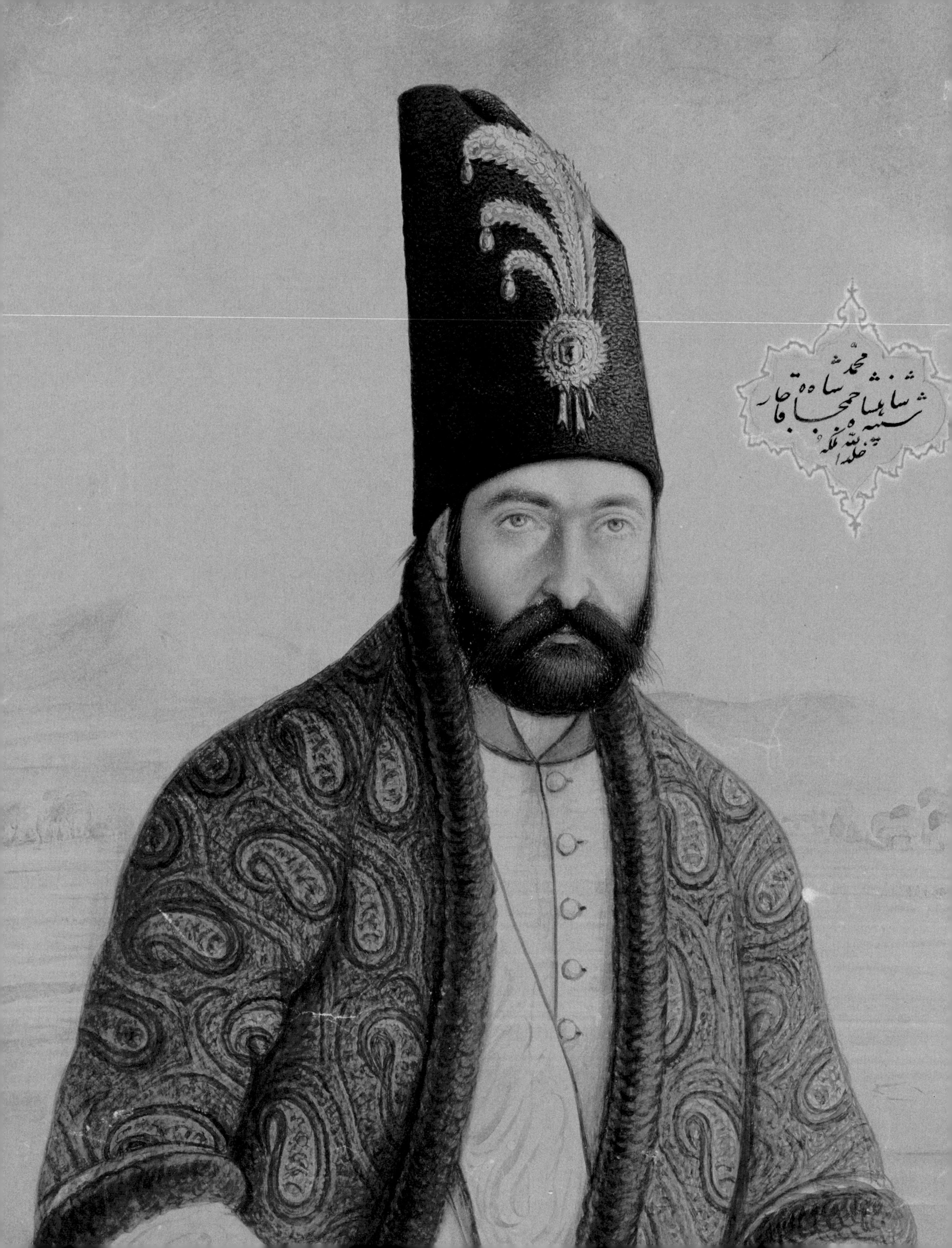
شبیه شاهنشاه محمد شاه قاجار
خلد الله ملکه

5 Painting after Photography in 19th-Century Iran

David J. Roxburgh[1]

Muhammad Shah had sent an artist to Rome to learn the secrets and processes of European art, which the Persians freely acknowledge as being superior to theirs. Unfortunately, the choice of the student did not appear to be very fortunate. The painter had neither been touched nor had understood anything. The only result of his trip was to transport a copy of the *Vièrge à la chaise*, which was very popular, and is copied everywhere nowadays. Besides, for a long time now European engravings and lithographs are being copied. One sees them on qalyans, inkpots, mirrors, and mainly pictures of a saintly nature.

JOSEPH ARTHUR, COMTE DE GOBINEAU,
Trois ans en Asie (1859)[2]

Since photography was discovered, it has been of great service to the art of design [*ṣanaʿat-i taṣvīr*]. The art of landscape rendering [*dūrnamā-sāzī*], of portraiture [*shabīh-kashī*], of light and shade [*vānimūdan sāya va rawshan*] and the use of the laws of perspective [*qānūn-i tanāsub*] as well as other aspects of this technique [*va sāyir nukāt-i īn fann hama az ʿaks*]: all have found their originality and have been perfected.

MUHAMMAD HASAN KHAN IʿTIMAD AL-SALTANA,
Kitāb al-maʾāthir wa al-āthār (1888–89)[3]

Detail: *Muhammad Shah Qajar*, dated 1262 H (1845–46). For full information, see cat. 1, p. 131.

The opinions expressed here by Joseph Arthur, comte de Gobineau (1816–1882), during his tenure as Ambassador of the French Legation in Tehran are entirely consistent with the majority view of European visitors to Qajar Iran. We find the same judgments of perceived artistic failure and a model in which cross-cultural interaction is understood reductively as one of simple copying, a process then facilitated by the dissemination of new mediums. Gobineau's opinions refer specifically to the artist Mirza ʿAli Akbar Khan Muzayyin al-Dawla, who is credited with bringing European images to Iran, a process long since under way but of increased incidence in the 1860s.[4] Gobineau's views were echoed by those of Julien de Rochechouart, his successor at the French Legation, and reverberated in the later writings of other Europeans, especially Lord George Curzon, who was as concerned about the loss of indigenous, national, and traditional art forms as he was perplexed by the apparent proliferation of duplicates, multiples that seemed in every instance to be identical to each other (see the introduction to this volume and cats. 28, 33).[5] And yet an entirely different view of art—of the affairs of the image—was voiced by Muhammad Hasan Khan I'timad al-Saltana (d. 1896), court chronicler during the reign of Nasir al-Din Shah (r. 1848–1896). In the section of his book devoted to "Progress in Art" (*taraqqī-yi naqqāshī*), he stated that photography had been of particular advantage to the arts of depiction in Iran because it afforded valuable instruction in such techniques as modeling (light and shade) and perspective. The years between Gobineau's and I'timad al-Saltana's statements, spanning the long reign of Nasir al-Din Shah, witnessed a rapid expansion not only in imported images and image technologies but also in the entirely fluid and mobile systems by which images moved across mediums in Qajar lands (Figs. 1, 2).

Though recent scholarship has given the art of the Qajar period the serious consideration it merits, some of the prejudice and criticism expressed by the likes of Gobineau, Rochechouart, and Curzon has found its way into an academic discourse and continues today, fortunately in reduced measure.[6] In different ways, 19th-century Europeans commented on the aesthetics, practices, and production of Persianate painting—including oil on canvas, watercolor on paper, and lacquer—of the Qajar period to draw contrasts with European models. But they also confronted evidence of intersections between the practice of painting and new technologies of mechanical or semi-mechanical image reproduction, including lithography, photography, and chromolithography. European writers reacted to these effects through an idea of an "authentic," historical Persian art and always considered the results detrimental. Writers of the period spanning the time of Gobineau and Curzon, and some art historians since, identified exchanges between Europe and Iran as initiating the downfall of a historical Persianate painting, a decline identified by some as beginning in the Safavid period of the early 1600s. From the perspective of a decline model, the adaptation of lithography and photography into Qajar art only hastened the loss of a native Persian tradition.

Another attitude to innovation and invention in Qajar art approaches the artist's choice as one of modernity and emphasizes the medium of photography. While Iranians eagerly embraced photography and its various technical innovations (introduced in Mira Xenia Schwerda's essay in this volume), the scholar Ali Behdad accepts Europe's *a priori* ownership of the medium and argues that Qajar-era photographers were co-opted agents. They could only reproduce a way of seeing and showing the "East" in "Western" terms (whatever value these binaries might possess should be debated). Such was the power of Orientalism that "native" Persian photography was "indebted to, and mimetic of, Orientalism's aesthetic values and ideological assumptions."[7]

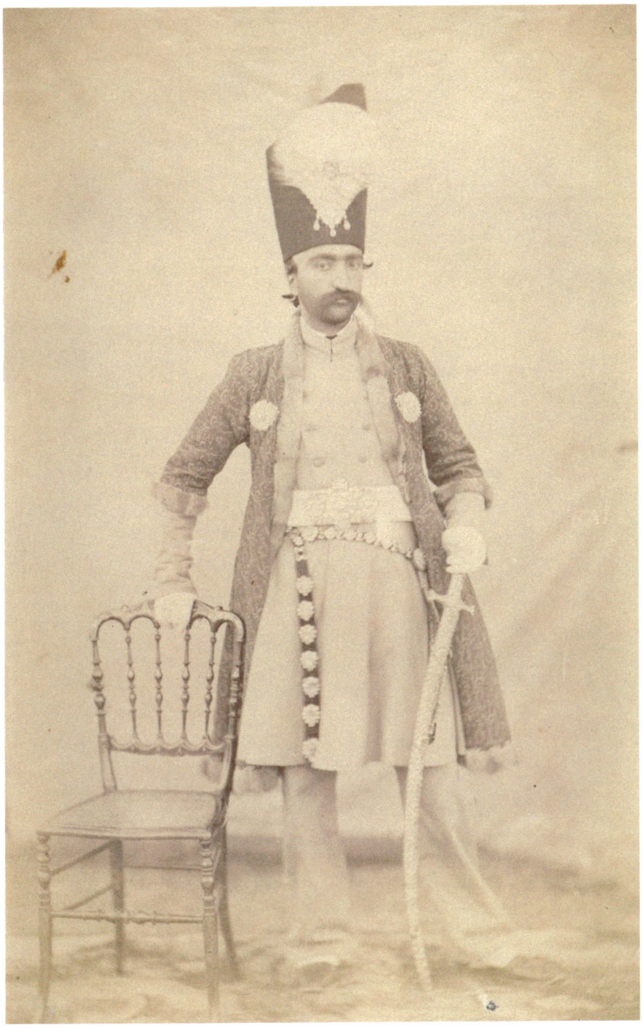

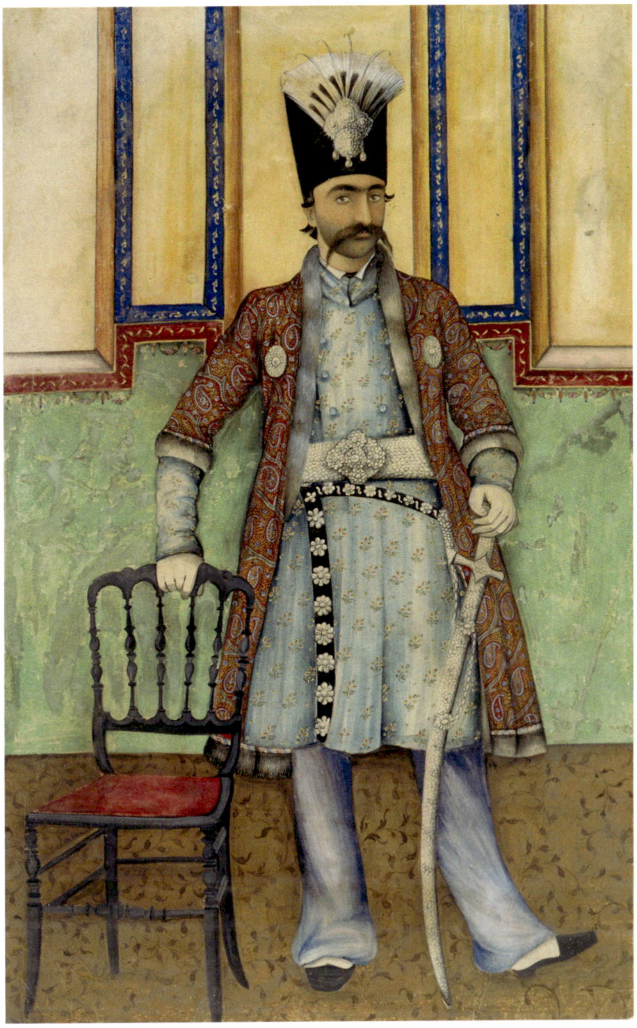

1 *Portrait of Nasir al-Din Shah*, Iran, c. 1852–55. Salted paper print from glass negative, 33.7 × 21.2 cm (13¼ × 8⅜ in.). The Metropolitan Museum of Art, New York, Gift of Charles K. and Irina B. Wilkinson, 1977, 1977.683.22.

2 *Portrait of Nasir al-Din Shah*, Iran, c. 1855. Watercolor and gold on paper, 29.8 × 19.2 cm (11¾ × 7⁹⁄₁₆ in.). Musée du Louvre, Paris, MAO778.

Behdad goes so far as to argue for the displacement of painting by photography during the reign of Nasir al-Din Shah, a shift of emphasis and priority that he considered to be embodied in a watercolor of about 1853 (Fig. 3).[8]

Both views are shaped by the notion of a rupture in the 19th century, a watershed in artistic tradition and practice caused by greater access to European art, visual culture, commodities, and technology. These perspectives, however, would benefit from a grounding in the close study of a broad range of visual materials, from objects made through or under the auspices of elite institutions and courtly patrons to those fashioned in the bazaar and purchased by the members of a general public. As noted in the introduction to this volume, these objects manifest highly complex intersections of mediums as well as their remediation.[9] How were lithographic and photographic images assimilated, remediated, and recast in and through the medium of painting, and what can we make of such processes?[10] Examples abound of images fashioned in one medium emulated in another, a process that deeply troubled most 19th-century

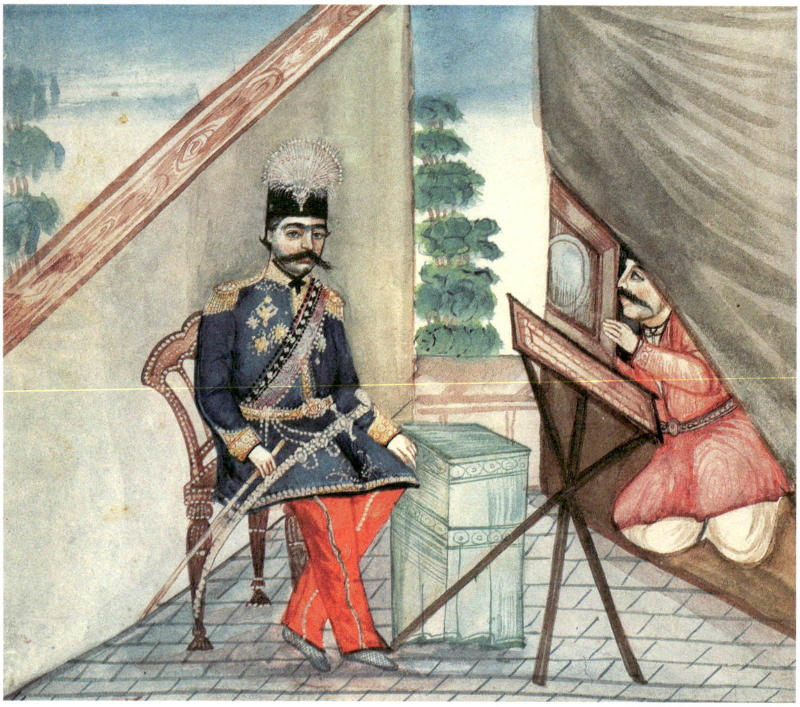

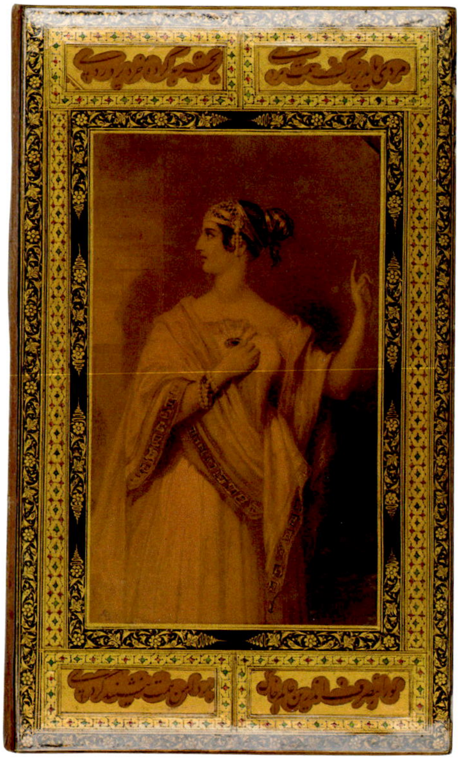

European visitors to Iran. In the case of lacquer wares, these include subjects adopted from European engravings and rendered in opaque watercolor under tinted varnish as well as the direct use of prints that were selected, trimmed, and pasted onto the paper substrate of lacquered objects (Fig. 4).[11]

The same processes were applied to the photograph shortly after its invention. One of the most striking examples of direct use is a pen box with applied photographs of Nasir al-Din Shah and views of Paris and Tehran, which were lacquered after being trimmed and attached to the wooden box (Fig. 5).[12] The restrained decoration used to complete the object—floral scrolls and cartouches of Persian poetry written in cursive *nastaʿlīq* script alternating between gold on black and black on gold—complements the monochrome photographs. Another example of photography under lacquer—but one that produces a different effect—consists of portraits of prince Dust Muhammad Khan Muʿayyir al-Mamalik attached to the binding of a *dīvān* (collection) of poetry by Hakim Manuchihri Damghani dated 1877–78 (Fig. 6).[13] While the varnish, ornamental scrolls, and epigraphic borders maintain the inherent monochrome of the mass-produced image, here the lacquer has an overall softening effect and transmutes the hard-edged photograph into something resembling a fully handmade thing. The refractive properties of the colored varnish render the photograph painterly. Also implicated in this transformation is the better known fact that the compositions of posed, highly controlled studio photography emulated the conventions of oil painting.

3 *Nasir al-Din Shah Being Photographed*, Iran, c. 1853. Watercolor on paper. (Image after Yaḥyā Ẕukā, *Tārīkh-i ʿakkāsī va ʿakkāsān-i pīshgām dar Īrān* [The History of Photography and Pioneer Photographers in Iran] [Tehran: Shirkat-i Intishārāt-i ʿIlmī va Farhangī, 1997], pl. 1.)

4 *Lower Cover of the Binding of a Prayer Book with a European Print*, Iran, 1825–50. Papier-mâché boards, 21.4 × 12.8 cm (8⁷⁄₁₆ × 5¹⁄₁₆ in.). Nasser D. Khalili Collection of Islamic Art, London, MSS.408.

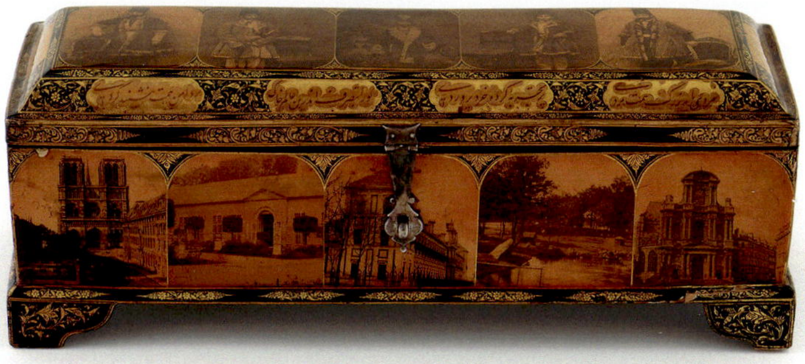

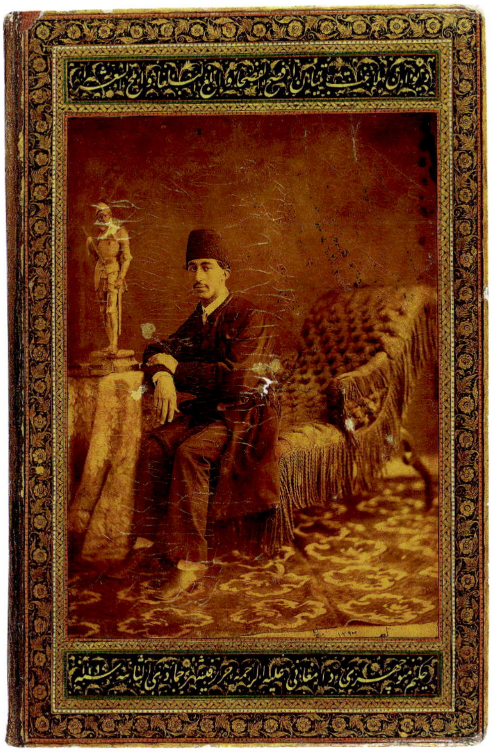

5 *Writing Box with Utensils, Decorated with Photographs of Nasir al-Din Shah, His Court, and Views of Paris and Tehran*, Iran, 1860–65. Lacquered and gilded wood with applied photographs and brass fittings, 11.1 × 30.8 × 10.3 cm (4⅜ × 12⅛ × 4¹⁄₁₆ in.). Freer Gallery of Art and Arthur M. Sackler Gallery, Smithsonian Institution, Washington, D.C., Purchase funds provided by the Friends of the Freer and Sackler Galleries, S2014.11.1.

6 *Lacquer Binding with a Photograph Portrait of Prince Dust Muhammad Khan, Mu'ayyir al-Mamalik*, Iran, 1877–78. Bonhams, London, *Islamic & Indian Art*, April 28, 2005, lot 88.

Other objects resulted from layered systems of material translation, some of which are difficult to disentangle (Fig. 7). The graphic techniques of lithographs—which were themselves made after, and often simulated the qualities of, paintings, drawings, prints, and photographs—are often found in ceramic tiles.[14] The choice of a monochrome palette in the face of easy access to polychrome offers the strongest evidence in this example of lithographic or photographic mediums as models and objects of reference. While these selected examples demonstrate some of the outcomes of cross-medium interaction, they also show that Qajar artists in the period from the mid-1800s to the early 1900s were not troubled by new technologies of image production, particularly photography.[15]

An additional question stems from the privileged place occupied by photography. Heralded as the epitome of modernity, the medium challenged the East not only for its reproductive potential but also because it appeared to confirm perspective and modes of representation based on optical naturalism characteristic of European painting. These questions are examined in the essay through three lines of approach: first, the early institutional histories of lithography and photography in Iran; second, the mediations of photography and lithography in Qajar painting; and third, the longer view of a history of art, which alters our understanding of developments in 19th-century Qajar art. Qajar artists' responses to mechanically produced and reproducible images can be viewed as another example of the assimilation of reproductive technologies, as another remediation, and hence can be understood as a continuity in the Persian artist's creative procedures.[16] Aside from emerging ideas about what it meant to be modern—and the means by which modernity was signaled—the proliferation of repeated images made possible through technologies scalable to mass production can in fact be understood as conceptually and practically systemic to Persianate art. In other words, artists largely continued to work in ways that they had before their exposure to the latest technologies of the image birthed in European centers: the principal shift lay in certain aesthetic outcomes of those exchanges as they crossed from one medium to another.

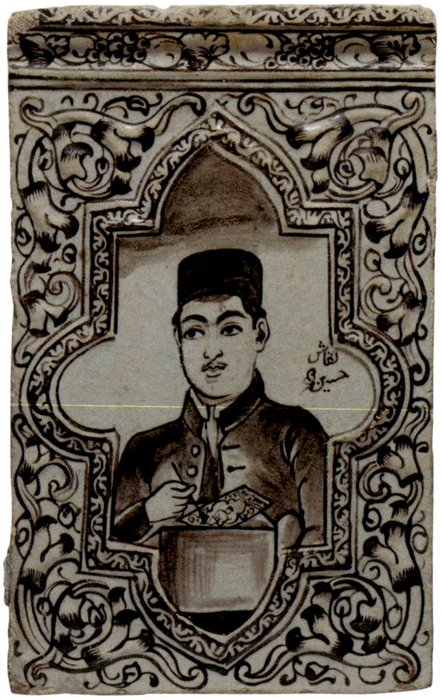

7 *Self-Portrait of the Artist Husayn*, Iran, Tehran, c. 1900. Fritware with painting under clear glaze, 49.2 × 31.8 × 3.8 cm (19⅜ × 12½ × 1½ in.). Harvard Art Museums/Arthur M. Sackler Museum, The Edwin Binney, 3rd Collection of Turkish Art at the Harvard Art Museums, 2017.19.

Institutional Histories of Lithography and Photography in Iran

The first press, using movable metal type (*chāp-i surbī*), was imported into Iran in 1817 and was soon followed by a few others through the 1830s. This printing technology was quickly superseded by lithography, however. A certain Ja'far Khan was sent to Moscow to study the technique of lithography (*chap-i sangī*) and returned to Tabriz, Iran, with a lithograph press in 1824. Soon thereafter, Mirza Asad Allah Shirazi was dispatched to St. Petersburg with the same objective. Lithography easily outstripped metal type for the purpose of producing printed text because its technique was naturally and materially closer to the calligrapher's act of writing in ink on paper.[17] As far as mass-produced illustration went, developments in the lithographic crayon—moving from the delineating pencil to a fat crayon—expanded the repertoire of graphic marks from lines and stippling to shading as gradations of light and dark.[18] Farshid Emami discusses the history of printing, and especially lithography, in his essay in this volume.

Knowledge of photography and its techniques was quickly made available to the royal court in Iran and was gradually disseminated from it in the second half of the 19th century. The practice spread to Iran only a few years after the official presentation of the daguerreotype to the French Académie des sciences in 1839. The arrival of photographic apparatus in 1842 through gifts made to Qajar ruler Muhammad Shah (r. 1834–1848) by Queen Victoria of England and Tsar Nicholas I of Russia is enshrined in the history of photography in Iran. Sources also inform us that Jules Richard (1816–1891) was invited to the Qajar court in 1844 to explain the operation and principles of photographic equipment and to demonstrate their use. Other Europeans followed, including Frances Carlhian (1818–1870), who arrived in 1858 and instructed the young Nasir al-Din Shah in photography. While European residents in Iran played a critical role in spreading and propagating knowledge of photography, its support by members of the royal house—the king as well as princes—led to the training of Persians in the medium. Nasir al-Din Shah devoted a building in the royal palace to photography (*'akkās-khāna-yi mubāraka-yi humāyūnī*) in 1862, and in the next year created the office of Chief Photographer (*'Akkās-Bāshī*).[19] Nasir al-Din Shah continued to support the position of Chief Painter (*Naqqāsh-Bāshī*). Photography won the enthusiastic attention of the courtly elite who stimulated its propagation, leading ultimately to the growth of commercial studios throughout Iran.[20] Further aspects related to the history of Qajar-period photography and its dissemination are discussed by Mira Xenia Schwerda in her essay in this volume.

One of the most important early sites for photography was Iran's first polytechnic, the Dar al-Funun (Abode of Sciences), which was established on December 28, 1851, and began operations in 1852. At the inauguration, I'timad al-Saltana stated, "[A]s of this date the useful discoveries of European nations will spread in this country."[21] The institution was initially conceived as an instrument to develop knowledge of Western sciences and military training so as to modernize Iran through internal reform, but by the early 1860s the curriculum adjusted its emphasis toward non-military subjects to include photography, lithography, painting, and music. Photography was added to the curriculum in 1860—located in the Department of Chemistry—and painting in 1861. The move away from a strict emphasis on subjects applicable to military study continued into the 1880s.

Though much more is to be learned about the pedagogy of painting at the Dar al-Funun, it is clear that students were exposed to techniques associated with European painting, printing, and lithography. They studied directly from photographs, paintings, sculptures, and engravings of works by European masters to understand and internalize the effects and principles of realism, perspective, and modeling.[22] Abu al-Hasan Ghaffari Kashani (1814–1866), bestowed with the titles Chief Painter some time before 1846 and Craftsman of the Kingdom (*Ṣāniʿ al-Mulk*) in 1861, had trained in Iran before journeying to Rome and Florence, where he studied painting, printing, and lithography between 1846 and 1850. Two years after his return to Tehran, he was appointed director of the Majmaʿ al-Sanayiʿ, a handicrafts center founded in the bazaar in 1850 by the reform-oriented prime minister Amir Kabir; the principal purpose of the masters of individual crafts assembled at the center was to impart their knowledge to apprentices, largely through court commissioned projects.[23] The addition of painting to the Dar al-Funun curriculum in 1861 coincided with the formation of the Ministry of Industries and Sciences, led by ʿAli Quli Mirza I'tizad al-Saltana, and the bestowing of yet another responsibility on Abu al-Hasan Ghaffari Kashani: to edit and direct production of the renamed state newspaper (*Rūznāma-yi dawlat-i ʿalīya-yi Īrān*), which was mostly illustrated with lithographed portraits of the Qajar elite.[24] As Maryam Ekhtiar argues, the curriculum developed by Abu al-Hasan Ghaffari for painting at the Dar al-Funun was adapted to Persian systems of artistic pedagogy because it excluded "life drawing, anatomy, geometry, and art theory."[25] Ekhtiar also observes that learning through imitation and the value of replication were similar in the fine art–oriented Dar al-Funun and the craft-oriented Majmaʿ al-Sanayiʿ. Although there was a division between institutions, principles of artistic pedagogy were shared.[26]

The sequence of developments in Iran in the 1850s and 1860s demonstrates an unquestionably strong degree of centralization in the formation of government institutions related to the practices of painting, photography, and lithography, and a robust connection among them. Continuity existed from the levels of administration to pedagogy and practice. It is also notable that the very concept of craft was formed in Qajar domains in light of the effects of industrialization and in the face of new technologies of the image. There is ample evidence to indicate that artists made lithographs from paintings, engravings, and photographs, and that paintings were in turn made from photographs and prints (both intaglio and lithographs).[27] It was also possible to directly use actual prints and photographs in the manufacture of objects (Figs. 4–6).

Before turning to examples of Qajar painting, mostly from the period of Nasir al-Din Shah's reign, it is useful to mention some of the reactions to photography recorded in Persian written sources. ʿAli Quli Mirza Iʿtizad al-Saltana, Nasir al-Din Shah's uncle, director of Dar al-Funun and Minister of Industries and Sciences, first styled the medium as a "kind of painting" and described it in terms related to painting.[28] Court historian Iʿtimad al-Saltana offered expanded accounts of photography, such as those given in his *Kitāb al-ma'āthir wa al-āthār* (1888–89), where he lists the names of the chief photographers and locations of the court's photographic studios and offers synopses of the arrival and early history of photography in Iran.[29] His famous statement about the impact of photography on the visual arts, quoted at the beginning of this essay, stressed its positive and progressive value: how it had enhanced the genres of landscape and portraiture and how it had aided in the comprehension of modeling and perspective. Here, and elsewhere, Iʿtimad al-Saltana championed the modernizing value of photography on Qajar art.

The only ostensible exception to this appears in Iʿtimad al-Saltana's entry on "The Production of Illustrated Newspapers" (*ījād-i jarīda-yi muṣavvara*) in the *Kitāb al-ma'āthir wa al-āthār*. Here Abu al-Hasan Ghaffari Kashani, by then deceased, is extolled as the leading figure of the country in this field, and it is further stated that he made "arrangements of figures" (*shabīh-sāzī*) and "portrait compositions" (*chihrā-pardāzī*) "without the assistance of photography" (*bidūn-i muʿāvanat-i ʿaks*), a capacity that gradually came to an end after his death.[30] But in the same entry, Iʿtimad al-Saltana describes his personal effort to restore the quality of illustrations in newspapers and credits the success of the newspaper *Sharaf* precisely to photography when it was applied to the "art of making figural compositions" (*fann-i shabīh-sāzī*).[31] It would seem that Iʿtimad al-Saltana's main concern was to emphasize Abu al-Hasan Ghaffari Kashani's unequaled artistic mastery and not to deny the utility of the photograph, or even the artist's outright use of them. His statement also indicates the increased use of photography in lithographic practice by the 1880s.

In his travel diary, Nasir al-Din Shah writes that photography is a "reflection and imprint of images of objects on external surfaces" and notes its usefulness as a "device in the demonstration of the science of perspective."[32] Such remarks convey the belief that photography naturalized perspective—it seemed to confirm the optical and perceptual truth of post-Renaissance European painting—but more curiously, one also senses that the photographic medium was a more effective transmitter of lessons in pictorial conventions than European paintings or direct study from life. The assessments of I'timad al-Saltana and Nasir al-Din Shah suggest that photography enabled Qajar artists to see in a way that they apparently could not by direct vision or through existing pictorial models, whether Persian or European.[33] Other comments made by contemporaries, particularly Hajji Mulla Hadi Sabzavari, dealt with philosophical questions that issued from the capacity of a manmade mechanical apparatus to produce images on paper.[34] As Stephen Vernoit has observed, "Theologians and jurists argued that a photographer was not rivaling God in the creative act because a photograph was brought about by the agency of the sun and was the result of divine activity," contrasting a passive "mechanical reflection" with an active "artist's creation."[35]

Remediations of the Mass-Produced Image in Painting

Even constructive assessments of the effects of lithography and photography on painting give short shrift to the formal features of Qajar painting and often reproduce habitual themes of contemporary writing: namely, that Qajar artists merely attempted to assimilate European pictorial conventions, reproduced their chosen prototypes, and relied on photographs as instruments of instruction.[36] These observations give little emphasis to a crucial point. Paintings made after photographic or lithographic models, themselves regarded as intermediaries, were never direct reproductions but in specific ways exhibit traces, material and visual memories, of their models.

So what of the practice of painting in the second half of the 19th century? Some scholars have suggested the slow eclipse of painting after the arrival of photography, while others have argued for the continuity of painting at the court and in other contexts. The position of Chief Painter continued under Nasir al-Din Shah even as the interest in photography intensified: the chief painter's mandate included oversight of the royal workshops and the guilds in the city's bazaar, as well as instructing the ruler in painting.[37] Painting continued to be practiced in a variety of venues, formats, and mediums—life-size panel paintings in oil, enamels, lacquer objects, paintings in manuscripts, and lithographed books—though the rupture paradigm obscures continuities in practice.

The brief survey of pedagogy in the Dar al-Funun pointed to the close intersection of painting, photography, and lithography from around 1860 onward. Evidence of their interaction is apparent outside of the Dar al-Funun curriculum in the decade before. Painters' use of photographs as prototypes is amply attested, and there are a few examples that can be matched as a pair, such as a salt print portrait of Nasir al-Din Shah dated to roughly 1852–55 and a watercolor done after it from about 1855 (Figs. 2, 3).[38] We cannot take the watercolor painting for a photograph, and we cannot treat it simply as a colored/tinted photograph. Visual study of the watercolor leaves one questioning how the photograph could have imparted lessons in shading and modeling while the tightly framed composition abrogates the understanding of perspective given that signs of spatial recession are eliminated. Artistic incompetence does not explain away this issue, as several other paintings attest. The photograph supplied data about relative scale, the outline of a figure, possible compositional elements—an imported spindle side chair but not a backdrop—and a skein of lit and shaded passages. The translation toward a painting required not only an imagined palette and invention of pattern, but also a choice of which tonal passages to mimic, which to invent, and which to ignore.[39]

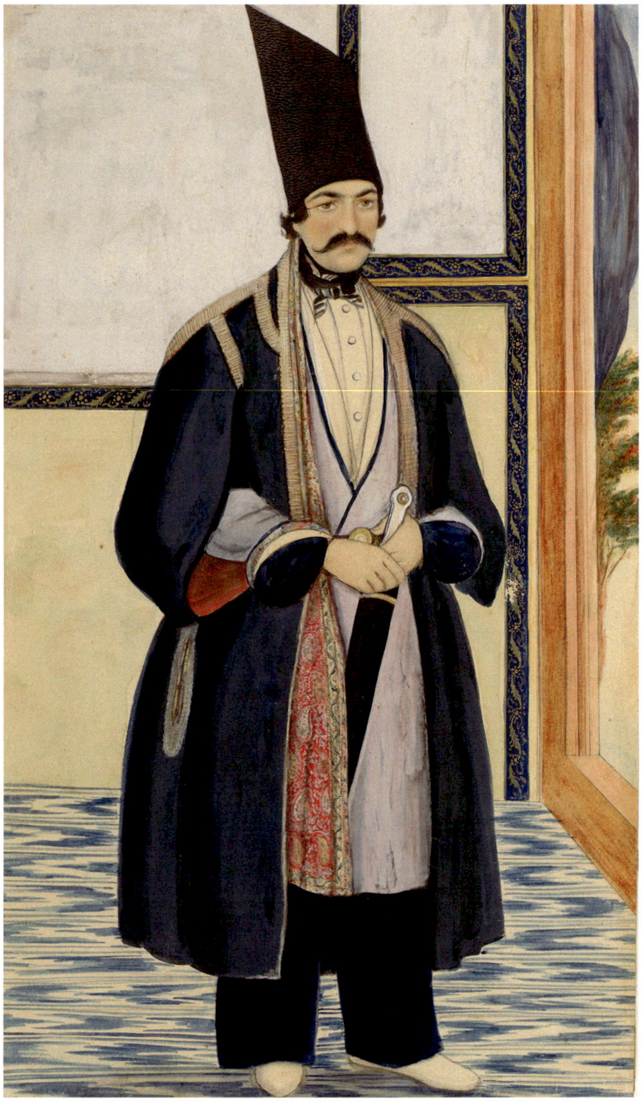

8 *Standing Courtier*, mid-19th century. For full information, see cat. 5, p. 132.

The single-sheet portrait, mostly of a single figure posed in an interior setting (of which the c. 1855 Nasir al-Din Shah painting is one example), was among the most common formats adopted by Qajar artists. It had a deep history in Persianate painting and had been thoroughly developed during the reign of Fath ʿAli Shah. Generally, those early 19th-century depictions showed the Qajar ruler in an interior space with any background architecture parallel to the picture plane. Spatial depth was sometimes suggested by the receding, but also parallel, lines of objects such as a throne or a carpet, shown axonometrically, or by cutaway views from an interior to the exterior. Elements of the painting tradition long since adopted from European art included an increased emphasis on the individual traits of physiognomy and the effects of light and shade. But none of these systems was applied systematically through the entire matrix of the image. Visible effects of light and shade or spatial recession, for example, were applied locally, affecting selected components of the image; and while the subject's face might suggest realism, intentional distortions in the proportions of the body—a slender waist, broad shoulders—reflected Qajar physiognomic ideals. For examples of these selective adoptions of European representational modes, see Figures 6 and 25 in Mary McWilliams's essay earlier in this volume.

A group of single-sheet portraits from the 1850s, many of them by Abu al-Hasan Ghaffari Kashani, demonstrate adaptations to the earlier Qajar paradigm. Rather than setting the figure in a space parallel to the pictorial space,

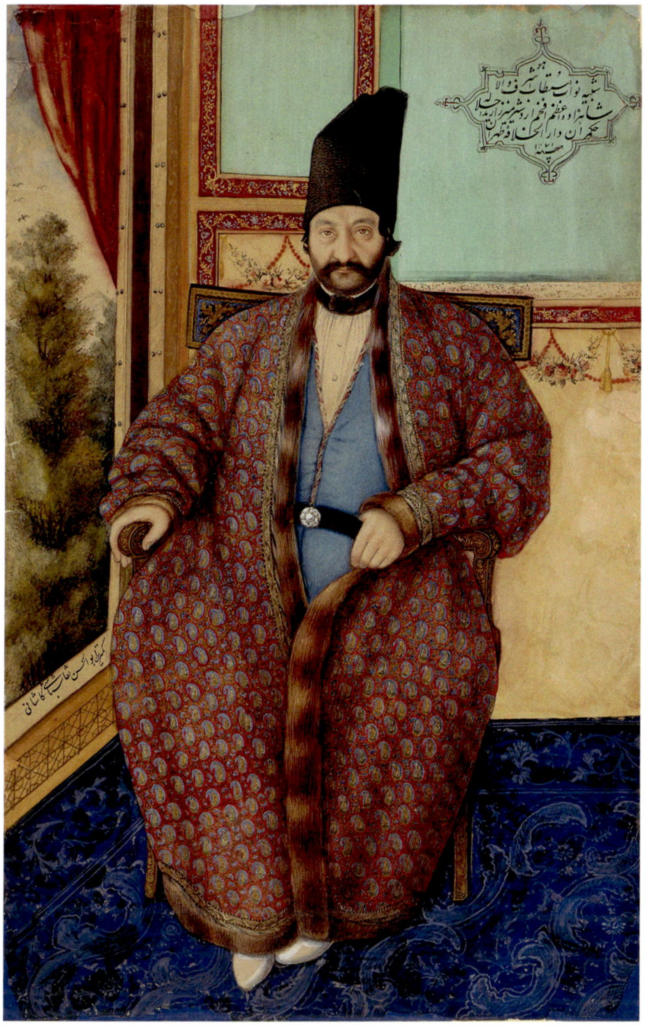

9 *Prince Ardashir Mirza, Governor of Tehran,* Abu al-Hasan Ghaffari Kashani, Iran, Tehran, 1854. Opaque and transparent watercolor on paper, 31.6 × 20.4 cm (12 7/16 × 8 in.). Musée du Louvre, Paris, MAO788.

the corner of a room is now frequently depicted, a window opening revealing an outdoor landscape, and the point of contact between the walls usually obscured by the sitter and furnishings (Figs. 8, 9).[40] The framing of the image is tight and the space is tipped up, heightening a sense of intimacy and immediacy. The figure stands or sits in a setting that is decorated with lavish floor and wall coverings, painted dadoes with borders and patterned drapes, and often furnished with a table and other objects.

In a painting made shortly after his return from training in Europe, Abu al-Hasan Ghaffari depicts Prince Ardashir Mirza (Fig. 9),[41] complete with all the elements of spatial construction outlined above. The work carries a customary inscription in *nastaʿlīq* script identifying the subject by name and titles and providing the artist's signature. Prince Ardashir Mirza dominates the composition, and his volume in space is conveyed through a tonal modeling integrated with networks of rich patterning and fields of flat color. Close attention is paid to the texture of the face and the beard, and a subtle execution of the face and hands is achieved. But for an artist trained in the West it cannot be accepted as a complete assimilation of post-Renaissance artistic conventions—consider the handling of linear perspective and the basic incongruities of spatial logic—nor as a full imitation of a painted or a photographic model. Despite our perception of a volume integrated in space and the sharp contrast between figure and ground, aspects of shading and shadow give the impression of an overall illumination. Two viewpoints, one for the room, the other for the figure, are collapsed and unified into a single image. It is clearly a combinatory visual form. In spatial conception, coloring, pattern, and facture it reflects the conventions of historical Persianate painting. The arrangement of the body—the unique contour that defines its edge against the background—the handling of the face and hands, and the close cropping of the subject: all suggest the mediation of a photographic image.

The same compositional setting was applied throughout multiple examples of portraits of Nasir al-Din Shah and his courtiers. In a work from the late 1850s, Nasir al-Din Shah is depicted in an interior (Fig. 10). This painting is similar in many details, especially the stacked bolster cushions and the oval end table carrying a bowl of flowers, to another portrait of Ardashir Mirza painted by Abu al-Hasan Ghaffari Kashani and dated 1852–53.[42] An inscription set in a cartouche above the sitter in Figure 10 identifies the subject as "the sultan, son of the sultan, Nasir al-Din Shah Qajar" (*al-Sulṭān ibn al-sulṭān Nāṣir al-Dīn*

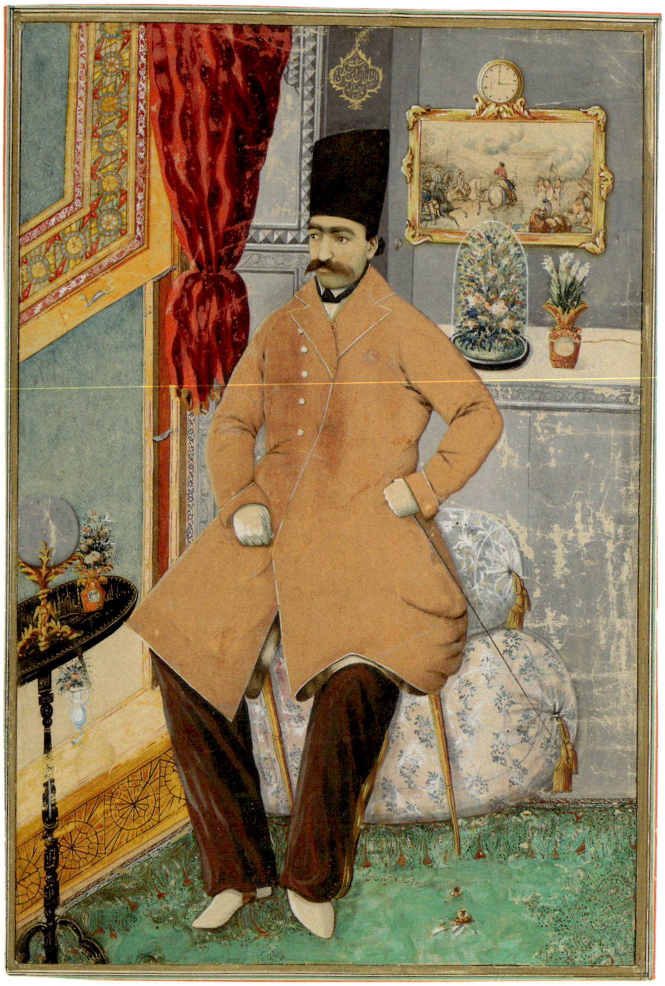

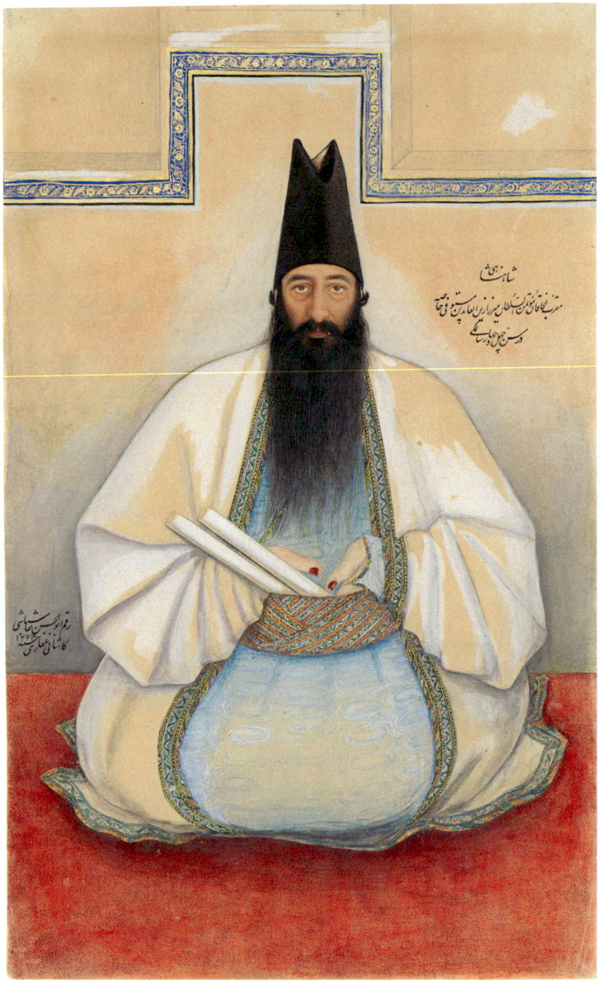

Shāh Qājār), while another at the ruler's feet provides the artist's signature, "rendering by the slave of the court Mubarak b. Mahmud" (*raqm-i banda-yi dargāh Mubārak ibn Maḥmūd*).[43] The room is populated with many objects, a glass globe set on a gilded stand, two small jugs of flowers, an artificial floral arrangement under a glass dome, and a painting of a Napoleonic battle set in a gilded frame surmounted by a clock. Elsewhere, rich colors and patterns provide texture to the bolster cushions, the wooden trim of the window, the carved plaster window frame and walls, the hanging crimson drape, and the green carpet. The posture of Nasir al-Din Shah shares the same effect of recent images of Ardashir Mirza, among others, a highly particularized contour that corresponds to a real body. This measure of reality is signaled also in the close treatment given to the mustachioed face and gloved hands. The face is built up from layers of wash and stippling that deftly model the facial features, the set of the ruler's eyes, and the careful calibration of difference between his barbered moustache, trimmed eyebrows, and shaved beard. Overall, the body of the ruler has the appearance of being cut out and inserted into an oft-repeated

10 *Nasir al-Din Shah Qajar*, late 1850s. For full information, see cat. 2, p. 131.

11 *Mirza Zayn al-ʿAbidin*, dated 1273 H (1856–57). For full information, see cat. 3, p. 132.

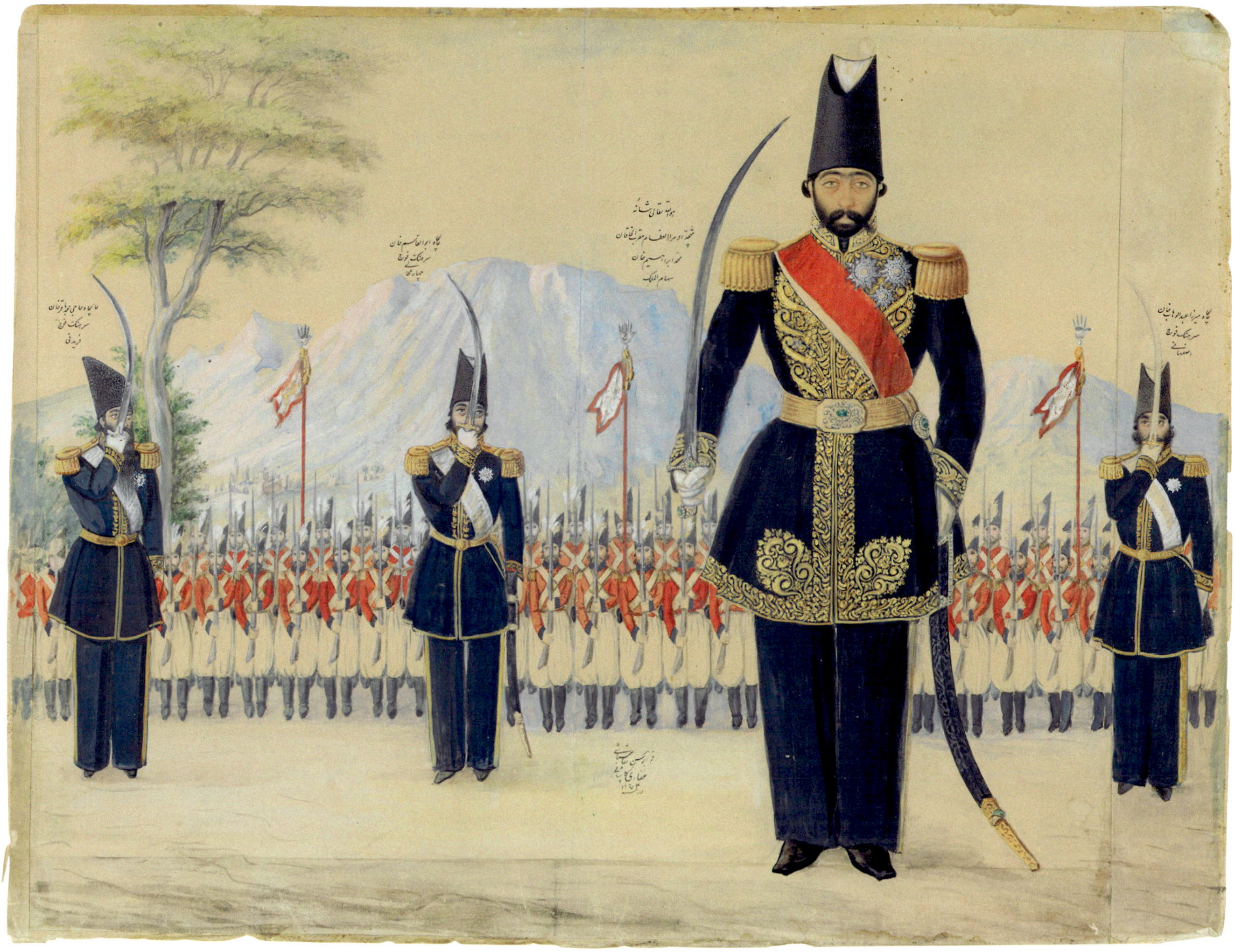

12 *Muhammad Ibrahim Khan Siham al-Mulk, Commander of the Isfahan Division*, dated 1274 H (1857–58). For full information, see cat. 4, p. 132.

composition, a space customized through the objects that populate it. The painting combines a conventional Persianate pictorial practice with the effects of the photograph, principally the unique contour of the body shown in a relaxed informal pose and the equally particularized features of the face, hands, and feet.[44] The rich polychrome of the room contrasts the near monochrome of the face, a distinction emphasized by shifts in the facture of paint. The habit of making an image by the selective appropriation and adaptation of components of existing models, sutured together into new compositions and further distinguished by aspects of detail, handling, and coloring, was an entirely normal procedure in Persianate artistic practice.

Two other works by Abu al-Hasan Ghaffari, both dated 1857–58, point to the breadth of the artist's capacities (Figs. 11, 12). They both depict strictly frontal views of their subjects: one a single figure seated in a narrow and constricted space (Fig. 11); the other an outdoor military review with prominent generals in the foreground and their infantry arranged in rows behind (Fig. 12). The paintings are labeled with the subjects' names and the artist's signatures.[45]

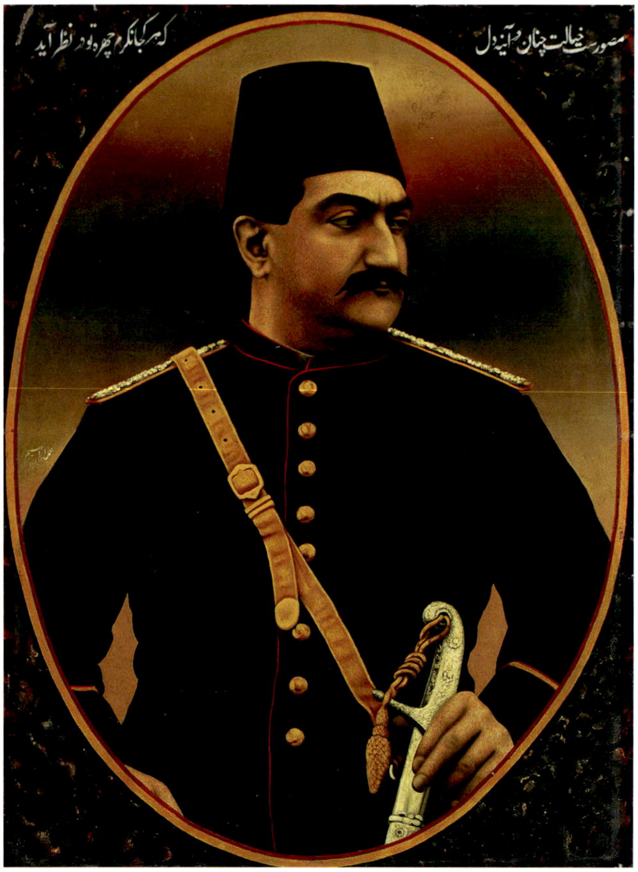

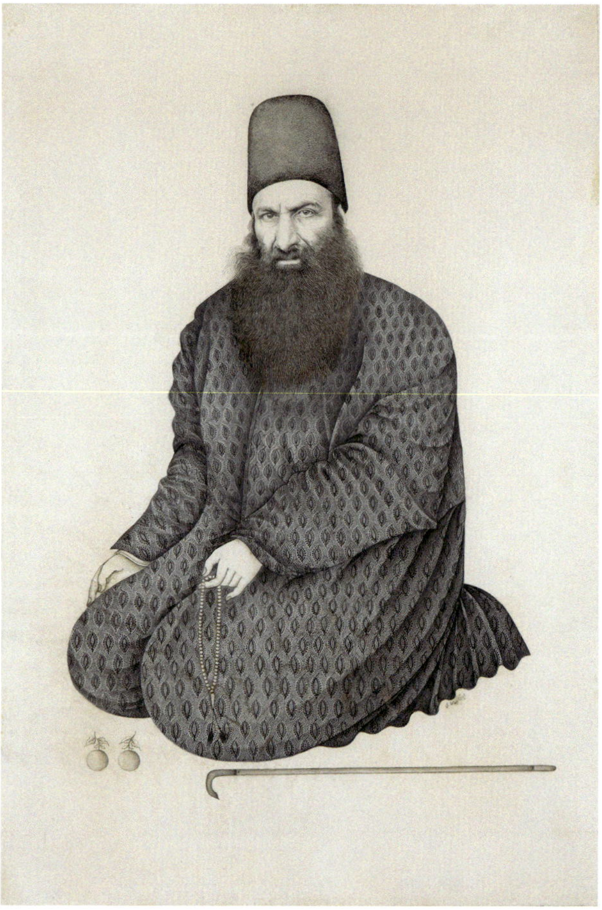

Both works show a sensitive command of watercolor applied opaquely as layers of wash. Like the earlier examples, the psychological intensity of the figures and their physiognomic specificity indicate the use of photographs. The effects of aerial perspective and recession, captured in photographs, are also visible in Figure 12.

Two other paintings offer a still more complex layering by showing interactions across and among the mediums of painting, photography, lithography, and lacquer (Figs. 13, 14). Some of their effects were already registered in an early work of Abu al-Hasan Ghaffari made the year before his departure to Europe for study (Fig. 15). The very fact that the portrait of Muhammad Shah (r. 1834–1848), dated 1845–46, is done in monochrome is highly unusual within Persianate pictorial practice, while its level of carefully drawn detail is modeled after the graphic features of printed models.[46] The general conception of the image, radically cropped to show only the torso of the ruler set against a tinted sky, equally suggests the impact of the daguerreotype—though perhaps not one of Muhammad Shah—or the rendering of the portrait as an imitation of the lithograph.

13 *Zill-i Sultan*, Ibrahim, Iran, 1890–91. Oil on tin, 76 × 57 cm (29 15/16 × 22 7/16 in.). Private collection.

14 *Haji Mirza Sulayman Khan Rukn al-Mulk*, Abu Turab Ghaffari, Iran, 1880–89. Watercolor on paper, 39 × 27 cm (15 3/8 × 10 5/8 in.). Musée du Louvre, Paris, MAO775.

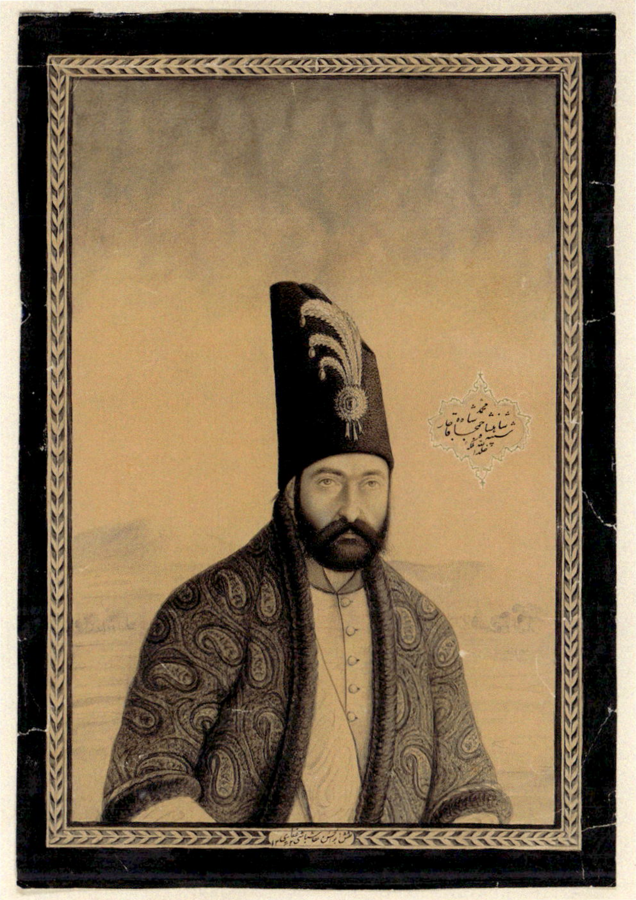

15 *Muhammad Shah Qajar*, dated 1262 H (1845–46). For full information, see cat. 1, p. 131.

The two later paintings (Figs. 13, 14) manifest a profound attention to the individuation of subjects set in casual poses, figures caught in time and congealed for posterity. Ibrahim's portrait of Zill-i Sultan (the eldest son of Nasir al-Din Shah), dated 1890–91, is an object designed to preserve the full effect of a photographic object and not only its mimetic properties—consider the oval frame outlined in red and yellow resembling gold, the mottled corners of a *trompe l'oeil* stone, the inscription (a caption in white *nasta'līq*), as well as how the frame crops the subject (Fig. 13).[47] The format of the medallion portrait resembles a photograph, while the frame partly mimics the presentation cases used to protect daguerreotypes and tintypes. (Tintypes were direct positives made on thin sheets of metal coated with lacquer and photographic emulsion.) The painting is in oil on tin by a painter also known for his lacquer work, and there are some of the honey-toned and amber hues of lacquer wares found in this painting. Without direct access to the portrait, it is not possible to determine whether it is a tinted tintype or a painted simulation of the optical naturalism of photography (strongly evident in the face, hands and background, and the nebulous mist of purples, grays, and browns that resembles a studio backdrop). The large format of the portrait suggests that it is less likely to be a tinted tintype, but that is not out of the question. If it is a tinted tintype, the large format brought the photograph into scale with the conventional size of presentation portraits executed in oil on canvas.[48]

The watercolor portrait of Haji Mirza Sulayman Khan, chief secretary to Zill al-Sultan, is a virtual monochrome in black and blue, dramatically opposing the figure against a blank ground (Fig. 14). The stark contrast between the modes of execution applied to the head and hands and the drapery-covered body suggests a fusion of visual effects and techniques associated with painting, photography, and lithography. The artist—Abu Turab Ghaffari (1862–1889), brother of Muhammad Ghaffari (Kamal al-Mulk) and nephew of Abu al-Hasan Ghaffari—was trained as a painter and lithographer in the Dar al-Funun and produced large paintings by commission and images for the newspaper *Sharaf*.[49] As a painted watercolor, the painting carries the trace of reproductive processes redolent of both lithography and photography. A rare description of process sheds light on Abu Turab's working method:

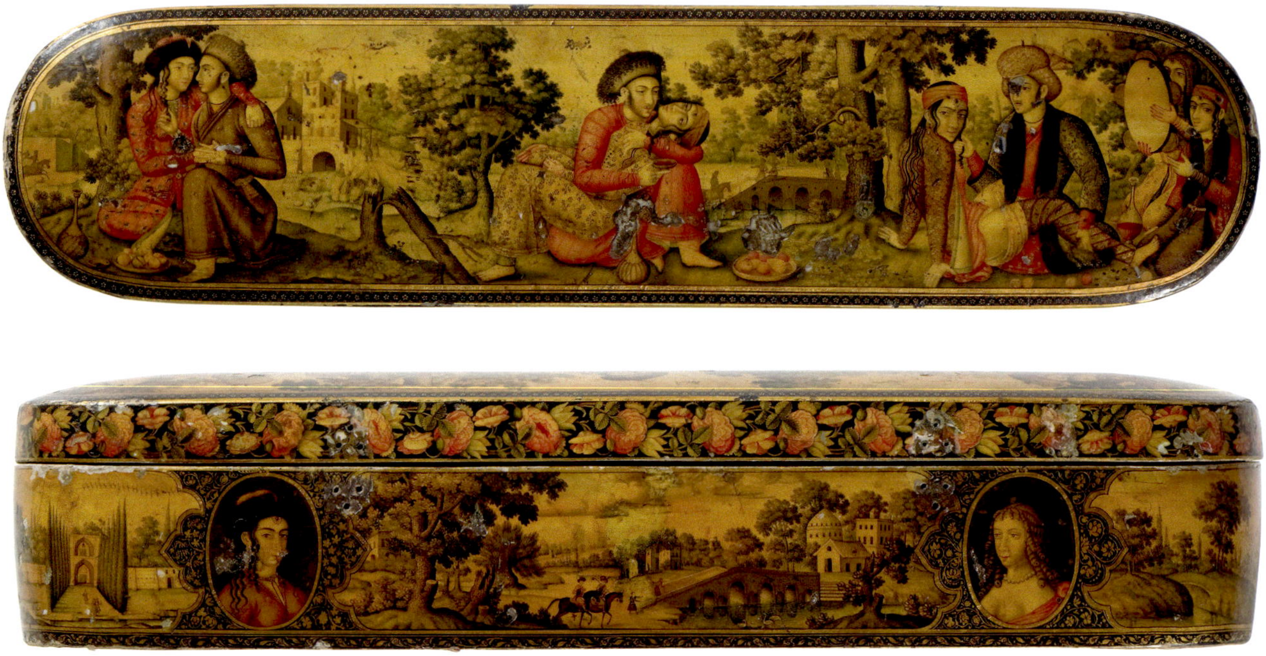

16 *Pen Box* (lid and side), Hajji Muhammad, Iran, Isfahan, dated 1124 H (1712–13). Opaque watercolor and lacquer on papier-mâché, 36.5 × 8.8 × 8.2 cm (14⅜ × 3⁷⁄₁₆ × 3¼ in.). Nasser D. Khalili Collection of Islamic Art, London, LAQ 361.

> Sitting . . . with a photograph, he had placed a mirror in front of it and was painting the reflection in the mirror on a marble slab; Mirzā Abutorāb Khan was the first to use this technique on stone or at least revive this old technique that had gone out of practice. He would work on the slab, *dān dān mīkard* [chisel], prepare it for direct application of ink and the printing of the image, and since the text or image appears in reverse during printing, he would work from the reflected image in the mirror to obtain the original after printing.[50]

Although the last two works (Figs. 13, 14) appear to be less connected to historical precedent than other paintings that mediated photographs, they prompt consideration of a longer history despite being conspicuously modern. A lacquer pen box of the late Safavid period, dated 1712–13, exemplifies what some art historians regard as the terrible effects of exposure to post-Renaissance European art (Fig. 16). In their minds, the reception of Western art led to incongruous fusions, incompletely absorbed pictorial conventions, and the death of "traditional" practices that had been characterized by coherent modes of representation. From the late 1500s, Persian artists increasingly responded to imported European art in the form of panel paintings, portrait miniatures, and prints to produce a "European style" (*farangī-sāz*), as it was named in Persian.[51] The pen box displays a composition of amorous couples set before a perspective landscape, a floral border around the lid, and sides composed of portrait busts and sweeping landscapes with Italianate and Persianate architecture.

The importance of this example, and numerous others of its kind, lies in the evidence it offers of an earlier time in Persianate art when prints—a reproductive image technology—functioned as intermediaries of representation. The Persian artists engaged this visual mode in their production of lacquers and other mediums. On the pen box, the artist combined dual modes of painted polychrome (for details of clothing, flowers) and stippled monochrome (for faces, exposed body parts, details of the environment). The pen box resulted from a creative process, a working methodology, based on the use of models (drawings, paintings, prints) and the fluid movement across mediums. Similar traces of adaptations from prints can be seen in the painted landscapes of many Qajar lacquer objects and are discussed in the earlier essay by Mary McWilliams.

Artists of Qajar Iran continued to emulate selected examples of Safavid art, adopting their subject matters and styles in an imitative form of creativity developed since the early 15th century, perhaps even earlier. As they did this, they also had an eye to the nearer past and the contemporary age.[52] They drew their subjects from lithographed books and single sheets, newspapers, photographs, photolithographs, and chromolithographs. An expanded universe of subjects, compositions, expressive modes, and the new affective nature of some images—especially photographic portraits characterized by descriptive detail and psychological intensity manifest in the direct gaze and/or facial expression—became available to Qajar artists from foreign and domestic contemporary sources. Some of these were translated—in the sense of being both *moved* and *changed*—to lacquer objects with or without the visual traces of the original medium being preserved (Fig. 17). The full-length portrait of a man on the lid of a pen box attributed to artist Muhammad Baqir Samirumi retains the traces of a photograph, transposed onto the surface of the lacquer, where it is embedded in a system of kinds of painting ranging from the mimetic to the abstract. While the painted portrait relates to photography, other painted compositions—the landscapes on the sides—stem from historical conventions of Persian lacquer painting. Another example of a lacquer pen box (cat. 76), signed by Mubarraz al-Shuʿara, and dated 1903–4, shows a similar combination of pictorial modes from historical Persianate painting. The composition of clerics and students in the central cartouche on the lid reflects the use of a photographic source through its complex overlapping and variation in relative size with respect to distance.

As yet, it is difficult to reconstruct fully the visual world of Qajar artists and to convey the intricate networks of image production between mediums, as lacquer objects simultaneously remediated a historical practice of Persianate painting (developed in books and on objects) and waves of new mediums in the form of various kinds of prints, lithographs, and photographs. And these forms were often in themselves blended. General observations of affinities of form and subject between mediums go only so far to explain Qajar artists'

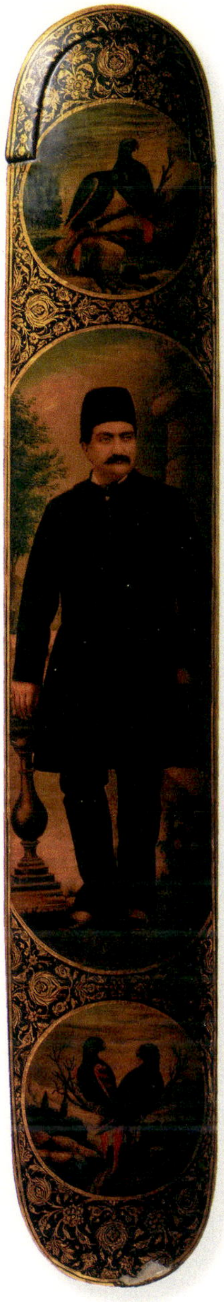

17 *Pen Box*, attributed to Muhammad Baqir Samirumi, Iran, early 1900s. Opaque watercolor and lacquer on papier-mâché, 23.4 × 4.1 × 4.1 cm (9³⁄₁₆ × 1⅝ × 1⅝ in.). Nasser D. Khalili Collection of Islamic Art, London, LAQ 518. (Image after Nasser D. Khalili, B. W. Robinson, and Tim Stanley, *Lacquer of the Islamic Lands*, pt. 2, The Nasser D. Khalili Collection of Islamic Art, vol. 22 [London; New York: Nour Foundation in association with Azimuth Editions and Oxford University Press, 1996–97], cat. 486, p. 246.)

creative intersection in a 19th-century world characterized by an escalating market for commodities and various regimes of mechanical reproduction. From this expanded world of images, Qajar lacquer artists reconfigured prototypes into new arrangements and combinations, shifted their palette, and supplied fresh details to the basic outlines presented in a design. (Some of these systems and procedures are outlined in McWilliams's essay.) While this form of production was not new—manuscript paintings since the early 1400s were conceived and executed in a comparable way—Qajar artists applied it to their great advantage.

It is useful now to return to the criticisms of Rochechouart presented in the introductory essay to this catalogue, because they actually illuminate key aspects of image production in Qajar times. Rochechouart took Qajar artists to task for their failure to distinguish between classes of images that were mapped against classes of consumer. (After all, in Iran artists treated with equal value "low brow" images used as shop displays in village wig stores or decorative accents in taverns and "high brow" paintings by the likes of Raphael and Titian.) They failed to make the appropriate aesthetic distinctions and also risked an association between their paintings and the world of commerce. The free process of sourcing imagery from various mediums and recombining them was also viewed with disdain by Rochechouart and many others, who perhaps considered it akin in process to the *découpage* of Victorian-era scrapbookers—cutting out and excerpting readymade compositions and fashioning them into new configurations—and hence also low class. Nonetheless, the procedure was well suited to the demands of efficient production in a competitive market, especially for an industrial art in which the artist was both "seller" and "worker," as Rochechouart would have it; for Qajar artists and patrons alike, it was a wholly legitimate and culturally approved form of creativity.

In aesthetic effect and means of production, the Qajar lacquers are comparable to contemporary paintings that mediated photographs. Qajar works on paper offer an intriguing parallel to the uses of photographs in late 19th-century India, where *cartes de visite* and other photographs were commonly painted with opaque watercolor. There are examples of painted and tinted Qajar photographs (see cat. 26), but typically they are sparsely colored with pigment used to enrich details of pattern and texture without covering the entire surface.[53] Similar treatments are indicated for lithographs. One example is a portrait of Muzaffar al-Din Shah (r. 1896–1907) dated to 1896–97 (see cat. 46, p. 146). The lithographic portrait has been delicately tinted with watercolor and set inside an elaborate frame composed of floral scrolls in polychrome and gold, resembling in its presentation historical albums (*muraqqaʿ*) of the Persian tradition.[54] The signature appearing below the portrait bust—"Life-scattering Mahdi, court painter, 1896–97" (*jān-niṣ̱ār Mahdī naqqāsh-i makhṣūṣ 1314*)—reflects the artist's work of coloring the mass-produced portrait.

The habit of painting Indian photographs was widespread and exceeded European and Persian conventions of retouching negatives or tinting prints. In India, paint was "much more than a supplement to the photographic image; rather, the overlay of paint completely replaces the photographic image in such a way that all or most of it is 'obscured.'"[55] In numerous examples, only the subject's face, hands, and feet are left unpainted, which produces a duality of modes—bright polychrome with pattern, subdued monochrome with subtle modulations of tone—in the painted photographs. This duality is comparable, in effect, to the fully painted Qajar portraits that used photographs as one of their source mediums.

An evaluation of the relationship between mechanical/semi-mechanical and handmade images cannot accept the conjecture that Qajar painters merely emulated and tried to reproduce photographs. Despite assessments made by contemporary Qajars that photographs offered an objective medium for instruction in proportion, light and shade, and perspective (aerial and linear), painters did not use them in this way. Rather, photographs were assimilated into painting in a manner consistent with practices that had a long historical precedent, a deep structure in the habits of artistic conception and production whether one looks at the output of court-sponsored workshops or the bazaar. Rather than opening the way for an entirely new artistic culture and a break with the past, one of the effects of photography and lithography was to reinvigorate the historical practice and format of the painted portrait—in Qajar eyes, a form of progress and modernity.[56] Far from being threatened by the reproductive and empirical promise of the new technology, photography was eagerly embraced as one of several techniques of art-making based on the use of models. Qajar artists across the social hierarchy preferred to engage their subject matters through pre-fabricated images—regardless of original medium—and not from their direct life study. The Qajar artists' general response to the new mediums of lithography and photography in the 19th century repeated earlier generations of Persian artists in the assimilation of print culture in the 17th century and after. In harnessing these new technologies, Qajar artists made doubly indexical objects: their paintings combined features simulating the photographic index—as the chemical impression of a sitter's real presence—with the abstract modes of historical Persian painting—which favored pattern, bright color, and isometric space—united by the medium of paint applied by the hand. In translating the chemical residues of the photograph's monochrome into the painting's polychrome, subtle adaptations of the photographic source mutated its status from a reproducible image into a unique object fashioned by the painter's hand.

David J. Roxburgh is the Prince Alwaleed Bin Talal Professor of Islamic Art History and Chair of the Department of History of Art and Architecture at Harvard University.

Notes

1 This essay is a revised and expanded version of a paper that I delivered at the Clark Art Institute in 2012 (video available at https://www.youtube.com/watch?v=PW7xTf2ByPk), and later published as David J. Roxburgh, "Troubles with Perspective: Case Studies in Picture-Making from Qajar Iran," in *Art History in the Wake of the Global Turn*, ed. Jill H. Casid and Aruna D'Souza (Williamstown, Mass.: Sterling and Francine Clark Art Institute, 2014).

2 Quoted in Willem Floor, "Art (*Naqqash*) and Artists (*Naqqashan*) in Qajar Persia," *Muqarnas* 16 (1999): 146. For the original, see Joseph Arthur, comte de Gobineau, *Trois ans en Asie (de 1855 à 1858) par le Cte. A. de Gobineau* (Paris: L. Hachette et Cie, 1859), 466.

3 Iʿtimad al-Saltana wrote the "Book of Histories and Traditions" in the 40th year of Nasir al-Din Shah's reign (1304 H [1886–87]) and published it two years later. Layla S. Diba, "The Qajar Court Painter Yahya Ghaffari: His Life and Times," in *Persian Painting from the Mongols to the Qajars: Studies in Honour of Basil W. Robinson*, ed. Robert Hillenbrand (London: I. B. Tauris, 2000), 85. For the Persian text, see Muḥammad Ḥasan Khān Iʿtimād al-Salṭana, *Ma'āthir wa al-āthār: Chihil sāl-i tārīkh-i Īrān: dar dawra-yi Pādishāh Nāṣir al-Dīn Shāh*, ed. Īrāj Āfshār, vol. 1 (Tehran: Shirkat-i Intishārāt-i Asāṭīr, 1363– H [1984–]), 168.

4 The artist was sent to study at the École des Beaux-Arts in Paris in 1858–59, when he was 12 years old. He later became Chief Painter (*Naqqāsh-Bāshī*) in 1871–72. For further details of his biography, see Floor, "Art (*Naqqash*) and Artists (*Naqqashan*) in Qajar Persia," 144, 146.

5 Gobineau had in the years before his appointment to Persia published *Essai sur l'inégalité des races humaines*, 4 vols. (Paris: Librairie de Firmin Didot, 1853–55), which organized the world into three races, placing the white Aryan race at its pinnacle and asserting that the mixing of races had caused the end of civilizations. His assessment of the Qajars and their art is shaped by his racial theories.

6 Tracing the impact of European visual art on those in Iran, John Carswell laments the adoption of "Western concepts of perspective and chiaroscuro," which resulted in a "lamentable failure" and provided one example "of the corruption of Eastern taste by Western influence." The result was a "deadly blow at what was admirable in Eastern painting." See John Carswell, "Eastern and Western Influence on Art of the Seventeenth Century in Iran," in *The Memorial Volume of the Vth International Congress of Iranian Art & Archaeology*, vol. 2, ed. A. Tajvidi and M. Y. Kiani (Tehran: Ministry of Culture and Arts, 1972), 277, 281. More recently, similar judgments were made about "the spectacular breakdown of the centuries-old system of artistic principles during the Qajar period." See Iván Szántó, "The Dying Days of Persian Book Painting," in *Artisans at the Crossroads: Persian Arts of the Qajar Period (1796–1925)*, ed. Béla Kelényi and Iván Szántó (Budapest: Ferenc Hopp Museum of Eastern Asiatic Arts, 2010). For summaries of prejudicial views and the problems they present to the study of Qajar art, see Floor, "Art (*Naqqashi*) and Artists (*Naqqashan*) in Qajar Persia," 125; Layla S. Diba, "An Encounter between Qajar Iran and the West: The Rashtrapati Bhavan Painting of Fath ʿAli Shah at the Hunt," in *Islamic Art in the 19th Century: Tradition, Innovation, and Eclecticism*, ed. Doris Behrens-Abouseif and Stephen Vernoit (Leiden, The Netherlands: Brill, 2006), 288; and Abbas Amanat, "Court Patronage and Public Space: Abu'l-Hasan Saniʿ al-Mulk and the Art of Persianizing the Other in Qajar Iran," in *Court Cultures in the Muslim World: Seventh to Nineteenth Centuries*, ed. Albrecht Fuess and Jan-Peter Hartung (New York: Routledge, 2011).

7 Ali Behdad, "The Power-ful Art of Qajar Photography: Orientalism and (Self)-Orientalizing in

Nineteenth-Century Iran," *Iranian Studies* 34 (1–4) (2001): 145.

8 Ibid., 141–42, and pl. 1. Behdad assigns the watercolor a symbolism and significance that I consider to be excessive. This painting and a second example signed by Mirza Riza Tabrizi, depicting a European photographer taking a daguerreotype of Mansur Khan, are published in Yaḥyā Ẕukā, *Tārīkh-i ʿakkāsī va ʿakkāsān-i pīshgām dar Īrān* (Tehran: Shirkat-i Intishārāt-i ʿIlmī va Farhangī, 1997), frontispiece and pl. 1. The relation between photography as practiced by Europeans throughout the Islamic lands and forms of local engagement is now being studied with greater nuance, especially in the Ottoman Empire. For one example, see Mary Roberts, "The Limits of Circumscription," in *Photography's Orientalism: New Essays on Colonial Representation*, ed. Ali Behdad and Luke Gartlan (Los Angeles: Getty Research Institute, 2013).

9 The term "remediation" is discussed in the introduction to this volume. The key study on remediation is Jay David Bolter and Richard Grusin, *Remediation: Understanding New Media* (Cambridge, Mass.: MIT Press, 1999). This essay is obviously of restricted scope and does not claim comprehensive coverage of all available materials. The study of Qajar art is still in a nascent state of development, and many large collections and archives are barely touched and await research and publication.

10 While this essay is not the first to comment on the impact of photography and lithography on painting in Iran, it reaches different conclusions than existing literature and applies pressure to some existing formulations advanced by other scholars. The most important commentaries include Behdad, "The Power-ful Art of Qajar Photography"; Layla S. Diba with Maryam Ekhtiar, eds., *Royal Persian Paintings: The Qajar Epoch, 1785–1925* (London: I. B. Tauris Publishers in association with Brooklyn Museum of Art, 1998); Stephen Vernoit, "The Visual Arts in Nineteenth-Century Visual Thought," in Behrens-Abouseif and Vernoit, *Islamic Art in the 19th Century*, 26–27; Julian Raby, *Qajar Portraits* (London: Azimuth Editions in association with the Iran Heritage Foundation, 1999), esp. 7, 17–18, and 56; and Floor, "Art (*Naqqashi*) and Artists (*Naqqashan*) in Qajar Persia," 131–34. In the face of increased interest in the interactions between photography and painting, Layla Diba has offered a revisionist view in which she questions some of the evidence and proposes that the naturalism seen in the work of an artist like Muhammad Ghaffari (Kamal al-Mulk) reflects the result of academic training in painting and not photography. See Layla S. Diba, "Qajar Photography and Its Relationship to Iranian Art: A Reassessment," *History of Photography* 37 (1) (2013). Diba further questions whether the range of Qajar art across mediums should in fact be considered together, re-inscribing divisions between the fine and decorative arts (which has forestalled the examination of Qajar materials in relation to one another), and suggests that the true impact of photography be found in the "commercial sphere, where photographs were widely disseminated, specifically in the production of tile-work portraits" (p. 98).

11 The binding of the prayer book seen in Figure 4 has early 19th-century European prints of women on its upper and lower covers. See Nasser D. Khalili, B. W. Robinson, and Tim Stanley, *Lacquer of the Islamic Lands*, pt. 2, The Nasser D. Khalili Collection of Islamic Art, vol. 22 (London and Oxford: Nour Foundation in association with Azimuth Editions and Oxford University Press, 1996–7), 163–64, cat. 378. For another example of the same process, a pen box covered with prints of women dating to the late 1800s, see Reingard Neumann, ed., *Aus 1001 Nacht: Islamische Lackkunst in deutschen Museen und Bibliotheken* (Münster, Germany: Museum für Lackkunst, 2009), 185, cat. 89. For an example of a print transformed into paint under lacquer, see Khalili, Robinson, and Stanley, *Lacquer of the Islamic Lands*, pt. 2, cat. 238. It is a mirror case (dated 1858–59) with a shutter signed by the artist Najaf ʿAli and made for Mirza Hasan Khan, the younger brother of Mirza Taqi Khan Amir Kabir, Nasir al-Din Shah's first prime minister.

12 The box was sold at Ader Nordmann, Paris, *Arts de l'Orient et de l'Inde*, May 28, 2014, lot 50. The figures on the lid are identified as Nasir al-Din Shah (at center) and to his right his son Kamran Mirza and prince Iʿtizad al-Saltana. There are two portraits of Qajar courtiers to the king's left. Carmen Pérez González and Reza Sheikh, "From the Inner Sanctum: Men Who Were Trusted by the Kings," in *The Eye of the Shah: Qajar Court Photography and the Persian Past*, ed. Jennifer Y. Chi (New York: Institute for the Study of the Ancient World at New York University, 2015), 145, note Nasir al-Din Shah's habit of collecting European photographs, lithographs, and albums during his travels throughout Europe.

13 The *dīvān* was offered for sale at Bonhams, London, *Islamic & Indian Art*, April 28, 2005, lot 88.

14 For examples of tiles reflecting the intermediaries of lithographs and photographs, see Jennifer M. Scarce, "Ancestral Themes in the Art of Qajar Iran, 1785–1925," in Behrens-Abouseif and Vernoit, *Islamic Art in the 19th Century*, 244–45; and Jennifer M. Scarce, "The Role of Architecture in the Creation of Tehran," in *Téhéran: Capitale bicentenaire*, ed. Charyhar Adle and Bernard Hourcade (Paris: Institut français de recherche en Iran, 1992), 87, 90.

15 Similar effects were noted for contemporary Europe by Michel Foucault.

See Sarah Mirseyedi, "Aesthetic Innovation and Conditions of Modernity in Nineteenth-Century Iran," in *An Album of Artists' Drawings from Qajar Iran*, ed. David J. Roxburgh (Cambridge, Mass.: Harvard Art Museums, 2017).

16 The gamut of cultural and artistic practices under the Qajars has been described as a form of eclecticism found in other 19th-century societies. See Diba, "An Encounter between Qajar Iran and the West," 287; Oleg Grabar, "Reflections on Qajar Art and Its Significance," *Iranian Studies* 34 (1–4) (2001); Maryam Ekhtiar, "Innovation and Revivalism in Later Persian Calligraphy: The Visal Family of Shiraz," in Behrens-Abouseif and Vernoit, *Islamic Art in the 19th Century*; and J. P. Luft, "The Qajar Rock Reliefs," *Iranian Studies* 34 (1–4) (2001).

17 See Peter Avery, "Printing, the Press, and Literature in Modern Iran," in *The Cambridge History of Iran*, vol. 7, *From Nadir Shah to the Islamic Republic*, ed. P. Avery, G. R. G. Hambly, and Charles Melville (Cambridge: Cambridge University Press, 1991), esp. 815–22.

18 The change is discussed by Floor, who dates it to the late 1860s and links the emergence of the fat crayon to the development of photography. See Floor, "Art (*Naqqash*) and Artists (*Naqqashan*) in Qajar Persia," 133.

19 The first court photographer was Aqa Riza Iqbal al-Saltana (1843–1889); he received the appointment in 1863. See Pérez González and Sheikh, "From the Inner Sanctum," 138.

20 Outlines of this history are presented in Iraj Afshar, "Some Remarks on the Early History of Photography in Iran," in *Qajar Iran: Political, Social, and Cultural Change, 1800–1925*, ed. Edmond Bosworth and Carole Hillenbrand (Costa Mesa, Calif.: Mazda, 1983), 261–90; Chahryar Adle and Yahya Zoka, "Notes et documents sur la photographie iranienne et son histoire," *Studia Iranica* 12 (2) (1983); Donna Stein, "Three Photographic Traditions in Nineteenth-Century Iran," *Muqarnas* 6 (1989); Behdad, "The Power-ful Art of Qajar Photography," 144–46; Ẕukā, *Tārīkh-i ʿakkāsī va ʿakkāsān-i pīshgām dar Īrān*; Maryam Ekhtiar, "Nasir al-Din Shah and the Dar al-Funun: The Evolution of an Institution," *Iranian Studies* 34 (1–4) (2001); Pérez González and Sheikh, "From the Inner Sanctum"; Mohammad Sattari and Houshang Salamat, "Photography and the Illustrated Journals *Sharaf* and *Sharāfat*," *History of Photography* 37 (1) (2013); and Mohammad Reza Tahmasbpour, "Photography in Iran: A Chronology," *History of Photography* 37 (1) (2013).

21 Ekhtiar, "Nasir al-Din Shah and the Dar al-Funun," 153.

22 Maryam Ekhtiar, "From Workshop and Bazaar to Academy: Art Training and Production in Qajar Iran," in Diba, *Royal Persian Paintings*, 60.

23 For further details on Abu al-Hasan Ghaffari's biography, see Raby, *Qajar Portraits*, 56; Floor, "Art (*Naqqashi*) and Artists (*Naqqashan*) in Qajar Persia," 141–44; *Encyclopaedia Iranica*, s.v. "Abu'l-Ḥasan Khan Gaffārī," by B. W. Robinson; and Yahya Zoka, *Life and Works of Saniʿ Ol-Molk: Abol-Hassan Ghaffari 1814–1866*, ed. Cyrus Parham (Tehran: Iran University Press, 2003).

24 For a reprint of issues of the newspaper, see *Rūznāma-yi dawlat-i ʿalīya-yi Īrān* (Tehran: Kitāb khāna-yi Millī-yi Jumhūrī-yi Islāmī-yi Īrān, 1992–93).

25 Ekhtiar, "From Workshop and Bazaar to Academy," 59.

26 It is important to emphasize the extent to which artists were skilled in multiple mediums. For examples of these crossovers, studied from the primary perspective of lithographic practice, see the artists' biographies in Ulrich Marzolph, *Narrative Illustration in Persian Lithographed Books* (Leiden, The Netherlands: Brill, 2001), 28–48. The close working relations of photographers and painters (working in lithography) is discussed in Sattari and Salamat, "Photography and the Illustrated Journals *Sharaf* and *Sharāfat*." In the late period of Nasir al-Din Shah's reign, photographers often complained that the painters did not reproduce their images adequately (p. 79).

27 The recent study by Sattari and Salamat, "Photography and the Illustrated Journals *Sharaf* and *Sharāfat*," investigates some of these materialist operations and intersections between institutions and people who worked to produce the newspapers *Sharaf* and *Sharāfat*. They have been able to match numerous lithographed images to their photographic models. This was a global phenomenon in the 19th century. For a comparable study treating the *Dianshizhai Pictorial*, a magazine published in Shanghai between 1884 and 1898, see Hongfeng Tang, "Zhaoxiang Dianshizhai Dianshizhai huabao zhong de zaimejie wenti" (Photolithography in Dianshizhai: The Issue of Remediation in *Dianshizhai Pictorial*), *Meishu Yanjiu* 1 (2016). I thank Hongfeng Tang for sharing her work with me. Her article discusses the complex process of imagery translation between photography and print. Equipped with the imported technology of photolithography, the artists of the magazine developed processes of copying, collaging, translating, and recreating images.

28 ʿAlī Qūlī Mīrzā Iʿtiżād al-Salṭana, *Akṣīr al-tawārīkh*, ed. Jamshīd Kīyānfar (Tehran: Vīsman, 1370 H [1991]); Afshar, "Some Remarks on the Early History of Photography in Iran," 262; Floor, "Art (*Naqqash*) and Artists (*Naqqashan*) in Qajar Persia," 133 and n. 102; and Sattari and Salamat, "Photography and the Illustrated Journals *Sharaf* and *Sharāfat*," 74.

29 Many of the commentaries made by Iʿtimad al-Saltana in several of his texts are presented in Afshar, "Some Remarks on the Early History of Photography in Iran."

30 The general meaning of the passage is conveyed by Sattari and Salamat, "Photography and the Illustrated

Journals *Sharaf* and *Sharāfat*," 76. For the original Persian, see Iʿtimād al-Salṭana, *Maʾāthir wa al-āthār*, 1:146. Diba also mentions this statement but as a means to minimize the impact of photography on painting; see "Qajar Photography and Its Relationship to Iranian Art," 92.

31 In the original Persian: *va az anjā ki ṣanaʿat-i ʿaks bi fann-i shabīh-sāzī takmīlan va tashīlan khidmatī sakht-i buzurg namūda ast*. Iʿtimād al-Salṭana, *Maʾāthir wa al-āthār*, 1:146.

32 Afshar, "Some Remarks on the Early History of Photography in Iran," 264.

33 This raises the complex issue of drawing and painting from life. There is little direct evidence of Qajar artists working from life—whether in the Dar al-Funun or outside it—though Nasir al-Din Shah himself kept sketchbooks. See Fāṭima Qāżīhā, *Nāṣir al-Dīn Shāh va Naqqāshī* (Tehran: Sāzmān-i Asnād va Kitāb-khāna-yi Millī-yi Jumhūrī-yi Islāmī-yi Īrān, 1394 H [2015]).

34 As Afshar notes, the mulla's reaction was shaped by a psychological notion that made photography impossible, "for the ancients believed that it was only the human spirit which was capable of imprinting and recording images, and this facility was beyond the scope of any man-made machine"; see Afshar, "Some Remarks on the Early History of Photography in Iran," 264.

35 Vernoit, "Visual Arts in Nineteenth-Century Visual Thought," 26.

36 This is the only shortcoming I can find in Sattari and Salamat's study "Photography and the Illustrated Journals *Sharaf* and *Sharāfat*." Perhaps future work on the translation from photograph to lithograph in Iran can take a closer materialist approach.

37 Ekhtiar, "From Workshop and Bazaar to Academy," 56, 60–61.

38 Adle and Zoka, "Notes et documents sur la photographie iranienne et son histoire," 258–60, 273. Examples include two portraits (oil on canvas) of Nasir al-Din Shah executed by Muhammad Ghaffari (Kamal al-Mulk) in 1881 for the Shams al-ʿImara, Gulistan Palace, Tehran. Inscriptions on the paintings identified the sources as daguerreotypes made by Jules Richard in 1844 and 1853–54. This evidence, based on Zoka's memory of the two portraits, has been questioned recently by Diba, "Qajar Photography and Its Relationship to Iranian Art," 87 and passim. Diba's essay focuses on the work of Muhammad Ghaffari and suggests that the realism of his portraits results from his academic training more than photography. However, there are several clear-cut examples of his portraits of Nasir al-Din Shah in oil (dated 1891–92 and 1889–90) and watercolor (1889) made after photographic models. See Raby, *Qajar Portraits*, cats. 126, 127; and Sotheby's, London, *Arts of the Islamic World*, October 7, 2015, lot 299. For the photograph, see Chi, *Eye of the Shah*, cat. 17.

39 For further details about the photograph, see Diba, *Royal Persian Paintings*, 264.

40 Cat. 5 was auctioned in 1976. See Sotheby's, London, *Catalogue of Fine Oriental Miniatures, Manuscripts, and Qajar Paintings*, April 13, 1976, lot 202.

41 Ardashir Mirza (1805–1866) was Nasir al-Din Shah's uncle and governor of Tehran. The painting is published in Diba, *Royal Persian Paintings*, cat. 78; for the earlier painting dated 1852–53, see cat. 79. A third example by the same artist is a portrait of Husayn ʿAli Khan Muʿayyir al-Mamalik dated 1853–54 and described as evidence of "a new level of psychological realism in Iranian portraiture." See Stephen Vernoit, *Occidentalism: Islamic Art in the 19th Century,* The Nasser D. Khalili Collection of Islamic Art, vol. 23 (London: Nour Foundation in association with Azimuth Editions and Oxford University Press, 1997), cat. 67.

42 For its illustration, see Diba, *Royal Persian Paintings*, cat. 79; and Roxburgh, "Troubles with Perspective," 115.

43 The painting was previously published in Abbas Amanat, *Pivot of the Universe: Nasir al-Din Shah and the Iranian Monarchy, 1831–1896* (London: I. B. Tauris, 2008), 175, pl. 7.

44 For a discussion of the spatial conception of Persianate painting, whose techniques are applicable in many aspects to the Qajar single-sheet portraits, see David J. Roxburgh, "Micrographia: Toward a Visual Logic of Persianate Painting," *RES: Anthropology and Aesthetics* 43 (2003). In her recent book, Carmen Pérez González compares historical Persianate painting with Qajar photography and makes many insightful observations about the relation between the two, especially with respect to the affinities between Qajar single-sheet painted portraits and photographs in the nature of poses adopted, treatments of the face, gestures, and the furnishings of interior spaces; see Carmen Pérez González, *Local Portraiture: Through the Lens of the 19th-Century Iranian Photographers* (Leiden, The Netherlands: Leiden University Press, 2012), chap. 3. But I disagree with her argument that the isometric space of Persianate painting determined the framing of Qajar photographs. The same spatial effects are evident in photographs taken worldwide at the same time.

45 For the inscriptions, see cats. 3 and 4.

46 For the inscription, see cat. 1.

47 The painting was offered for sale at Christie's, London, *Islamic Art and Indian Miniatures*, October 14, 1997, lot 159.

48 Little work has been done on the tintype (melainotype or ferrotype) and the practice of retouching, painting, and tinting photographs in Iran, with a few passing remarks in Floor, "Art (*Naqqashi*) and Artists (*Naqqashan*) in Qajar Persia," 133. Study of American tintypes suggest an upper plate size of 11 × 14 in., with the smaller sized "bon-ton" of 2⅜ × 3½ in. or 4 × 5¾ in. being most popular. Floyd Rinhart, Marion

Rinhart, and Robert W. Wagner, *The American Tintype* (Columbus: Ohio State University Press, 1999), 43, 74, and app. 3.

49 Diba notes the dual modes of execution in the image and suggests its execution by two artists. She also compares it to a near identical image on a ceramic tile that highlights the replication of imagery "in different formats and disseminated throughout the country." Diba, *Royal Persian Portraits*, cat. 81.

50 The recollection of Abu Turab's method was offered by Muhammad ʿAli Furughi; quoted in and translated by Sattari and Salamat, "Photography and the Illustrated Journals *Sharaf* and *Sharāfat*," 76.

51 Rochechouart, *Souvenirs d'un voyage en Perse* (Paris: Challamel Aîné, 1867), 264.

52 For the imitation of Safavid art in Qajar lacquers, see Iván Szántó, "Qajar Lacquerware and the Related Art Forms," in Kelényi and Szántó, *Artisans at the Crossroads*, 51; and B. W. Robinson, "Qajar Lacquer," *Muqarnas* 6 (1989): 143. Representative examples of the forms taken by Qajar imitations of Safavid lacquers are published in Khalili, Robinson, and Stanley, *Lacquer of the Islamic Lands*, part 2, cats. 314–20.

53 Pérez González and Sheikh ("From the Inner Sanctum," 150) describe the need for detailed study of hand-colored photography in Iran. Their essay is illustrated by several examples that demonstrate the scope of the painting and tinting of photographs between the reigns of Nasir al-Din Shah and Ahmad Shah. See Chi, *Eye of the Shah*, cats. 5, 43, 120, and Fig. 10.

54 Earlier in the century, artists in the Majmaʿ-i Sanayiʿ had applied the same techniques to the production of photographic albums. See Pérez González and Sheikh, "From the Inner Sanctum," 142.

55 Christopher Pinney, *Camera Indica: The Social Life of Indian Photographs* (Chicago: University of Chicago Press, 1997), 77–78, Figs. 43–44.

56 At the conclusion of her essay "Qajar Photography and Its Relationship to Iranian Art," Diba writes that "photography was fundamentally not beneficial to the evolution of Persian painting towards an authentic modernity, although it responded clearly to long-held Persian aesthetic values and aspirations towards realism as expressed by Eʿtemād-os-Saltane" (p. 98).

Works in the Exhibition

PAINTINGS

1. Muhammad Shah Qajar

Signed by Abu al-Hasan Ghaffari Naqqash-Bashi
Iran, dated 1262 H (1845–46)
Black ink, graphite, and watercolor on beige wove paper
30 × 23.8 cm (11 13/16 × 9 3/8 in.)
Collection of Vahid Kooros

INSCRIBED:

shabīh-i shāhanshāh-i jamjāh Muḥammad Shāh Qājār khallada Allāh mulkahu naqsh-i Abū al-Ḥasan Naqqāsh-Bāshī Ghaffārī 1262

Portrait of the King of Kings who resembles Jamshid, Muhammad Shah Qajar, may God perpetuate his kingdom. Painted by Abu al-Hasan Ghaffari, the Chief Painter, 1845–46

2. Nasir al-Din Shah Qajar

Signed by Mubarak Mirza b. Mahmud
Iran, late 1850s
Watercolor, gold, and graphite on beige wove paper
31.9 × 22.1 cm (12 9/16 × 8 11/16 in.)
Collection of Saeed Kouros

INSCRIBED:

al-Sulṭān ibn al-sulṭān Nāṣir al-Dīn Shāh Qājār raqm-i banda-yi dargāh Mubārak ibn Maḥmūd

The sultan, son of the sultan, Nasir al-Din Shah Qajar. Rendering by the slave of the court Mubarak b. Mahmud

PUBLISHED:

Abbas Amanat, *Pivot of the Universe: Nasir al-Din Shah and the Iranian Monarchy, 1831–1896* (Berkeley: University of California Press, 2008), 175, pl. 7.

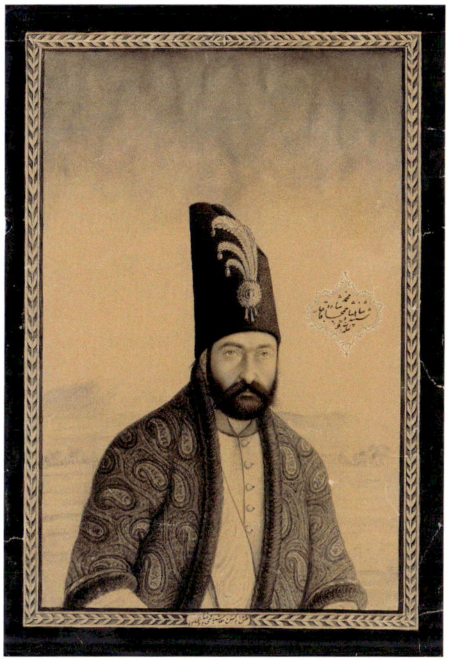

1

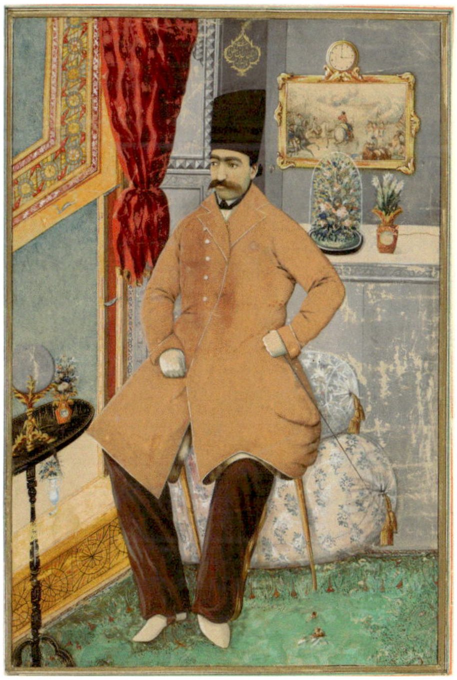

2

3. Mirza Zayn al-ʿAbidin

Signed by Abu al-Hasan Ghaffari Kashani Naqqash-Bashi
Iran, dated 1274 H (1857–58)
Black ink, watercolor, and graphite on beige wove paper
31.8 × 19.5 cm (12½ × 7¹¹⁄₁₆ in.)
Harvard Art Museums / Arthur M. Sackler Museum, Gift of Vahid Kooros in honor of Thomas W. Lentz, 2015.32

INSCRIBED:

shāhanshāhī muqarrab al-khāqān mu'tamin al-sulṭān Mīrzā Zayn al-ʿĀbidīn mustawfī-i khāṣṣa dar sinn-i chihil va chahār sāligī raqm-i Abū al-Ḥasan Naqqāsh-Bāshī Kāshānī Ghaffārī sana 1274

Royal intimate of the emperor, confidante of the sultan, Mirza Zayn al-ʿAbidin, comptroller of the crown at the age of 44. Painted by Abu al-Hasan Kashani Ghaffari, the Chief Painter, [in] the year 1857–58

4. Muhammad Ibrahim Khan Siham al-Mulk, Commander of the Isfahan Division

Signed by Abu al-Hasan Ghaffari Kashani Naqqash-Bashi
Iran, dated 1274 H (1857–58)
Black ink, watercolor, gold, and graphite on beige wove paper
36.6 × 49.2 cm (14⁷⁄₁₆ × 19⅜ in.)
Collection of Saeed Kouros

INSCRIBED:

LEFT: *ʿālījāh Abū al-Qāsim Khān sarhang-i fawj-i Chahārmaḥanī*

His Excellency Abu al-Qasim Khan, Commander of the Chaharmahani battalion

CENTER: *huwa Allāh taʿālā shā'nahu natīja al-umarā' al-ʿaẓẓām muqarrab al-khāqān Muḥammad Ibrāhīm Khān Sihām al-Mulk*

He is God, may His importance be exalted, offspring of the greatest amirs, intimate of the emperor, Muhammad Ibrahim Khan, Arrows of the Kingdom

RIGHT: *ʿālījāh Mīrzā ʿAbd al-Wahhāb Khān sarhang-i fawj-i Iṣfahānī*

His Excellency Mirza ʿAbd al-Wahhab Khan, Commander of the Isfahan battalion

BOTTOM CENTER: *raqm-i Abū al-Ḥasan Naqqāsh-Bāshī Ghaffārī Kashānī dar sana 1274*

Painted by Abu al-Hasan Ghaffari Kashani, the Chief Painter, in the year 1857–58

PUBLISHED:

Yahya Zoka, *Life and Works of Saniʿ ol-Molk Abol-Hassan Ghaffari 1814–1866*, ed. Cyrus Parham (Tehran: Iran University Press, 2003), 46, 80, cat. 10 (English section).

5. Standing Courtier

Iran, mid-19th century
Watercolor and graphite on beige wove paper
34.5 × 20.8 cm (13⁹⁄₁₆ × 8³⁄₁₆ in.)
Collection of Hamid Kooros

PUBLISHED:

Sotheby's, London, *Fine Oriental Miniatures, Manuscripts, and Qajar Paintings*, April 13–14, 1976, 40–41, lot 202.

6. ʿAli, Hasan, and Husayn

Signed by Muhammad Baqi [. . .]
Iran, late 19th century
Watercolor and gold on beige wove paper; illuminated page with punchwork; medallion insert
49.7 × 31.3 cm (19⁹⁄₁₆ × 12⁵⁄₁₆ in.)
Collection of Saeed Kouros

INSCRIBED:

MARGINS (prayer in Arabic invoking the Prophet and Shiʿi imams): *bi-nabīyi ʿarabī wa rasūl madanī wa akhīha asad Allāh . . .*

By the Arab prophet and messenger of Medina, and by his brother, Lion of God . . .

TOP (hadith in Arabic): *Qāla bi qawl Allāh ʿazza wa jalla wilāyat ʿAli b. Abī Ṭālib ḥiṣnī fa-man dakhala ḥiṣnī āmina min adhābī*

He said in God's words, may He be Honored and Glorified: "The guardianship of ʿAli b. Abi Talib is my fort. Whoever enters my fort is safe from my torment."

BOTTOM (couplet from a 14th-century poem in praise of ʿAli):
Ṣuratī gardad mujassam, fatḥ guyad āshkār
Lā fatā illā ʿAlī, lā sayf illā Dhū al-Fiqār
An image becomes incarnated, the divine grace proclaims:
There is no generous youth but ʿAli, no sword but *Dhu al-Fiqār* (ʿAli's double-edged sword)
ʿamal-i ḥaqir Muḥammad Baqī [. . .]
Work of the lowliest Muhammad Baqi [. . .]

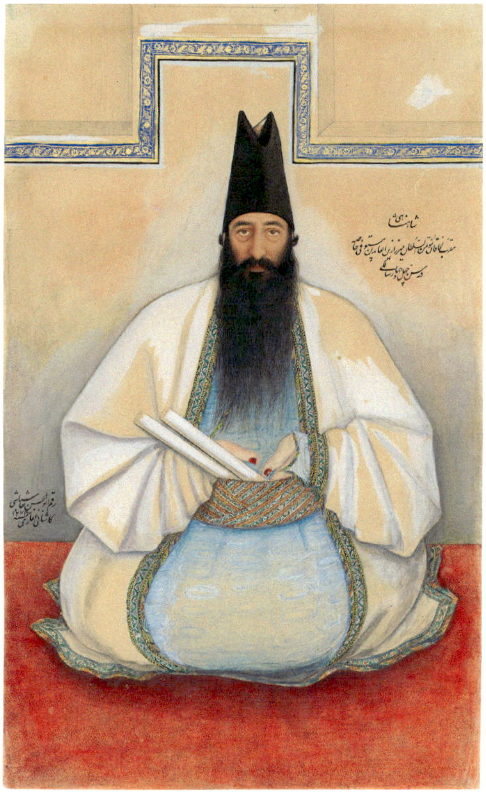

3

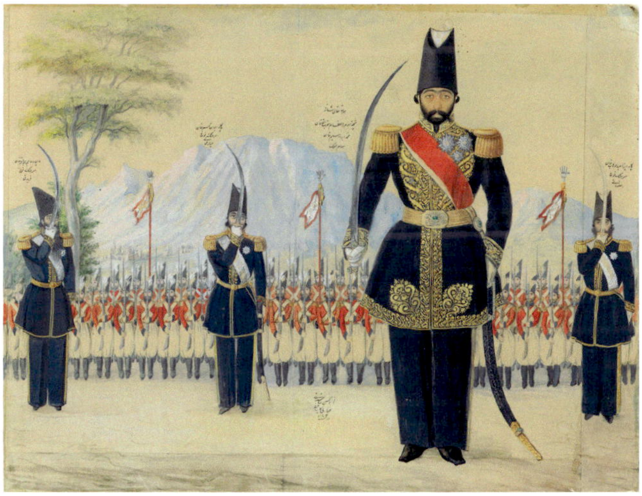

4

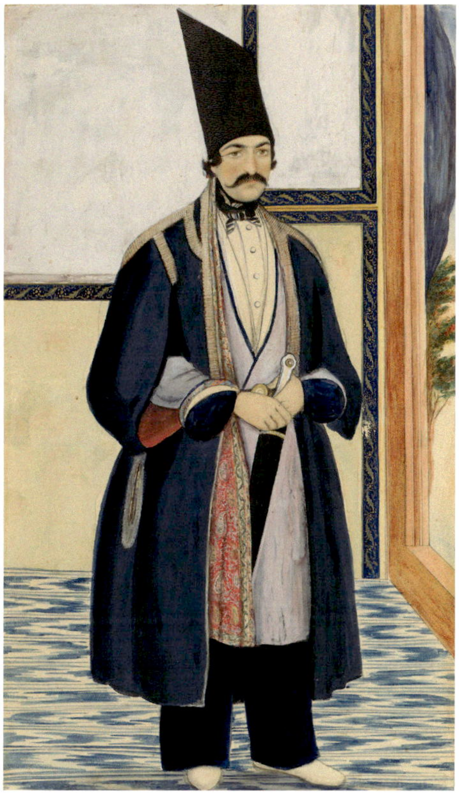

5

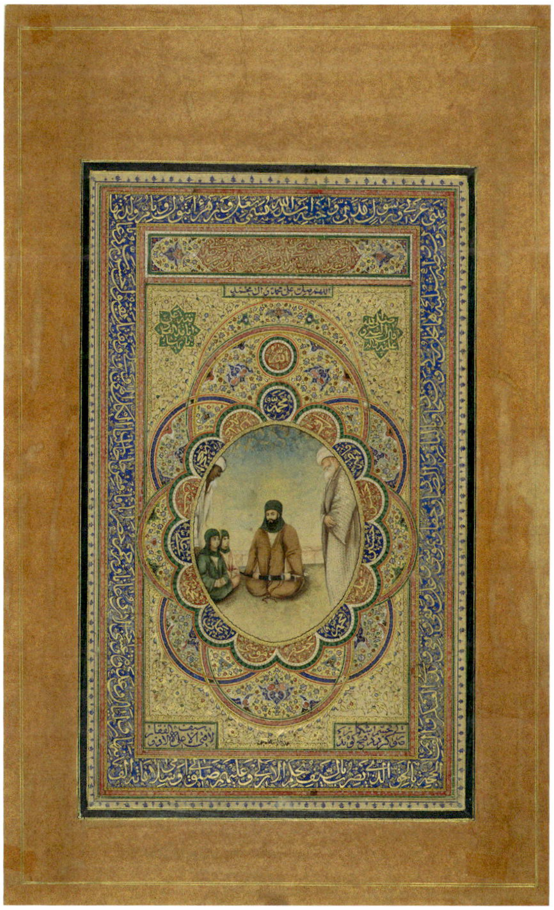

6

MANUSCRIPTS

7. Farhad Receives a Visitor at Mount Bisutun (*right*) and Farhad Shows the Rock Relief of Shirin to His Visitor (*left*)

Double page from a manuscript with poetry by Maktabi Shirazi, Vahshi Bafqi, and Naw'i Khabushani
Iran, Shiraz, text dated 22 Shawwal 1254 H (January 8, 1838)
Paintings: ink, watercolor, and gold on off-white laid paper; cover: watercolor, gold-colored pigments, and lacquer on pasteboard
16 × 10 cm (6 5/16 × 3 15/16 in.)
Harvard Art Museums / Arthur M. Sackler Museum, Gift of A. Soudavar in memory of his mother Ezzat-Malek Soudavar, 2014.401

8. Jamshid Explains the Wearing of Rings

Folio from a manuscript of the *Gulistān* (Rose Garden) by Sa'di
Signed by Ibrahim
Iran, late 19th century
Colored ink, watercolor, and gold on off-white laid paper (coated and burnished)
Folio: 22.8 × 15 cm (9 × 5 7/8 in.)
Harvard Art Museums / Arthur M. Sackler Museum, Loan from A. Soudavar in memory of his mother Ezzat-Malek Soudavar, 28.2015
INSCRIBED:
raqm-i Ibrāhīm
Painted by Ibrahim

9. Study of a Rose Balsam (*Impatiens balsamina*) (*right*) and Study of a Rose Balsam (*Impatiens balsamina*) (*left*)

Signed by Muhammad Hadi (left)
Folios 9b and 10a from *An Album of Persian Paintings and Drawings*
Iran, 18th–19th century
Right: watercolor and traces of black chalk on off-white wove paper; left: watercolor and graphite on off-white wove paper
Each folio: 30 × 20 cm (11 13/16 × 7 7/8 in.)
Harvard Art Museums / Arthur M. Sackler Museum, Loan from A. Soudavar in memory of his mother Ezzat-Malek Soudavar, 19.2015
INSCRIBED (left):
raqm-i kamtarīn Muḥammad Hādī
Painted by the most humble Muhammad Hadi

10. Birds, Flowers, and Butterflies

Folio 2b from *An Album of Artists' Drawings from Qajar Iran*
Iran, c. 1775–1850
Black ink on off-white modern laid paper, pricked
Folio: 32.5 × 22 cm (12 13/16 × 8 11/16 in.)
Harvard Art Museums / Arthur M. Sackler Museum, Alpheus Hyatt Purchasing Fund, 1960.161.2

11. Medallion with Portrait Bust of a European Woman, Enclosed in Symmetrical Composition of Scrollwork, Flowers, Birds, and Insects

Folio 3a from *An Album of Artists' Drawings from Qajar Iran*
Iran, c. 1805–30
Black ink, watercolor, and graphite on beige wove paper, burnished
Folio: 32.5 × 22 cm (12 13/16 × 8 11/16 in.)
Harvard Art Museums / Arthur M. Sackler Museum, Alpheus Hyatt Purchasing Fund, 1960.161.3

12. Virgin and Child with Three Old Men, Angel, Female Companion, and Putto in the Sky

Folio 6a from *An Album of Artists' Drawings from Qajar Iran*
Iran, 1780–1850
Black counterproof with touches of black ink on off-white wove paper
Folio: 32.5 × 22 cm (12 13/16 × 8 11/16 in.)
Harvard Art Museums / Arthur M. Sackler Museum, Alpheus Hyatt Purchasing Fund, 1960.161.6

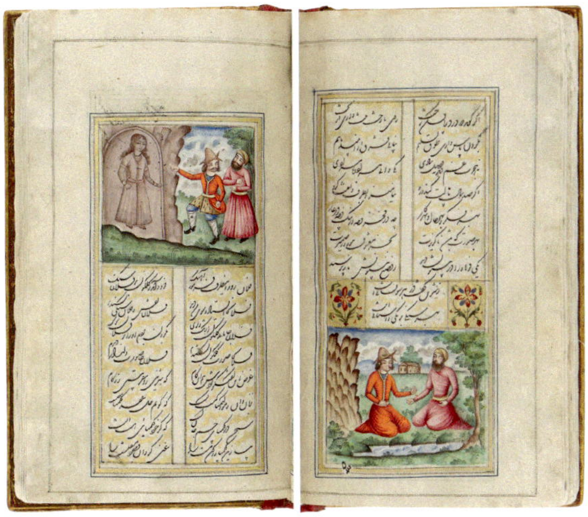

7

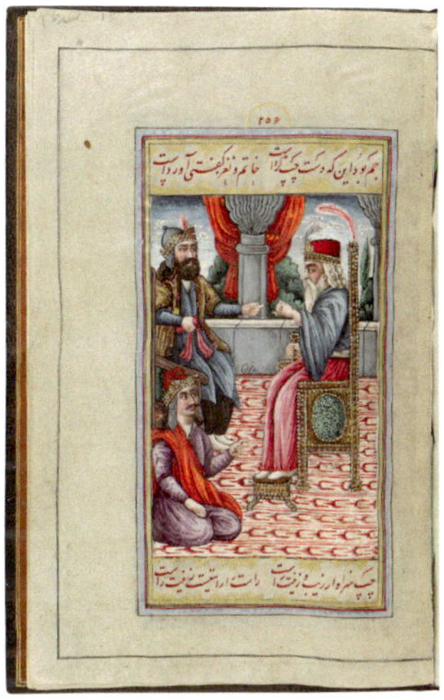

8

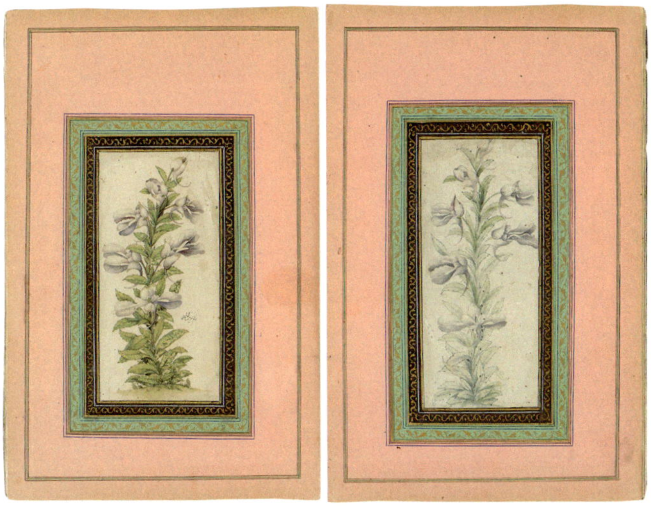

9

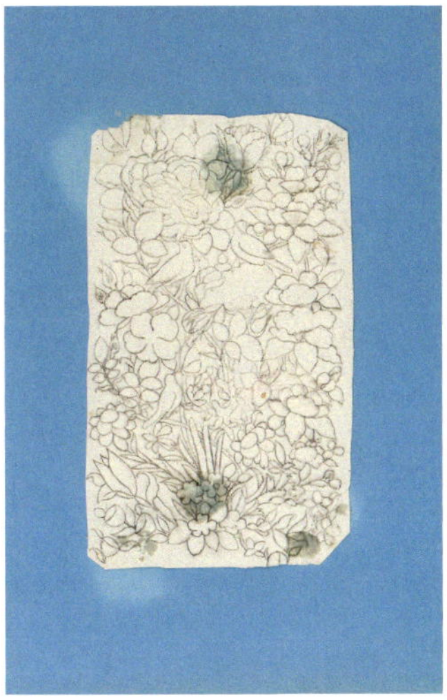

10

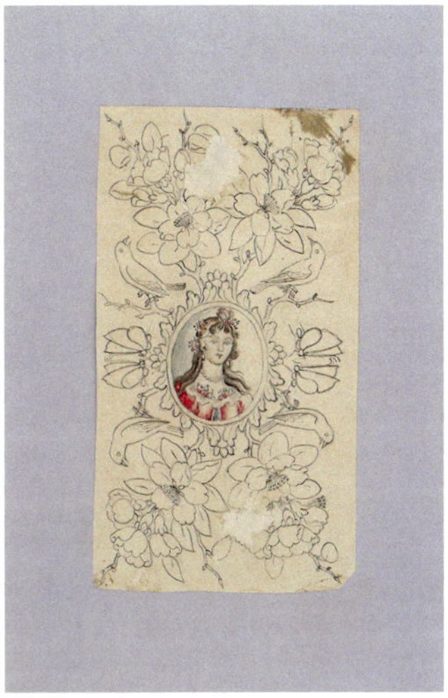

11

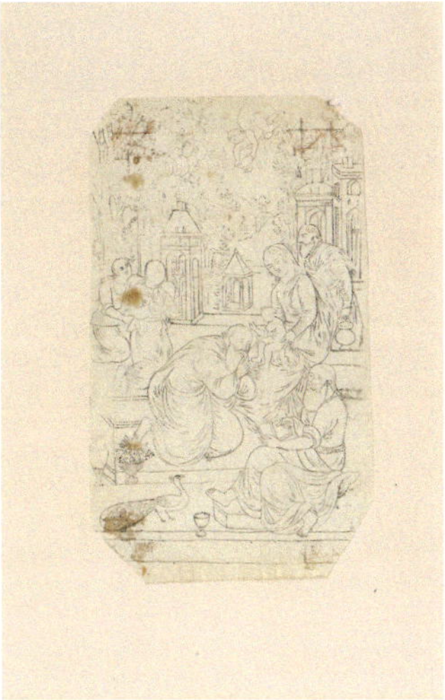

12

13. Embracing Couple on a Terrace, Attended by Male and Female Servants, a Musician, and a Dancer

Folio 7a from *An Album of Artists' Drawings from Qajar Iran*
Iran, 1820s–50s
Black counterproof on beige paper, pricked and rubbed with red chalk
Folio: 32.5 × 22 cm ($12\frac{13}{16} \times 8\frac{11}{16}$ in.)
Harvard Art Museums / Arthur M. Sackler Museum, Alpheus Hyatt Purchasing Fund, 1960.161.7

14. Virgin and Child with Attendants

Folio 42a from *An Album of Artists' Drawings from Qajar Iran*
Iran, 1780s–1870s
Black counterproof on off-white laid paper
Folio: 32.5 × 22 cm ($12\frac{13}{16} \times 8\frac{11}{16}$ in.)
Harvard Art Museums / Arthur M. Sackler Museum, Alpheus Hyatt Purchasing Fund, 1960.161.42

15. Couple with Male and Female Attendants Entertained by Musicians and a Dancer

Folio 10b from *An Album of Artists' Drawings from Qajar Iran*
Iran, 1820s–50s
Black counterproof on off-white modern laid paper, with gold and ink ruling, pricked and selectively pounced with red chalk
Folio: 32.5 × 22 cm ($12\frac{13}{16} \times 8\frac{11}{16}$ in.)
Harvard Art Museums / Arthur M. Sackler Museum, Alpheus Hyatt Purchasing Fund, 1960.161.10

16. The Meeting of Shams Tabrizi and Mawlana Jalal al-Din Rumi, from Haci Bektaş Veli's *Maqālāt* (Conversations) (*top*) and Shaykh San'an and the Christian Maiden, from Farid al-Din 'Attar's *Manṭiq al-ṭayr* (Conference of the Birds) (*bottom*)

Folio 18a from *An Album of Artists' Drawings from Qajar Iran*
Iran, 1850–1900
Displayed side: brown ink and graphite on off-white wove paper, edges pricked; adhered side: rubbed with red chalk
Folio: 32.5 × 22 cm ($12\frac{13}{16} \times 8\frac{11}{16}$ in.)
Harvard Art Museums / Arthur M. Sackler Museum, Alpheus Hyatt Purchasing Fund, 1960.161.18

17. Study Sheet with Flowers and Female Portraits and Figures

Folio 21b from *An Album of Artists' Drawings from Qajar Iran*
Iran, 1850–75
Displayed side: brown ink and graphite on off-white wove paper; adhered side: graphite
Folio: 32.5 × 22 cm ($12\frac{13}{16} \times 8\frac{11}{16}$ in.)
Harvard Art Museums / Arthur M. Sackler Museum, Alpheus Hyatt Purchasing Fund, 1960.161.21

18. Design for a Pen Box Composed of a Landscape and Audience Scene Divided by Portrait Roundels (*top*), King Bahram Gur in One of the Seven Pavilions, from Nizami's *Haft paykar* (Seven Beauties) (*center*), and Design for a Pen Box Composed of a Perspectival Architectural Landscape Divided by Portrait Medallions (*bottom*)

Folio 30a from *An Album of Artists' Drawings from Qajar Iran*
Iran, 1830–75
Top: red ink on off-white modern laid paper, pricked and rubbed with red chalk; center: brown ink on off-white wove paper; bottom: red and blue-black inks on off-white modern laid paper, pricked and rubbed with red chalk
Folio: 32.5 × 22 cm ($12\frac{13}{16} \times 8\frac{11}{16}$ in.)
Harvard Art Museums / Arthur M. Sackler Museum, Alpheus Hyatt Purchasing Fund, 1960.161.30
PUBLISHED:
David J. Roxburgh, "The Qajar Lacquer Object," in *In Harmony: The Norma Jean Calderwood Collection of Islamic Art*, ed. Mary McWilliams (Cambridge, Mass.: Harvard Art Museums, 2013), 72, pl. 8.

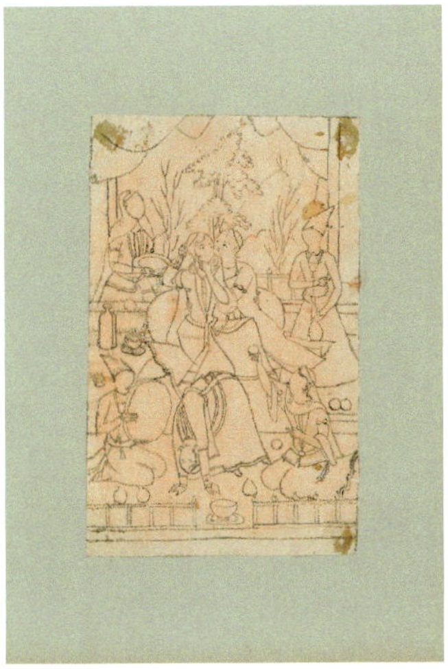

13

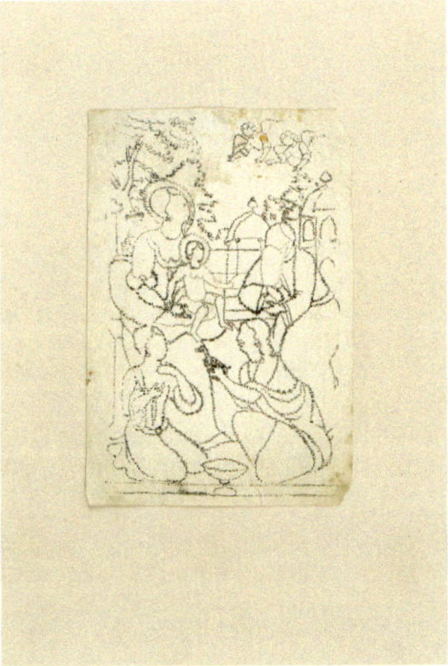

14

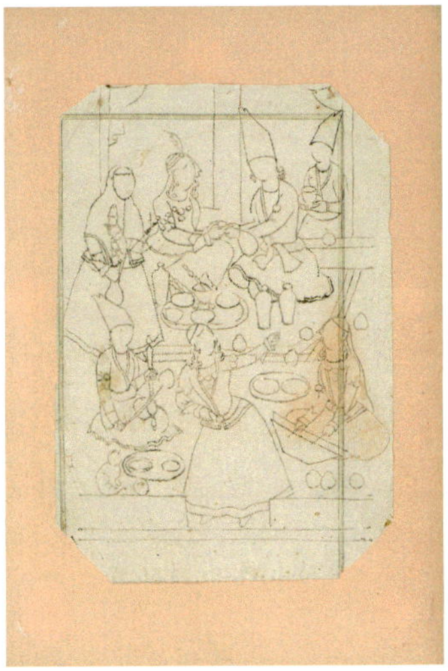

15

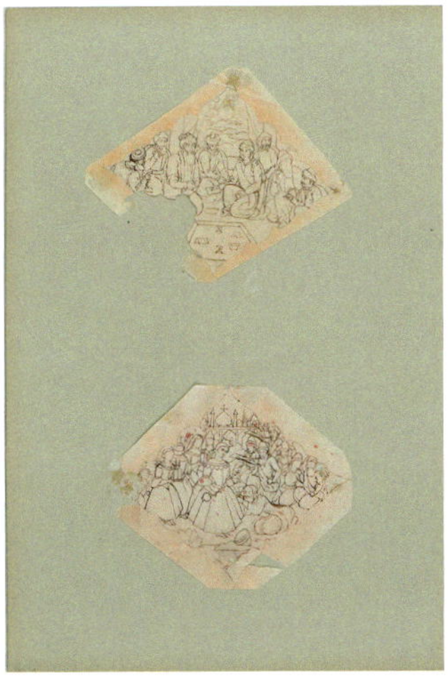

16

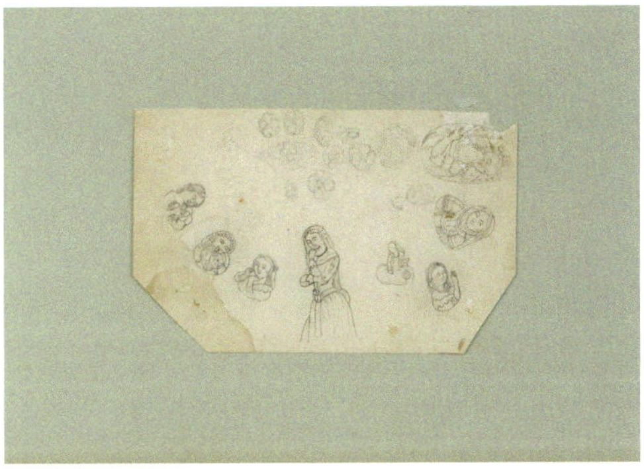

17

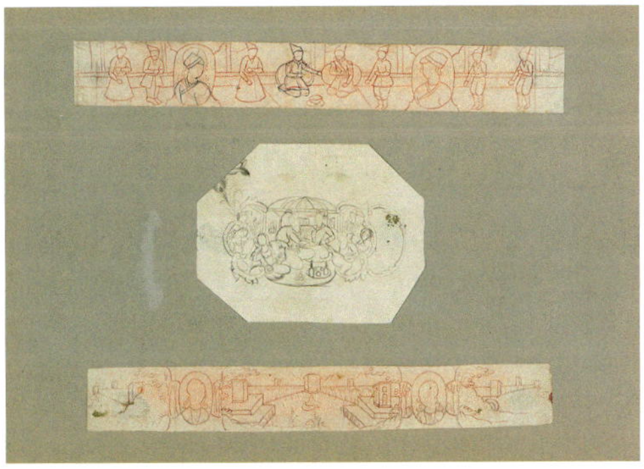

18

19. Design for a Pen Box Organized as Three Scenes around a Reclining Female with Angels and Male and Female Figures (*top*), Portrait Bust of Muhammad Shah Qajar (r. 1834–1848) (*center, left*), European Woman Holding a Bouquet and Enclosed by a Shawl (*center, right*), and Design for a Pen Box Composed of Male and Female Portrait Medallions Dividing Three Scenes Organized around a Reclining Female with Attendants (*bottom*)

Folio 41a from *An Album of Artists' Drawings from Qajar Iran*
Iran, 1780–1860
Top: black counterproof, red ink, and watercolor on laid paper, pricked (adhered side rubbed with red chalk); center, left: graphite on off-white wove paper; center, right: black counterproof on off-white wove paper, pricked; bottom: brown counterproof, brown ink, and graphite on off-white wove paper
Folio: 32.5 × 22 cm ($12\frac{13}{16} \times 8\frac{11}{16}$ in.)
Harvard Art Museums / Arthur M. Sackler Museum, Alpheus Hyatt Purchasing Fund, 1960.161.41

20. Cuckolded Husband Discovers His Wife with a Young Man

Folio 49a from *An Album of Artists' Drawings from Qajar Iran*
Iran, mid-19th century
Graphite on beige wove paper
Folio: 32.5 × 22 cm ($12\frac{13}{16} \times 8\frac{11}{16}$ in.)
Harvard Art Museums / Arthur M. Sackler Museum, Alpheus Hyatt Purchasing Fund, 1960.161.49

21. Study of a Rose (*top*) and Study of an Iris (*bottom*)

Folio 56b from *An Album of Artists' Drawings from Qajar Iran*
Iran, 1780–1860
Top: pink and green inks on beige wove paper; bottom: green and brown inks on beige laid paper
Folio: 32.5 × 22 cm ($12\frac{13}{16} \times 8\frac{11}{16}$ in.)
Harvard Art Museums / Arthur M. Sackler Museum, Alpheus Hyatt Purchasing Fund, 1960.161.56

PHOTOGRAPHS

22. An Unidentified Qajar Gentleman

Wilhelm Schönfeld
Russia, St. Petersburg, 1843–51
Daguerreotype, half plate; hand-colored
Overall: 28.5 × 24.2 cm ($11\frac{1}{4} \times 9\frac{1}{2}$ in.); photograph: 14.7 × 11 cm ($5\frac{3}{4} \times 4\frac{3}{8}$ in.)
Collection of Azita Bina and Elmar W. Seibel
LABELED (back):
Portraits au Daguerréotype éxécutés [sic] *par Giullaume* [sic] *Schonfeldt. Petite Morskaia, maison Veltsine en face l'hôtel de Paris.*
Vil'gel'm Shenfel't. Snimaet portrety posredstvom Dagerotipa v Maloi Morskoi v dome Vel'tsynoi protiv Gostinitsy Parizh.
Daguerreotype portraits taken by Wilhelm Schönfeld. House of Mme. Vel'tsyna, Malaia Morskaia St., across from Hotel Paris.
PUBLISHED:
Jennifer Y. Chi, ed., *The Eye of the Shah: Qajar Court Photography and the Persian Past* (New York: Institute for the Study of the Ancient World at New York University, 2015), cat. 1.
Muhammad Rizā Ṭahmāsbpūr, "Kashf-i nakhustīn dāgiru'tīp, az taṣvīr-i yik Irānī," *'Aks* 244 (Khordād 1388/June 2009): 33–35.

23. *Carte de Visite* of Two Qajar Gentlemen

Probably Russia, St. Petersburg, 1843–51
Albumen silver print
10 × 6.3 cm ($3\frac{15}{16} \times 2\frac{1}{2}$ in.)
Collection of Azita Bina and Elmar W. Seibel
LABELED:
105
PUBLISHED:
Jennifer Y. Chi, ed., *The Eye of the Shah: Qajar Court Photography and the Persian Past* (New York: Institute for the Study of the Ancient World at New York University, 2015), cat. 115.

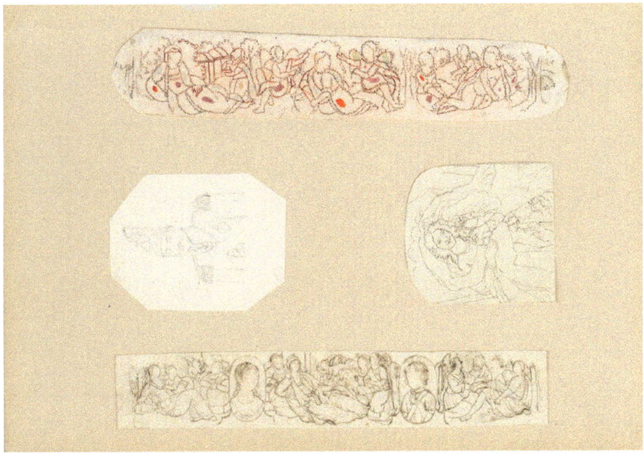

19

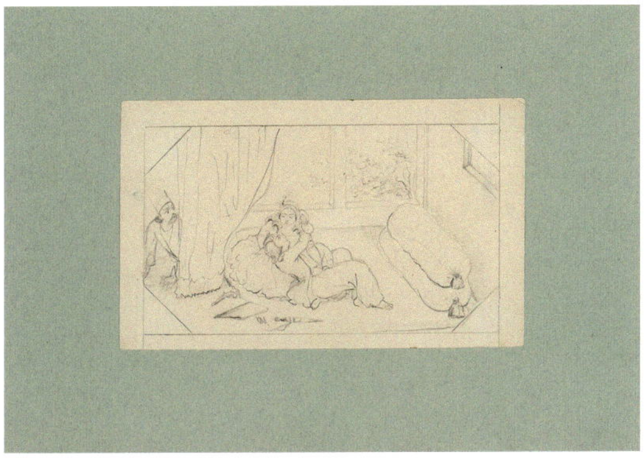

20

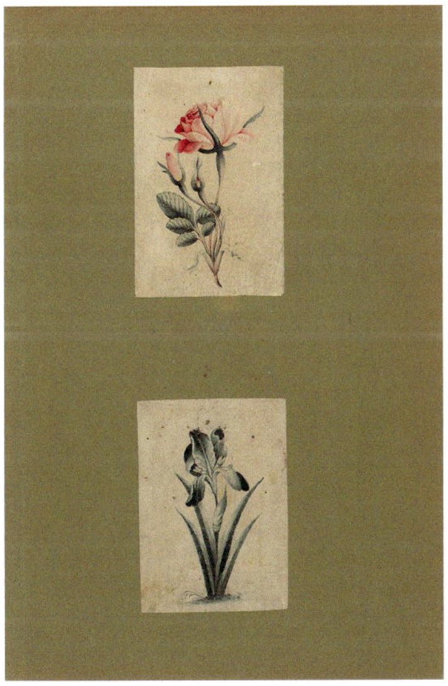

21

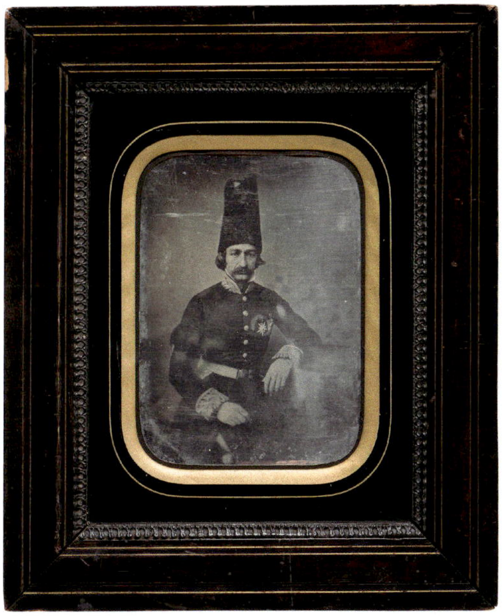

22

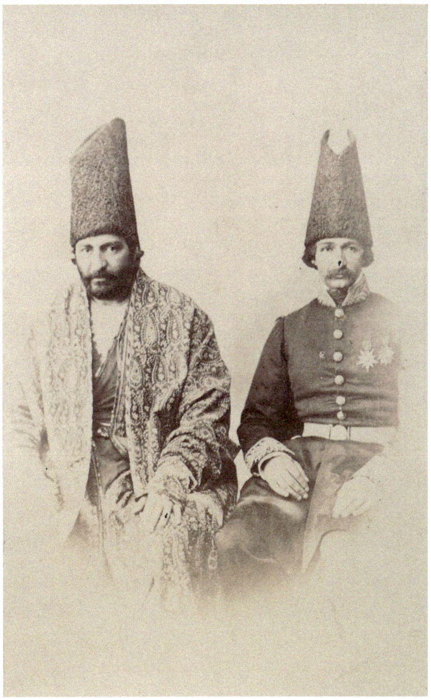

23

24. Pages 2, 3, 44, 45 from the Album of Photographs by ʿAli Khan Vali

Iran and Russia, 1862–1900
Albumen silver prints mounted on sailcloth
Folio: 30 × 45 cm (11 13/16 × 17 3/4 in.)
Special Collections, Fine Arts Library, Harvard University, AKP111
Inscribed with descriptive information by ʿAli Khan Vali

PUBLISHED:

Layla S. Diba, "Qajar Photography and Its Relationship to Iranian Art: A Reassessment," *History of Photography* 37 (1) (2013): 90–91.

Aṣghar Muḥammad'zāda, ed., *Āzarbāyjan va Vālī-i ʿakkās: bar asās-i nuskha'hā-yi khaṭṭī va ālbūm-i ʿAlī Khān Vālī* (Tehran: Nashr-i Awḥadī, 1390 H [2011]).

Yaḥyā Ẕukā, *Tārīkh-i ʿakkāsī va ʿakkāsān-i pīshgām dar Īrān* (Tehran: Shirkat-i Intishārāt-i ʿIlmī va Farhangī, 1997), 66–74.

25. Mecca. View of the Kaʿba and the Sacred Enclosure (*Hijr*) and Its Surroundings

Muhammad Sadiq Bey (1822–1903)
Saudi Arabia, Mecca, 1880–81
Albumen silver print
18 × 21 cm (7 1/16 × 8 1/4 in.)
Special Collections, Fine Arts Library, Harvard University, AKP106

26. Barber (*right*); Persian Bath (*left*)

Attributable to Antoin Sevruguin (1830–1933)
Iran, late 19th century
Hand-colored albumen silver prints
Folio: 27 × 36 cm (10 5/8 × 14 3/16 in.); each photograph: 16 × 11.5 cm (6 5/16 × 4 1/2 in.)
Collection of Azita Bina and Elmar W. Seibel

LABELED:

Barbier
Barber
Bain persan
Persian Bath

27. Small Album with Photographs of Women

Iran, late 19th century
Gelatin silver prints
Folio: 23 × 17.5 cm (9 1/16 × 6 7/8 in.); each photograph: 4.5 × 3 cm (1 3/4 × 1 1/8 in.)
Collection of Azita Bina and Elmar W. Seibel

INSCRIBED:

ʿAṭṭā, dasta-yi ʿAzīz, Ṣadīqa Rīshī, ʿAzīz Aqā
ʿAtta, group of ʿAziz, Sadiqa Rishi, ʿAziz Aqa

28. A Photographer's Room

Attributable to Antoin Sevruguin (1830–1933)
Iran, late 19th century
Albumen silver print
Folio: 30.2 × 24 cm (11 7/8 × 9 7/16 in.); photograph: 21.5 × 16.5 cm (8 1/2 × 6 3/8 in.)
Collection of Azita Bina and Elmar W. Seibel

INSCRIBED:

99

LABELED:

The room of the photographer who took these pictures.

PUBLISHED:

Yaḥya Ẕukā, *Tārīkh-i ʿakkāsī va ʿakkāsān-i pīshgām dar Īrān* (Tehran: Shirkat-i Intishārāt-i ʿIlmī va Farhangī, 1997), 198.

Jennifer Y. Chi, ed., *The Eye of the Shah: Qajar Court Photography and the Persian Past* (New York: Institute for the Study of the Ancient World at New York University, 2015), 77, cat. 138.

29. Woman Smoking a Water Pipe

Attributable to Antoin Sevruguin (1830–1933)
Iran, late 19th century
Albumen silver print, with graphite
36 × 26 cm (14 1/4 × 10 1/4 in.)
Collection of Azita Bina and Elmar W. Seibel

INSCRIBED:

49

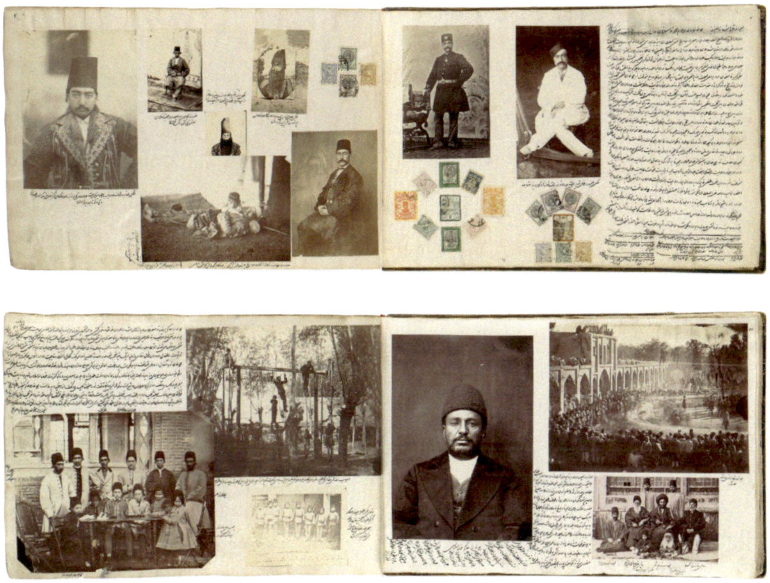

24

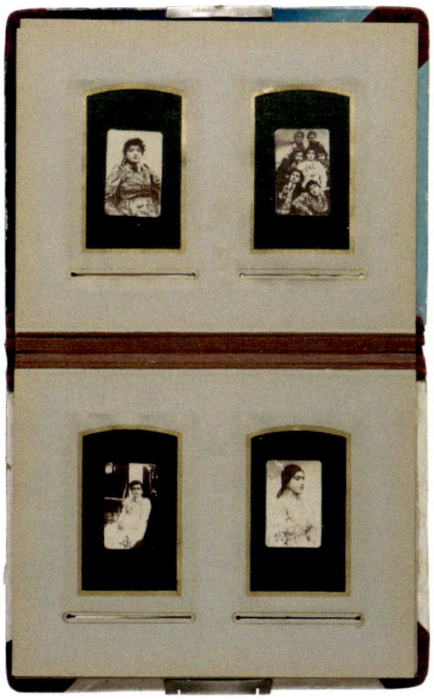

27

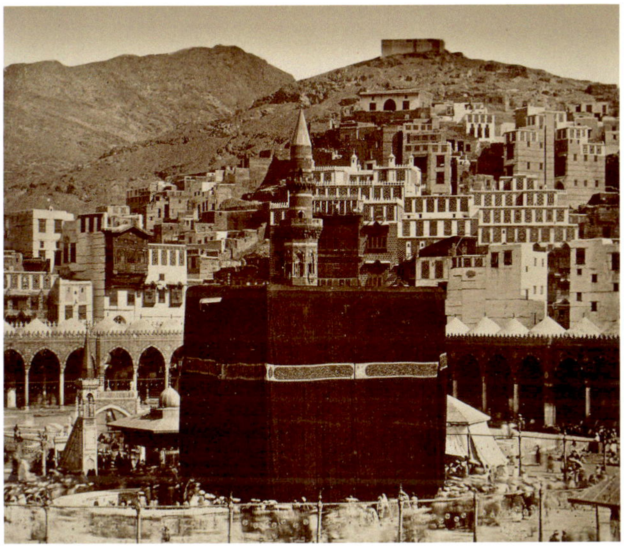

25

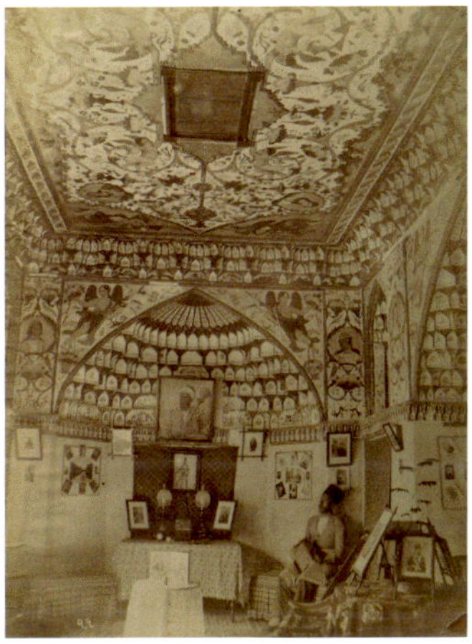

28

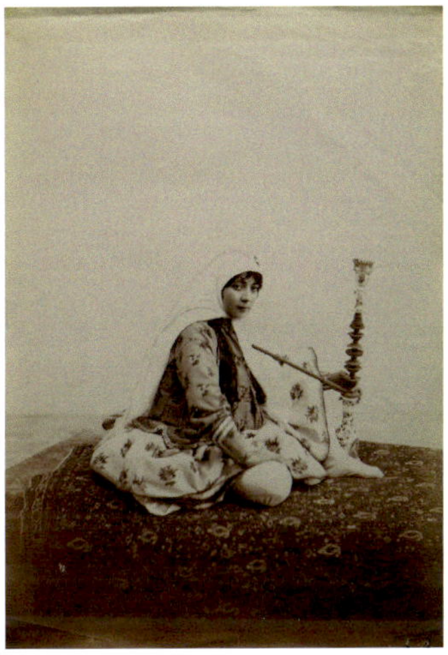

29

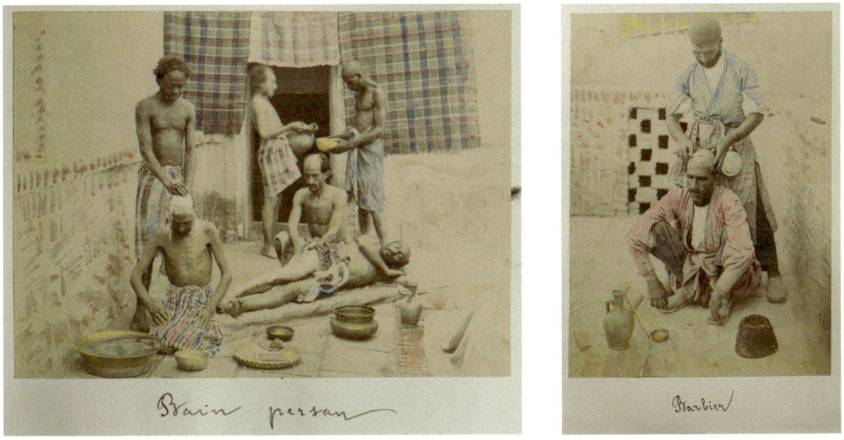

26

30. The Persian Family

Attributable to Antoin Sevruguin (1830–1933)
Iran, late 19th century
Albumen silver print
Folio: 32 × 39.5 cm (15¾ × 12¾ in); photograph: 16 × 21 cm (6⅝ × 8⅜ in.)
Collection of Azita Bina and Elmar W. Seibel

31. The Persian Family

Switzerland, Zurich, 1904–12
Chromolithograph (photochrome)
16.6 × 22.5 cm (6$\frac{9}{16}$ × 8⅞ in.)
Collection of Azita Bina and Elmar W. Seibel

LABELED:

9013. P.Z. – TÉHÉRAN. FAMILLE PERSANE
9013. P.Z. – Tehran. A Persian Family
9013. Persiia. Tegeran. Rebenok v verevochnoi liul'ke i dve zhenshchiny s devochkoi vokrug nego.
9013. Persia, Tehran. A child in a rope cradle and two women and a girl around it.

PUBLISHED:

Béla Kelényi and Iván Szántó, eds., *Artisans at the Crossroads: Persian Arts of the Qajar Period* (Budapest: Ferenc Hopp Museum of Eastern Asiatic Arts, 2010), 122, C.9.1.1.

32. Women Attending a Public Performance

Iran, late 19th century
Albumen silver print
23.2 × 29.8 cm (9⅛ × 11¾ in.)
Collection of Azita Bina and Elmar W. Seibel

33. Fruit Sellers Preparing for Festivities

F. Hoveepiantz
Iran, Tabriz, late 19th century
Albumen silver print
19 × 21.7 cm (7½ × 8$\frac{9}{16}$ in.)
Collection of Azita Bina and Elmar W. Seibel

INSCRIBED:

Le fruitier pendant la fête qui prepare. F. Hoveepiantz, Tauris
The fruit stand during festival preparations. F. Hoveepiantz, Tabriz

34. *Ta'zīya* Performers

Iran, late 19th century
Albumen silver print
Folio: 15.8 × 20.4 cm (6¼ × 8 in.)
Collection of Azita Bina and Elmar W. Seibel

INSCRIBED:

5921

35. Rock Relief of Nasir al-Din Shah Commemorating the Reconstruction of the Old Road to Mazandaran

Antoin Sevruguin (1830–1933)
Iran, c. 1880s–90s
Albumen silver print
Folio: 23.2 × 29.8 cm (9⅛ × 11¾ in.); photograph: 18 × 23.9 cm (7 × 9$\frac{9}{16}$ in.)
Collection of Azita Bina and Elmar W. Seibel

PUBLISHED:

Jennifer Y. Chi, ed., *The Eye of the Shah: Qajar Court Photography and the Persian Past* (New York: Institute for the Study of the Ancient World at New York University, 2015), cat. 187.

L. A. Ferydoun Barjesteh van Waalwijk van Doorn and Gillian M. Vogelsang-Eastwood, eds., *Sevruguin's Iran: Late Nineteenth Century Photographs of Iran from the National Museum of Ethnology in Leiden, the Netherlands* (Tehran: Zaman; Rotterdam: Barjesteh van Waalwijk van Doorn, 1999), 157.

36. Rock Relief of the Triumph of Shapur I over Valerian

Antoin Sevruguin (1830–1933)
Iran, c. 1880s–1930s
Albumen silver print
Folio: 23.2 × 29.8 cm (9⅛ × 11¾ in.); photograph: 16.3 × 21.2 cm (6$\frac{7}{16}$ × 8$\frac{5}{16}$ in.)
Collection of Azita Bina and Elmar W. Seibel

INSCRIBED:

133

PUBLISHED:

Jennifer Y. Chi, ed., *The Eye of the Shah: Qajar Court Photography and the Persian Past* (New York: Institute for the Study of the Ancient World at New York University, 2015), cat. 178.

L. A. Ferydoun Barjesteh van Waalwijk van Doorn and Gillian M. Vogelsang-Eastwood, eds., *Sevruguin's Iran: Late Nineteenth Century Photographs of Iran from the National Museum of Ethnology in Leiden, the Netherlands* (Tehran: Zaman; Rotterdam: Barjesteh van Waalwijk van Doorn, 1999), 154.

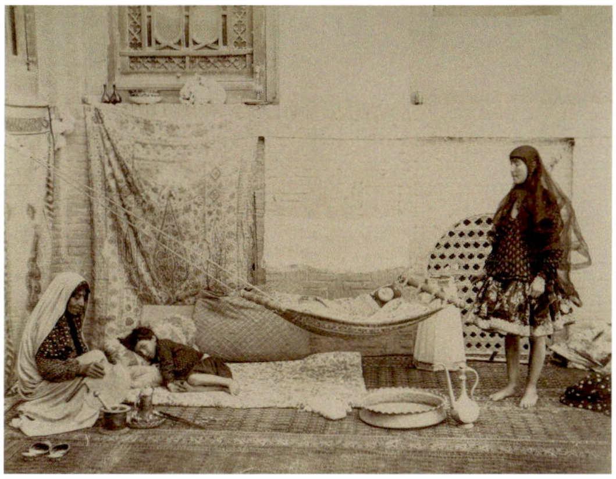

30

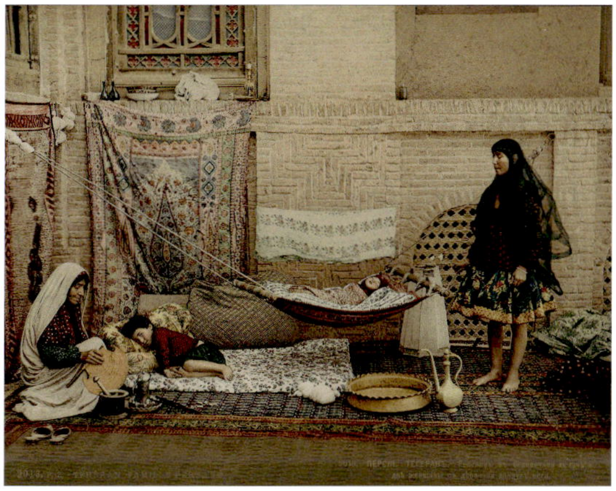

31

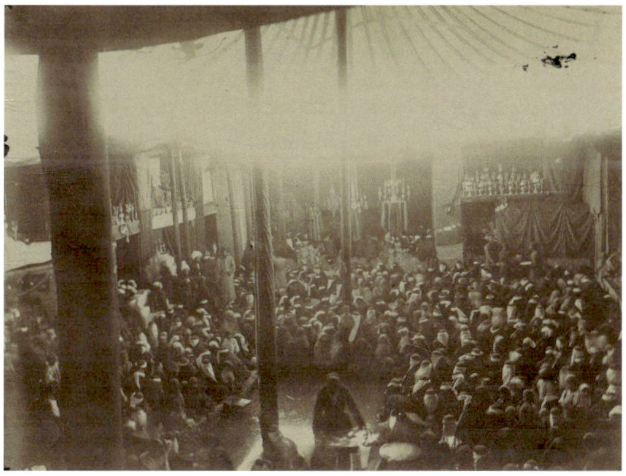

32

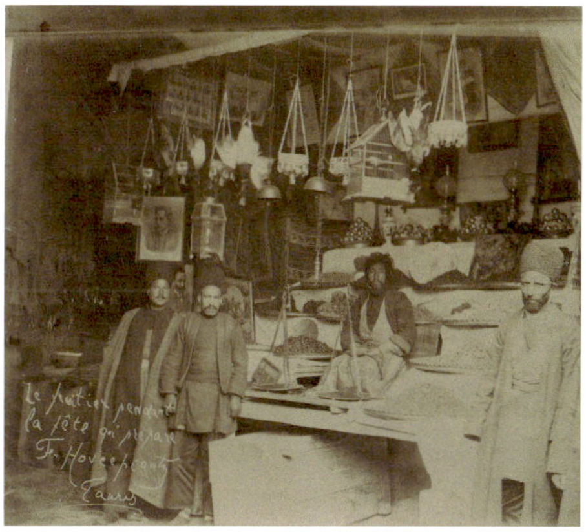

33

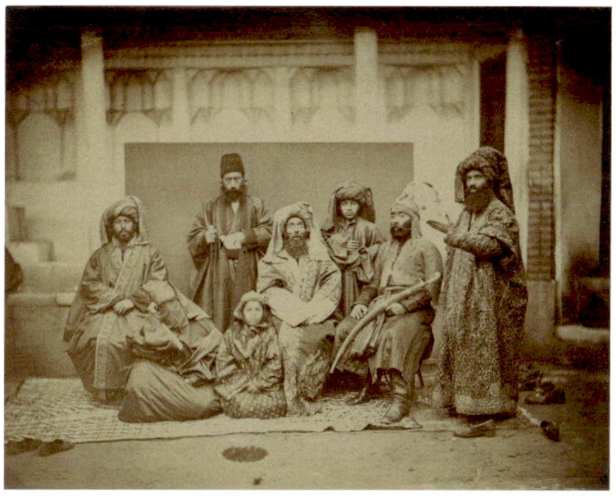

34

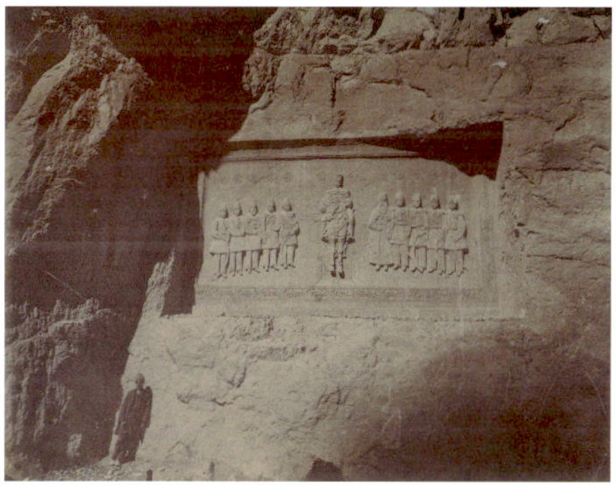

35

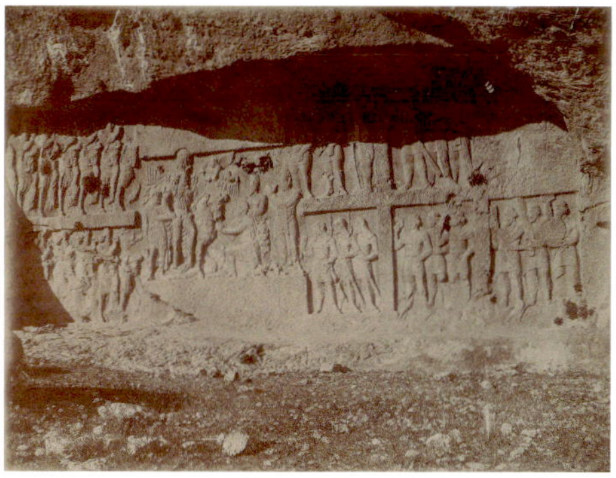

36

37. Reclining Woman with Dancer and Musicians

Antoin Sevruguin (1830–1933)
Iran, 1880s–1930s
Albumen silver print
Folio: 30.2 × 24 cm (11⅞ × 9 7/16 in.); photograph: 14.3 × 21.5 cm (5⅝ × 8½ in.)
Collection of Azita Bina and Elmar W. Seibel
PUBLISHED:
Jennifer Y. Chi, ed., *The Eye of the Shah: Qajar Court Photography and the Persian Past* (New York: Institute for the Study of the Ancient World at New York University, 2015), cat. 110.

38. Persepolis (Iran): Throne Hall, Northern Wall, West Jamb of Eastern Doorway: View of Relief Picturing Enthroned King Giving Audience, as well as Registers Picturing Persian and Median Guards

Antoin Sevruguin (1830–1933)
Iran, 1902–5
Gelatin silver print
17.5 × 12.5 cm (6⅞ × 4 15/16 in.)
Myron Bement Smith Collection: Antoin Sevruguin Photographs, Freer Gallery of Art and Arthur M. Sackler Gallery Archives, Smithsonian Institution, Washington D.C., Gift of Katherine Dennis Smith, 1973–85, FSA A.4 2.12.Sm.28
INSCRIBED:
914

39. Interior Views of Toko Department Store (Tehran)

Folios 48 and 49 from the *Albert Hotz Photograph Album*
Iran, Tehran, 1893–1903
Albumen silver print
Folio: 30 × 25.5 cm (11 13/16 × 10 1/16 in.); each photograph: 23 × 17 cm (9 × 6 11/16 in.)
Collection of Azita Bina and Elmar W. Seibel
PUBLISHED:
Corien Vuurman, *Nineteenth-Century Persia in the Photographs of Albert Hotz* (Rotterdam: Barjesteh van Waalwijk van Doorn, 2011), 24.

40. Procession with Portrait of Muhammad ʿAli Shah at the Opening of the Parliament in Tehran

Published by Sayyid ʿAbd al-Rahim Kashani
Iran, Tehran, c. 1907
Collotype postcard
9 × 13 cm (3 9/16 × 5⅛ in.)
Kenneth & Joyce Robbins Collection
LABELED:
FRONT: *Le portrait du roi detrôné* [sic] *de la Perse à illumination au parlement au lieu de lui-même.*
The portrait of the dethroned king of Persia presented to parliament in place of himself.
Portret shahka, nizvedennogo s prestola v parlamente.
Portrait of the shah, dethroned in parliament.
Rūzī ki ʿaks-i Muḥammad ʿAlī Shāh rā bi-majlis-i muqaddas bi-ʿavaż-i khūd-i shāh mīburdand.
The day when they were carrying the picture of Muhammad ʿAli Shah to the sacred parliament, in place of the Shah himself.
BACK: *Maḥall-i furūsh Tihrān sarā-yi Amīr hujra-yi Sayyid ʿAbd al-Raḥīm Kāshānī.*
Place of selling: Tehran, the Amir Saray, shop of Sayyid ʿAbd al-Rahim Kashani.
Séyéd Abdor Rahime Kachani, seraïé Amir, Téhéran, Perse.
Sayyid ʿAbd al-Rahim Kashani, Amir Saray, Tehran, Persia.
PUBLISHED:
Layla S. Diba with Maryam Ekhtiar, eds., *Royal Persian Paintings: The Qajar Epoch, 1785–1925* (London: I. B. Tauris Publishers in association with Brooklyn Museum of Art, 1998), 42, Fig. 12.
Sassan Pejhan, "A Picture Postcard View of the Persian Constitutional Revolution," *Journal of Persianate Studies* 3 (2) (2010): 192–221, Fig. 17.

41. Destroyed Palace in Rasht

Published by Sayyid ʿAbd al-Rahim Kashani
Iran, Tehran, 1906–11
Collotype postcard
9 × 13 cm (3 9/16 × 5⅛ in.)
Kenneth & Joyce Robbins Collection
LABELED:
FRONT: *Palais du Gouvernement à Recht, dans le temps de la révolution.*
Governmental palace in Rasht during the time of the revolution.
16 Muḥarram 1327; ẓulm-i jūr īn . . . dar Gīlān va Rasht bi-himmat-i mujāhidīn kūhī az ātish namūd yādgār. Ḥusayn Kasmāī Rasht-i yādgār
7th of February 1909; A mountain of fire turned the injustice and tyranny of this building into a memorial, thanks to the efforts of the Mujahidin. Husayn Kasmai; Souvenir of Rasht
BACK: *Maḥall-i furūsh Tihrān sarā-yi Amīr hujra-yi Sayyid ʿAbd al-Raḥīm Kāshānī.*
Place of selling: Tehran, the Amir Saray, shop of Sayyid ʿAbd al-Rahim Kashani.
Séyéd Abdor Rahime Kachani, seraïé Amir, Téhéran, Perse.
Sayyid ʿAbd al-Rahim Kashani, Amir Saray, Tehran, Persia.

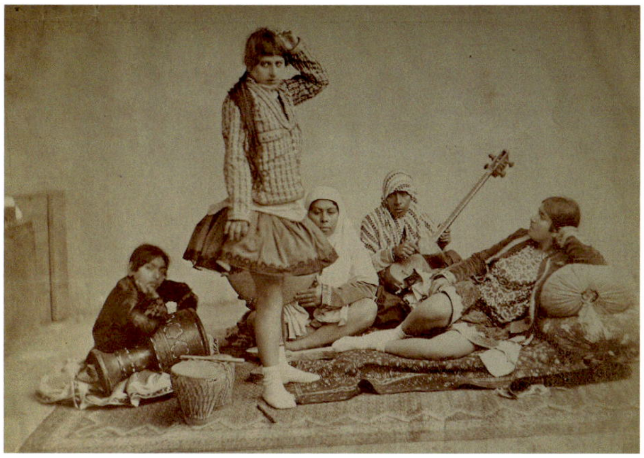

37

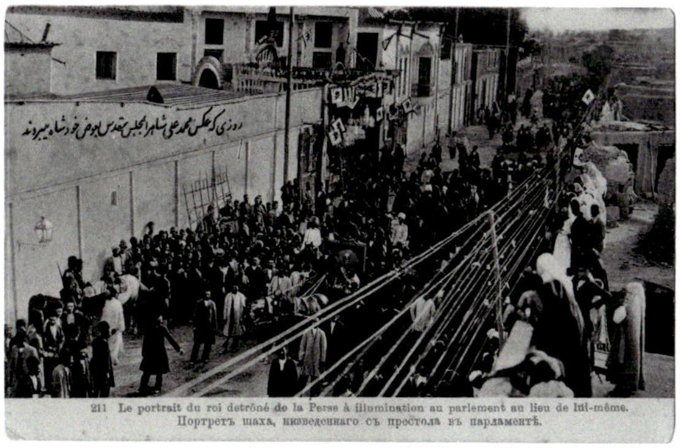
211 Le portrait du roi detrôné de la Perse à illumination au parlement au lieu de lui-même.
Портретъ шаха, низведеннаго съ престола въ парламентѣ.

40

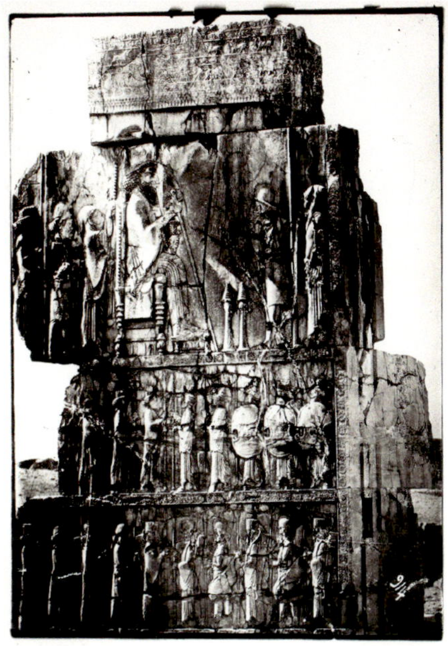

38

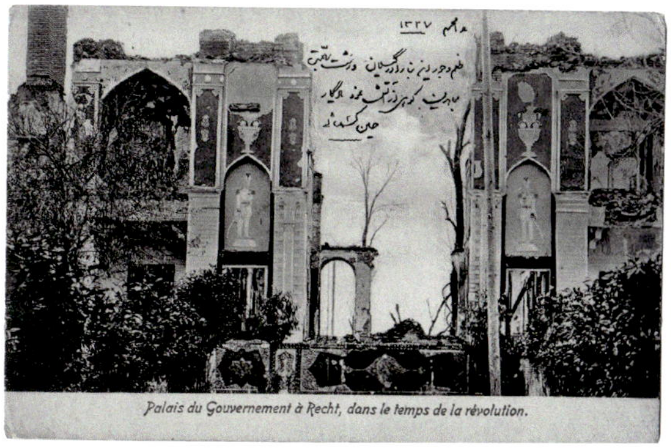
Palais du Gouvernement à Recht, dans le temps de la révolution.

41

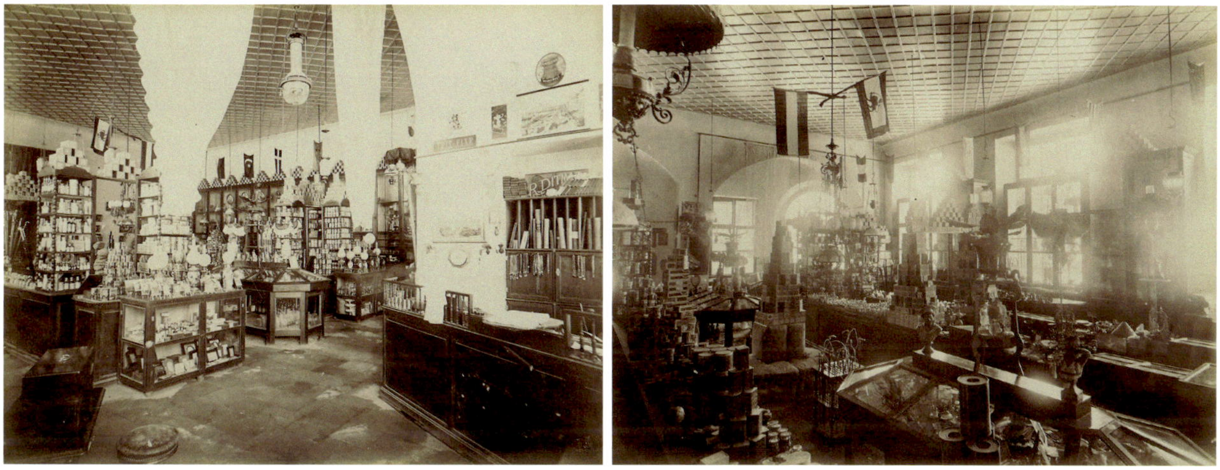

39

PRINTED WORKS: ENGRAVINGS, ETCHINGS, LITHOGRAPHS

42. The Bower of Venus

G. Kellaway, after Richard Westall (1765–1836)
England, London, 1825
Engraving and etching, chine collé
Image: 11.1 × 14.2 cm (4⅜ × 5⁹⁄₁₆ in.)
Museum of Fine Arts, Boston, Harvey D. Parker Collection—Harvey Drury Parker Fund, 97.1205

INSCRIBED:

R. Westall, Esq. R. A. Pinx London, Published Sept 1, 1825, by W. J. White, Brownlow Street, Holborn G. Kellaway, Sculp
The Bower of Venus.
Hither the laughing loves resort,
Hence wing their mystic darts.

43. Golden Eagle

Folio from *The Natural History of the Birds of Great Britain and Ireland, Part 1: Birds of Prey*, The Naturalist's Library, vol. 9, ed. Sir William Jardine
Edinburgh, 1838
Hand-colored wood engraving
Folio: 18 × 11.3 (7¹⁄₁₆ × 4⁷⁄₁₆ × 1⅜ in.)
Ernst Mayr Library and MCZ Archives, Museum of Comparative Zoology, Harvard University, 3302

44. Farhad at Mount Bisutun (*right*) and Ibrahim's Sacrifice (*left*)

Double page from the *ʿAjāʾib al-makhlūqāt wa gharāʾib al-mawjūdāt* (The Wonders of Creation and Oddities of Existence) by al-Qazwini
Illustrations by Mirza ʿAli Quli Khawʾi
Iran, dated 1264 H (1847–48)
Lithographed text and illustrations
Folio: 30.2 × 19.8 cm (11⅞ × 7¹³⁄₁₆ in.)
Collection of Azita Bina and Elmar W. Seibel

45. Title Page (*top right*) and Zoroaster Offering the Eternal Fire to Gushtasb (*top left*); Battle of Gudarz and Piran (*bottom right*)

Double page from the *Shāhnāma* (Book of Kings) by Firdawsi (*Shāhnāma-yi kajūrī*)
Illustrations by Mirza ʿAli Quli Khawʾi, calligraphy by Mustafa Quli b. Muhammad Hadi Sultan Kajuri
Iran, Tehran, dated 1265–67 H (1848–50)
Lithographed text and illustrations
Overall: 35.7 × 22.5 × 7 cm (14¹⁄₁₆ × 8⅞ × 2¾ in.);
folio: 34.5 × 21 cm (13⁹⁄₁₆ × 8¼ in.);
print: 26.5 × 15.5 cm (10⁷⁄₁₆ × 6⅛ in.)
Houghton Library, Harvard University, Typ 883.49.7856

46. Muzaffar al-Din Shah Qajar

Signed by Mahdi (Mahdi Musavvir al-Mulk)
Iran, dated 1314 H (1896–97)
Lithograph, hand-colored
41 × 30.9 cm (16⅛ × 12³⁄₁₆ in.)
Collection of Hamid Kooros

INSCRIBED:

Jān-niṣār Mahdī naqqāsh-i makhṣūṣ 1314
Life-scattering Mahdi, court painter, 1896–97

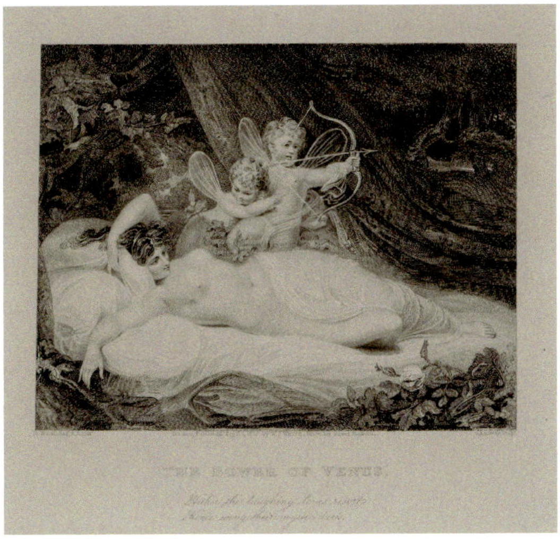

42

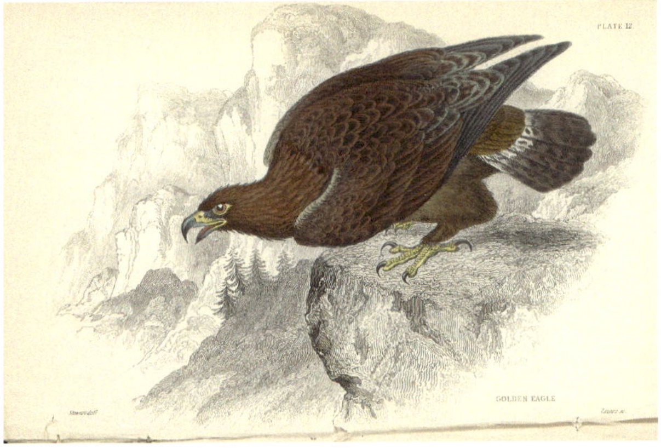

43

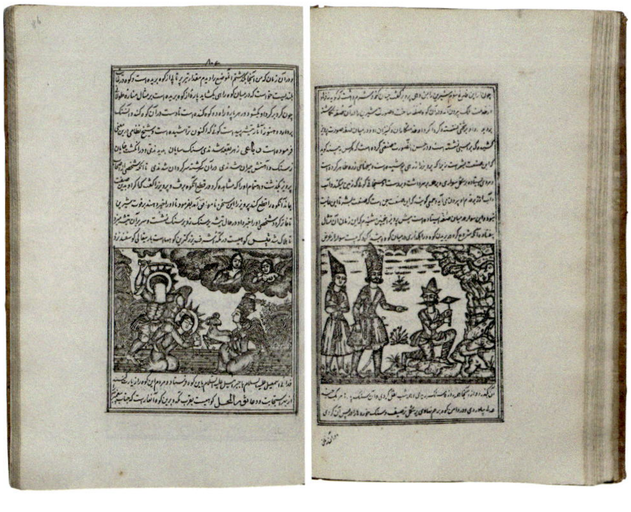

44

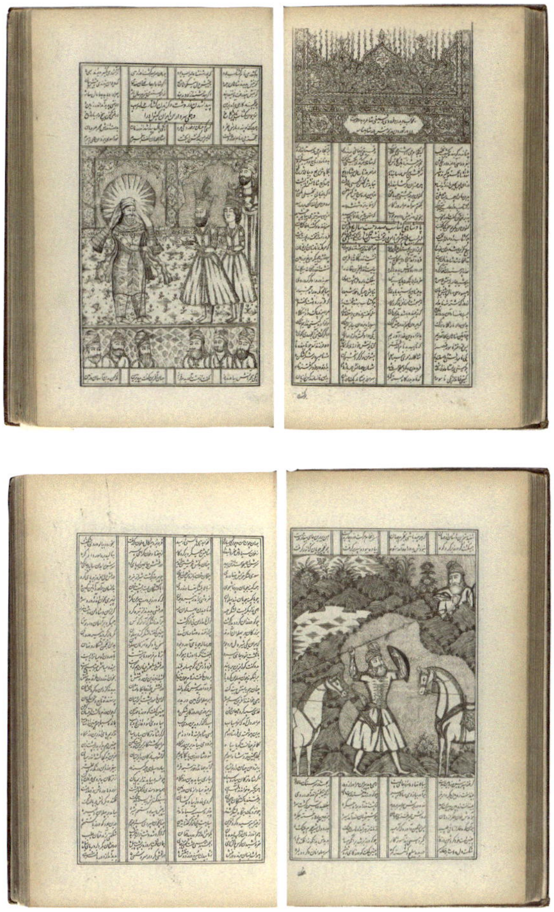

45

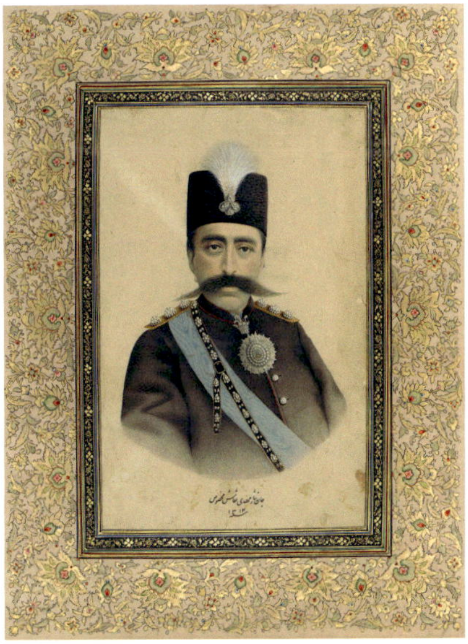

46

47. Jamshid Enthroned

Folio from the *Shāhnāma* (Book of Kings) by Firdawsi (*Shāhnāma-yi bahādurī*)
Iran, Tehran, 1901–4
Lithographed text and illustrations
Folio: 43.2 × 33 cm (17 × 13 in.)
Collection of Azita Bina and Elmar W. Seibel

48. Battle of Karbala

Sayyid ʿArab (Husayn Zaydi Latifi)
Iran, c. 1950
Color relief print
Overall: 36 × 45 cm (14 3/16 × 17 11/16 in.)
Special Collections, Fine Arts Library, Harvard University, AKP254

49. Ibrahim's Sacrifice

Sayyid ʿArab (Husayn Zaydi Latifi)
Iran, c. 1950
Color relief print
Overall: 45 × 34 cm (17 3/4 × 14 3/16 in.)
Special Collections, Fine Arts Library, Harvard University, AKP254

LACQUER

50. Pen Box with Medallions on Floral Ground

Signed by Haji Muhammad
Iran, Isfahan, dated 1102 H (1692–93)
Watercolor, gold-colored pigments, copper particles, and lacquer over silver layer on pasteboard
3.7 × 4.2 × 23.9 cm (1 7/16 × 1 5/8 × 9 7/16 in.)
Harvard Art Museums/Arthur M. Sackler Museum, Gift of A. Soudavar in memory of his mother Ezzat-Malek Soudavar, 2014.303
INSCRIBED:
Huwa al-ʿalā illā ʿalī raqamahu Ḥājī Muḥammad fī 1102
He! The Most High. It was painted by Haji Muhammad in 1692–93
PUBLISHED:
Layla S. Diba, *Lacquerwork of Safavid Persia and Its Relationship to Persian Painting*, Ph.D. dissertation, New York University, 1994, vol. 2, 601, cat. 76.

51. Large Box with Fath ʿAli Shah Seated on the Sun Throne (*Takht-i khurshīd*)

Iran, 1820s–30s
Watercolor, gold-colored pigments, and lacquer on pasteboard
19.5 × 29.9 × 42 cm (7 11/16 × 11 3/4 × 16 9/16 in.)
Collection of Vahid Kooros

52. Large Book Cover with Entertainment Scenes on a Terrace (*front and back*)

Iran, 1820s–40s
Watercolor, gold-colored pigments, and lacquer over brass layer on pasteboard
44.9 × 30.5 × 0.9 cm (17 11/16 × 12 × 3/8 in.)
Collection of Saeed Kouros
Inscribed (exterior) with poetry by Saʿdi

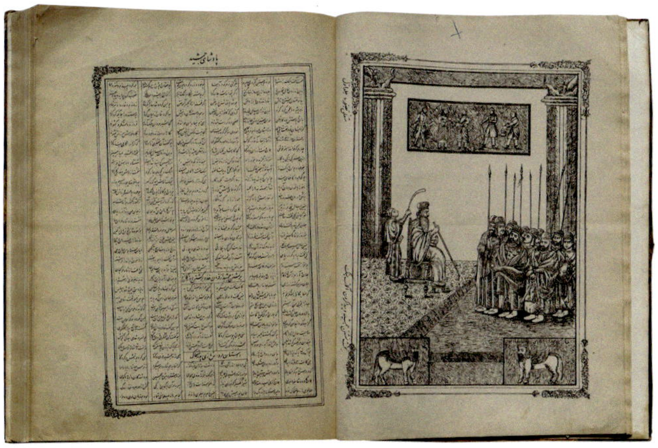

47

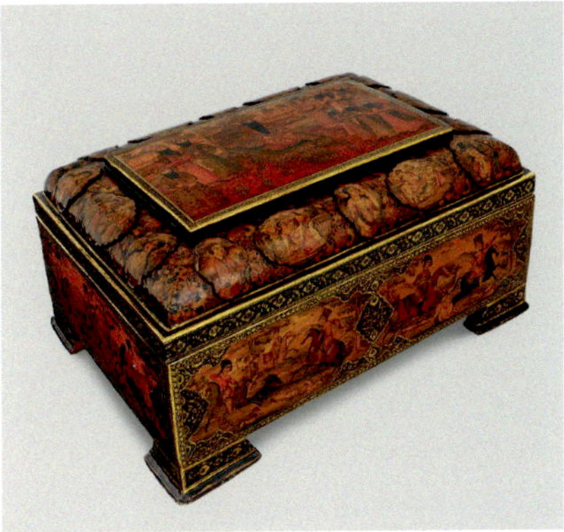

51

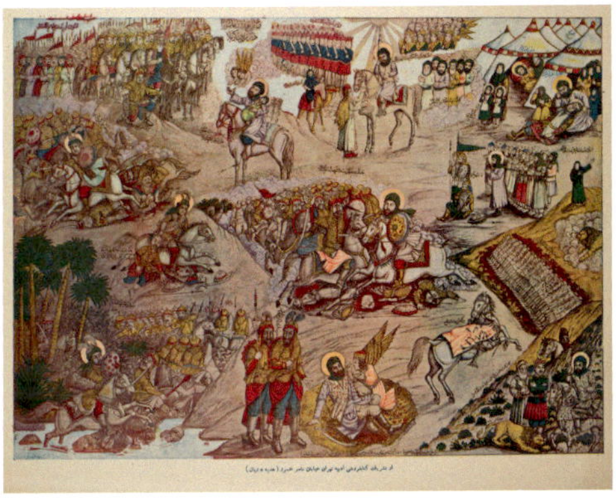

48

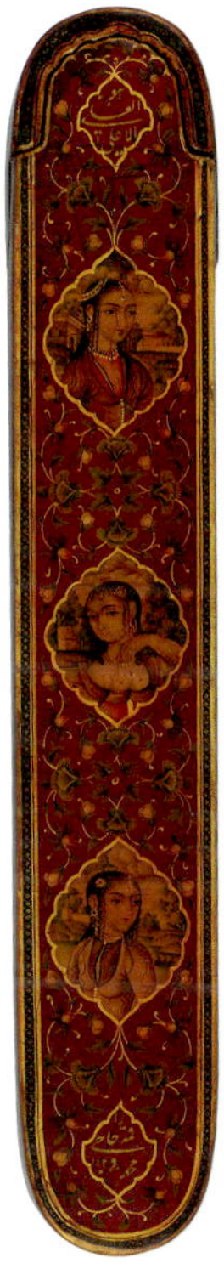

50

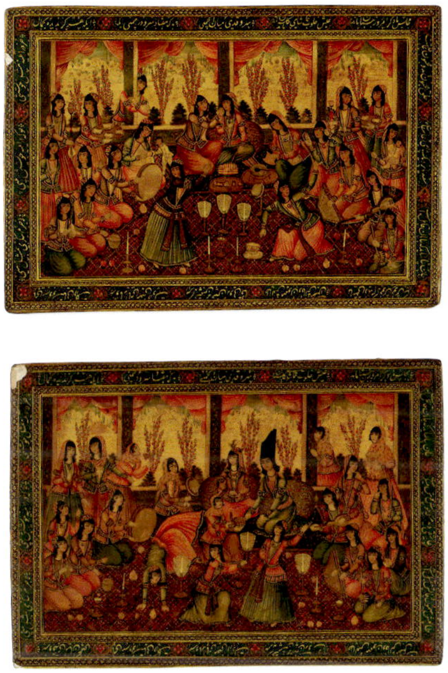

52

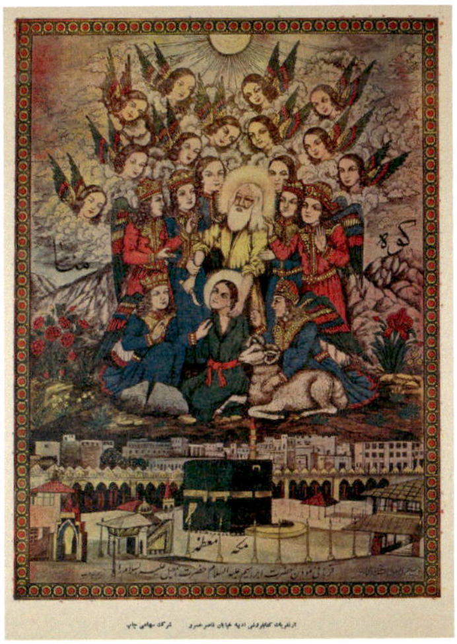

49

53. Large Book Cover with Enthronement Scenes of Fath ʿAli Shah and Muhammad Shah (*front and back*)

Iran, 1830s–40s
Watercolor, gold-colored pigments, and lacquer over brass layer on pasteboard
Each: 40.5 × 29.5 cm (15 15/16 × 11 5/8 in.)
Collection of Hamid Kooros
Inscribed (interior) with poems by Saʿdi

54. Rectangular Mirror Case with Scenes of a Baby Boy's Birth and Circumcision (*front and back*)

Iran, 1830s–40s
Watercolor, gold-colored pigments, and lacquer on pasteboard
Frame: 1.6 × 15.3 × 23.8 cm (5/8 × 6 × 9 3/8 in.)
Harvard Art Museums / Arthur M. Sackler Museum, Gift of A. Soudavar in memory of his mother Ezzat-Malek Soudavar, 2014.383

55. Rectangular Mirror Case with Mir Findiriski, Shaykh Baha'i, Companions, and a Lion

Iran, 1830s–40s
Watercolor, gold-colored pigments, and lacquer on pasteboard
Frame: 23.2 × 15 cm (9 1/8 × 5 7/8 in.)
Museum für Lackkunst, Münster, Germany, 1982–221
PUBLISHED:
Reingard Neumann, ed., *Aus 1001 Nacht: Islamische Lackkunst in deutschen Museen und Bibliotheken* (Münster, Germany: Museum für Lackkunst, 2009), 81, fig. 5.

56. Pen Box with Medallions on Floral Ground

Signed by Muhammad Ismaʿil
Iran, probably Isfahan, mid-19th century
Watercolor, gold-colored pigments, lacquer, and copper ribbons over brass layer on pasteboard
4 × 3.9 × 23 cm (1 9/16 × 1 9/16 × 9 1/16 in.)
Harvard Art Museums / Arthur M. Sackler Museum, Gift of A. Soudavar in memory of his mother Ezzat-Malek Soudavar, 2014.324
INSCRIBED:
huwa Allāh taʿalā subḥānahu / muṣawwiruhu Muḥammad Ismāʿīl
He, Praise to God, the Almighty / His painter is Muhammad Ismaʿil

57. Rectangular Mirror Case with Flowers, Butterfly, and Sleeping Bird

Signed by Muhammad Riza [al-Imami]
Iran, probably Isfahan, dated 1263 H (1847–48)
Exterior: watercolor, gold-colored pigments, and lacquer on pasteboard; interior: watercolor, gold-colored pigments, brass particles, and lacquer over brass layer on pasteboard
Frame: 27.7 × 18.1 × 2.1 cm (10 7/8 × 7 1/8 in.)
Collection of Hamid Kooros
INSCRIBED:
EXTERIOR: *banda-yi dargāh Muḥammad Riza sana 1263*
Slave of the threshold, Muhammad Riza, year 1847–48
INTERIOR: *bar āyina tā ki ʿaks-i rūy-i shāh ast. Uftāda dar-ū shuʿā-yi mihr u māh ast. Yā nūr-i ilāhī ast dar viy ẓāhir. Yā rushani-yi jamāl-i ẓill Allāh ast.*
As long as the shah's face is in the mirror. Rays of the sun and moon are reflected in it. Either divine light is apparent in it, or it is the brightness of the beauty of the shadow of God.

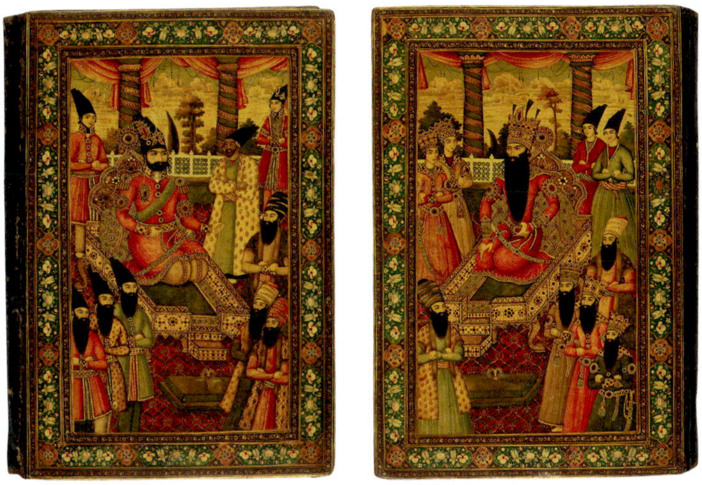

53

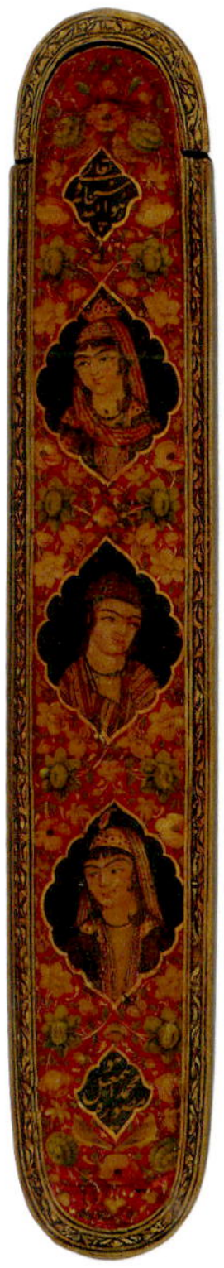

56

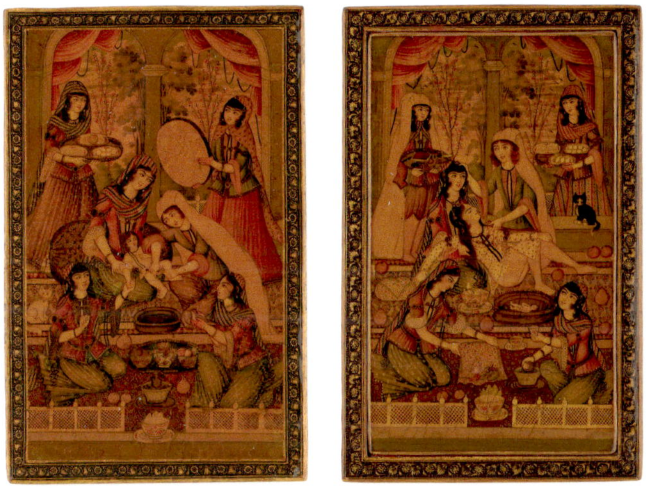

54

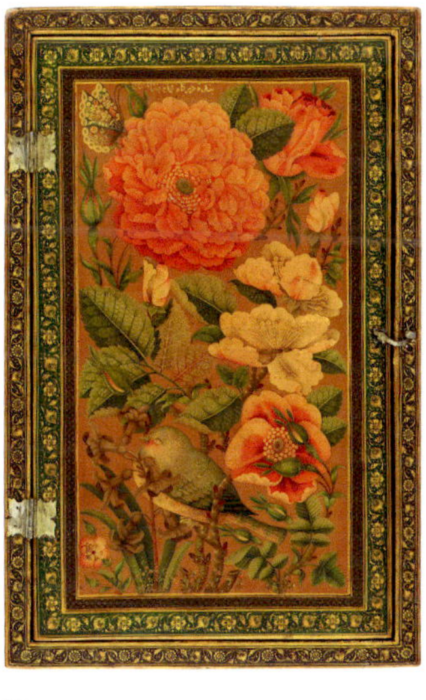

57

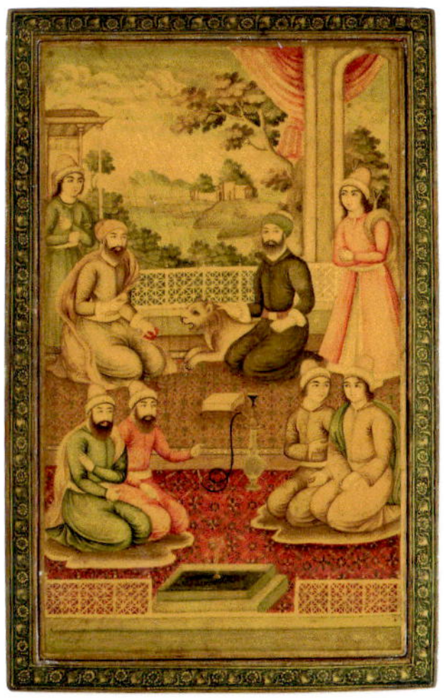

55

58. Rectangular Mirror Case with Bird, Flowers, and Two Butterflies

Attributable to the circle of Najaf ʿAli
Iran, probably Isfahan, first half 19th century
Watercolor, gold-colored pigments, and lacquer over brass layer on pasteboard
Frame: 1.6 × 15.6 × 24 cm (5⁄8 × 6 1⁄8 × 9 7⁄16 in.)
Harvard Art Museums / Arthur M. Sackler Museum, Gift of A. Soudavar in memory of his mother Ezzat-Malek Soudavar, 2014.385

59. Octagonal Mirror Case with Birds and Flowers (*exterior*) and The Bower of Venus (*interior*)

Signed by Mirza Jani b. Ahmad
Iran, 1825–50
Watercolor, platy hematite particles, and lacquer on pasteboard
Frame: 1.4 × 16.3 × 19.4 cm (9⁄16 × 6 7⁄16 × 7 5⁄8 in.)
Harvard Art Museums / Arthur M. Sackler Museum, Gift of A. Soudavar in memory of his mother Ezzat-Malek Soudavar, 2014.384
INSCRIBED:
raqm-i kamtarīn Mīrzā Jānī ibn Ahmad
Painted by the most humble Mirza Jani b. Ahmad

60. Rectangular Mirror Case with Virgin and Child (*front and back*)

Attributable to the circle of Najaf ʿAli
Iran, Isfahan, first half 19th century
Watercolor, gold-colored pigments, and lacquer on pasteboard
Frame: 1.7 × 15 × 23.4 cm (11⁄16 × 5 7⁄8 × 9 3⁄16 in.)
Harvard Art Museums / Arthur M. Sackler Museum, Gift of A. Soudavar in memory of his mother Ezzat-Malek Soudavar, 2014.387

61. Octagonal Mirror Case with Virgin and Child

Attributable to the circle of Najaf ʿAli
Iran, Isfahan, first half 19th century
Watercolor, gold-colored pigments, and lacquer on pasteboard
Frame: 20 × 16 × 1.6 cm (7 7⁄8 × 6 5⁄16 × 5⁄8 in.)
Collection of Hamid Kooros

62. Pen Box with Medallions on Floral Ground

Signed by Zayn al-ʿAbidin [al-Imami]
Iran, probably Isfahan, dated 1270 H (1853–54)
Watercolor, gold-colored pigments, and lacquer over brass layer on pasteboard
3.8 × 3.9 × 22.4 cm (1 1⁄2 × 1 9⁄16 × 8 13⁄16 in.)
Collection of Saeed Kouros
INSCRIBED:
kamtarīn Zayn al-ʿĀbidīn 1270
The most humble Zayn al-ʿAbidin, 1853–54

63. Pen Box with Virgin and Child and Illumination

Painting signed by Abu al-Hasan al-Ghaffari Naqqash-Bashi; illumination signed by ʿAbd al-Vahhab Muzahhib-Bashi Shirazi
Iran, 1271 H (1854–55)
Watercolor, gold-colored pigments, and lacquer over brass and tin layers (top) on pasteboard
3.2 × 3.6 × 21.8 cm (1 1⁄4 × 1 7⁄16 × 8 9⁄16 in.)
Harvard Art Museums / Arthur M. Sackler Museum, Gift of A. Soudavar in memory of his mother Ezzat-Malek Soudavar, 2014.340
INSCRIBED:
rāqimahu Abū al-Ḥasan al-Ghaffārī Naqqāsh-Bāshī
yā wahhāb 1271
Painted by Abu al-Hasan al-Ghaffari, the Chief Painter
O Munificent One! 1854–55

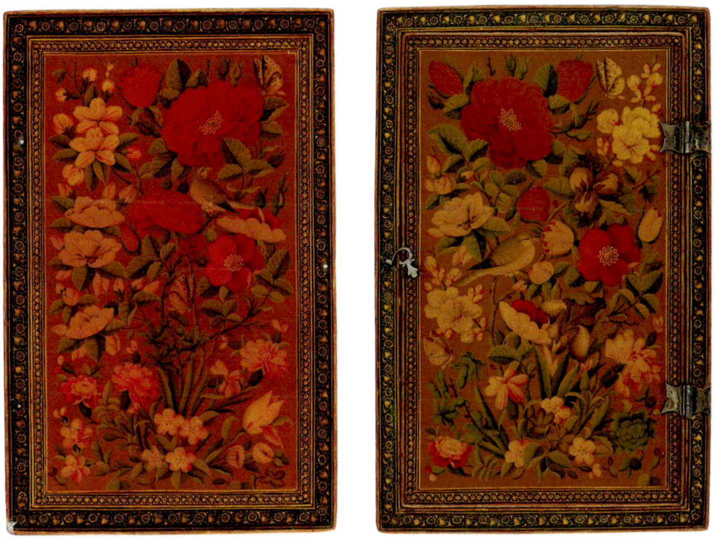

58

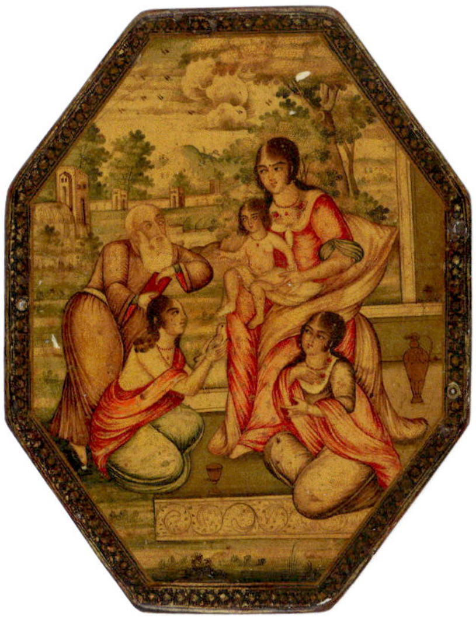

61

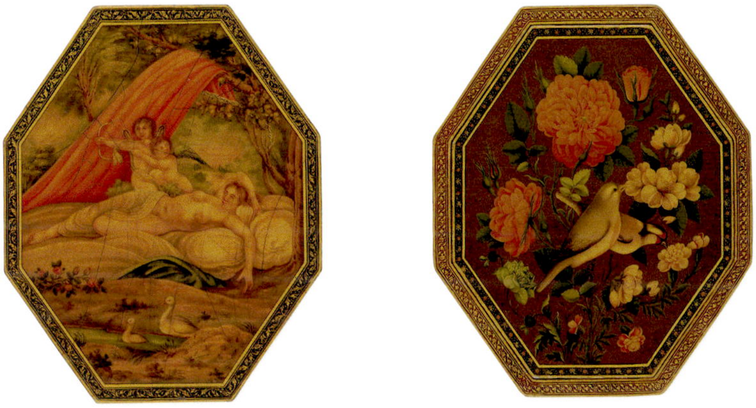

59

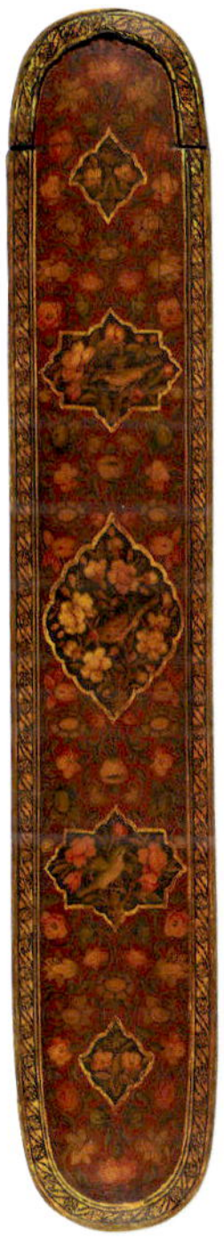

62

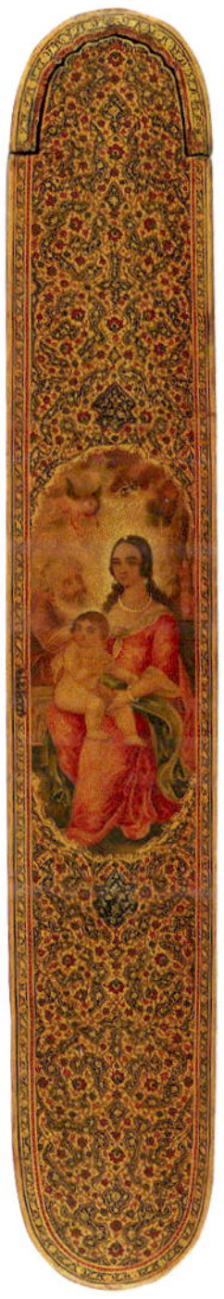

63

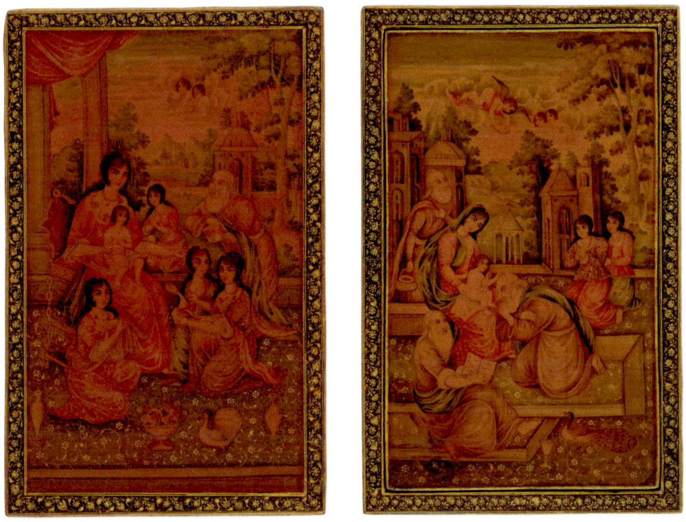

60

64. Snuff Box with Lovers Discovered

Iran, mid-19th century
Watercolor, gold-colored pigments, and lacquer over brass layer on pasteboard
2.4 × 6.4 × 9.2 cm (15⁄16 × 2½ × 3⅝ in.)
Collection of Saeed Kouros

65. Pen Box with Scenes of Shaykh San'an and the Christian Maiden, Khusraw and Shirin, and Shirin and Farhad

Signed by Ja'far b. Najaf 'Ali
Iran, probably Isfahan, 1850–75
Watercolor, gold-colored pigments, metallic particles, and lacquer over brass layer on pasteboard
3.7 × 3.8 × 23.1 cm (1 7⁄16 × 1½ × 9⅛ in.)
Harvard Art Museums / Arthur M. Sackler Museum, Gift of A. Soudavar in memory of his mother Ezzat-Malek Soudavar, 2014.328
INSCRIBED:
Ja'far ibn Najaf 'Alī

66. Pen Box with Scenes from Nizami's Tale of Bahram Gur and the Seven Princesses

Signed by Muhammad Kazim b. Najaf 'Ali
Iran, Isfahan, dated 1276 H (1859–60)
Watercolor, gold-colored pigments, and lacquer on pasteboard
4.1 × 4 × 24 cm (1⅝ × 1 9⁄16 × 9 7⁄16 in.)
Harvard Art Museums / Arthur M. Sackler Museum, Gift of John Goelet, 1958.260
INSCRIBED:
raqm-i kamtarīn Muḥammad Kāẓim sana 1296
Painted by the most humble Muhammad Kazim, year 1859–60
On the top and sides, multiple Persian inscriptions identify the images of Bahram Gur and the princesses.
PUBLISHED:
Habibeh Rahim, *Inscription as Art in the World of Islam: Unity in Diversity* (Hempstead, N.Y.: Hofstra Museum, Hofstra University, 1996), 46.
David J. Roxburgh, "The Qajar Lacquer Object," in *In Harmony: The Norma Jean Calderwood Collection of Islamic Art*, ed. Mary McWilliams (Cambridge, Mass.: Harvard Art Museums, 2013), 68, Fig. 3.

67. Cover for a Small Qur'an with Floral Composition (*exterior*) and Portrait of 'Ali, Hasan, and Husayn (*interior*)

Signed by Muhammad Isma'il
Iran, probably Isfahan, dated 1279 H (1862–63)
Watercolor, gold-colored pigments, and lacquer over brass layer on pasteboard
8.2 × 5.1 × 1.8 cm (3¼ × 2 × 11⁄16 in.)
Collection of Saeed Kouros
INSCRIBED:
'amal-i Ismā'īl Naqqāsh-Bāshī 1279
The work of Isma'il, the Chief Painter, 1862–63

68. Pen Box with Amorous Couples and Female Portraits in Medallions

Signed by Ahmad b. Najaf 'Ali
Iran, probably Isfahan, 1281 H (1864–65)
Watercolor, gold-colored pigments, and lacquer over brass layer on pasteboard
3.7 × 3.6 × 23.6 cm (1 7⁄16 × 1 7⁄16 × 9 5⁄16 in.)
Harvard Art Museums / Arthur M. Sackler Museum, Gift of A. Soudavar in memory of his mother Ezzat-Malek Soudavar, 2014.326
INSCRIBED:
Aḥmad ibn Najaf 'Alī 1281
Ahmad b. Najaf 'Ali 1864–65

69. Pen Box with Reclining Women and Female Portraits in Medallions

Circle of Najaf 'Ali
Iran, probably Isfahan, dated 1287 H (1870–71)
Watercolor, gold-colored pigments, and lacquer on pasteboard
3.9 × 3.9 × 22.7 cm (1 9⁄16 × 1 9⁄16 × 8 15⁄16 in.)
Collection of Saeed Kouros
INSCRIBED:
yā shāh-i Najaf 1287
O King of Najaf! 1870–71

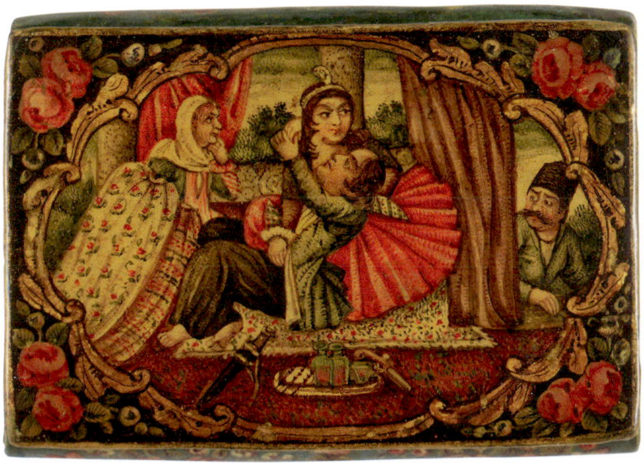

64

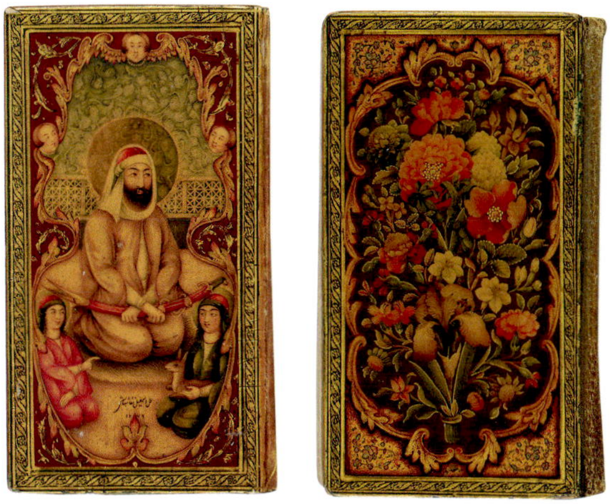

67

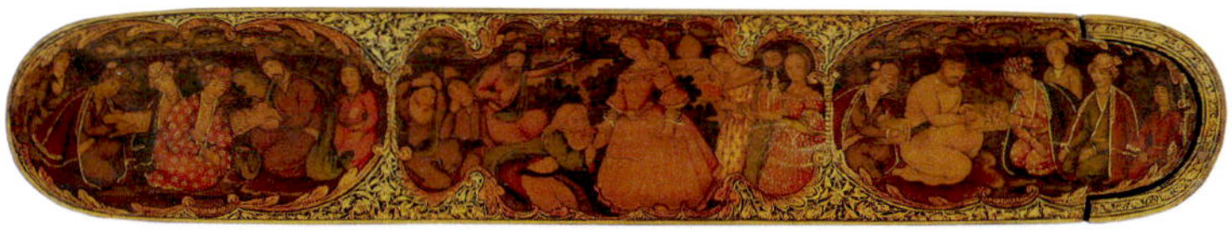

65

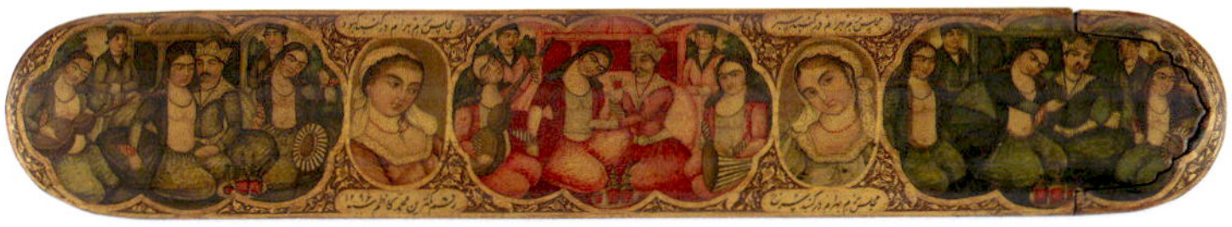

66

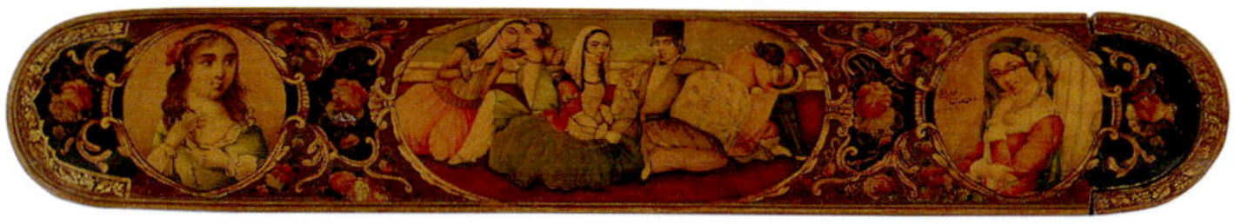

68

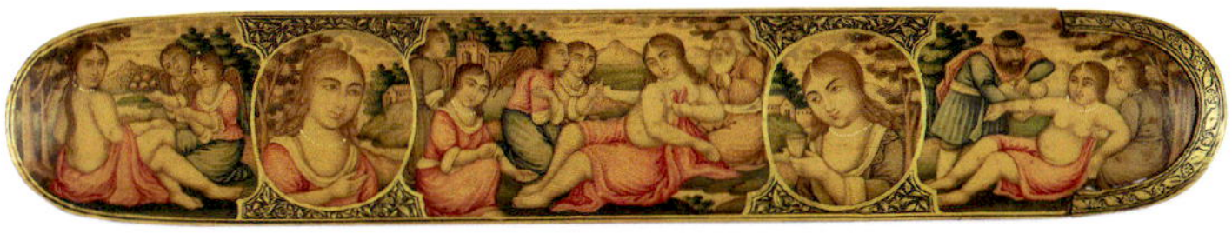

69

70. Pen Box with Reclining Women and Female Portraits in Medallions

Attributable to the circle of Najaf ʿAli
Iran, probably Isfahan, 1850–75
Watercolor, gold-colored pigments, platy hematite particles, and lacquer on pasteboard
3.7 × 3.7 × 23.3 cm (1 7/16 × 1 7/16 × 9 3/16 in.)
Harvard Art Museums / Arthur M. Sackler Museum, Gift of A. Soudavar in memory of his mother Ezzat-Malek Soudavar, 2014.321

71. Pen Box with European Woman and Eagles

Signed by ʿAbbas Shirazi
Iran, Shiraz, dated 1295 H (1878–79)
Watercolor, gold-colored pigments, and lacquer on pasteboard
3.9 × 3.9 × 23.6 cm (1 9/16 × 1 9/16 × 9 5/16 in.)
Harvard Art Museums / Arthur M. Sackler Museum, Gift of A. Soudavar in memory of his mother Ezzat-Malek Soudavar, 2014.355
INSCRIBED:
yā ʿAbbās 1295
O ʿAbbas! 1878–79

72. Pen Box with Portraits of Nasir al-Din Shah and Legendary Rulers from the *Shāhnāma*

Signed by Muhammad Kazim b. Najaf ʿAli
Iran, probably Isfahan, dated 1296 H (1879–80)
Watercolor, gold-colored pigments, and lacquer over brass layer on pasteboard
4.1 × 4 × 23.7 cm (1 5/8 × 1 9/16 × 9 5/16 in.)
Harvard Art Museums / Arthur M. Sackler Museum, Gift of A. Soudavar in memory of his mother Ezzat-Malek Soudavar, 2014.327
INSCRIBED:
raqm-i kamtarīn Muḥammad Kāẓim fī tarīkh sana 1296
Painted by the most humble Muhammad Kazim in the year 1879–80
Multiple Persian inscriptions identify the figures in the vignettes.

73. Pen Box with Young Woman

Russia, Lukutin factory, c. 1880
Lacquer, oil paint, and applied silver on pasteboard
3.9 × 4.1 × 23 cm (1 1/2 × 1 5/8 × 9 in.)
Museum für Lackkunst, Münster, Germany, 2011–37
PUBLISHED:
Monika Kopplin, *Russian Lacquer: The Collection of the Museum für Lackkunst* (Münster, Germany: Museum für Lackkunst; Munich: Hirmer Verlag, 2016), 174, cat. 95.

74. Pen Box with Seated and Reclining Women

Iran, second half 19th century
Watercolor, gold-colored pigments, and lacquer on pasteboard
3.5 × 3.4 × 22.3 cm (1 3/8 × 1 5/16 × 8 3/4 in.)
Collection of Vahid Kooros

75. Pen Box with Women, Men, and Children in Domestic Scenes

Iran, second half 19th century
Watercolor, gold-colored pigments, and lacquer on pasteboard
3.9 × 3.8 × 22.8 cm (1 9/16 × 1 1/2 × 9 in.)
Collection of Hamid Kooros

76. Pen Box with Figures in Indoor and Outdoor Settings, and Medallions

Signed by Mubarraz al-Shuʿara
Iran, dated 1321 H (1903–4)
Watercolor, gold-colored pigments, and lacquer over brass layer on pasteboard
3.6 × 3.7 × 21.6 cm (1 7/16 × 1 7/16 × 8 1/2 in.)
Collection of Hamid Kooros
INSCRIBED:
ʿamal-i mubarraz al-shuʿarā 1321
The work of Mubarraz al-Shuʿara, 1903–4

77. Pen Box with Women in Medallions

Signed by Muhammad Baqir Samirumi
Iran, Isfahan, dated 1327 H (1909–10)
Oil paint, gold-colored pigments, and lacquer on pasteboard
3.5 × 3.2 × 19.9 cm (1 3/8 × 1 1/4 × 7 13/16 in.)
Harvard Art Museums / Arthur M. Sackler Museum, Gift of A. Soudavar in memory of his mother Ezzat-Malek Soudavar, 2014.361
INSCRIBED:
303 Samīrumī 1327
303 Samirumi, 1909–10

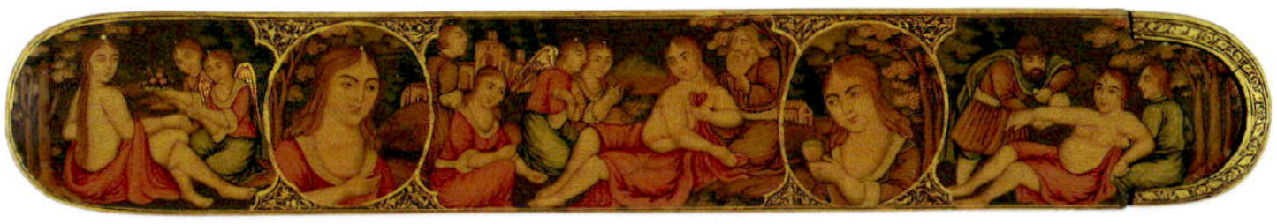

70

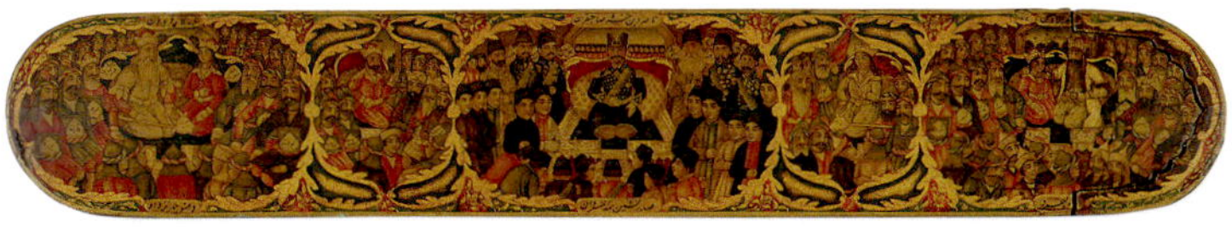

72

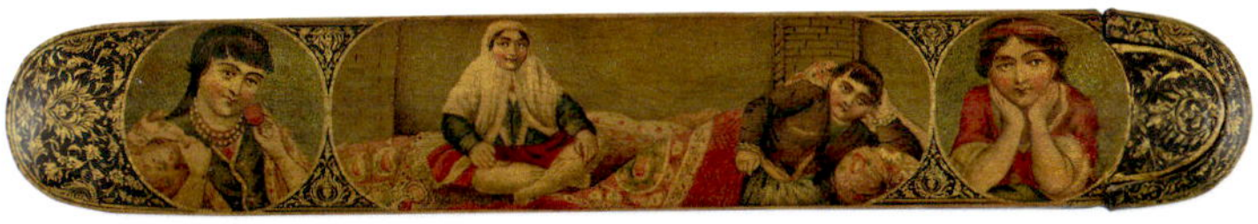

74

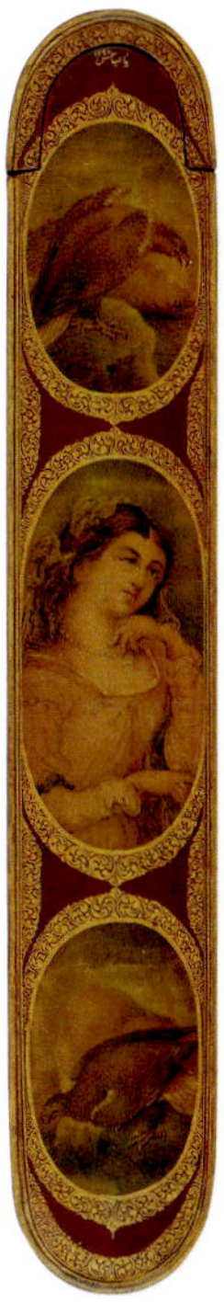

71

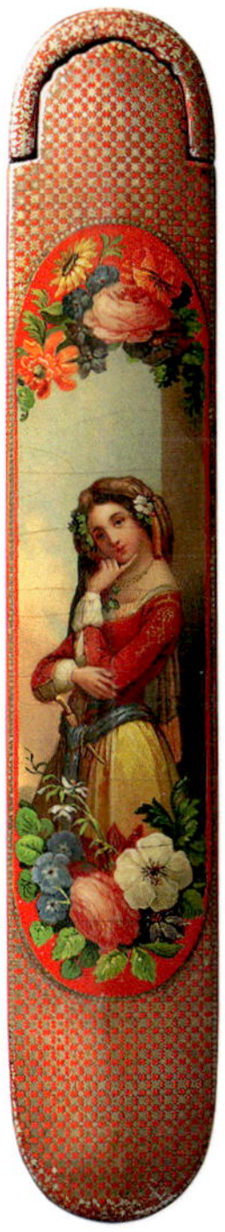

73

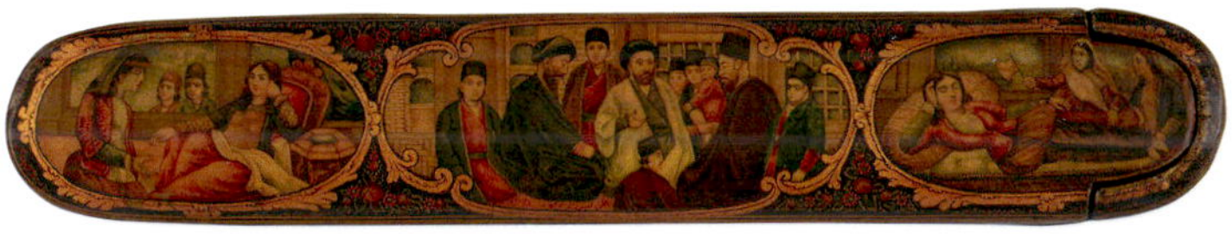

76

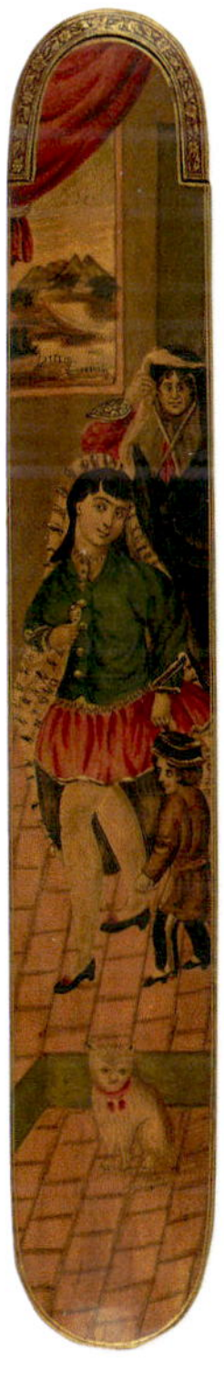

75

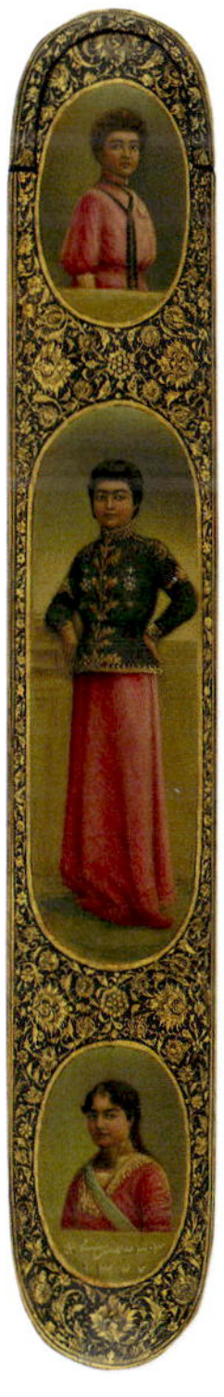

77

Bibliography

Adle, Chahryar. "Ṣāḥib-i Nasq, 'Alī Khān Vālī va sardār-i Humāyūn Vālī." *Bukhārā* 28 (1381 H [2002]): 36–55.

Adle, Chahryar, and Yahya Zoka. "Notes et documents sur la photographie Iranienne et son histoire." *Studia Iranica* 12 (2) (1983): 249–80.

Afshar, Iraj. "Some Remarks on the Early History of Photography in Iran." In *Qajar Iran: Political, Social, and Cultural Change, 1800–1925*, ed. Clifford Edmund Bosworth and Carole Hillenbrand, 261–90. Costa Mesa, Calif.: Mazda, 1983.

Aitken, Molly Emma. "Parataxis and the Practice of Reuse, from Mughal Margins to Mīr Kalān Khān." *Archives of Asian Art* 59 (2009): 81–103.

Ala'i, Cyrus. "Hotz, Albert Paul Herman." In *Encyclopaedia Iranica*, Online Edition. http://www.iranicaonline.org/articles/hotz-albert-paul-herman. Accessed September 11, 2016.

Alschuler, William R. "Color Theory and Practice. 1800–1860." In *Encyclopedia of Nineteenth-Century Photography*, vol. 1, ed. John Hannavy, 315–18. London: Routledge, 2007.

Amanat, Abbas. "Court Patronage and Public Space: Abu'l-Hasan Sani' al-Mulk and the Art of Persianizing the Other in Qajar Iran." In *Court Cultures in the Muslim World: Seventh to Nineteenth Centuries*, ed. Albrecht Fuess and Jan-Peter Hartung, 408–44. New York: Routledge, 2011.

———. *Pivot of the Universe: Nasir al-Din Shah Qajar and the Iranian Monarchy, 1831–1896*. Berkeley: University of California Press, 1997.

———. "Pūr-i khāqān va andīsha-yi bāzyābī-yi tārīkh-i millī-yi Īrān: Jalāl-al-Dīn Mīrzā va *Nāma-yi Khusravān*." *Īrān-nāma* 17 (1) (1999): 5–54.

Amanat, Abbas, and Farzin Vejdani. "Jalāl-al-Din Mirzā." In *Encyclopaedia Iranica*, Online Edition. http://www.iranicaonline.org/articles/jalal-al-din-mirza. Accessed December 6, 2016.

Amir-Moezzi, Mohammad Ali. "Icon and Meditation: Between Popular Art and Sufism in Imami Shi'ism." In *The Art and Material Culture of Iranian Shi'ism: Iconography and Religious Devotion in Shi'i Islam*, ed. Pedram Khosronejad, 25–45. New York: I. B. Tauris, 2012.

Arberry, A. J. *Fifty Poems of Hafiz*. Cambridge: Cambridge University Press, 1947.

Avery, Peter. "Printing, the Press, and Literature in Modern Iran." In *The Cambridge History of Iran*, vol. 7, *From Nadir Shah to the Islamic Republic*, ed. P. Avery, G. R. G. Hambly, and Charles Melville, 815–69. Cambridge: Cambridge University Press, 1991.

Bābāzāda, Shahlā. *Tārīkh-i chāp dar Īrān*. Tehran: Ṭahūrī, 1999.

Baghdiantz McCabe, Ina. *The Shah's Silk for Europe's Silver: The Eurasian Trade of the Julfa Armenians in Safavid Iran*

and India, 1530–1750. Atlanta: Scholars Press, 1999.
Barjesteh van Waalwijk van Doorn, L. A. Ferydoun, and Gillian M. Vogelsang-Eastwood, eds. *Sevruguin's Iran: Late Nineteenth Century Photographs of Iran from the National Museum of Ethnology in Leiden, the Netherlands*. Tehran: Zaman; Rotterdam: Barjesteh van Waalwijk van Doorn, 1999.
Batchen, Geoffrey. *Burning with Desire: The Conception of Photography*. Cambridge, Mass.: MIT Press, 1997.
Bayer, Thomas M., and John R. Page. *The Development of the Art Market in England: Money as Muse, 1730–1900*. London: Pickering & Chatto, 2011.
Behdad, Ali. "The Power-ful Art of Qajar Photography: Orientalism and (Self)-Orientalizing in Nineteenth-Century Iran." *Iranian Studies* 34 (1–4) (2001): 141–51.
Benjamin, S. G. W. *Persia and the Persians*. Boston: Ticknor and Co., 1887.
Berlekamp, Persis. *Wonder, Image, and Cosmos in Medieval Islam*. New Haven, Conn.: Yale University Press, 2011.
Bohrer, Fredrick N., ed. *Sevruguin and the Persian Image: Photographs of Iran, 1870–1930*. Washington, D.C.: Arthur M. Sackler Gallery, Smithsonian Institution; Seattle: University of Washington Press, 1999.
Bolter, Jay David, and Richard Grusin. *Remediation: Understanding New Media*. Cambridge, Mass.: MIT Press, 1999.
Bradley-Birt, F. B. *Persia: Through Persia from the Gulf to the Caspian*. Boston: J. B. Millet, 1910.
Būẕarī, ʿAlī. *Chihil ṭūfān: barrasī-yi taṣāvīr-i chāp-i sangī-yi Ṭūfān al-bukāʾ fī maqātil al-shuhadā*. Tehran: Kitābkhāna, Mūzih va Markaz-i Asnād-i Majlis-i Shūrā-yi Islāmī, 2011.
———. "Sketching and Copying in the Niello-Prints of the Qajar Period." *Nāma-yi bahāristān* 10 (15) (2009): 343–48.
Būẕarī, ʿAlī, and Muḥammad Āzādī. *Ma'khaz-shināsī-yi kitābhā-yi chāp-i sangī va surbī*. Tehran: Kitābdār, 1390 H (2011–12).
Carswell, John. "Eastern and Western Influence on Art of the Seventeenth Century in Iran." In *The Memorial Volume of the Vth International Congress of Iranian Art & Archaeology*, vol. 2, ed. A. Tajvidi and M. Y. Kiani, 277–81. Tehran: Ministry of Culture and Arts, 1972.
———. *New Julfa: The Armenian Churches and Other Buildings*. Oxford: Clarendon Press, 1968.
Chelkowski, Peter J., ed. *Eternal Performance: Taʿziyeh and Other Shiite Rituals*. London: Seagull, 2010.
Chi, Jennifer Y., ed. *The Eye of the Shah: Qajar Court Photography and the Persian Past*. New York: Institute for the Study of the Ancient World at New York University, 2015.
Corbin, Henry. "Āẕar Kayvān." In *Encyclopaedia Iranica*, Online Edition. http://www.iranicaonline.org/articles/azar-kayvan-priest. Accessed on December 6, 2016.
Coste, Pascal. *Monuments modernes de la Perse*. Paris: A. Morel, 1867.
Dailami, Pezhmann. "Kasmā'i, Mirzā Hosayn." In *Encyclopaedia Iranica*, Online Edition. http://www.iranicaonline.org/articles/kasmai_mirza. Accessed September 11, 2016.
D'Allemagne, Henry-René. *Du Khorassan au pays des Backhtiaris: Trois mois de voyage en Perse*. Paris: Hachette et Cie, 1911.
Diba, Layla S. "An Encounter between Qajar Iran and the West: The Rashtrapati Bhavan Painting of Fath ʿAli Shah at the Hunt." In *Islamic Art in the 19th Century: Tradition, Innovation, and Eclecticism*, ed. Doris Behrens-Abouseif and Stephen Vernoit, 281–304. Leiden, The Netherlands: Brill, 2006.
———. "Lacquerwork." In *The Arts of Persia*, ed. R. W. Ferrier, 243–54. New Haven, Conn.: Yale University Press, 1989.
———. "Lacquerwork of Safavid Persia and Its Relationship to Persian Painting." Ph.D. dissertation, 2 vols., New York University, 1994.
———. "Persian Painting in the Eighteenth Century: Tradition and Transmission." *Muqarnas* 6 (1989): 147–60.
———. "The Qajar Court Painter Yahya Ghaffari: His Life and Times." In *Persian Painting from the Mongols to the Qajars: Studies in Honour of Basil W. Robinson*, ed. Robert Hillenbrand, 83–96. London: I. B. Tauris, 2000.
———. "Qajar Photography and Its Relationship to Iranian Art: A Reassessment." *History of Photography* 37 (1) (2013): 85–98.
Diba, Layla S., with Maryam Ekhtiar, eds. *Royal Persian Paintings: The Qajar Epoch, 1785–1925*. London: I. B. Tauris Publishers in association with Brooklyn Museum of Art, 1998.
Ekhtiar, Maryam. "Innovation and Revivalism in Later Persian Calligraphy: The Visal Family of Shiraz." In *Islamic Art in the 19th Century: Tradition, Innovation, and Eclecticism*, ed. Doris Behrens-Abouseif and Stephen Vernoit, 257–79. Leiden, The Netherlands: Brill, 2006.
———. "Muhammad Ismaʿil Isfahani: Master Lacquer Painter." In *Persian Masters: Five Centuries of Painting*, ed. Sheila R. Canby, 129–43. Bombay: Marg Publications, 1990.
———. "Nasir al-Din Shah and the Dar al-Funun: The Evolution of an Institution." *Iranian Studies* 34 (1–4) (2001): 153–63.
Engelberts, Theresia H. E. *A Persian from a Distant Land: Albertus Paulus Hermanus Hotz: A Memoir*. The Hague: Ansureß Press, 2000.
Eremin, Katherine, and Claire Grech. "Technical and Chemical Examinations of Persian Lacquer in the Ezzat-Malek Soudavar Collection." In *A Collector's Passion: Ezzat-Malek Soudavar and Persian Lacquer*, ed. Massumeh Farhad and Mary McWilliams. Washington, D.C.: Smithsonian Institution, 2017.
Ettehadieh, Mansureh (Nezam Mafi). "The Social Condition of Women in

Qajar Society." In *Society and Culture in Qajar Iran: Studies in Honor of Hafez Farmayan*, ed. Elton L. Daniel, 69–98. Costa Mesa, Calif.: Mazda Publishers, 2002.

Ettehadieh, Mansureh (Nezam Mafi), and Bahman Farman Farmaian. "The Beginnings of Illustrated Journals during the Reign of Nasser ed-Din Shah, and the Work of Sani ol-Molk." *Qajar Studies: Journal of the International Qajar Studies Association* 6 (2006): 67–97.

Farhad, Massumeh, and Mary McWilliams, eds. *A Collector's Passion: Ezzat-Malek Soudavar and Persian Lacquer*. Washington, D.C.: Smithsonian Institution, 2017.

Fehervari, Geza. "The Near East, the Middle East and India." In *Lacquer: An International History and Collector's Guide*, ed. Jonathan Bourne, 150–69. Marlborough, Wiltshire, U.K.: Crowood in association with Phoebe Phillips Editions, 1984.

Feuvrier, Jean-Baptiste. *Trois ans à la cour de Perse*. Paris: Impr. nationale, 1906.

Flandin, Eugène. *Voyage en Perse de mm. Eugène Flandin, peintre, et Pascal Coste, architecte*. 2 vols. Paris: Gide et J. Baudry, 1851.

Floor, Willem. "Art (*Naqqashi*) and Artists (*Naqqashan*) in Qajar Persia." *Muqarnas* 16 (1999): 125–54.

———. "Čāp." In *Encyclopaedia Iranica*, Online Edition. http://www.iranicaonline.org/articles/cap-print-printing-a-persian-word-probably-derived-from-hindi-chapna-to-print-see-turner-no. Accessed on December 6, 2016.

———. "Dutch-Persian Relations." In *Encyclopaedia Iranica*, Online Edition. http://www.iranicaonline.org/articles/dutch-persian-relations. Accessed on September 11, 2016.

———. *Wall Paintings and Other Figurative Mural Art in Qajar Iran*. Costa Mesa, Calif.: Mazda, 2005.

Gaffary, F. "Amīn-al-Dawla, Farrok Khan Gaffārī." In *Encyclopaedia Iranica*, Online Edition. http://www.iranicaonline.org/articles/amin-al-dawla-abu-taleb-farrok-khan-gaffari-1227-88-1812-71-a-high-ranking-qajar-official. Accessed on September 11, 2016.

George, Henri. *La belle histoire des images d'Épinal*. Paris: Cherche midi éditeur, 1996.

Gobineau, Joseph Arthur, comte de. *Essai sur l'inégalité des races humaines*. 4 vols. Paris: Libraririe de Firmin Didot, 1853–55.

———. *Trois ans en Asie (de 1855 à 1858) par le Cte. A. de Gobineau*. Paris: L. Hachette et Cie, 1859.

Gosudarstvennyi tsentr fotografii. *Sankt-Peterburg v fotografiiakh serediny XIX-nachala XX veka: katalog vystavki*. St. Petersburg: Rosfoto, 2008.

Grabar, Oleg. "Reflections on Qajar Art and Its Significance." *Iranian Studies* 34 (1–4) (2001): 183–86.

Green, Bryan Clark. "Wet Collodion Negative." In *Encyclopedia of Nineteenth-Century Photography*, vol. 1, ed. John Hannavy, 1485–86. London: Routledge, 2007.

Green, Nile. "Stone from Bavaria: Iranian Lithography in Its Global Context." *Iranian Studies* 43 (3) (2010): 305–31.

Gruber, Christiane. "Introduction: Islamic Book Arts in Indiana University Collections." In *The Islamic Manuscript Tradition: Ten Centuries of Book Arts in Indiana University Collections*, ed. Christiane Gruber, 2–51. Bloomington: Indiana University Press, 2010.

Gulbun, Muḥammad. *Sarguẕasht va āṡār-i taṣvīrgar-i buzurg, Mīrzā Abū Turāb Khān Ghaffārī Kāshānī, 1263–1307, H. Q.* Tehran: Anjuman-i Āṡār va Mafākhir-i Farhangī, 1386 H (2007–8).

Gulpāyagānī, Ḥusayn Mīrzā. *Tārīkh-i chāp va chāp-khāna dar Īrān: (1050 Qamarī tā 1320 Shamsī)*. Tehran: Nashr-i Gulshān, 1378 H (1999).

Gurney, John, and Negin Nabavi. "Dār al-Fonūn." In *Encyclopaedia Iranica*, Online Edition. http://www.iranicaonline.org/articles/dar-al-fonun-lit. Accessed on September 11, 2016.

Hambly, G. R. G. "Iran during the Reigns of Fath ʿAli Shah and Muhammad Shah." In *The Cambridge History of Iran*, vol. 7, *From Nadir Shah to the Islamic Republic*, ed. Peter Avery, G. R. G. Hambly, and Charles Melville, 144–73. Cambridge: Cambridge University Press, 1991.

———. "The Traditional Iranian City in the Qajar Period." In *The Cambridge History of Iran*, vol. 7, *From Nadir Shah to the Islamic Republic*, ed. Peter Avery, G. R. G. Hambly, and Charles Melville, 542–89. Cambridge, Cambridge University Press, 1991.

Hanaway, William L. "Persian Travel Narratives: Notes toward the Definition of a Nineteenth-Century Genre." In *Society and Culture in Qajar Iran: Studies in Honor of Hafez Farmayan*, ed. Elton L. Daniel, 249–68. Costa Mesa, Calif.: Mazda Publishers, 2002.

Hanaway, William L., Jr. "Paradise on Earth: The Terrestrial Garden in Persian Literature." In *The Islamic Garden*, ed. Elisabeth B. MacDougall and Richard Ettinghausen, 41–68. Washington, D.C.: Dumbarton Oaks, Trustees for Harvard University, 1976.

Höltzer, Ernst. *Persien vor 113 Jahren: Text und Bilder*. Edited by Mohammad Assemi. Tehran: Kultur- und Kunstministeriums, Zentrum für die Persische Ethnologie, 1975.

Hults, Linda C. *The Print in the Western World: An Introductory History*. Madison: University of Wisconsin Press, 1996.

Impey, Oliver, and Christiaan Jörg. *Japanese Export Lacquer: 1580–1850*. Amsterdam: Hotei Publishing, 2005.

Iṣfahānī, Muḥammad Maḥdī b. Muḥammad Riżā. *Niṣf-i jahān fī taʿrīf al-Iṣfahān*. Edited by Manūchihr Sutūdah. Isfahan, Iran: Ta'yīd, 1340 H [1961].

Iʿtimād al-Salṭana, Muḥammad Ḥasan Khān Mir'āt. *Mirāt al-buldān-i nāṣirī*. 4 vols. Tehran: n.p., 1295 H (1878–79).

———. *Ma'āṣir wa al-āṣār: Chihil sāl-i tārīkh-i Īrān: dar dawra-yi Pādishāh-i Nāṣir al-Dīn Shāh*, ed. Īrāj Āfshār. 3 vols. Tehran: Shirkat-i Intishārāt-i Asāṭīr, 1363– H (1984–).

Iʿtiẓād al-Salṭana, ʿAlī Qūlī Mīrzā. *Akṣīr al-tawārīkh*. Edited by Jamshīd Kīyānfar. Tehran: Vīsman, 1370 H (1991).

Jackson, Christine Elisabeth, and Peter Davis. *Sir William Jardine: A Life in Natural History*. Leicester, U.K.: Leicester University Press, 2001.

Jalāl al-Dīn Mīrzā. *Nāma-yi khusravān: dāstān-i pādshāhān-i Pārs*. 3 vols. Tehran: n.p., 1868–72.

James, David. "Lacquer Items in the Chester Beatty Library." In *Lacquerwork in Asia and Beyond*, ed. William Watson, 318–27. London: Percival David Foundation and the University of London, 1982.

Jardine, Sir William. *Birds of Great Britain and Ireland, Part 1: Birds of Prey*. The Naturalist's Library, vol. 9. Edinburgh: W. H. Lizars, 1838.

———. *Mammalia. Ruminating Animals, Part 1: Deer, Antelopes, Camels, & C*. The Naturalist's Library, vol. 21. Edinburgh: W. H. Lizars, 1866.

Kamal, Muhammad. *Mulla Sadra's Transcendent Philosophy*. Aldershot, U.K.: Ashgate, 2006.

Karimi, Pamela. *Domesticity and Consumer Culture in Iran: Interior Revolutions of the Modern Era*. London: Routledge, 2013.

Karīmzāda Tabrīzī, Muḥammad. *Aḥvāl va āṣār-i naqqāshān-i qadīm-i Īran va barkhī az mashāhīr-i nigārgar-i Hind va ʿUṣmānī*. 3 vols. London: Interlink Longraph, 1363 H (1985–1991).

Kazemzadeh, Firuz. *Russia and Britain in Persia: Imperial Ambitions in Qajar Iran*. New York: I. B. Tauris, 2013.

Khalili, Nasser D., B. W. Robinson, and Tim Stanley. *Lacquer of the Islamic Lands*. 2 pts. The Nasser D. Khalili Collection of Islamic Art, vol. 22. London: Nour Foundation in association with Azimuth Editions and Oxford University Press, 1996–97.

Kopplin, Monika. *Russian Lacquer: The Collection of the Museum für Lackkunst*. Münster, Germany: Museum für Lackkunst; Munich: Hirmer Verlag, 2016.

Kunz, Peter, and Bruno Weber. "The 19th-century Photochrom Printing Process." In *Voyage en couleur: Photochromie, 1876–1914*, ed. Sabine Arqué et al., 180–87. Paris: Éditions Eyrolles, 2009.

Landau, Amy S. "Visibly Foreign, Visibly Female: The Eroticization of *Zan-i Farangi* in Seventeenth-Century Persian Painting." In *Eros and Sexuality in Islamic Art*, ed. Francesca Leoni and Mika Natif, 99–130. Burlington, Vt.: Ashgate Publishing Company, 2013.

Landor, A. Henry Savage. *Across Coveted Lands: Or a Journey from Flushing (Holland) to Calcutta, Overland*. 2 vols. New York: Scribner's Sons, 1903.

Langer, Axel. "European Influences on Seventeenth-Century Persian Painting: Of Handsome Europeans, Naked Ladies, and Parisian Timepieces." In *The Fascination of Persia: The Persian-European Dialogue in Seventeenth-Century Art and Contemporary Art of Teheran*, ed. Axel Langer, 170–237. Zurich: Museum Rietberg, 2013.

Loginov, Alexei. "Russian Empire." In *Encyclopedia of Nineteenth-Century Photography*, vol. 2, ed. John Hannavy, 1227–23. London: Routledge, 2007.

Luft, J. P. "The Qajar Rock Reliefs." *Iranian Studies* 34 (1–4) (2001): 31–49.

Mahdavi, Shireen. "Rishār Khan." In *Encyclopaedia Iranica*, Online Edition. http://www.iranicaonline.org/articles/rishar-khan. Accessed August 22, 2016.

Mamatsashvili, Lika, and Herman Maes. *Masters of 19th Century Photography: Dimitri Ermakov, Photographer and Collector*. Amsterdam: Pegasus, 2014.

Marzolph, Ulrich. "From Mecca to Mashhad: The Narrative of an Illustrated Shiʿi Pilgrimage Scroll from the Qajar Period." *Muqarnas* 31 (2014): 207–42.

———. "Illustrated Persian Lithographic Editions of the *Shânâme*." *Edebiyât* 13 (2) (2003): 177–98.

———. "The Last Great *Shahnama*: The *Shahnama-yi Bahaduri* (1319–26/1901–8)." In *Shahnama Studies I*, ed. Charles Melville, 259–76. Cambridge: Cambridge University Press, 2006.

———. "Mirzā ʿAli-Qoli Xu'i: Master of Lithograph Illustration." *Annali (Istituto Orientale di Napoli)* 57 (1–2) (1997): 183–202.

———. *Narrative Illustration in Persian Lithographed Books*. Leiden, The Netherlands: Brill, 2001.

———. "The Pictorial Representation of Shiʿi Themes in Lithographed Books of the Qajar Period." In *The Art and Material Culture of Iranian Shiʿism: Iconography and Religious Devotion in Shiʿi Islam*, ed. Pedram Khosronejad, 74–103. London: I. B. Tauris, 2012.

———. "The *Shahnama* in Print: Lithographed Editions of the Persian National Epic." In *Heroic Times: A Thousand Years of the Persian Book of Kings*, ed. Julia Gonnella and Christoph Rauch, 64–71. Munich: Edition Minerva, 2012.

Marzolph, Ulrich, and Muḥammad Hādī Muḥammadī. *Ālbūm-i Shāhnāma: Taṣvīrhā-yi chāp-i sangī-yi Shāhnāma-yi Firdawsī*. Tehran: Chīstā, 1384 H (2005–6).

Matthee, Rudi. *The Pursuit of Pleasure: Drugs and Stimulants in Iranian History, 1500–1900*. Princeton, N.J.: Princeton University Press, 2005.

McWilliams, Mary. "Reflections of the Najaf Circle of Artists in Isfahan." In *An Album of Artists' Drawings from Qajar Iran*, ed. David J. Roxburgh. Cambridge, Mass.: Harvard Art Museums, 2017.

Meisami, Julie Scott. "Allegorical Gardens in the Persian Poetic Tradition: Nezami, Rumi, Hafez." *International Journal of Middle East Studies* 17 (2) (1985): 229–60.

Mihrābī, Muʿīn al-Dīn. "Sayyid ʿAbd al-Rahīm Kāshānī. Namāvanda-yi Tihrān dar dawrahā-yi haftum va hashtum-i majlis-i shawrā-yi millī." *Asnād-i bahāristān dawra-yi jadīd* 3 (1392 H [2013–14]): 89–107.

Mirseyedi, Sarah. "Aesthetic Innovation and Conditions of Modernity in 19th-Century Iran." In *An Album of Artists' Drawings from Qajar Iran*, ed. David J. Roxburgh. Cambridge, Mass.: Harvard Art Museums, 2017.

Muḥammad'zāda, Aṣghar, ed. *Āẕarbāyjan va Vālī-yi ʿakkās: Bar asās-i nuskhah'hā-yi khaṭṭī va ālbūm-i ʿAlī Khān Vālī*. Tehran: Nashr-i Awḥadī, 1390 H (2011).

Nafīsī, Saʿīd. "Ṣanʿat-i chāp-i muṣavvar dar Īrān." *Payām-i naw* 2 (5) (1945–46): 22–35.

Neumann, Reingard, ed. *Aus 1001 Nacht: Islamische Lackkunst in deutschen Museen and Bibliotheken*. Münster, Germany: Museum für Lackkunst, 2009.

Neumann-Henneberg, Erika. "Technologische Untersuchungen an Lackarbeiten aus Persien." In *Zeitschrift für Kunsttechnologie und Konservierung* 18 (2004): 349–70.

Nouraei, Morteza. "Ordinary People and the Reception of British Culture in Iran, 1906–41." In *Anglo-Iranian Relations since 1800*, ed. Vanessa Martin, 67–79. New York: Routledge, 2005.

Ouseley, Sir William. *Travels into Various Countries of the East, More Particularly Persia*. 3 vols. London: Rodwell and Martin, 1823.

Pejhan, Sassan. "A Picture Postcard View of the Persian Constitutional Revolution." *Journal of Persianate Studies* 3 (2) (2010): 192–221.

Pérez González, Carmen. *Local Portraiture: Through the Lens of the 19th-Century Iranian Photographers*. Leiden, The Netherlands: Leiden University Press, 2012.

Pérez González, Carmen, and Reza Sheikh. "From the Inner Sanctum: Men Who Were Trusted by the Kings." In *The Eye of the Shah: Qajar Court Photography and the Persian Past*, ed. Jennifer Y. Chi, 132–57. New York: Institute for the Study of the Ancient World at New York University, 2015.

Pinney, Christopher. *Camera Indica: The Social Life of Indian Photographs*. Chicago: University of Chicago Press, 1997.

Plunkett, John. "Carte-de-visite." In *Encyclopedia of Nineteenth-Century Photography*, vol. 1, ed. John Hannavy, 276–77. London: Routledge, 2007.

———. *Queen Victoria: First Media Monarch*. Oxford: Oxford University Press, 2003.

Porter, Sir Robert Ker. *Travels in Georgia, Persia, Armenia, Ancient Babylonia, &c. &c. during the Years 1817, 1818, 1819, and 1820*. 2 vols. London: Longman, Hurst, Rees, Orme, and Brown, 1821–22.

Qāsimī, Farīd, ed. *Sarguzasht-i matbūʿāt-i Īrān: Rūzgār-i Muḥammad Shāh va Nāṣir al-Dīn Shāh*. Tehran: Sāzmān-i Chāp va Intishārāt, Vizarāt-i Farhang va Irshād-i Islāmī, 1380 H (2001).

Qāżīhā, Fāṭima. *Nāṣir al-Dīn Shāh va Naqqāshī*. Tehran: Sāzmān-i Asnād va Kitābkhāna-yi Millī-yi Jumhūrī-yi Islāmī-yi Īrān, 1394 H (2015).

Raby, Julian. *Qajar Portraits*. London: Azimuth Editions in association with the Iran Heritage Foundation, 1999.

Rahim, Habibeh. *Inscription as Art in the World of Islam: Unity in Diversity*. Hempstead, N.Y.: Hofstra Museum, Hofstra University, 1996.

Rahimi-Golkhandan, Shabnam. "Ali Khan Vali: The Histories of an Archive." In *Photography's Shifting Terrain: Conference Proceedings*, ed. Shamoon Zamir and Nassar Issam. London: I. B. Tauris, 2017.

Raīsī Mubāraka, Suhaylā, and Mahbūba Bābāī. *Muṭālaʿātī dar tārīkh-i chāp dar Īrān*. Tehran: Gulshan-i Rāz, 1378 H (1999).

Rajabzadeh, Hashem. "Japan as Seen by Qajar Travellers." In *Society and Culture in Qajar Iran: Studies in Honor of Hafez Farmayan*, ed. Elton L. Daniel, 285–310. Costa Mesa, Calif.: Mazda Publishers, 2002.

Razpush, Shahnaz, "Galyân," In *Encyclopaedia Iranica*, Online Edition. http://www.iranicaonline.org/articles/galyan-. Accessed September 11, 2016.

Rinhart, Floyd, Marion Rinhart, and Robert W. Wagner. *The American Tintype*. Columbus: Ohio State University Press, 1999.

Roberts, Mary. "The Limits of Circumscription." In *Photography's Orientalism: New Essays on Colonial Representation*, ed. Ali Behdad and Luke Gartlan, 53–74. Los Angeles: Getty Research Institute, 2013.

Robinson, B. W. "Abu'l-Ḥasan Khan Gaffārī." In *Encyclopaedia Iranica*, Online Edition. http://www.iranicaonline.org/articles/abul-hasan-khan-gaffari-sani-al-molk-1814-66-painter-in-oils-and-miniature-lacquer-artist-and-book-illustrator. Accessed December 6, 2016.

———. *An Exhibition of 50 Pieces of Persian, Indian, and Turkish Lacquer at Bernheimer Fine Arts Ltd. from 10 June to 27 June 1986*. London: Bernheimer Fine Arts, 1986.

———. "Lacquer in the University of Oxford." In *Islamic Art in the Ashmolean Museum*, part 2, ed. James Allan, 45–61. Oxford Studies in Islamic Art, vol. 10. Oxford: Oxford University Press, 1995.

———. "A Lacquer Mirror Case of 1854." *Iran* 5 (1967): 1–6.

———. "Persian Painting under the Zand and Qājār Dynasties." In *The Cambridge History of Iran*, vol. 7, *From Nadir Shah to the Islamic Republic*, ed. Peter Avery, G. R. G. Hambly, and Charles Melville, 870–89. Cambridge: Cambridge University Press, 1991.

———. "Qajar Lacquer." *Muqarnas* 6 (1989): 131–46.

Rochechouart, Julien de. *Souvenirs d'un voyage en Perse*. Paris: Challamel Aîné, 1867.

Roxburgh, David J., ed. *An Album of Artists' Drawings from Qajar Iran*. Cambridge, Mass.: Harvard Art Museums, 2017.

———. "Micrographia: Toward a Visual Logic of Persianate Painting." *RES: Anthropology and Aesthetics* 43 (2003): 12–30.

———. "The Qajar Lacquer Object." In *In Harmony: The Norma Jean Calderwood Collection of Islamic Art*, ed. Mary McWilliams, 65–76. Cambridge, Mass.: Harvard Art Museums, 2013.

———. "Troubles with Perspective: Case Studies in Picture-Making from Qajar Iran," in *Art History in the Wake of the Global Turn*, ed. Jill H. Casid and Aruna d'Souza, 107–25. Williamstown, Mass.: Sterling and Francine Clark Art Institute, 2014.

Rūznāma-yi dawlat-i ʿalīya-yi Īrān. Tehran: Kitābkhāna-yi millī Jumhūrī Islāmī-yi Īrān, 1992–93.

Saburova, T. G. *Dagerotip v Rossii: Sobranie Istoricheskogo muzeia: katalog*. Moscow: Gosudarstvennyi istoricheskii muzei, 2014.

———. *U istokov fotoiskusstva: sobranie dagereotipov Gosudarstvennogo Istoricheskogo muzeia*. Moscow: Izd-vo Art-Rodnik, 1999.

Sāfī, Qāsim. *Kārt pustāl'hā-yi tārīkhī-yi Īrān*. Tehran: Mu'assasa-yi Farhangī-yi Gustarish-i Hunar, 1989.

Ṣafīnizhād, Javād, ed. *Dawra-yi rūznāma-i Sharaf va Sharāfat*. Tehran: Yasāvulī, 1363 H (1984).

Sattari, Mohammad, and Houshang Salamat. "Photography and the Illustrated Journals *Sharaf* and *Sharāfat*." *History of Photography* 37 (1) (2013): 74–84.

Savory, Roger. "Last of the Qezelbāš." In *Society and Culture in Qajar Iran: Studies in Honor of Hafez Farmayan*, ed. Elton L. Daniel, 3–34. Costa Mesa, Calif.: Mazda Publishers, 2002.

Sayf, Hādī. *Naqqāshī-yi qahva-khāna*. Tehran: Vizārat-i Farhang va Āmūzish-i ʿĀlī, 1369 H (1990).

Scarce, Jennifer M. "Ancestral Themes in the Art of Qajar Iran, 1785–1925." In *Islamic Art in the 19th Century: Tradition, Innovation, and Eclecticism*, ed. Doris Behrens-Abouseif and Stephen Vernoit, 231–56. Leiden, The Netherlands: Brill, 2006.

———. "Čīt." In *Encyclopaedia Iranica*, Online Edition. http://www.iranicaonline.org/articles/cit-borrowed-from-indian-where-it-occurs-in-many-dialects-with-the-meaning-spotted-cloth-probably-of-non-indo-aryan-orig. Accessed December 6, 2016.

———. "Major-General Sir Robert Murdoch Smith KCMG and Anglo-Iranian Relations in Art and Culture." In *Anglo-Iranian Relations since 1800*, ed. Vanessa Martin, 21–35. New York: Routledge, 2005.

———. "Persian Art through the Eyes of Nineteenth-Century British Travellers." *Bulletin of the British Society for Middle Eastern Studies* 8 (1) (1981): 38–60.

———. "The Role of Architecture in the Creation of Tehran." In *Téhéran: Capitale bicentenaire*, ed. Chahryar Adle and Bernard Hourcade, 75–94. Paris: Institut français de recherche en Iran, 1992.

Schwartz, Gary. "Between Court and Company: Dutch Artists in Persia." In *The Fascination of Persia: The Persian-European Dialogue in Seventeenth-Century Art and Contemporary Art of Teheran*, ed. Axel Langer, 152–60. Zurich: Museum Rietberg, 2013.

Schwerda, Mira Xenia. "Death on Display: Mirza Riza Kirmani, Prison Portraiture and the Depiction of Public Executions in Qajar Iran." *Middle East Journal of Culture and Communication* 8 (2–3) (2015): 172–91.

Senefelder, Alois. *The Invention of Lithography*. Translated by J. W. Muller. New York: The Fuchs & Lang Manufacturing Company, 1911.

Shcheglova, Olimpiada P. "Lithography, i. In Persia." In *Encyclopaedia Iranica*, Online Edition. http://www.iranicaonline.org/articles/lithography-i-in-persia. Accessed December 6, 2016.

Sheikh, Reza. "The Rise of the Kingly Citizen." In *Portrait Photographs from Isfahan: Faces in Transition, 1920–1950*, ed. Parisa Damandan, 231–54. London: Saqi; The Hague: Prince Claus Fund Library, 2004.

Smith, Sir Robert Murdoch. *Persian Art*. New York: Scribner, Welford, and Armstrong, 1877.

Stanley, Tim. "Lacquer in the Islamic World." In *The World of Lacquer: 2000 Years of History*, ed. Pedro de Moura Carvalho, 157–90. Lisbon: Calouste Gulbenkian Museum, 2001.

———. "The Rise of the Lacquer Binding." In *Hunt for Paradise: Court Arts of Safavid Iran, 1501–1576*, ed. Jon Thompson and Sheila R. Canby, 185–202. New York: Rizzoli, 2003.

Stein, Donna. "Three Photographic Traditions in Nineteenth-Century Iran." *Muqarnas* 6 (1989): 112–30.

Sykes, Ella C. *Through Persia on a Side-Saddle*. Philadelphia: J. B. Lippincott, 1898.

Szántó, Iván. "The Dying Days of Persian Book Painting." In *Artisans at the Crossroads: Persian Arts of the Qajar Period (1796–1925)*, ed. Béla Kelényi and Iván Szántó, 34–43. Budapest: Ferenc Hopp Museum of Eastern Asiatic Arts, 2010.

———. "Qajar Lacquerware and the Related Art Forms." In *Artisans at the Crossroads: Persian Arts of the Qajar Period (1796–1925)*, ed. Béla Kelényi and Iván Szántó, 51–61. Budapest: Ferenc Hopp Museum of Eastern Asiatic Arts, 2010.

Tahmasbpour, Mohammad Reza. "Photography in Iran: A Chronology." *History of Photography* 37 (1) (2013): 7–13.

Ṭahmāsbpūr, Muḥammad Riżā. "Kashf-i nakhustīn dāgiru'tīp, az taṣvīr-i yik Irānī." *ʿAks* 244 (Khurdād 1388 H [June 2009]): 33–35.

Tanavoli, Parviz. *European Women in Persian Houses: Western Images in Safavid and Qajar Iran*. Edited by Sarah B. Sherrill and Moya Carey. New York: I. B. Tauris, 2015.

Tang, Hongfeng. "Zhaoxiang Dianshizhai Dianshizhai huabao zhong de zaimejie wenti" (Photolithography in Dianshizhai: The Issue of Remediation in *Dianshizhai Pictorial*). *Meishu Yanjiu* 1 (2016): 75–83.

Tavakoli-Targhi, Mohammad. "Contested Memories: Narrative Structures and Allegorical Meanings of Iran's Pre-Islamic History." *Iranian Studies* 29 (1–2) (1996): 149–75.

———. "Eroticizing Europe." In *Society and Culture in Qajar Iran: Studies in Honor of Hafez Farmayan*, ed. Elton L. Daniel, 311–46. Costa Mesa, Calif.: Mazda Publishers, 2002.

———. "Women of the West Imagined: The *Farangi* Other and the Emergence of the Women Question in Iran." In *Identity Politics and Women: Cultural Reassertions and Feminisms in International Perspective*, ed. Valentine Moghadam, 98–120. Boulder, Col.: Westview Press, 1994.

Vejdani, Farzin. *Making History in Iran: Education, Nationalism, and Print Culture*. Stanford, Calif.: Stanford University Press, 2015.

Vernoit, Stephen. *Occidentalism: Islamic Art in the 19th Century*. The Nasser D. Khalili Collection of Islamic Art, vol. 23. London: Nour Foundation in association with Azimuth Editions and Oxford University Press, 1997.

———. "The Visual Arts in Nineteenth-Century Visual Thought." In *Islamic Art in the 19th Century: Tradition, Innovation, and Eclecticism*, ed. Doris Behrens-Abouseif and Stephen Vernoit, 19–36. Leiden, The Netherlands: Brill, 2006.

Voigt, Jochen. *Der gefrorene Augenblick: Daguerreotypie in Sachsen 1839–1860. Inkunabeln der Photographie in sächsischen Sammlungen*. Chemnitz, Germany: Edition Mobilis, 2004.

Vuurman, Corien. "Antoin Sevruguin (ca. 1840–1933). A Beloved Photographer, in Iran and the West." In *Sevruguin's Iran: Late Nineteenth Century Photographs of Iran from the National Museum of Ethnology in Leiden, the Netherlands*, ed. L. A. Ferydoun Barjesteh van Waalwijk van Doorn and Gillian M. Vogelsang-Eastwood, 166–71. Tehran: Zaman; Rotterdam: Barjesteh van Waalwijk van Doorn, 1999.

———. *Nineteenth-Century Persia in the Photographs of Albert Hotz: Images from the Hotz Photograph Collection of Leiden University Library, the Netherlands*. Rotterdam: Barjesteh van Waalwijk van Doorn, 2011.

Yūsufīfar, Shahrām. "Majmaʿ al-ṣanāyiʿ (tajrubī-yi nawgarāʾī dar mashāghil-i kārgāh'hā-yi salṭanatī-yi dawra-yi Qājār)." *Ganjīna-yi asnād* 21 (3) (2011): 42–64.

Zebrowski, Mark. "Indian Lacquerwork and the Antecedents of the Qajar Style." In *Lacquerwork in Asia and Beyond: A Colloquy Held 22–24 June 1981*, ed. William Watson, 333–45. Colloquies on Art and Archaeology in Asia 11. London: Percival David Foundation of Chinese Art, School of Oriental and African Studies, University of London, 1982.

Zoka, Yahya. *Life and Works of Saniʿ Ol-Molk: Abol-Hassan Ghaffari 1814–1866*. Edited by Cyrus Parham. Tehran: Iran University Press, 2003.

Ẕukā, Yaḥya. *Tārīkh-i ʿakkāsī va ʿakkāsān-i pīshgām dar Īrān* (History of Photography and Pioneer Photographers in Iran). Tehran: Shirkat-i Intishārāt-i ʿIlmī va Farhangī, 1997.

———. *Zindagī va āṡār-i ustād Ṣanīʿ al-Mulk Abū al-Ḥasan Ghaffārī (1229–83 Q.)*. Tehran: Markaz-i Nashr-i Dānishgāhī, 1382 H (2003–4).

Zutphen, Marjolijn van. "Lithographed Editions of Firdawsī's *Shāhnāma*: A Comparative Study." *Oriens* 37 (2009): 65–101.

Index

Italicized page numbers indicate illustrations; bold italicized page numbers indicate catalogue entries.

N

Image Credits

"Technologies of the Image: Art in 19th-Century Iran," David J. Roxburgh

Fig. 1: Courtesy of Harry Elkins Widener Memorial Library, Harvard University; Figs. 2 and 3: Courtesy of Special Collections, Fine Arts Library, Harvard University; Fig. 4: Courtesy of Freer Gallery of Art and Arthur M. Sackler Gallery Archives, Smithsonian Institution, Washington, D.C.; Figs. 5–10: Courtesy of David J. Roxburgh; Fig. 11: Courtesy of Elmar W. Seibel; Fig. 12: Courtesy of Special Collections, Fine Arts Library, Harvard University; Fig. 13: Courtesy of Elmar W. Seibel.

"Qajar Lacquer as a Medium of Exchange," Mary McWilliams

Fig. 6: © Institute of Oriental Manuscripts, Russian Academy of Sciences; Fig. 7: Courtesy of Special Collections, Fine Arts Library, Harvard University; Fig. 14: Photograph © 2017 Museum of Fine Arts, Boston; Fig. 16: Courtesy of Ernst Mayr Library and MCZ Archives, Museum of Comparative Zoology, Harvard University; Fig. 25: Courtesy Sotheby's; Fig. 26: © The Trustees of the British Museum. All rights reserved; Fig. 31: © Victoria and Albert Museum, London; Fig. 33: Courtesy of Museum für Lackkunst, Münster, Germany; Fig. 40: © 2017 by Benaki Museum, Athens; Fig. 41: Courtesy of Museum für Lackkunst, Münster, Germany.

"The Lithographic Image and Its Audiences," Farshid Emami

Fig. 1: Courtesy of Elmar W. Seibel; Figs. 3 and 4: Courtesy of Harry Elkins Widener Memorial Library, Harvard University; Fig. 5: Courtesy of Houghton Library, Harvard University; Figs. 7 and 8: Courtesy of Houghton Library, Harvard University; Fig. 9: Courtesy of Elmar W. Seibel; Fig. 10: Courtesy of Harry Elkins Widener Memorial Library, Harvard University; Fig. 13: Courtesy of Butler Library, Columbia University in the City of New York; Fig. 14: Courtesy of Freer Gallery of Art and Arthur M. Sackler Gallery Archives, Smithsonian Institution, Washington, D.C.; Fig. 16: Courtesy of Elmar W. Seibel; Fig. 19: Courtesy of Special Collections, Fine Arts Library, Harvard University; Fig. 20: Courtesy of Elmar W. Seibel; Figs. 21 and 22: Courtesy of Special Collections, Fine Arts Library, Harvard University.

"Iranian Photography: From the Court, to the Studio, to the Street," Mira Xenia Schwerda

Fig. 1: Courtesy of Elmar W. Seibel; Fig. 2: © State Historical Museum, Moscow; Fig. 3: Courtesy of Elmar W. Seibel; Fig. 4: Courtesy of Matenadaran Mesrop Mashtots Institute of Ancient Manuscripts, Yerevan; Figs. 5–9 and 11–12: Courtesy of Elmar W. Seibel; Fig. 13: Courtesy of Library of Congress; Figs. 14 and 15: Courtesy of Elmar W. Seibel; Figs. 16 and 17: Courtesy of Special Collections, Fine Arts Library, Harvard University; Fig. 18: Courtesy of Elmar W. Seibel: Figs. 19 and 20: Courtesy of Kenneth Robbins.

"Painting after Photography in 19th-Century Iran," David J. Roxburgh

Fig. 1: © The Metropolitan Museum of Art. Image source: Art Resource, NY; Fig. 2: © RMN-Grand Palais/Art Resource, NY; Fig. 4: Nasser D. Khalili Collection of Islamic Art, © Khalili Family Trust; Fig. 5: Courtesy of Freer Gallery of Art and Arthur M. Sackler Gallery, Smithsonian Institution, Washington, D.C.; Fig. 6: Courtesy of Bonhams; Fig. 9: © RMN-Grand Palais/Art Resource, NY; Fig. 13: Private collection. Photo © Christie's Images/Bridgeman Images; Fig. 14: © Musée du Louvre, Dist. RMN-Grand Palais/Raphaël Chipault/Art Resource, NY; Fig. 16: Nasser D. Khalili Collection of Islamic Art, © Khalili Family Trust.

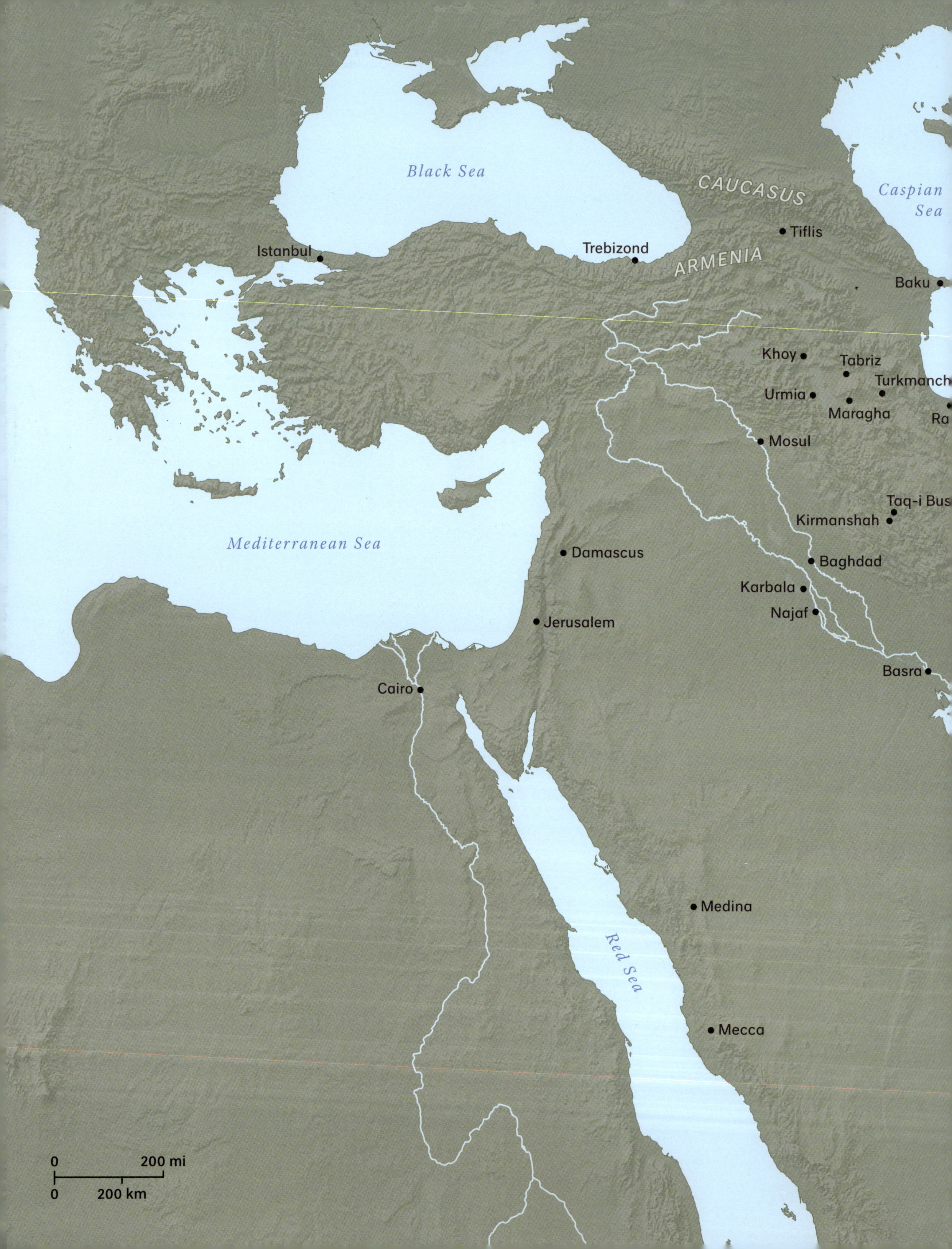
Black Sea
CAUCASUS
Caspian Sea
Tiflis
Istanbul
Trebizond
ARMENIA
Baku
Khoy
Tabriz
Turkmanch
Urmia
Maragha
Ra
Mosul
Taq-i Bus
Kirmanshah
Mediterranean Sea
Damascus
Baghdad
Karbala
Najaf
Jerusalem
Basra
Cairo
Medina
Red Sea
Mecca
0
200 mi
0
200 km